615044

940.27104093 JEN

Revolution and the Antiquarian Book

D1338825

At the end of the eighteenth century, nobl.   ....u revolutionaries spent extravagant sums of money or precious military resources competing to acquire old books, which until then had often been regarded as worthless. These books, called incunabula, achieved cultural and political importance as luxury commodities and as tools for mastering a controversial past. Men of different classes met in a new, shared marketplace, creating a competition for authority, as books were seen no longer merely as sources of textual information but as a way of controlling the past in the service of contemporary concerns. The old books themselves were often changed to meet new expectations of what important historic objects should be.

Focusing on Paris and London, but taking a resolutely pan-European view, this book examines the emergence of this commodity and of a new historical discipline created by traders and craftsmen.

KRISTIAN JENSEN is Head of Arts and Humanities at the British Library. He was elected Lyell Reader at the University of Oxford for 2008, and this book is based on his Lyell Lectures.

WITHDRAWN FROM LIBRARY STORE.

Revolution and the Antiquarian Book

Reshaping the Past, 1780–1815

———

KRISTIAN JENSEN

CAMBRIDGE
UNIVERSITY PRESS

CAMBRIDGE
UNIVERSITY PRESS

University Printing House, Cambridge CB2 8BS, United Kingdom

Published in the United States of America by Cambridge University Press, New York

Cambridge University Press is part of the University of Cambridge.

It furthers the University's mission by disseminating knowledge in the pursuit of education, learning and research at the highest international levels of excellence.

www.cambridge.org
Information on this title: www.cambridge.org/9781107687837

© Kristian Jensen 2011

This publication is in copyright. Subject to statutory exception and to the provisions of relevant collective licensing agreements, no reproduction of any part may take place without the written permission of Cambridge University Press.

First published 2011
First paperback edition 2014

A catalogue record for this publication is available from the British Library

Library of Congress Cataloguing in Publication data
Jensen, Kristian, 1954–
     Revolution and the antiquarian book : reshaping the past, 1780–1815 / Kristian Jensen.
          p.   cm.
     Includes bibliographical references and index.
     ISBN 978-1-107-00051-3
     1. Book collecting–Social aspects–Europe–History–18th century.   2. Book collecting–Social aspects–Europe–History–19th century.   3. Incunabula–Collectors and collecting–Europe–History–18th century.   4. Incunabula–Collectors and collecting–Europe–History–19th century.   5. Antiquarian booksellers–Europe–History–18th century.   6. Antiquarian booksellers–Europe–History–19th century.   7. Books and reading–Social aspects–Europe–History.   8. Printing–Social aspects–Europe–History.   9. Enlightenment–Europe. 10. Europe–Intellectual life–18th century.   I. Title.
     Z987.5.E85J46 2010
     093.075–dc22
     2010040404

ISBN 978-1-107-00051-3 Hardback
ISBN 978-1-107-68783-7 Paperback

Cambridge University Press has no responsibility for the persistence or accuracy of URLs for external or third-party internet websites referred to in this publication, and does not guarantee that any content on such websites is, or will remain, accurate or appropriate.

Contents

Figures

Acknowledgements

This book is a revised version of the Lyell Lectures which I gave in Oxford in 2008. I am grateful to the Lyell Electors, for electing me Lyell Reader, and subsequently for providing a subsidy towards the inclusion of illustrations in this book. As Electors, Richard Sharpe and Sarah Robert, Bodley's Librarian, supported me, in their different ways, as did Richard Ovenden and Alexandra Franklin.

The British Library granted me a research break of six months, without which I could have completed neither the lectures nor this book. For this I am very grateful.

The book is the fruit of research carried out in various contexts and over the years I have had the immense privilege of learning from discussions with colleagues and friends in the UK and abroad, in museums, libraries, universities, and in the rare books trade. I could not have worked without this stimulating international environment. I cannot mention them all, but I would like to thank Lilian Armstrong, Ivan Boserup, Annie Charon, Isabelle de Conihout, Dominique Coq, Cristina Dondi, Mirjam Foot, Meg Ford, John Goldfinch, Lotte Hellinga, Anthony Hobson, Monique Hulvey, Roland Kany, Martin Kauffmann, Eckhard Kessler, Richard Linenthal, Maria-Luisa Lopez, David McKitterick, Pascal Ract Madoux, Giles Mandelbrote, Philippa Marks, Nigel Palmer, Nicolas Petit, Richard Sharpe, Yann Sordet, and Bettina Wagner. I would like to thank Emma Wildsmith for her careful copy editing, her corrections, and for her numerous improvements to my text. I am very grateful to them all. Special thanks are of course due to Richard Simpson, my partner, who over twenty-five years has listened and advised, criticised and revised my work, combining moral and practical support with sharp analysis.

The book has been immensely enhanced by the generosity in use of images of the British Library (Figures 2.5, 3.1, 3.5, 3.6, 4.1, 4.5, 4.6, 5.2, 5.7–5.12, 5.15 and 5.16), the Bodleian Library (Figures 2.5, 2.7, 3.2, 3.3 and 5.6); Biblioteca Medicea Laurenziana (Figure 5.14); the National Trust (Figure 2.6); the Réunion des musées nationaux (the cover and Figures 5.5 and 5.17); and Lord Rothschild (Figure 5.13). I am grateful to all for their support. Figures 2.8–2.10, 3.4, 4.3, 4.4, 5.1, and 5.4 are reproduced courtesy of the University Librarian and Director, The John Rylands University Library, The University of Manchester; Figures 2.2 and 5.3 courtesy of the Bibliothèque nationale de France; Figure 4.7 courtesy of Musée des Beaux-Arts de Lyon; Figures 2.1, 2.3, and 4.2 courtesy of the Earl Spencer.

Introduction

During the eighteenth century the past was radically reassessed in order to understand and to influence changing political and social structures. The remaking of the past was often expressed through a physical remaking of the most treasured historical art objects but it also required a remaking of the physical environment in which the past was presented. Much excellent work has been undertaken on the development of museums emerging as institutions which were not only public but owned and funded by the state. A new model for museums expressing the state's cultural ambitions for the nation was firmly established during and after the French Revolution, presenting newly acquired art in a way which ensured that its interpretation was consistent with the intellectual, political, and aesthetic requirements of their new owners, while their original functions were marginalised or even deliberately obscured.

Historic books and their meanings underwent a similar transformation in the eighteenth century and in the years leading up to the formation of public and national institutions in the early nineteenth century: in the process this too had a physical, visible impact on the books. There are many similarities with the development of the way in which art was understood and used, but books have characteristics of their own so their role in the transformation of the past was specific to them, as were the ways in which they were collected and treated. Many of the issues which relate to the use of historic books can be associated with a conflict between the understanding of books as merchandise, as physical objects, and as conveyors of textual meaning that can be detached from the object which carries it, which in turn becomes a trivial manifestation of the independently existing text.

The invention of printing was often celebrated as the liberation of the text from the manuscript form, where it had been private and object specific. Much of the discussion of the function of the book as an expression of the past can therefore be found articulated through interpretations of the invention of printing and through the collecting of the earliest printed books. The late eighteenth century is one of the very few moments in history when incunabula and the invention of printing achieved a prominence

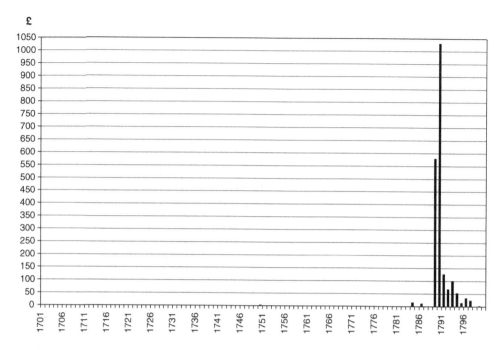

Figure I.1 Bodleian expenditure on incunabula 1700–1801.

which took the discourse about them far beyond the world of collectors, historians, and dealers.

Incunabula are books printed in the fifteenth century, but very often this is well hidden. Many of them look, and not only from the outside, like eighteenth-century books, for the simple reason that prominent parts of the surviving physical structure are from the eighteenth century. One may deplore the loss of fifteenth-century evidence, but the material which we actually have is also historical evidence in its own right. Incunabula were eighteenth-century books in the sense that they were sold, bought, confiscated, and transformed in the eighteenth century. Through these books we can explore how people approached their past and their present, how books were part of the reshaping of their world, and part of their rewriting of the past.

The scale of reassessment of fifteenth-century books in the last decades of the eighteenth century is made evident by the acquisitions made by the Bodleian Library in Oxford, which has the largest collection held by any European university library, a collection formed as a result of deliberate decisions about what to buy, unlike most other university collections which often acquired their historic books largely as a result of external circumstances.[1]

£

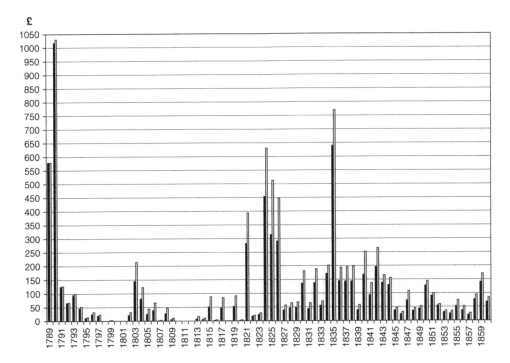

Figure I.2 Bodleian expenditure on incunabula, 1789–1861. Grey columns are adjusted for inflation, baseline 1789.

The Bodleian Library did not buy any incunabula until the last eleven years of the century,[2] but then began to spend significant sums, the level of expenditure of 1789–90 never to be surpassed, especially when figures are adjusted for inflation.[3]

The same is true in terms of the expenditure on incunabula as a percentage of the entire Bodleian purchasing budget. Yet, at the same time, these graphs show that the acquisitions of the late eighteenth century did not constitute an isolated phenomenon, but a 'big bang' at the beginning of a new and lasting approach to collecting.

At first the Bodleian Library set out to buy the first and best editions of the classical authors, the intention being to provide a working tool for the preparation of classical texts to be published by the University Press.[4] They were not acquired because they were incunabula. Yet one of the most expensive acquisitions was Duranti on the divine office, printed in 1459, a medieval text of no classical significance, bought in 1790 for £80 10s.[5] That is a substantial amount of money, for instance the equivalent of over twenty years' rent for a room off the Tottenham Court Road, or dinner for four and a half years, at the rates paid by Chateaubriand when he was a poor refugee

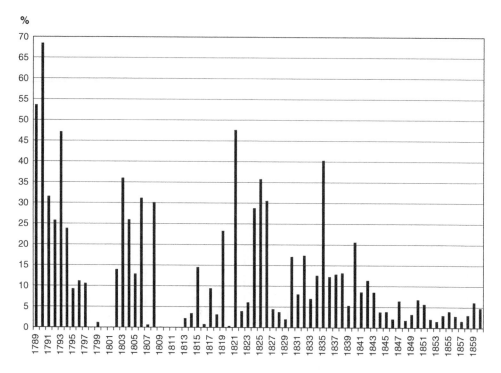

Figure I.3 Expenditure on incunabula as a percentage of the Bodleian book budget 1789–1861.

in London in 1793.[6] The price paid for Duranti no longer makes sense when measured against the prices of books; it now belonged among objects which were priced for their cultural importance.

The acquisition of such medieval books grew more frequent during the 1790s and by about 1810 it was no longer an exception. A similar pattern is suggested by the purchases of the second Earl Spencer, owner of the most outstanding collection of rare printed books ever created by a private person in Britain. In 1789 he bought a large collection of classical texts from Count Reviczky, envoy of the Holy Roman Emperor to the Court of St James. Although at first insisting on only wanting first editions of the classics, a few years later Spencer spent significant amounts of money on books printed in the fifteenth century which were anything but classical.

The transformation was rapid and the impact on the distribution of early printed books in Europe was profound. The fate of the Gutenberg Bible is symptomatic. In 1790 there was half a copy of the Gutenberg Bible in Britain, in Lambeth Palace, unidentified and unnoticed. In 1815, by the end of the Napoleonic wars, there were at least nine and possibly more. The first copy to make the move was bought by Spencer some time before June 1792;[7] the second was acquired by the Bodleian Library in 1793 for £100.[8] Similarly, in 1792 all but two of the surviving ten copies of the 1457 Psalter, the first printed book to contain a date of imprint, were still in the possession of religious institutions.[9] By the end of the Napoleonic wars none was; two had made their way to Britain by 1802, followed by one more by 1824. We are witnessing a reclassification of objects and see the importance of the newly found cultural property expressed in their prices and in their concomitant redistribution. The cultural and financial value of a class of objects had been comprehensively reassessed.

And England was far from alone. In Paris in the spring of 1792 the Bibliothèque royale, as it was still called, spent 39,615 livres and 6 sols on 550 incunabula, the equivalent of about £1,584, its largest ever acquisition of incunabula, despite the deep financial troubles of the period.[10]

Like the history of the book, the history of collecting has often been approached from a perspective defined by nationality. Without losing sight of different cultural, economic, and political circumstances, this book seeks to explore a shared international marketplace where the aspirations of collectors, dealers, and scholars met, competed, were formed and reformed. The Paris and London markets for books were intimately linked, as were French and English collectors; they were also connected with markets and collectors throughout Europe, where the interest of collectors from the two great centres for luxury trade and consumption in turn had a dramatic impact. This wider European environment, not least the German-speaking lands, is crucial for the understanding which this study seeks to achieve of the relations between the different participants in this cultural and economic activity. The relation of agents throughout Europe, from Copenhagen to Vienna to Rome, is central to my analysis.

This Europe-wide interest continued into the twentieth century which saw the creation, but not quite the completion, of two ambitious state-funded projects to describe incunabula, each with their distinct ideological backgrounds: the Prussian *Gesamtkatalog der Wiegendrucke* and the catalogue of incunabula in the library of the British Museum, now the British Library, major monuments to twentieth-century scholarship. These projects, remarkable both for their quality and for their ability to survive and retain financial support through a turbulent century, have so dominated the twentieth-century engagement with books from the fifteenth century that it can be difficult to achieve a different view from the analysis which they imply. A third project, the French national union catalogue, was privately funded, had yet a third ideological hinterland, and was discontinued at the death of its author and sponsor. The Bodleian Library's catalogue of incunabula, which I initiated and edited, set out to use the achievements of these catalogues to construct a fundamentally different approach. Similarly, this book does not seek to contribute to the history of these and other related projects: it seeks to understand the intensive eighteenth-century engagement with fifteenth-century book production in its own right. However, it inevitably contributes, simultaneously, to our understanding of the formation and the function of the collections which constituted the working material for those grand twentieth-century projects, and, as we shall see, also used methodologies which were reformulated but based on fundamental intellectual and social assumptions which were articulated during the eighteenth century.

The first chapter explores the way in which the invention of printing was used by philosophers and politicians to explain significant changes which were seen to be taking place in eighteenth-century society, whether these changes were applauded or deplored. It focuses on thoughts about books, and less on individual historic books. This chapter sets a wider scene for the explanation of why discussions of incunabula became part of a modern and modernising discourse in the late eighteenth century.

The second chapter takes Earl Spencer and the French Bibliothèque nationale as its two focal points, the two most significant collectors of this type of book in the late eighteenth century. It investigates the implications of a national institution of revolutionary France and of a rich British aristocrat, who led the naval war effort against France, competing for the same books in a shared market. It seeks to understand to what extent their motives were perceived to be different or were in fact different, and to what extent they had different impacts on the market. Institutions and individuals, across Europe, who supplied the books, through confiscations or sale, emerge as often playing a sophisticated role in a complex market.

The third chapter sees the events of the second half of the century in a broader historical perspective. It explores the emergence of a new category of collectables – incunabula – as an intellectual construct. It outlines a process where different intellectual and economic currents gradually came together over quite a long period of time, simultaneously defining a new type of commodity and a new discipline which, largely created outside established institutions, was able to engage with objects as historical evidence. The financial and intellectual values of the markets for luxury in Paris and London are central, but they are again set in a wider European context.

Chapter 4 examines the often fierce polemic about who had the right to make judgements about books. This debate developed between the various social groups who encountered each other in the same market, over the same merchandise. The centre of this discussion was often incunabula: they provided a shared environment which exposed the confrontation between the behaviour required in a marketplace and the behaviour appropriate to different social classes. This permits a fuller articulation of a theme which runs though the previous chapters, the increasing differentiation between the perceived functions of private and public collections, the emergence of the truly public and national library, in parallel to the emergence of public, national museums, as private knowledge increasingly cannot be construed, without challenge, as an unproblematic social benefit.

Chapter 5 examines how eighteenth-century collectors' perceptions of the texts from the past were expressed through the historical objects which they collected. It seeks to understand how they made them conform to expectations of the past which were formed by eighteenth-century polit-ical, intellectual, and aesthetic concerns, as part of a process which both commemorated the past and suppressed it. While ancient art was restored to look ancient and placed in architectural environments which aspired to classical forms, early books were effectively modernised, expressing their relevance in the modern world. The themes of the first chapter recur, but now firmly rooted in the examination of books, reflecting an often contra-dictory but shared approach to fifteenth-century books as one single type of merchandise.

As a conclusion Chapter 6 briefly explores how this resolutely mod-ernising discourse about incunabula was modified as the past was yet again reassessed in the early nineteenth century. Yet an analysis of prices and of collecting patterns indicates that while the modernising discourse was challenged, the reinvention of the Middle Ages did not have a com-prehensive effect on the market. This was the point at which some of the world's greatest public collections of incunabula were built. The conclusion explores the crucial role which the eighteenth-century reformulation of the importance of historic books played for the establishment of a new function for national institutions now accessible to a new audience, which sought for itself the same control of the use of history as the wealthiest private collec-tors of the past.

1 | Enlightenment ideas and revolutionary practice: incunabula and freedom

In the late summer of 1792 the young Republic of France was fighting for its survival. Enemy troops had reached as far as Verdun. The fight-back had begun, but the situation remained perilous. At this moment of supreme national danger, the keeper of printed books at the newly renamed Bibliothèque nationale wrote to his minister:

Citizen Minister. Allow me to bring myself to your recollection, and to ask you to have the kindness to inform general Custine,[1] who is marching on Mainz, that there is in the Metropolitan Chapter Library a copy of the earliest dated printed book, of which I add the title. It is the famous Psalter of Mainz, from 1457, in folio. May it be convenient for him to procure it or to have it presented to him. In the Bibliothèque nationale, it would complete our collection of the early editions from the city of Mainz, the cradle of printing. Please, accept my request with your accustomed kindness to me. Desaulnays, keeper at the Bibliothèque nationale. 22 October, year one of the French Republic.[2]

Desaulnays's letter was timely: Custine had taken Mainz the previous day. Written a month after the Republic had been declared, the letter preceded by nearly two years the establishment of the formal bureaucratic structures facilitating the systematic spoliation of cultural property outside France, which began after the fall of the Jacobin republic in the summer of 1794. It is, I believe, the earliest written evidence of the formation of a policy which, going far beyond Desaulnays's suggestion, was to transform the distribution throughout Europe of cultural objects, paintings, and sculpture, as well as of books, dislocating them from earlier contexts, and leading to their radical reinterpretation.[3]

Leaving aside any larger discussion of the intellectual or cultural causes of the French revolution, Desaulnays's letter shows that the Bibliothèque nationale was not the passive beneficiary of a policy formulated elsewhere but that, very early on, the institution actively sought a policy of cultural spoliation.[4] It draws attention to how strands of thinking about the past which had developed during the earlier decades of the century were at the root of decisions about the treatment of historic objects during the years of revolutionary upheaval and how these decisions were carried out by men who had been formed under the *Ancien Régime*.[5] Desaulnays had been a royal censor before he was appointed to the Bibliothèque du roi in 1774, on the recommendation of Turgot. Two central figures in ensuring the spoliation of books from abroad were Jean-Augustin Capperonnier and Joseph-François-Bernard Van Praet, joint keepers of printed books from 1795.[6] They too had been employed while the library was still the Bibliothèque du roi and, in different ways, both had strong roots in pre-revolutionary book culture. Capperonnier came from a family associated with the administration of the library and had been helped into his position by his uncle, Jean Capperonnier, director of the Bibliothèque du roi from 1761 to 1775. Van Praet, on the other hand, came from the trade. The son of a bookseller in Bruges, he was appointed by Desaulnays in 1784, having begun his Parisian career in the up-market bookshop of Guillaume Debure, l'aîné.

As it developed in the years after the end of the Terror, the policy of spoliation of foreign libraries was not officially confined to rare books. Especially in the early years there was also a focus on books of contemporary practical use. But when it came to these more practical books, it seems that the initiative often came from outside the library. For instance, between October 1794 and January 1795 Gaspard Michel, known as Leblond, visited Brussels, Mechelen, Liège, Aachen, Cologne, Bonn, Koblenz, and, in March 1795, The Hague. This was part of his work as Commissioner for the arts, attached to the army, but working to the orders of the Comité d'instruction.[7] Amongst printed books, he was directed to concentrate on two categories, each at opposite ends of the spectrum: on the one hand, the first monuments of printing, that is the earliest incunabula, and on the other hand, modern works which could be useful for the advancement of learning and science, categories which had also been deemed worthy of preservation from literary depots where libraries confiscated in France itself were being sorted through.[8] He followed his instructions closely.

Anton Keil (born 1769) was Commissioner for the search of scientific and artistic objects in the conquered countries of Germany. The numerous books which he confiscated were mainly modern useful works.[9] He even organised sales of confiscated older books from the State Library of Trier, in order to raise funds for buying more recent German books which were not in the Bibliothèque nationale, in conformity with his orders from the Directoire éxécutif, then the highest body of authority in the country.[10] In September 1797 he instructed Van Praet to draw up lists of useful works in addition to his frequent lists of rare books, the clear implication being that he and Van Praet did not have the same priorities.[11]

This does not mean that Van Praet and his colleagues at the Bibliothèque nationale were uninterested in modern books. When they made their choice of books from the vast depots of libraries confiscated from emigrants and religious institutions, they sought to ensure as complete a collection as possible of modern books, resisting pressure from the ministry which sought to restrict the library to claiming only one edition of each text. Capperonnier politely explained the distinction between duplicates and different editions of the same text to Pierre Bénezech, minister of the interior. He defended the library's policy as part of the revolutionary project:

> May we be allowed to express our disappointment in this respect, to have encountered obstacles in the implementation of a project which was already created at the beginning of the Revolution and which several famous men of letters have always applauded. This project aimed to form in the Bibliothèque nationale a collection as complete as possible of books in all fields and in all languages, and to collect as many different editions of these same books as possible, taking advantage of a unique situation which no other government in Europe has yet faced.[12]

On occasion, in making their selections of modern books for purchase, staff seem to have been able to rely on expert users, for instance, when a list of modern foreign books, mainly German, on mineralogy, was submitted by Charles Coquebert, professor of physical geography and mineral stratification at the École des mines from 1796 to 1797, and editor of the *Journal des mines* from 1794 to 1800.[13] But the staff themselves drew up very extensive lists of contemporary books to be bought from Italy, Holland, Germany, and especially England. Their bid for an acquisition grant from the ministry for the funding period of year IX and X, the brief period of peace in 1802, survives in the archives of the Bibliothèque nationale de France. They requested the equivalent of about £840 for modern books from Germany and £220 from Italy, while they asked for the staggering sum of about £3,520, for the purchase of modern books from England, probably to catch up with books published during the years of conflict.[14] This application for funds appears to have been backed up by extensive lists of books individually priced, based both on booksellers' catalogues, and on what we may consider almost as trade literature, the *Analytical Review* and for the most recently published volumes, the *Monthly Review*.[15] Seen within this context of a well-funded policy of acquisitions, it becomes clear that incunabula were a class apart among printed books. The judgement of the staff in the Bibliothèque nationale seems to have been that incunabula belonged to a category of objects which merited resource-intensive confiscation, rather than the relatively simple process of purchasing.

Not only were the parameters for the selection of books for confiscation set in Paris, individual books were selected by the official specialists in the metropolis. This guidance could be very detailed. Take, for instance, a letter of 31 March 1799 to the Minister of the Interior:

Citizen minister. We have the honour to place before you a list of precious books which are found in several libraries in Germany and which are mainly wanting in the Bibliothèque nationale, where the sequence of books from the fifteenth century is already very considerable. These typographical rarities would serve to fill some gaps. We recommend them, citizen minister, to the keen interest which you take for our institution and to your love for all those things which brings glory to our nation and for the good of public instruction. As our armies penetrate into Germany, we ask you, therefore, to give the orders necessary for these monuments of the art of printing also to become monuments of our victories. Greetings and respect. Van Praet and Capperonnier.[16]

The lists which went with the letter were systematic. For each town there was a list of libraries, thirty-nine in all; for each library there was a list of individual books, every single one an incunable, except for a few fifteenth-century blockbooks. The 1457 Psalter, the book which Custine was supposed to have confiscated in Mainz, featured prominently, the copy kept in the monastery of Roth being at the top of the lists. It was described as 'The most interesting book in existence, as it is the earliest of all. Note: nothing must be spared in assuring for the Republic the possession of this important edition, for which we will happily sacrifice all the other books on the present list.'[17] In the case of Nuremberg city library they even gave shelfmarks. This was where they hoped to acquire the then only known copy of Turrecremata's *Meditationes* from 1467, described by Van Praet as 'the rarest of all editions and the only copy known'.[18] This book featured as frequently on lists and in correspondence and was nearly as desirable as the Mainz Psalter, and it too escaped confiscation.

Whereas the selection of modern books for purchase was informed either by external experts or by staff relying on standard tools provided for the booktrade, when it came to confiscations, incunabula were the clear priority and the staff of the Bibliothèque nationale here relied on their own extensive expert knowledge, much of which was based on information which had become available fairly recently.

Thus Desaulnays would have known about the copy of the 1457 Psalter in the Mainz Chapter library from a catalogue printed in 1789,[19] while Van Praet and Capperonnier would have known the copy of the same book in Roth from von Heinecken's work on woodcuts from 1770.[20] It was possible to include the highlights from the libraries of the canon regulars at both

Rebdorf and Neustift in Tyrol in the list of books to be confiscated because, in 1792, the Bibliothèque nationale had bought two recently published catalogues of the historic books in those collections at the Frankfurt book fair, and at least one very recent catalogue of incunabula was among the useful modern books confiscated by Keil.[21]

The list which went with Capperonnier's letter of 31 March 1799 is marked 'to wait for a more convenient moment'. When, in the summer of 1800, that more favourable moment came, the library was prepared and supplied an augmented list, now with forty-five different libraries.[22] In September 1800, Neveu, Commissioner of the French government in Germany for sciences and art, reported that he had acquired the majority of the books on the list, but not quite all.[23] Unlike Keil, who had insisted on modern books,[24] Neveu allowed himself to be guided by the criteria of the experts at the library and was commended to the minister for his zeal by Capperonnier.[25]

The operation was monitored in Paris through a system of verification and accountability, ensuring a complete audit trail from confiscation to incorporation into the collections. When the confiscated books were dispatched they were accompanied by packing notices listing each item, signed by representatives both of the French authorities and of the former owner.[26] Upon arrival in Paris the sealed chests were opened in the presence of representatives from the ministry and the library who jointly checked each item on the lists, noting any irregularity.[27] The difficulty which was experienced, on occasion, in bringing together representatives from the two parties is an indication both of how seriously this was taken and of the burden in terms of staff time which this insistence on accountability inevitably caused.[28]

The Italian campaign was no less organised; the confiscation of books was even stipulated as part of the treaty of 16 May 1797 between the French and the Venetian republic: it allowed for the confiscation of 500 manuscripts at the choice of the French; in the end it came to 241 manuscripts, supplemented by 120 incunabula, fifty-nine editions printed by Aldus Manutius, and fifty volumes of music.[29] Incunabula also predominated among the books confiscated in the Italian campaign. This is confirmed by the twenty-six boxes of books which arrived at the Bibliothèque nationale 3 Frimaire of year V (23 November 1796). They had been confiscated by Monge in Milan and Bologna and almost exclusively consisted of incunabula.[30]

Although both random looting and looting organised as a punitive measure did take place, this has nothing to do with what we see here; incunabula were collected as part of a carefully planned, long-term, and closely controlled bureaucratic process which relied on high-level political support and was sustained over a significant period of time, although it was expensive in resources at the point of confiscation, during transport, as well as when the books were delivered in Paris.

Although dramatic and ruthless, the confiscation of foreign books and works of art by the French central authorities is part of the centuries-long process of appropriation by increasingly powerful and centralised secular states of the worldly property of European religious institutions, as well as of a tradition that victorious powers loot luxury goods. However, the process was different from the wholesale appropriation of entire libraries, for instance, the conquest of the Bibliotheca palatina by the Papal State, or from the effects of monastic dissolution. It was characterised by an expert selectivity, conducted by the Bibliothèque nationale, based on accumulated knowledge, expertise, and attitudes which had been formed in the preceding decades. With their sharply focused policy of confiscations, the staff of the Bibliothèque nationale can be seen to align incunabula less with modern – useful – books, and more closely with the understanding of art objects which was expressed through the formation of a historical, chronological museum of French art. The confiscation of foreign highlights aimed to express the grandeur of the new republic by demonstrating its appreciation of cultural objects, in part in reaction to the iconoclastic trends of the Jacobin republic.[31]

Van Praet and Capperonnier prioritised the use of the available resources by focusing their confiscation lists on incunabula, items which were disproportionately expensive to buy through the trade, while seeking to use their financial resources for acquiring modern books; and they were able to rely on expensive bureaucratic and military structures to support their aim. Bearing in mind that the librarians had complex motives, I wish to explore how it came about that men in high office deemed old printed books to be so important for public instruction and national glory that they merited the expenditure of a vital national resource, the manpower of the army, and why they constituted a class of objects of cultural importance for the Revolution which, after all, set out to achieve a radical break with the past.

The invention of printing analysed in eighteenth-century France

During the latter part of the eighteenth century, the invention of printing was the subject of lively debate among specialists in most of Western Europe; in France, in addition, it was discussed by men who were not primarily interested in the history of books, but in the nature of society as a whole, by philosophers and politicians. In England, to a lesser extent, political activists were to use the theme in polemical works. The invention of printing was politically significant. It was used as a way of explaining what was happening in their own eighteenth-century world. While they did not discuss individual books, this is perhaps the only point in history when the invention of printing has achieved such importance outside the narrow field of specialists, a phenomenon which can only be understood in the wider context of how they understood the function of books in their own society.

In pre-revolutionary France the booktrade was heavily regulated, both in terms of corporate control of the profession, permissions and privileges, and in terms of censorship of individual books. This was administered through the Bureau de la librairie, relying on administrative structures which had begun to have their full force in the 1670s and 1680s.[32] The system of control was supported by the academies which had been created by Colbert and his successors as institutions loyal to the crown, constituting an integrated system of control, protection, and encouragement. The academies were institutionally close to the Bureau de la librairie, and also drew on the same social group for their members. The function of ensuring the continued viability of established economic structures of the printing and publishing industry had to be balanced with the requirements of the other important role of the Bureau, that of implementing a control of the production and distribution of books, in the form of pre- and post-publication censorship. If too strict a regime of pre-publication censorship was imposed, undesirable books would be printed abroad and imported, to the detriment of a publishing industry which could otherwise be kept largely favourable to the regime.

In 1689, a hundred years before the Revolution, in his history of printing in Paris, Jean de la Caille could view the invention of printing as an uncomplicated advantage to society. The spread of knowledge which it occasioned was an undisputed benefit for society and there was no question of hostility to printing or publishing as such. While some people might not admire printing as much as it deserved, that was simply because they did not appreciate something which was so much part of their everyday lives that they took it for granted: 'If ignorant persons look at printing without admiring it, it is because they see it without understanding it.'[33]

By the mid eighteenth century, however, those critical of the regime were becoming more vocal, not least within the institutions designed to foster loyalty. In parallel, disquiet grew over the disregard of God, king, and morality which was displayed in the output of contemporary publishers, whether legal or illegal, imported or produced in France. This renewed polarisation can be detected in contrasting attitudes to the invention of printing displayed by authors who, to a greater or lesser extent, supported or opposed existing power structures.

The Bureau de la librairie exercised functions of regulation not unlike those which had been imposed on the Stationers in London by the Act of 1662, until it lapsed in 1694. While it is easy to see the similarity of the tension between protection and control, different political structures led to utterly different approaches in the two countries. Eighteenth-century French observers, authorities and reformers alike, saw the situation in England as one of freedom of the press, and used it as a counter-image to the situation in their own country, although in England itself, the less structured control exercised through a post-publication legal process involving lawsuits for libel or treason was often highly controversial.[34]

Formey, the son of French Huguenot refugees in Berlin, played an active role in French philosophical debate, if from a distance. He was hostile to French enlightenment philosophy, not least to Diderot. In his *Principes élémentaires des belles-lettres*, from 1763, and published in English in 1766, he maintained that, while the invention of printing in itself could have been a positive development, in practice its exploitation had been determined by greed, a cardinal sin.[35] The commercial nature of publishing, the need of printers and publishers to make a living, was the root of its evil. Economic considerations were inherently opposed to the promotion of truth, which was well known and well established. The invention of printing was part of a history of decline from our divinely inspired potential, fully in conformity with an orthodox Augustinian understanding which viewed all of the Divine creation as good but susceptible to abuse through man's sinful abuse of his free will. The inherent faults of human nature derived from the original fall of man, and they explained why the invention of printing had turned out to be less of a blessing than it might have been.

While the degree and the methods of control or suppression were a theme open for discussion, it was rare totally to deny that the invention of printing was an improvement but, writing in 1761, Louis Bollioud-Mermet came close to espousing this radical view. He moved seamlessly from the invention of printing to its contemporary effects and to the debate about the freedom of the press. He too saw the invention of printing as part of a history determined by mankind's sinful nature. Reflecting our flawed nature, our books are insolent in presuming knowledge and they will mislead others into error:

It is still an undecided question, knowing if the invention of printing contributed more to the progress of letters and the perfection of morality than it has brought damage to them. This is not the place either to examine this question or to resolve it – all one can say is that the number of books is immense and that those which are good are very few ... Out of the shapeless and monstrous farrago of frivolous and audacious works which human nature in its waywardness engenders, what remains for the avid and unreflecting reader but a confused accumulation of ideas, of a nature much less apt to enrich his spirit than to trouble and corrupt his imagination?[36]

The Christian, authoritarian, view of printing was also expressed by men closer to the world of early books. In the late 1770s François-Xavier Laire wrote a history of printing in Rome in the fifteenth century.[37] A Franciscan and a specialist in the earliest printed books, he sought to reconcile the divergent views on printing. The issues of his own day were the reason why his theme was important:

No invention has been more important than typography. Nothing more desirable could ever happen to mankind. Let us recall those dismal times when all knowledge was contained in the evanescent spoken word or in easily destroyed manuscripts. Let us then consider the insecure and precarious state of letters which then prevailed. The light of knowledge had to be spread with slow steps to very distant, savage nations, on the way impeded by numerous dangerous obstacles. Only a man brought up in the wild as an ignorant enemy of knowledge can deny the advantages of the art of printing. It is true, however, that everything useful becomes damagingly destructive. No tears are sufficient to deplore it. But what conclusion can we draw from that? Abuse must be suppressed and proper use carefully preserved. If that rule cannot be observed, our whole society must collapse and it would be preferable to banish the greatest advantages of human existence. Anyone can see how stupidly destructive that would be. As that is the case, it will be useful to examine the origin and development of the most excellent of crafts.[38]

Laire knew that the abuse of a divine instrument was an inevitable consequence of human nature and he saw the current situation, created by the invention of printing, as acutely dangerous to social stability. His solution was one often adopted by the Church and others when in power, repression. But he also realised that there was a need for a balanced approach:

May printers display a genuine affection for their craft, and may princes and true lovers of learning guard this knowledge with their authority and promote it with their beneficence. Then we will soon have the happiness to see this art liberated and purged, to the benefit of mankind, from the sinful misuse by which it is shamefully stained.[39]

Laire's solution to this consequence of original sin was not original. His notion of 'sinful misuse', *vitia et abusus*, is the equivalent of the *mauvais livres* which the Bureau de la librairie attempted to stamp out, in return granting royal protection of privileges and patronage to the learned, especially to those whose learning focused on antiquity. He recommended the system of control, protection, and encouragement which was collapsing in France as he wrote.

Formey and Laire used theology as a tool for social analysis. They presented and analysed observations about issues which confronted contemporary society within a theological explanatory model. But both writers indirectly acknowledged that their account of the invention of printing depended on a view of mankind which was, by then, less widely accepted as obviously true, not least since the concept of original sin had been so famously rejected in the *Essay on Man* by Alexander Pope, an author whose works were frequently owned by the ruling elite in France as in England.[40] Laire and Formey's view of history and of the present was far removed from that of the men behind the *Encyclopédie*.

In his *Discours préliminaire*, d'Alembert repeatedly explained the historic shortcomings of human understanding as problems of structures of communication, rather than as consequences of sin. Conversely, human communication was a causal factor in the formation of society. The darkness of the Middle Ages was eventually dispelled, and the new model of communication brought about by printing had been a significant instrument in achieving this. Notably, however, in a cursory passage, he expressed the traditional view that printing had enabled mankind to regain the lost insights of the ancient Greeks and Romans.[41]

The *Discours préliminaire* was familiar to Malesherbes, Director of the Bureau de la librairie from 1750 to 1763, a function which included the role of censor-in-chief. In this role, on the one hand, he presided over a vastly expanded number of censors and sent many more members of the booktrade to the Bastille than his predecessors, especially members of the lowest rungs of the trade, both because of the dramatic growth in the published output, and because of the increasingly vociferous opposition to the absolutist monarchy.[42] On the other hand, he was an intellectual of his time, deeply engaged with Enlightenment ideas, and he administered censorship much more selectively than before, concentrating his resources on the more flagrant offences against God, king, or decency. His work as censor-in-chief embodied the conflict between the *philosophes* and the exercise of actual political power, as described by Daniel Roche.[43] His controversial approval of the publication of the *Encyclopédie* itself exemplifies this ambiguity.

The invention of printing features prominently in two of his political writings. They are not works of historiography, but practical proposals for the improvement of the affairs of the state written by an enlightened member of the elite who was deeply involved with its administration. While Malesherbes's works have been well discussed, less attention has been paid to the way in which he formulated his contemporary concerns through a discussion of the invention of printing. The same is true of Condorcet, to whom I shall shortly turn. However, for both men their discussion of the invention of printing formed a crucial part of their understanding of their own times. Not only did they use the past to express and to legitimise contemporary political views but, much more profoundly, it was part of their analytical process of understanding matters of central concern in contemporary society.

In 1775, working at the Cour des aides which dealt with issues concerning the collection of taxes, Malesherbes published a remonstrance addressed to the king about the administration of justice in relation to taxation, especially the secrecy surrounding the process of decision-making in the courts of law.[44]

Just as it was natural for Laire and Formey to discuss the invention of printing in terms of the present-day problem of subversive publications, it was equally natural for Malesherbes, administrator and *philosophe*, to discuss the problems of the day in terms of the invention of the press. Instead of theology, he used history as a tool for analysis of contemporary problems which we today might think of as sociological.

Outlining the historical development which had led to the present situation, Malesherbes argued that, before the invention of writing, laws had been orally transmitted and had consequently been subject to great uncertainty. Justice had been arbitrary, entirely dependent on individual judges but, on the other hand, it had been administered in public. Often the law had been applied by the king in front of his people: his decisions were thus informed by their views. With the age of writing, the codification of laws had reduced the arbitrary nature of justice but, again, it had created laws so complicated that they were impenetrable, except after long study. As a consequence legal decisions were made in private by men who all belonged to the same new class, the *Gens de Loi*.

It was a crucial part of Malesherbes's argument that the present situation was both oppressive and new, deliberately evoking themes which were associated with the earliest days of the French monarchy. The age of printing could have overcome the disadvantages which the manuscript era had created. The availability of laws in printed form meant that the population as a whole was no longer ignorant; an informed public could now in its turn be a sort of tribunal which judged the decisions of judges.

The age of printing has thus given to writing the same public exposure which the spoken word had in the first age, in the middle of the assembly of the nation. But it took several centuries for the invention to have its effect on all men. It was necessary for the entire nation to acquire the taste and habit of educating itself through reading, and for enough people to be skilled in the art of writing to lend their service to all the public and to take up the place of those who, endowed with a natural eloquence, let themselves be heard on the Champ de Mars or in public pleas.[45]

However, political structures had not yet adapted to the new reality. Couched in terms of a reversion to an original, better state of things, when justice was administered in public, he presented a request for a profound reform of the legal system, which would be based on the effects of the social changes brought about by the invention of printing, but to which the political structures of society had not yet fully adapted.

In 1788 Malesherbes wrote another contribution to contemporary political debate, *Mémoire sur la liberté de la presse*. It was written at the occasion of the convocation of the estates general, on 2 August. Malesherbes advocated a moderate approach to control and suppression, without favouring the complete absence of pre-publication control which he saw as the English model: there was still a need to suppress abuse.[46] In this context he developed his thoughts on the long-term impact of the invention, that of ensuring an ever-increasing level of literacy. By this he meant not an ability to read but more specifically an ability to take part in the discussion of issues of political importance. Soldiers were now so brave that they dared to publish their opinions. Even among artisans surprising literary talents were found. He did not claim that everybody could read and write but that there were people who had their own way of thought and who were capable of holding their own against no matter whom, at all levels of society and in all parts of the country.

Malesherbes explained the widespread participation in public debate not as a consequence of an educational system, but as a result of the new system of communication. He saw the changes in his own times as part of a historic development begun with the invention of printing, such a radical event that even 350 years later society was still in the process of adapting to its consequences:

This is the happy effect of the art of printing. This art has existed but three and a half centuries. This is not too much time to have enabled entire nations to have acquired this level of education, of which the time has come to harvest the fruits.[47]

Society was grappling not so much with the effects of the printing of oppositional literature, as with the ongoing process of adapting to the changes caused by its invention. One of the most fundamental conceptual changes which were to be crystallised by the Revolution, the reformulation of the relationship between people, nation, and state, was necessitated by the effects of the invention of printing: 'Let us in our day no longer look at the people with the same eye as we did in the past.'

Malesherbes's view of a wide discussing public was undoubtedly informed by his experience as a censor which had challenged the view that literary engagement was reserved for the privileged few. The social distribution of literary activity which he described is recognisably the same world as the one described by Robert Darnton in his analysis of the files of Joseph d'Hémery, a police inspector of the booktrade, who compiled his notes from 1748 to 1753.[48] The extent to which literacy spread is another matter. The point here is that an important group of people noticed, and thought it problematic, that literacy was not confined to those who had been trained to use it for the purpose of maintaining the stability of society. Despite Malesherbes's position as a senior administrator of the absolutist monarchy, he was closer to the more radical world of Diderot and d'Holbach than to that of Voltaire, and saw this new development as entirely positive.[49]

Condorcet's *Esquisse d'un tableau historique des progrès de l'esprit humain* was published in 1794 immediately after his death and, in contrast to the works of Malesherbes, Condorcet's views had a significant contemporary distribution in printed form. The work's centrality for the self-understanding of the Republic was given official expression when, on 2 April 1795, after the fall of the Jacobin republic, the Convention nationale ordered the purchase of 3,000 copies, as if to make up for his death and that of so many others.[50] It continued to be of direct importance until new restrictions on freedom were imposed under Napoleon. It also appeared in English already in 1795 under the title *Outlines of an Historical View of the Progress of the Human Mind*.

It is highly likely that Condorcet was familiar with the two political works in which Malesherbes discussed the invention of printing. The two men had been close for a long time and Condorcet had dedicated one of his political treatises to Malesherbes as early as 1775.[51] For both, the invention of printing was still contemporary in the sense that its effects were still in active progress. The invention may be used as shorthand for its effect, but this reflects a perception of the contemporary world as located within a process begun by the invention, and only now about to be completed. Yet there are also profound differences between them. Malesherbes placed his account of change within the context of an essentially stable human society where innovation enabled a return to former, better monarchical practices. For Condorcet a return to a golden age, when the king was close to his people, or a revival of ancient learning, were no more plausible than a return to an antelapsarian, ignorant innocence. Condorcet set out a new periodisation of human history. It was structured according to the development of communication, for it was communication that determined the nature of human society.[52]

He was deeply involved with the reforms of weights and measures, including the measurement of time itself. His recasting of the way in which the past was structured is analogous to the reorganisation of how we structure and measure the world around us. Like the political world, the organisation of history was liberated from the domination of the Church and of monarchs and their dynasties. Human history did not begin with the fall to end with redemption; nor was it structured by the rise and fall of empires. Beginning with the period of hunters and fishers, who recognised some sort of social cohesion and therefore developed the use of language, human history would culminate in the tenth epoch, in the future, when national languages would be replaced with an international scientific language, free of all ambiguities and all potential for manipulation. Condorcet did not discuss the invention or the origin of language, but the social structures which were associated with the types of communication prevalent in each period.

Condorcet was quite aware of a long tradition of celebrating the invention of printing as a benefit for mankind. In his life of Turgot, he suggested that Turgot had held views on the invention of printing similar to those which Condorcet was later to express himself, referring to a sermon delivered by Turgot at the Sorbonne in 1750. However, there Turgot had provided an entirely conventional, humanist account of printing as the beginning of the revival of learning.[53] Condorcet's acknowledgement of his indebtedness to this passage provides a measure of the radical nature of his reformulation and reinterpretation of this well-known theme.

Within his historical system the invention of printing represented the most important turning point in human history. It had radically changed the world, constituting the beginning of the eighth epoch. Condorcet described this period in the chapter entitled 'From the invention of printing until the time when the sciences and philosophy threw off the yoke of authority'. The new system of communication had affected all aspects of society, and put the relationship between its different constituent groups onto a new footing.

It was of central importance to Condorcet that private knowledge did not increase enlightenment. Improvements in knowledge which did not affect people at large were not progress. On the contrary, they might lead to fear and secrecy. The proper measure of progress was how widespread knowledge is, how the truths discovered by science and how its unmasking of superstitions are communicated to a wide section of the population.[54]

Condorcet deployed a well-established theme that printing had made books much cheaper and much more accessible but, again, he developed it in his own direction. While others deplored the commercial nature of printing and expressed a wish to control printing to make it rise above commerce, for Condorcet it was the commercial nature of the booktrade which enabled enlightenment to be universal and public rather than restricted or private: 'Enlightenment has become the object of an active, universal trade.'[55] It was the commercial multiplication of identical texts which enabled many to engage with the same political and scientific debate, despite geographical or social distances. Condorcet was therefore not worried about the printing of erroneous ideas. On the contrary, their multiplication would enable a discussing public to discard them, and to do so quickly. This was a radical, secular, and non-hierarchical solution to Laire's theological worry about how to control error.

Most especially, printing had enabled people to shake off the chains of superstition for it had enabled them to reject texts which political and religious institutions had sought to impose on them, not least trying in vain to use schools for stamping out dissent. Condorcet's understanding of the invention of printing as a structural, potential force for popular control of the powerful must therefore also be read in the context of his plans for a revolutionary system of public instruction providing the public with knowledge and appropriate tools with which they themselves could uncover truth. He wished to see schools becoming a tool in the creation and the defence of freedom, as distinct from their past function as a tool for socialisation within a system which educated the population by inculcating values and attitudes, whether of a religious or national nature. With this view of schooling under the *Ancien Régime*, it becomes clear why he identified the invention of printing, not education, as having created the parameters for freedom.[56]

A similar dichotomy between education and instruction had worried the educational establishments of the Church. While the Assemblée du clergé in the 1760s initially wished for religious schools to replace those of the disbanded Jesuits, in the 1770s it began to change its point of view as it realised that education could no longer be relied upon to teach religion and suppress heresy. In a popular collection of homilies, François-Léon Réguis saw education as the cause of literacy and consequently of the lack of Christian piety:

Having examined the matter closely, I find, and my colleagues find likewise, that the greater portion whom we judge to be least Christian in our parishes is constituted

by those who have been to school, whereas those who are most simple, most innocent, most Christian can neither read nor write.[57]

Schools were failing as institutions which could provide controlled 'education'. Condorcet had again taken up a theme which was of contemporary
concern, but reinterpreted it radically as an integral part of his understanding of the emerging new world made possible by the invention of printing.
Again the methods of historiography provided the analytical tools used for
understanding contemporary concerns.

The *Esquisse* is marked by a belief in our potential as human beings to
progress through the use of reason, collectively as a society. But this is not
the naive account of history as an uninterrupted linear process of progress,
which some critics assume that men and women of the Enlightenment proposed. Condorcet saw a world where the mighty exercised their oppression, even beyond their own continent, through slavery and colonisation.
They could do this because their power was unchecked by equal access to
information.[58] Oppression was possible because communication had not
developed to its full potential. The restriction on commerce imposed by
monopolistic trade was parallel to the restrictions imposed on communication, through the control of the press, which impeded the spread of
knowledge and the ability to challenge those in power. Progress was not
inevitable, but a potential which could be thwarted by tyrants, uncontrolled
by a free press.

Relationships between human understanding and change in society were
also fundamental for the discussion of historiography which Volney presented
in a series of lectures originally given between 22 January and 23 March 1795.
His *Leçons d'histoire* were published in several contexts, but appeared as a
single book in 1800, also in an English translation.

He looked at the invention of printing not from the point of view
of a historian, but as a teacher of historiography. It was important for
the future historians whom he educated that their assessment of their
sources took into account the nature of the society which had created
them. Just as the invention of printing had changed the nature of communication, so it had also changed the nature of the writing of history.
Volney argued:

Such is the power of printing, such is its influence on civilisation, that is on the
development on all the faculties of man in the direction useful for society, that the
era of its invention divides into two distinct and divers systems the political and
moral state of peoples before and after its invention. The same is true of their historiographers. And its existence characterises to such an extent the enlightenment

that to establish whether a people is civilised or barbarian, all one need do is to ask: Have they got the use of printing? Is there freedom of press?[59]

Because printing created a new system of communication it also constituted a dividing point in our engagement with the past.[60] Volney's assessment of the invention of printing amounted to a critical theory of our understanding of history. Understanding the social function of printing is necessary if we are to apply our critical faculties to the assessment of the various types of evidence of human history. For instance, historiographers of the manuscript period had suffered numerous drawbacks. Their sources were often controlled by powerful families who only allowed use which was to their own advantage, and who might falsify or destroy evidence which went against their interest, a strong argument for collecting source material into public repositories. Restricted access to information meant that there could be no informed criticism of historiography, once published. The length of time it might take to produce and distribute a book in the manuscript period could mean that it was published so late that informed contemporaries could not criticise it. All this made it easier for writers in the manuscript period to distort or even to falsify their evidence.

In the past, reading and writing had been highly restricted to specific classes. Greek and Roman historiographers were, for instance, all either generals or magistrates. They had been formed by specific educational systems which had preconditioned them to think and write as they did. Their bias was thus not personal or deliberate, but deeply rooted in their aristocratic culture. All this was changed by the invention of printing. Admittedly printing had introduced a new commercial callousness which, in the manuscript era, had been contained by the tiresome complications of writing out books by hand, although there were charlatans in the manuscript era as well. But in the period after the invention of printing, it was much more difficult to rely unchallenged on false information, because of a general ability to verify and because of the very nature of public discussion in the printing era in which objections could get as much public notice as the work which they criticised.

Volney had been close to the circles of power during the directorate and the early consulate, but he was increasingly in opposition to prevailing political views as Napoleon strengthened his grip on power, the breach being complete when he opposed the reintroduction of slavery. The centrality of Volney's view of the invention of printing for the formation of modern society was confirmed in 1800 by Jondot, who was quick to celebrate the first Napoleonic moves towards the abolition of the freedom of expression. This took the form of an attack on Volney's account of the invention of printing, focusing on the damaging effects of the invention on human society. In the period of manuscripts there had been more '*simplicité, franchise, noblesse, et majesté*':

A truth too widely diffused is lost, or at least no longer has the merit of tradition. 'The circle of readers was very narrow' [it is argued, by Volney]. Yes, but comments were also wiser, the spirit of observation more correct, and criticism was healthier … Unfortunate the country where the largest number is minded to reason and to discuss! Where the focus of enlightenment is narrowest, that is where it is most ardent, that is where it shines most uniformly. It is the sacred fire of Vesta. It is immortal.

Jondot went much further than rejecting Volney's historiographical method. He rejected the whole of the eighteenth-century consensus that the invention of printing was a positive, if to some a problematic, part of the history of mankind. His attack on the invention of printing was the one central theme which carried his entire book forward, and which led to total rejection of the modern world. Indeed, he suggested that the uncritical certainties of the Middle Ages were to be preferred to the discussing society of his own times:

So what are the advantages derived from the art of printing? Where are 'the faculties of man developed in a direction most useful for society'? I see in this society much less virtue, much less morality, much less religion than before. On the contrary, I see discord agitating with greater fury. Without the invention of printing the errors of Luther, Münzer, Calvin, and Zwingli would not have been diffused with such rapidity, and would not have ignited everywhere the fire of civil war.[61]

The centrality of the invention of printing for the enlightened view of the nature of man and for human history is encapsulated in Jondot's attack on the freedom of expression, which reasserted the importance of all those things which the invention had undermined: authority, control, and religion.

The enlightened view that printing created a new type of social relationship and a new type of communication was based on the essentially non-religious notion that knowledge progresses through an open discussion of divergent ideas, that the publication of error was an integral part of the progress of knowledge. Jondot's counter-revolutionary criticism of the eighteenth-century freedoms points to a perceived link between eighteenth-century philosophical rejection of hierarchy and the Protestant rejection of the hierarchy of the Roman Church, a view which was to become much more current after the restoration of the monarchy in France in 1815.[62]

Evidently wrong to believe that the Revolution was simply a Protestant conspiracy, Jondot expressed a view which was also found among those whom he attacked. The defenders of freedom often referred to the heroes of the English Protestant revolutions against their monarchy, Thomas Harrison, the regicide, and Algernon Sidney being part of a recurring list of models for revolutionary behaviour, and Milton's *Areopagitica* regularly being referred to in discussions of the freedom of the press. In 1802 the Institut National announced the theme for its prize essay of the year: 'What was the influence of Luther's reformation on the political situation in the various countries of Europe and on the progress of enlightenment?' Charles Villers, who won the prize, was no Protestant, but saw his work as emanating from an enlightened nation. Yet his assessment of Protestantism was so positive that his work was instantly translated and published in England and Scotland.[63]

Enlightened views of printing as a tool of progress were undoubtedly related to Protestant notions of printing as a tool of God invented to ensure the fall of the Pope. But this religious view had become integrated into a secular view of human progress, and had in the process been profoundly transformed. Condorcet, Volney, and Malesherbes all used history as a tool for analysis of contemporary issues and their interpretations of the invention of printing were part of the framework which informed their action in the present. Eighteenth-century works which emphasised a causal link between modern freedom and the invention of printing belonged in the orbit of literature which sought to erode the foundations of the seemingly natural and unchallengeable hierarchy of traditional monarchical society. Important strands of the thinking about the past which had an impact on actual events during the Revolution were formulated before the Revolution, by men intimately involved with the administration and with reform of the *Ancien Régime*. Condorcet's and Volney's reinterpretations were more revolutionary in their intent than that of Malesherbes, while being a development of a model of understanding the past which had been explored in the last decades before the Revolution itself. Yet their conclusions are radically different in that they emphasise a link between freedom and truth which is not transmitted to a receptive, passive audience, in church or in school, but arrived at independently by an informed and communicating public.

A work claiming to be 'translated from a series of letters, written originally in French, and dedicated to the National Assembly', the *Reflections on the Causes and Probable Consequences of the Late Revolution in France*, by an unidentified Mons. B—de, were published in Edinburgh, London, and Dublin in 1790.[64] The book placed issues central for the French Revolution in a British context and made them available to anglophone readers. Discussing the invention of printing twice, the author seems to have been aware of Malesherbes's argument that printing created an informed public opinion, but he developed it within a specific British context by associating it with parliamentary representation. Representation could not reach its genuine form in a society which was based on oral communication, where political discussion took place in public meetings, with the menace of physical force. It was dependent on a public informed by a shared printed, textual universe. Printing had a continuous function as an instrument in curbing despotism and corruption. But much more profoundly it had been the necessary cause for a radical change in the structure of society which enabled liberty to develop fully. The book thus seems to present the view among many French reformers that the English constitution was a model for France to follow. In its English context, however, the author's view of the function of the invention of printing was far from revolutionary, but rather an assertion of the superiority of the English constitution which, in contrast to the French political system, seemed to have evolved to suit the new realities created by the invention of printing.

The invention of printing – the political analysis in eighteenth-century Britain

The more radicalised and assertively secular understanding of the invention of printing only emerged as a theme in England in the radical circles of the 1790s as restrictions on the press began to appear, not least with the royal proclamation against seditious writings of 21 May 1792. While in France thoughts on the wider impact on society of the invention of printing were expressed by leading politicians, in England they were formulated by men who were increasingly marginalised as the conflicts with France evolved.

In 1794 Daniel Isaac Eaton was prosecuted for treason because he had printed Thomas Paine's *Rights of Man*. In response he published a sarcastic volume, written in the voice of 'Antitype': *The Pernicious Effects of the Art of Printing Upon Society, Exposed. A Short Essay Addressed to the Friends of Social Order*. His fiery prose parodied the view of his oppressors that the invention of printing was the evil cause of the mounting challenge to the established hierarchical society. While he agreed with them on the fact of the matter, he disagreed about the assessment of it, mocking those who saw the invention of printing as part of a history of decline from a former state of greater virtue:

Before this diabolical art was introduced among men, there was social order, and as the great Locke expresses it, some subordination – man placed an implicit confidence in his temporal and spiritual directors – Princes and

Priests – entertained no doubts of their infallibility; or ever questioned their unerring wisdom. Indeed, the lower orders, though in other respects immersed in the most profound ignorance, knew full well (their superiors having taken care to inform them) that the existence of society depended upon distinctions of rank, fortune etc ... Since printing has been employed as the medium of diffusing sentiments etc. government has become more difficult – the governors are frequently, and insolently called upon to give an account of the national treasure, its expenditure etc. ... This, with a great deal more such stuff, is called the rights of man – blessed fruits of the art of printing – the scum of the earth, the swinish multitude, talking of their rights! ... With similar mistaken notions of liberty, even many women are infatuated; and the press, that grand prolific source of evil – that fruitful mother of mischief, has already favoured the public with several female productions on this very popular subject – one in particular called Rights of Women, and in which, as one of their rights, a share in legislation is claimed and asserted – gracious heaven! To what will this fatal delusion lead, and in what will it terminate.[65]

This passage may show that Eaton was familiar with Baron d'Holbach's sarcastic *Théologie portative*, which has an entry on 'Printing: The invention of the devil',[66] as well as with Malesherbes and Condorcet. But in the following passages he developed the theme in a way which had a specific resonance in an English context. Using the word 'diabolical' about printing, so often referred to as an art divinely inspired, Antitype turned on its head the English establishment theme, which to book people would have been known for instance from Lewis's life of Caxton,[67] that printing had dispelled the obscurantism of Popery:

But for printing, those two disturbers of the repose of society, and rascally innovators ... Calvin and Luther, would never have been able to propagate their ... rebellion against the spiritual jurisdiction of his Holiness, the Pope ... and had mankind remained ignorant of the use of types, those outcasts of society, Paine and Barlow, would not have been able to publish their wicked ... inflammatory books.

Making Antitype deplore the Reformation as an earlier instance of insolent rebellion against authority, Eaton implied that his opponents, who saw the invention of printing and its consequences as part of the history of the human fall from grace, were Popish and trying to subvert the 1688 settlement. The repression of Paine and Barlow was a parallel to the repression of Luther and Calvin. A positive attitude to the invention of printing was taken to imply support for the freedom of the press and became a sort of test of 'Britishness'. It was a theme running through his publications of those years that, far from being a traitor, it was he, not Pitt and the king, who represented true British values.

Thomas Paine himself was also aware of the Protestant theme that printing subverted Popish falsehoods, but he turned the argument round and made it more radical still. Far from being a gift of God, the invention of printing provided evidence against the divine status of the Bible. Printing fixed a text in many identical copies and made it more difficult, but not impossible, for changes made by individuals to gain currency. A passage had been interpolated into the second edition of Part I of his own *Age of Reason*: if this could happen within a year of publication in the relatively stable medium of printing, it showed that no reliance at all could be placed on texts which were transmitted in manuscript, the earliest of which were datable to centuries after their alleged composition: 'Can we suppose it is consistent with the wisdom of the Almighty, to commit himself and his will to man upon such precarious means as these; or is it consistent we should put our faith upon such uncertainty?'[68]

In the polarised Britain of the 1790s Eaton and Paine were not alone. In 1793 Thomas Cogan published *The Rhine*, which described a journey in 1791–2 in the form of a series of letters. He passed through Mainz and in four letters, more than seventy pages long, he discussed the invention of printing.[69] Despite the many pages devoted to the topic, his derivative and incoherent account, based on views by then long discredited, shows that he was not very concerned with who in fact invented printing. But, echoing Condorcet, he was very interested in the social impact of the invention, which had created a system of communication in which even the publication of error was beneficial for it would lead immediately to the publication of refutations.

Cogan's long history ends somewhat unexpectedly with a drinking song, toasting not the invention which he had been discussing, but the current use of printing. This placed the invention in the contemporary sphere of clubs or associations, which by now were increasingly repressed. In not so coded language Cogan attacked the oppressive legislation of the 1790s and the tyrannical system which had imposed them. A secular, non-hierarchical celebration of the invention of printing had become a way of expressing hostility to the monarchy and the war.

I
See riches circulate at will,
By coinage, and by minting:
The Printing Art is nobler still.
Truth circulates by printing.
    Chorus.
The Printing Art, etc.

II

Since truth is truth, as all allow
It cannot suffer *stinting*:
Pernicious Error rears her brow;
When tyrants limit printing.
    Chorus.
Pernicious Error etc.

III

Since Freedom's self sometimes runs mad,
The thought is well worth hinting:
Let useful truths be modest clad;
And then go on with printing.
    Chorus.
Let useful, etc.

IV

But Vice, you say, with hideous leer,
At Virtue will be *squinting!*
Well, if Vice squints and looks so queer:
We'll mend her sight with Printing.
    Chorus.
Well, if Vice squints and looks so queer:
We'll mend her sight with printing.

The French *philosophes* used the past to understand their present. Cogan made no such attempt and the new, enlightened interpretation of the invention of printing is reflected in a long account, so formulaic and out-of-date that it appears simply to be a vehicle for expressing contemporary political opinions. Its value to Cogan nonetheless depended on the invention of printing being politically meaningful.

Just as Cogan, despite devoting pages to the issue, showed no profound interest in who actually invented printing, the French political thinkers did not identify the books produced in the very first years as being themselves of great importance. Notably, in his article on printing in the *Encyclopédie*, Louis de Jaucourt discussed the implications for human society of the invention of printing, but dismissed the study of individual books as being of no wider interest, important only for royal librarians and book dealers.[70] Yet the reflections of men with wider political interests on the invention of printing formed part of the intellectual environment in which the staff of the Bibliothèque nationale could use state resources for collecting incunabula, in the years of the Revolution, whether they shared these political views or not. Equally, the expressed attribution of a philosophical and political importance to the invention of printing coincided chronologically with the emergence of incunabula as a separate category of merchandise and as a new type of historical evidence, and with the growth in their value, both financial and intellectual.

The account of the invention of printing which rejected the notion that the history of mankind was determined by original sin also reveals affinities with what was happening in the marketplace. For example, the debate about the invention of printing was related to the debate about whether profit and luxury were in sinful opposition to virtuous poverty, a theme discussed further in Chapter 4.[71] The invention of printing had gained additional meaning because the earliest printed books were becoming prominent parts of the commercial and cultural landscape. While the political and philosophical views which we have analysed explain in part why incunabula were regarded as they were in the 1790s, these views were also themselves part of the wider changes in attitudes and values which I seek to explain.

2 | Aristocratic aspirations and the wartime market: competing for the past and the future

In February 1798 Lord Glenbervie noted in his diary:

Edwards the bookseller dined with me yesterday. He says Lord Spencer's collection is richer in classics than even the National Library, enriched as it now is with the spoil of so many countries. I asked him what he thought Lord Spencer's may be worth. He thinks it may have cost him £25,000.[1]

Considering jointly the formation of the book collections of an English aristocrat and the French Bibliothèque nationale, Lord Glenbervie compared their means of acquisition, and measured the effects of the Europe-wide spoliation of the French troops against the purchasing power which resided in the dominant English economy. Money was often the more effective. This chapter will examine the collecting practices of the second Earl Spencer, an English aristocrat who was both rich and politically prominent, and of the national institution of revolutionary France, competing for the same books in a shared market in war-torn Europe.[2] This will be the point of departure for an analysis of the relationship between the intellectual importance attached to old books and their value in the market.

I will seek to understand to what extent the motives of the public institution and of the noble lord in creating their collections of essentially similar objects were perceived to be similar or different, and to what extent they were in fact different. This will highlight how the emergence to pre-eminence of public and national institutions, which were to become so important for the nations of Europe in the nineteenth century, played a role also in redefining the meaning of a private collection, the two types of collection now more readily understood as ideologically distinct.

This will in part emerge from an analysis of how they interacted with and through the market for rare books, in some obvious ways very differently while they were, simultaneously, interdependent. The analysis will in addition give a more nuanced view of the role of those who supplied the books, former owners as well as dealers, who contributed not only to the formation of a market but also to the construction of the category of incunabula.

The Revolution enabled the Bibliothèque nationale to collect, but things could have turned out very differently. In his 'Rapport sur l'instruction

Figure 2.1 Earl Spencer in his Garter robes, by John Singleton Copley, 1801. From the Collection at Althorp.

publique' of 1791, Talleyrand famously saw the intellectual efforts of the past as a series of experiments. Just as one discards the equipment of failed scientific experiments, so one discards books when they have served their purpose. Some books from the past are useful, others not: 'They are the numerous failures of a task which should not cloud the view once the work is over.' He also clarified the institutional responsibility for the ongoing process of throwing away outdated books: 'It is obvious that it is from within libraries that the means shall be found for accelerating the destruction.'[3]

Talleyrand's views were less unusual than they may sound, and they were not confined to men and women who favoured the Revolution. In Sénac de Meilhan's novel *L'émigré* from 1797, an exiled aristocrat finds stoic consolation for the sale of his confiscated library: he cannot regret the loss of something no longer useful. In post-revolutionary France his books have lost their meaning. Thus he comments extensively on how his law books are now of no use: 'This discipline will soon cease to occupy people's minds, for the Gothic edifice of which it is the description is undermined on all sides.'[4]

The impact of such attitudes is best measured, perhaps, in the market-place. Already in 1789 Guillaume Debure l'aîné, the bookseller, complained that he was losing money on law books. Another publisher complained to the Convention nationale that religious reforms had ruined his business in service books.[5] There was no market for books which were no longer useful. This also had an impact on the market for old books. Writing in 1860, Brunet, the dealer and bibliographer of rare books, looked back to his youth and explained how hostility to everything old had had an impact on the value of historic books and, consequently, on what he himself had included in the first edition from 1809 of his *Manuel du libraire et de l'amateur du livre* or, from the perspective of the older man, what he had excluded:

The philosophical spirit of the eighteenth century, or what passed for it, was then still dominant, with … its stupid disdain for the past … regarding the history of our ancestors only as the useless debris of feudal privilege.[6]

The link between ideological importance and market value was so clearly understood that it could be used in political satire, for instance by Eaton, Thomas Paine's publisher, in a spoof booksellers' catalogue which offered Magna Carta and other iconic texts for the struggle for freedom. The political danger to British freedoms could be signposted though a fiction of a fall in their commercial value:

These works, having formerly been much read, are consequently rather soiled, in consideration of which, and their being now *out of fashion* they will be sold exceeding cheap, and must of course be articles worthy the attention of trunkmakers, pastry cooks etc.[7]

Books were always vulnerable when their texts were seen to be of no use and to belong to a superseded, unlamented past. But now they could equally be vulnerable to destruction for being meaningful in another way, when they were judged as objects from a despised past. In 1792 and 1793, feudal symbols were prohibited in France in a number of decrees: as early as 14 August 1792 the Assemblée legislative voted for the destruction of the symbols of the *Ancien Régime*. Charters which detailed the rights of the nobility were among the first victims. Following the order of 4 July 1793 to remove royal marks from all public monuments the collection of the Bibliothèque nationale was seriously threatened with devastation. Unlike genealogical charters, its books were not to be burnt, but the decree still had significant consequences.[8] It would have meant removing the royal coat of arms from bindings made for the Bibliothèque du roi, as well as the arms of past noble owners from historic bindings. It would equally have meant the destruction

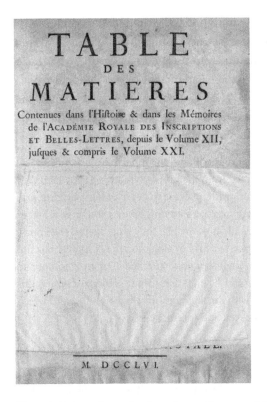

Figure 2.2 A crude repair where the royal arms and the royal imprint have been cut out. BnF, salle X, usuels, ACADi.

of feudal symbols within books, whether book-plates or Renaissance decorated title pages which so often incorporated the arms of their noble owners. The very paper on which books were printed was threatened, it was suggested, if watermarked for instance with the royal French fleur-de-lys. It was not the texts which were to be controlled or repressed, but the political allegiance attributed to the books as objects, conveyed by symbols which were seen to appropriate them for specific ideological purposes (see Figure 2.2).

A workshop was organised in the Louvre on 18 October 1793 to allow potential contractors to undertake a technical investigation in preparation for tendering for a contract for modifying the books to bring them into conformity with the new standards. The library received at least two bids for the job, including one from a consortium of three Parisian booksellers and binders, who quoted a price of one million livres, then the equivalent of about £40,000.[9] It is quite possible that this process was set in motion to scupper the project while appearing to comply with the law by presenting the ministry and the Comité d'instruction publique with a proposal which would have to be turned down for financial reasons.

Renouard, later to become a famous bookseller and bibliographer, composed a submission to the Comité d'instruction publique. Before submitting it on 16 October 1793, he ensured that it was signed by Charles Chardin, a bookseller, and Jean-Philippe-Victor Charlemagne, a schoolteacher, both prominent Jacobins in his part of Paris. Renouard warned against the destruction of books which had paved the way for the Revolution, but he also brought up a completely different argument:

For three years, the ferocious and cunning Pitt and the repulsive Catherine and all the capitalists of Europe have benefited from the prodigious advantage which they can draw from the changes. They work without cease to deprive us of our most precious pieces … Numerous agents are over here buying up everything which they believe will please their masters. This silent war which they wage against the France of letters is no less active than the one which they wage so cruelly against our liberty. How the proud jealousy of the English will be gratified … if an ignorant and sacrilegious hand brought disorder and degradation to our National Library, this monument which they cannot see without shaking with envy and rage and which they would be delighted to see destroyed and overturned.

In a footnote he added:

I have with my own eyes seen English people leave the National Library furious and downcast. They were as if burdened by the weight of the beautiful things of all sorts which one had endeavoured to show them and their mournful and wild eyes seemed to call for the destruction of this admirable monument.[10]

He was supported by Gilbert Romme, president of the Comité d'instruction publique, who reported to the Convention nationale that the royal symbol of the fleur-de-lys had been used by craftsmen not as a royal symbol, but as a 'type national pour les arts', the logo of the French national brand. Removing the symbols would hand a victory to the English: it was in fact a plot between the English and the émigrés to destroy what they could not possess.[11] This theme was to be repeated by the Abbé Grégoire in his report on the Bibliothèque nationale:

The strategy of our enemies was always to take from us all which they could, to destroy that which they could not take away; in a word to commit and to organise crimes for the pleasure of imputing them to us and to call us barbarians.[12]

Yet he also agreed that in noble collections the books had served an ideological purpose:

The scientific property of the nation comes from repositories which it possessed before the Revolution, from the former castles of the tyrant, from the suppression of the ecclesiastic and legal corporations, academies, emigrants and convicts … Rare and valuable objects had been accumulated, or rather hoarded, to serve the ambitions of the former nobility.[13]

The theory of an enemy plot was probably aided by a fire which broke out in the Théâtre Montausier in November 1793, when these discussions of ideological destruction were under way. In London *The Times* reported that the owner of the theatre was accused of having received 50,000 francs, some £2,000, from the former queen, and a large sum from the English, to begin a fire so that it should spread and burn the neighbouring National Library.[14]

We may find it difficult to accept that Renouard and his colleagues believed in a counter-revolutionary plot, but they were not the only ones to use such arguments. A report of 4 June 1793 suggested that public monuments were being destroyed by aristocrats and asked for penalties to be imposed for such actions. Conspiracy was a frequent way of explaining events on all sides of the Revolution.[15]

The preservation of historic books in a public repository was placed firmly in the context of the battle for the control of history.[16] One approach was similar to the Roman *damnatio memoriae*, the destruction of images or inscriptions which commemorated a past which had become undesirable. Renouard and his colleagues proposed a more sophisticated use of the past, not a suppression of its memory but its condemnation through a memorialisation of its iniquity, a controlled and redirected commemoration expressed through the surviving objects, which were open to competing interpretations and therefore relinquished to the enemies of progress at one's peril. The battle against feudalism was no longer only internal. It was part of a war, and intellectual issues in the battle for control over the French past were now merged with the battle against England. In the words of Romme:

A grand battle has been engaged between peoples and their kings. Our libraries are filled with works which provide evidence of their criminality. The history which most flatters their pride is to the same degree the history of their misdeeds.[17]

Undoubtedly Renouard and his colleagues sought out the arguments which he thought would be most persuasive and to our ears their words may sound like desperate rhetorical ploys, but Chardin, Charlemagne, Renouard, and Romme were all active Jacobins. Charlemagne represented the Section de Brutus at the Commune de Paris and it was he who, on behalf of the Section, delivered the funeral oration for Marat.[18] The published oration was countersigned by Chardin, who was commander-in-chief of the Section's militia. Renouard and Charlemagne both took part in the rota of citizens leading the armed guard of the Temple where the young Louis XVII was

kept prisoner.[19] After the end of the Terror Charlemagne remained firm in
his Jacobin views and was executed in 1794. Away from Paris at the coup of
9 Thermidor [27 July 1794], Romme killed himself, having been condemned
to death for continued Jacobin agitation as late as June 1795. Renouard himself got away with two spells of imprisonment in autumn and winter of 1794
and again early in the summer of 1795.[20] These were not men who wished to
undermine the revolutionary cultural policy. They genuinely believed that
what they proposed was part of their revolutionary agenda. If it did not use
the historic books of the Bibliothèque nationale to its own advantage, the
Republic would leave the field open to its enemies who would create collections where the books would be used to flatter their aristocratic pride.

The role of French nationalism has been well examined in discussions
of the political change from an iconoclastic programme to the creation
of the notion of a national heritage, which was formulated in opposition
to the iconoclasm of 1792 and 1793 and which was to become the intellectual foundation both for the spoliations of occupied countries and for
the creation of central national museums in Paris.[21] But the importance
of the economic relationship with England has not been much discussed
in this context. Yet it is obvious from the remarks of Renouard, Romme,
and Grégoire that the importance of the French past was conceived as
part of the battle for supremacy with England, cultural and economic.

This emphasis on national supremacy was associated with the, correct,
perception of a change in the balance between London and Paris as markets for goods which could be understood as cultural indicators: London
was becoming much more dominant. Thus there was an anxiety in France
about the commercial and cultural advantage which England drew from
the vases in the Etruscan style produced by Josiah Wedgwood, inspired by
Hamilton's collection of Greek vases; this was an important argument in
a joint report of the Committees of Finance and of Public Instruction in
June 1795, recommending the creation of a museum in Paris which might
inspire French manufacturers to compete.[22]

Closer to the field of books, English artists and manufacturers began to
pose a threat to French supremacy in the market for prints and engravings,
as well as in the manufacture of luxury paper, an anxiety which Renouard
expressed in vivid nationalistic terms in 1802.[23] Camus, who had been active
in the burning of aristocratic charters in 1792, chaired a special committee
set up to evaluate the edition of Virgil published by Pierre Didot in 1798.
In his report he paid the greatest attention to all aspects of the standards of
production, underlining how Didot enabled French manufacture to compete with the high quality of books produced in England.[24]

Even English fashion began to dominate, as evidenced by the fashion magazine *Le cabinet des modes* which changed its name in 1786 to *Magasin des modes nouvelles françaises et anglaises*.[25] These were the years when smart Frenchmen wore *un redingote* (a riding coat), or *un spencer*, named after the second Earl. Gouverneur Morris, soon-to-be minister of the embassy of the young United States of America to Paris, wrote in a letter to George Washington in March 1789 about life in the salons of Paris: 'Everything is à l'anglaise, and the desire to imitate the English prevails alike in the cut of a coat and in the form of a constitution.'[26] Contemporaries easily understood the wider political context for the changed balance between London and Paris in the market for luxury goods. This balance took on a new political meaning when England was no longer the model for progress but the henchman of the fallen feudal masters. Whether Renouard was right or not to see the sale of goods abroad to English aristocrats as part of the same phenomenon as the physical destruction of French national heritage, he was undoubtedly justified in thinking that it reflected a balance of power, economically and politically.

For a long time English buyers had been present at Parisian book sales just as French buyers had been at London sales.[27] What was new was that this was now considered so threatening that even German and Italian books were construed as French national cultural property. It is far from certain, however, that the Revolution initially created a situation where the English could dominate more than they had done before. Lord Palmerston, by the standards of many English noblemen a modest collector of art and antiques, was in Paris in 1791, shopping as well as observing, with growing distaste, debates in the Jacobin club. He found Paris expensive, commenting, for instance, that Sèvres porcelain cost more than corresponding pieces sold by Christie's in London, simply because they were the latest fashion, which was changing so fast that it really only mattered in Paris itself. His dislike of Jacobin politics did not put him off going back: next year he took his whole family to Paris. They paid their respects to Louis XVI and Marie Antoinette on 5 August, but the visit had to be cut short for reasons of safety and they left on 7 August, with too little time for shopping: 'We set out from Paris about 12 having been making purchases, a very few, having sadly been hurried away.'[28]

Similarly, when James Payne reported on his extensive purchases of books for Spencer at various sales in Paris in spring 1792 he did not find the prices very favourable, nor was the exchange rate invariably all that good. The value of the franc had, he believed, begun an irreversible recovery after its initial decline, and in the late autumn of 1792 he felt that it was close to the pre-revolutionary rate.[29]

When the incunabula of Cardinal Loménie de Brienne were auctioned in Paris in March 1792,[30] Count Reviczky, until recently Imperial envoy to the Court of St James, ensured a few items for Spencer via Eusebio Della Lena, making much of the difficulty of getting to Paris.[31] He suggested that the sale had not been fair because the Bibliothèque nationale could print the assignats which they used for paying.[32] Commercial relations were in fact relatively normal. Spencer received a copy of the catalogue in London in December 1791.[33] Leaving bids with the auctioneer in the normal way, the Bodleian Library acquired its copy of the Gutenberg Bible, paying £100, quite what one would expect, and using nearly exactly the standard, pre-revolutionary exchange rate.[34] The sale of 2,000 lots, all incunabula but a small part of the 100,000-volume library, fetched a total of 106,324 livres and 19 sous, the equivalent of some £4,250. Edwards claimed that the sale brought in more money than Loménie de Brienne had spent on creating his collection.[35] When Payne, in January 1792, bought a small Donatus for Spencer at Maguérard's sale, decidedly the sale of a man who wanted cash to leave France, he paid 450 francs, or £16 9s, an enormous price for a small undated school book.[36] There is nothing to suggest that the market in Paris was in crisis.

Although the political situation may have meant that more items were sent to be sold in London, it does not seem that this influx occasioned a noticeable downward pressure on prices there either, a powerful measure of the strength of the market. James Edwards was probably the dealer who brought most collections to England in this period. He had been one of the first to exploit the opportunities. Returning from Paris in June 1790 he organised the sale in London of a collection of books promoted as the Bibliotheca Parisiana in 1791. It was among the most spectacular London book sales of the 1790s,[37] and brought Edwards a staggering profit of £1,500.[38]

Clayton Mordaunt Cracherode was rich but, with an annual income of £3,600, roughly half the income of Lord Palmerston, not quite fabulously rich.[39] Yet he could spend money on luxury books, collecting, like so many others, mainly texts of classical authors. With his bequest of 1799 the British Museum for the first time acquired a collection of printed books selected by a bibliophile for being sumptuous. He wrote the date of acquisition into most of them and this enables us to establish that the three years in which he bought the most incunabula were 1790, 1797, and 1798, probably to some extent a reflection of availability, but an analysis of the individual items shows that it also represented a change in his collecting interest, incunabula supplementing his interest in editions of the classics.

One of his most spectacular purchases was made in 1791 at the sale of the Bibliotheca Parisiana, namely Fichet's *Rhetorica* printed in Paris in 1471, lavishly decorated and bound in red satin for presentation to Sixtus IV. It cost him £31 10s, marginally more than it had fetched in 1786 at the sale of Camus de Limare.[40] Just as they still held up in Paris, prices in London were not lowered by the influx of books from France.

Renouard was wrong in implying that the English profiteered in the normal sense of the word: as long as it was possible for English collectors to take part in the Paris market, prices held up. There were willing vendors and English buyers had money, but they paid the going market rate. This was all quite obvious to contemporary observers. Thorkelin, professor at the University of Copenhagen, knew why. In his new year's greetings for 1791 to Francis Douce, he wrote:

And may the God of Gold keep you in his divine graces in the same proportion as the public-spirited Edwards continues to enrich the first of nations with whatever is valuable in the literary world.[41]

The impact of this may be illustrated by an episode which took place at an auction in Paris in 1813. A French bookseller bought the Aldine Homer printed on vellum for 2,900 francs, that is about £116. The dealer was congratulated by a delighted public: at least this treasure would remain in France. But he was wounded by the delight of his colleagues who did not know his secret: he acted for Spencer. The bookseller was none other than Renouard, the opponent of England's aristocratic war against the France of letters.[42] He had to operate in a market presided over by the God of Gold, even when embodied in an English aristocratic war leader.

The events in Paris in the summer of 1792 made Spencer, like so many leading Whigs, abandon the faction of Fox, whose opposition to monarchical power had become uncomfortable as events unfolded in France. Spencer joined Pitt and one of his early tasks was a diplomatic mission to Vienna in 1794, accompanied by Thomas Grenville, another eminent book collector, and another Whig who had abandoned Fox. On his return Spencer was made First Lord of the Admiralty, from where he efficiently guided the British naval engagement with France until 1801. To complete the picture, Grenville was First Lord of the Admiralty for a brief spell in 1806–7 in the Government of All the Talents. Men who combined wealth with positions at the centre of British power were avid collectors of the very same books as those sought by the Bibliothèque nationale. There was some truth to the high-strung fear of Romme, Renouard, and their Jacobin allies that the war on the battlefield was equally fought in the field of rare books.

Figure 2.3 Earl Spencer as a man of learning, by John Hoppner, 1808. From the Collection at Althorp.

The foundation of Spencer's collection coincided with the beginning of the upheavals in France: at first sight his acquisition processes, through purchase, may seem entirely distinct from those of the Bibliothèque nationale, yet on closer inspection there were intimate connections between the two.

Until 1789 Spencer's book bills provide no evidence of an interest in rare books but in September that year he finalised his acquisition of the collection which had been formed by Count Reviczky.[43] This purchase was the beginning of one of the most remarkable and luxurious collections of books ever to be formed in the British Isles. According to Reviczky himself, his collection had been valued by several London booksellers at £10,000. He sold it to Spencer for an annuity of £600, on condition he had permanent access to the books.[44]

Spencer only paid the annuity for some four and a half years, for Reviczky died in 1793, so it turned out to be a good deal for Spencer but much more importantly, this form of purchase, unusual among peers, shows us that he attached such importance to owning the collection that he was prepared to pay not only a very large, but an unspecified sum of money.[45] This must be

seen in its context of the means available to Spencer. His annual expenditure has been assessed at some £60,000, against at income of *c.* £40,000. It
is not surprising that, having received his property largely unencumbered,
he died with debts of £147,806 11s.[46] During his life he sold property to the
value of at least £207,000, chiefly for his extravagant expenditure on his
library.[47] One creditor was Cracherode, who at his death forgave Spencer
a loan of £3,000, the equivalent of his total annual income.[48] Not only did
Spencer have an enormous annual income, he also had the means of spend-
ing substantially more. Both the sums paid by Spencer – set in the context
of his wealth – and the way in which he paid help us to understand the
place of books as part of a wider picture of expenditure on luxury in late
eighteenth-century England.

This level of expenditure is so far removed from the life of people who
bought what they needed to feed and clothe themselves that a comparison is as good as meaningless. To make sense of the price which Spencer
paid for Reviczky's collection we must see it in the context of other luxury
objects brought to England at the same time. In 1790 Lord Lansdowne
paid £600 for a statue of Hercules found in Hadrian's Villa in Tivoli, an
important statue which has given the name of its aristocratic owner to
one of the standard representations of Hercules (see Figure 2.4).[49] In 1791
Charles Townley paid £700 for the statue of the Discoboulos, now in
the British Museum, also from Hadrian's Villa.[50] One year of Reviczky's
annuity could buy one of the most celebrated pieces of antique sculpture.
It was a large sum of money, especially outside England, but it should
also be seen in the context where the English super-rich had money to
spend frivolously: Reviczky's annuity of £600 was exactly the same as
the pension which Sir Humphry Morice left in his will to provide for his
horses and dogs when he died in 1785. His favourite horse did better
than Reviczky: it lived at Grove House in Chiswick for twenty years after
Morice's death.[51]

We can gain an impression of what individual books in Reviczky's collection would have cost, for in 1789–90 the Bodleian Library bought extensively in exactly the same field. While some cost as little as 15s,[52] one the
most expensive, a copy of Aulus Gellius printed in Rome in 1469, cost
£58 16s (Figure 2.5).[53] By the way of comparison, a little earlier a statue of
Diana was offered for £60 by an agent of Lord Egremont to Charles Townley
(Figure 2.6).[54]

In 1794 on their way back to London from their diplomatic mission
to Vienna, Spencer and Grenville bought a large quantity of wine from a
Frankfurt wine merchant. Spencer's part of the bill came to £244 for some

Figure 2.4 'The Lansdowne Hercules', from Hadrian's Villa in Tivoli, *c.* 125–38 AD, with eighteenth-century restorations by Carlo Albacini, since removed but subsequently reinstated. *Catalogue of the Ancient Marbles of the Marquess of Lansdowne* (London: Christie's, 1930), lot 34.

717 litres of two different Rhenish wines, Hochheim (hock), 1726 vintage, and Johannisberg from 1783.[55] According to a wine book from 1825, 1726 and 1783 were among the five best years for Rhenish wine in the eighteenth century.[56] So instead of Aulus Gellius you could have bought about 205 bottles of one the most expensive wines.

In 1790 the Bodleian Library paid £38 17s for the third edition of Livy's Roman history,[57] a price comparable to the £41 16s (about 1,046 francs) which a clock by the innovative and fashionable clockmaker Lépine cost Lord Palmerston in Paris in 1791.[58]

Although Reviczky owned many books printed in the fifteenth century, he did not buy them because they were incunabula. He collected editions of classical authors in Greek or Latin, with one important exception: he excluded ancient authors who were Christian.[59] The collection was an assertion of the direct link of the eighteenth-century aristocratic governing elite to the classical world, bypassing the intervening period of theological

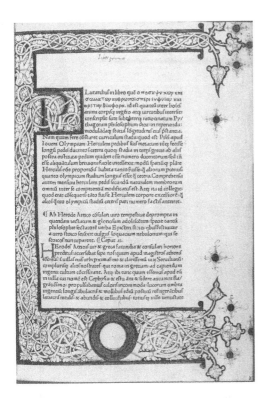

Figure 2.5 Aulus Gellius, *Noctes Atticae*, sig. [b]1 recto. [Rome]: Sweynheym and Pannartz, 11 April 1469. Bodleian, Auct. L 2.2.

domination. Reviczky had a great interest in classical literature but no interest in the culture of the fifteenth century. His pre-eminent interest in books which were genuinely first editions of the classics was widely shared and is reflected in the prices paid by the Bodleian Library. One of the few non-classical incunabula bought in those years was a copy of Gratianus's *Decretum*, splendidly bound and also illuminated, if rather crudely. It was printed in Strasbourg in 1471 by Eggestein, whose works were important in the debate about the invention of printing. Yet it cost the Bodleian Library only £3 at the sale of Loménie de Brienne (Figure 2.7).[60]

As we saw, in 1789 the first edition of Aulus Gellius, Rome 1469, cost £58 16s, but the first edition of the sermons of Leo I printed in Rome in 1470 only cost £4 6s. The difference in price is striking, not least bearing in mind that, if one attaches any importance to the early Church, Leo was a significant pope. Even if we take the size of the volume into consideration, the classical text was twelve times as expensive, sheet by sheet, as the papal sermons.[61] The relative importance was also reflected in the bindings which the Bodleian paid to have put on the two books, expensive red morocco on

Figure 2.6 A heavily restored Roman statue of Diana from about 100 AD. Petworth House. The National Trust. Reference: 180540. © National Trust/Andrew Fether.

the Aulus Gellius, brown calf on Leo, probably some ten price categories lower than red morocco.[62]

The relative importance can also be seen if we look at price changes. When in 1743–5 Thomas Osborne offered Harley's books for sale in London he asked, for instance, £2 2s for the first edition of Pliny's letters; in 1790, the Bodleian Library paid £23 3s 6d for its copy. By contrast, while Osborne had asked £3 3s for the first edition of Cyprianus from 1471, in 1789 the Bodleian Library paid £2 12s 6d for a handsomely decorated copy. While first editions of classical texts had increased by over 700 per cent, comparable patristic editions had not even maintained their price level, in this case costing over 30 per cent less.[63]

Spencer initially continued Reviczky's approach to collecting. Lists of books drawn up for him in Italy in the early 1790s contain almost entirely editions of the classics.[64] Yet there are a few signs that he soon explored an expansion of his horizons. The first of Spencer's bills to include incunabula is from 9 May 1789, and the first to include a reference work on early printed books is from 16 May 1789.[65] In 1790 he bought Maittaire's

Annales typographici, for £8 8s and in the same year he bought five central works of European scholarship specifically on fifteenth-century books.[66] The next year he acquired another set of indispensable tools, namely the most important catalogues produced by the doyen of the French book-trade: Guillaume-François Debure le jeune's *Bibliographie instructive,* his catalogue of the Gaignat sale, and Guillaume Debure l'aîné's catalogue of sale of the duc de La Vallière.[67]

When in Vienna in 1794 Spencer bought extensively from several dealers. His purchases centred on the contemporary situation in Europe, descriptions and histories of various countries and their political situation, and large numbers of maps. This conforms to an impression of Spencer as a man who took his new political role extremely seriously. Standing out from these political books are some of the most important eighteenth-century German studies on fifteenth-century books, studies which were often of a strong local flavour, sometimes in German, and generally difficult to acquire outside German-speaking lands.[68] Spencer's engagement with the very active German study of incunabula contrasts with Edwards's condescending lack of enthusiasm, which seems to have been based on the importance which he attached to the book culture of metropolitan London, compared with that of a decentralised Germany.[69]

However, when it came to rare books, Spencer still concentrated his buying on first editions of the classics.[70] The first reliable sign of a new development is from 17 December 1796, when he bought for £10 10s a copy of Albertus Magnus's work on medicine printed by William de Machlinia in London about 1483.[71] His new-found interest in early English printing is evident in subsequent bills and this is matched by how their price developed in the market. By 1799 prices for English incunabula had grown dramatically, only to grow even more precipitously by 1812, by which time they were as valuable as the most sought-after foreign treasures. For instance, in 1799 Spencer paid £75 for a copy of *The Book of Hawking, Hunting, and Heraldry;* in 1812, at the sale of John Ker, the Duke of Roxburghe, a copy fetched £147.[72] This is an indication of the supremacy of the English market, for in contrast to other categories, prices for Caxtons were maintained nearly exclusively by English collectors.[73]

Spencer soon expanded beyond English incunabula and by 1806 he was prepared to spend £60 on a volume of medieval devotion, Turrecremata's *Meditationes* from 1467. It was not for want of trying that both he and the French repeatedly failed to acquire this book from Nuremberg City Library.[74] After failed attempts at confiscation, Capperonnier sought to acquire it by exchange, offering books to the value of about £80, an indication that the earl and the Bibliothèque nationale had a shared view of the market value of the item.[75]

In 1800 and 1801 Spencer paid prices ranging between £40 and £60 for each of three scraps of vellum bought in rapid succession, indulgences, items for which there had been no market until then, and textually as far as you can get from his plan to concentrate on classical authors in first editions.[76] In ten years Spencer had moved from the collection strategy of Reviczky to one similar to that known from the duc de La Vallière, and even more similar to the one pursued by the French troops on behalf of the Bibliothèque nationale. Spencer's interests were, as we have seen, in part formed by a recent French and German appreciation of incunabula which he encountered through newly acquired reference works and sale catalogues, but must also be seen in the context of the war between Britain and France and the market which it enabled to prosper.

Spencer's developing interests as a collector began to be noticed. In January 1797 he received a letter written from Erfurt by Maugérard, one of the many whose careers were both unmade and made by the French Revolution.[77] By some he has been described as the worst of book thieves. More appropriately Anthony Hobson has referred to his 'sharp practice', a practice on which he did not have a monopoly, as we shall see. A Benedictine from Metz, Maugérard specialised in books from German religious houses: it seems that as early as 1767 he acquired from the Mainz Carthusians a copy of the Gutenberg Bible which was to be sold the following year with the collection of Gaignat.[78] He supplied the duc de La Vallière and, in the 1780s, Loménie de Brienne.[79] He wrote several contributions to learned journals about early printing, and it was he who established beyond reasonable doubt which of the early undated Bible editions was the one printed by Gutenberg. He did this on the basis of a manuscript note in a copy procured by himself for the Bibliothèque royale which was thus demonstrably earlier than the Psalter from 1457. In 1791 he refused to take the Oath of the Clergy, and in 1792 he sold his collection, or rather his stock.[80] In 1793 he was accused of seeking to leave France in possession of national property.[81] Although this was in fact true, he managed to get away, taking the goods with him, and finding safety mainly in Erfurt which became a base for his commercial activities. In 1800 he returned to France, and in 1802 he was given the official responsibility for the spoliation of libraries in the four new departments on the west bank of the Rhine annexed by France following the treaty of Luneville of 9 February 1801, a job which he performed vigorously and with his accustomed shrewdness, to the advantage of himself, the Bibliothèque nationale, and the English book-trade.[82]

In 1797 Maugérard presented himself to Spencer as a collector who was prepared to sell his books.[83] He sent Spencer a list of items including block-books and a copy of the earliest dated book in German and the earliest to carry woodcut illustrations. Spencer scrawled a draft response on the back of Maugérard's letter: the books were out of scope; books printed before 1470 were of no interest to him, unless they were truly the first editions of classical authors; he was not interested in papal decretals, which in the context of what was on offer must be shorthand for murky, medieval texts; and the prices were about a third too high. Instead he included a list of items which he wished Maugérard to seek out for him. The fiction that this was a correspondence between two collectors did not last long. Maugérard justified the prices by referring to the sale of the duc de La Vallière, by now a shared benchmark for the monetary value of early printed books. In 1791 the earl had bought a copy of the auction catalogue, with a price list. With splendid condescension, Maugérard suggested that perhaps the earl was used to lower prices because his taste was less exacting than the duke's. Nonetheless, he graciously offered a discount of 25 per cent, 'to assist the Earl's zeal for literature'.[84]

Being a good dealer, Maugérard pushed the boundaries of the earl's collecting criteria with considerable success. In August 1797 he sold him the illustrated German vernacular book which Spencer had earlier turned down so emphatically. It was a volume containing four tales based on the Old Testament, printed in Bamberg in 1462,[85] a book much talked about since it was first discovered in 1792,[86] but far removed from the earl's declared interest in the classics (Figure 2.8). The earl offered 1,000 livres [£40], but Maugérard was not easily daunted and insisted on sending it to him with an invoice for 1,800 livres [£72]. What Spencer in fact paid is not known.

Encouraged by this success, Maugérard told the earl that the narrow scope which he had set for his collection was 'a great loss to literature', and sought to shift his focus towards acquiring books that were fifteenth-century typographical specimens. He proposed an ambitious cataloguing project, and also tried to implant an idea in the mind of the earl that the developing nature of his collection required a different approach from the vast, newly published catalogue by Panzer.[87] It had to be based on real expert knowledge, and was to focus on typography, with engraved facsimiles of all the typefaces in the collection. But this would be viable only if the earl collected more widely. Maugérard evidently hoped for a post for himself, even beginning to suggest terms, including receiving a flat fee and all profits, while Spencer would carry the risks:

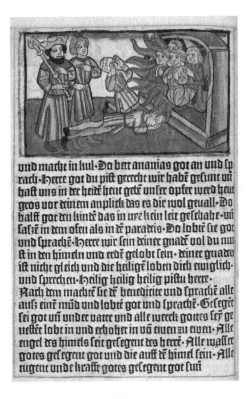

und machte in kul·Do het ananias got an und sp
rach·Herre got du pist gerecht wir habe gesunt vñ
hast uns in der heide heut getö unser opfer werd heut
gros vor deinem anplick das es dir wol geuall·Do
half got den kindö das in nre kein leit geschahe·vñ
saßö in dem ofen als in de paradis·Do lobte sie got
und sprachö·Herre wir sein deiner gnade vol du mu
ßt in den himeln und erde gelobt sein· deiner gnade
ist nicht gleich und die heilige loben dich ewiglich·
und sprechen·Heilig heilig heilig pistu herre·
Nach dem machte sie de benedicite und sprachö alle
auß einö mud und lobte got und sprachö·Gesegnet
sei got vñ under vater und alle werck gottes sey ge
neßet lobt in und erhohet in vö euen zu euen·Alle
engel des himels seit gesegent des herre·Alle wasser
gottes gesegnet got und die auff de himel sein·Alle
tugent unde krafft gottes gesegent got sun

Figure 2.8 *Historie von Joseph, Daniel, Judith und Esther*, sig. [c]3 verso, [fol. 17 verso]. Bamberg: Pfister, 1462. JRL, 9375.

We still have no good bibliography, for Panzer copied the errors of others, as I have told him. But he works to keep his family. Your Excellency is, I believe, the only person who combines a fully enlightened zeal with financial means adequate to enlighten ours and a future age on the art of printing and the printers whom we do not know yet by publishing your catalogue with engraved plates of some lines of all printers, to make their types known. I know that the engraving for this catalogue will be costly and demands advance payments, but it is certain that this bibliography, which cannot be pirated, will immediately give a good return, and that the learned world would render your Excellency the same gratitude which it will for ever render Mabillion and Montfaucon, for their work on the handwriting of different periods. The Duchess of Chatillon paid the expenses of the catalogue of the duc de La Vallière, her father, and when the costs had been covered, 18,000 francs remained which she surrendered to De Bure, on top of his salary. Excuse me, Sir, for these remarks, but it seems to me that making such a generous present to the public gives glory to a grand lord.[88]

The First Lord of the Admiralty was busy in 1797, a year which saw two major naval victories, St Vincent and Camperdown. His diary shows that when in London he had breakfast, dinner, and supper at the Admiralty every day. Although he had daily breaks for reading, there was little time for literary correspondence: his draft answer says: 'If I had had the time I would have liked to have a few questions asked to clarify two or three points in your letter, but for now I will limit myself to thanking you for the information which it contains, hoping to have another occasion to write in greater detail on those matters.'[89] But in his next letter, dated 17 October, six days after Camperdown,[90] he addressed Maugérard with the courtesy due to a man of learning, and offered him the opportunity to engage in a learned correspondence. It would be charming to have the time to compare books and discuss current views on them. In the meantime he would be delighted if Maugérard would explain his identification of the printer of the first Bible printed in German: it differed from the opinion of Placidus Braun, whose work Spencer had bought in Vienna.[91] Showing his familiarity with the best contemporary German scholarship Spencer demonstrated to Maugérard that he was not just a rich aristocrat, but also extremely well informed, just as Maugérard had sought to show Spencer that he was not just a dealer but a respectable scholar.[92] Without this shared bibliographical expertise it would not have been possible for the trade between occupied Germany and London to take place. Like the French confiscations, Spencer's purchases depended on his sharing with his suppliers an expertise which was often based on very recently published scholarly or commercial works.

There is little reason to doubt that Maugérard provided early inspiration for the direction of the lavish catalogue of Spencer's incunabula which Dibdin was later to write, at Spencer's expense, but circumstances did not allow Maugérard to engage in an unpaid correspondence, and his learned cataloguing project was never mentioned again. In the following correspondence Maugérard reverted to be being a dealer: like Panzer, he had to make a living. In October 1797 Spencer helpfully showed Maugérard's list to Edwards, for whom Maugérard increasingly became a supplier.[93] Thus in November 1798 he sent four boxes with about 150 books weighing 935 pounds, addressed to Spencer but destined for Edwards.[94] It seems likely that the bulk of this consignment was auctioned at Sotheby's six months later, perhaps after Spencer had creamed off what he needed, for it appears that none of the lots was sold to him. This was the first sale in London to consist exclusively of incunabula.[95]

If the war offered opportunities, it also made trade more difficult. In 1799, as French control of Europe became more entrenched, Maugérard asked to be paid in bills drawn on bankers in London rather than in Germany.

He explained the financial loss incurred when books paid for by him were confiscated by the French, how his suppliers ran the risk of being deported to Guyana for the crime of exporting state property, and how owners were reluctant to strike deals under such circumstances:

Apart from my steps to procure some rarities for you ... I had two well-informed friends, one in Trier, the other in Augsburg, who undertook to search; but the latter has just written that it is impossible to find anything; everything is hidden away because of the wartime panic. The former wrote that he had found several items, but then told me in enigmatic terms that it was impossible for him to risk sending anything under current conditions, indeed to do anything for me, because they are so oppressed by fear that he will soon be declared 'suspect and deported'. Another man sent a good chest of these items and wrote that they have arrived in Coblenz awaiting an opportunity to cross the Rhine; but having been declared suspect for this shipment, he only had time to save himself from being sent to Guiana. I do not know where he is. Unfortunately I do not know who has this chest now, although I paid for it. I have a strong suspicion that it was seized crossing the Rhine.[96]

Unless you lived by a major trade route, even at the best of times it could be difficult to send books abroad if you did not have connections to rely on. In 1786, for instance, Daniel Schmidt and Francis Douce struggled to work out how to send a book from Basel to London: the 'Voitures Suisses' did not accept books.[97] During the war the situation was so much more difficult, normal routes being blocked, as the Frankfurt wine merchant pointed out in 1794 when he charged Spencer and Grenville extra for shipping via Hamburg rather than down the Rhine. For the men sourcing books for the London market the whole export operation depended on official contacts, from 1798 to 1803 relying nearly exclusively on Charles Henry Fraser and then on Charles Gregan Craufurd, British Residents in Hamburg. Through them they sent shipments to Edwards and Payne, the booksellers, but addressed to Spencer, to ensure that they were part of the official mail.

The problems of the Frankfurt wine merchant and Maugérard reflect a wider picture of trade restrictions which badly affected the whole economy of the lands on both sides of the Rhine. They formed an integrated economic area created by a system of rivers flowing into the Rhine. After the imposition in 1798 of a customs barrier down the Rhine, the lands on the west bank were deprived of their natural trading partners while geography prevented them from redirecting their exports towards France.[98] This caused a steep economic decline which must have increased the willingness of owners of luxury objects to sell. English collectors benefited from the economic crisis created by the French occupation.

While Spencer eased Maugérard's access to the London market, he in his turn played a crucial role in turning Spencer's interest in the direction which had been current in France just before the Revolution. As a result, deals done between Maugérard, German owners, Spencer, and Edwards were not only undertaken in direct competition with the French occupation forces: they were simultaneously impeded by their controls and stimulated by the instability created by them.

The situation in Italy was essentially the same as in Germany. Although long-standing commercial contacts with the English trade in luxurious cultural merchandise meant that more established channels of supply were available, they were not necessarily very efficient. As we have seen, the trade in books required specialist knowledge which art dealers did not have.[99] The presence of expert book dealers was required; and they arrived, showing the close interconnection between spoliation and trade. Writing to Douce from Rome, on 4 November 1796, Edwards found that he had to pause in his own work:

I have no doubt that the Vatican contains MSS of every century, but at this moment there will be great difficulty in examining them. Our active enemies the French have already run thro the list and laid aside several hundred.[100]

Just like Renouard, Edwards compared the competition in the book market between English wealth and the forces of the French republic with the conflict on the battlefield. But when Edwards referred to the French troops as 'our active enemies', he undoubtedly meant enemies in the sense of competitors for books. He would not have wanted to provoke Douce, a good customer with well-known pro-French, republican views. But being near to the French troops was useful; Edwards wrote to Spencer from Turin on 22 February 1797, twenty days after the first French campaign in Italy came to an end with the surrender of the Austrian troops at Mantua.[101] The profit which Edwards derived from the ravages of the war was well known to his contemporaries. William Beloe wrote:

He determined to make a circuit of Europe, and proceeding from his native island with abundance of money, great acuteness, the most intimate and familiar acquaintance with the objects of his research, and above all, choosing the most auspicious moment for his purpose, when by following the rear of the French armies, he might on easy terms obtain his choice of what he most wanted.[102]

The opportunities available to the English booktrade in the wake of the French troops were so widely known that *The Times* referred to it casually, and without any hint of opprobrium.[103] Booksellers were of course not the only English traders to profit from French spoliation. In May 1800, for instance, Christie's sold forty-five chests of *objets d'art* which were said to have been taken by French troops from the papal collections, but which might well have been acquired by traders following them.[104] The trade in old books was becoming increasingly similar to the trade in art objects, and increasingly distinct from the trade in modern books.

Edwards's close proximity to the French activities is also borne out by his visit to France, three years later, in 1800, to negotiate the release of some of his merchandise, presumably books, which had been retained in Livorno, presumably in 1797.[105] His connections in France were no less impressive than his connections at home in England. He met Talleyrand, whom it would appear that he knew, as well as Leblond who was Commissioner for libraries. Quite consistently with his own interests, he remarked, in a letter to William Wyndham, Lord Grenville, the Foreign Secretary, how spoliation had spectacularly increased the holdings of the Bibliothèque nationale, with no indication that he thought this was in any way reprehensible.[106] Edwards was more devoted to commercial opportunities than to patriotic feeling. Commenting on his journey to Vienna in 1796, he wrote to Douce: 'Happily men of letters and virtuosi in this part of the world do not consider the politics of princes as their affair – neither is it mine, so that victory or defeat we leave to providence to arrange.'[107] In the highly polarised world of England of the mid 1790s 'the politics of princes' is a meaningful phrase: the war was, literally, none of his business.

In this he was not alone. James Payne, the younger son of the bookseller Thomas Payne (1719–99), had been working in Paris for Spencer and others, on his father's behalf, in 1792. He set up as an independent dealer in 1802, apparently in competition with his elder brother Thomas Payne (1752–1831), and immediately after the peace of Amiens, concluded on 27 March 1802, he went back to Paris where he struck deals with Van Praet at the Bibliothèque nationale.[108] In return Van Praet facilitated contacts with two of the library's more colourful suppliers of books. Payne went to Metz to meet Maugérard, now a commissioner of the French state.[109] They did not get on, for Payne did not think Maugérard a gentleman, and apparently did little to hide it; but that did not stop them from doing business.[110] Bargaining was evidently hard and Maugérard, whose account of the meeting also survives, claimed that he had only agreed to sell because of Payne's connection with Van Praet: 'Mr Ortolani arrived the other day with the very amiable Mr Payne who left us abruptly Friday evening, having set his own price for several of my old books which pleased him. It was enough that he is your friend for the prices to have pleased me.'[111] At the same time Payne asked Van Praet to act as an intermediary to obtain a book from Maugérard at a more reasonable price.[112] Maugérard, on his side, was at pains to underline to Van Praet that he only showed those books to Payne which he had not set aside for the Bibliothèque nationale.

Although now an agent of the state, Maugérard continued to trade with Van Praet in a private capacity and he used Payne's visit to suggest that Van Praet might in future also pay him in duplicates.[113] This made his commercial relationship with Van Praet much suppler than when he was paid in money. We can identify a triangular commercial relationship between Maugérard, the Bibliothèque nationale, and the London booktrade. Maugérard was soon to exploit his position so blatantly to his own advantage that Capperonnier attempted to call him to order requiring him at least to offer items to the Bibliothèque nationale before attempting to sell them on the open market.[114] Perhaps this was because Capperonnier was essentially from a civil service background, whereas Van Praet had a background in the booktrade; in any case, Maugérard preferred working with Van Praet, who did not seek to stop his private dealings; in return he flattered Van Praet by calling him the director of the library, slighting Capperonnier by calling him 'one of the staff'.

In addition to his dealings with Maugérard, Payne also acquired books from Gotthelf Fischer, zoologist and fawningly pro-French librarian at the University of Mainz, who abused his position to deal in incunabula, not least supplying Van Praet, who again acted as a point of contact between the two.[115] Payne went from Metz on to Vienna and Italy, remaining in close contact with Van Praet, seeking out incunabula printed on vellum, one of Van Praet's special delights. His signed his letter to Van Praet with a flourish: 'May you have vellum in abundance is the sincere wish of yours truly Jas Payne.' In 1803 the two worked on exchanges of books between the Bibliothèque nationale and Spencer, some actively proposed by Van Praet, who, without having to resort to scarce cash, could use confiscated books as a means of payment for books acquired by Spencer on the open market.[116] Van Praet's ability to make use of the Bibliothèque nationale as a clearing house for books, in association with the English trade, was specific for this turbulent time. In 1817, he had to admit: 'In those days we could take it upon ourselves to make such an arrangement, but today it is no longer possible for us.'[117]

The trade in cultural property was associated with grave risks, as Maugérard pointed out, but placing books in the English luxury market had the potential for such financial rewards that some judged it worth the risk. Edwards managed to do his business in close proximity to the French troops with great success, losing only some of his stock. Not all had his luck. James Payne made the fatal misjudgement of returning from Italy to France in 1803, after the short peace had come to an end. He was arrested as an enemy alien, some time before 30 August, and made a prisoner of war. The harsh conditions made him ill and he died in 1807, shortly after he had been given permission to live in Versailles. Renouard has recorded his death-bed scene. His friends in the Parisian booktrade came to report on a high-profile sale and told of a dealer who had missed out on an important item. Payne's last words are worthy of any bookseller: 'Dying, he raised himself up and said: "A man who wants to buy a César from 1469 does not go out for lunch." Two hours later he was dead.'[118]

The close interdependency with French activities becomes clearer from Spencer's dealings with Alexander Horn, who also provides us with important insights into attitudes to the ownership of early books in this period of conflict. Born in Scotland, he had since 1789 been librarian of the Benedictine monastery of St James in Regensburg, one of the monasteries populated by Scots. Like Maugérard, he supplied incunabula to Lord Spencer and to dealers in London, Edwards, Thomas and James Payne, and Nicol, who often worked for George III.[119] Horn also supplied Spencer with political information, as a paid spy, embodying the close association between the war and the trade in incunabula.

Spencer's acquisition of the Mainz Psalter from 1457 is only one example, but it is emblematic of the interdependence of English purchases and the spoliation which took place in the wake of French expansion. Spencer succeeded in buying where the policy of spoliation failed. Having asked General Custine to procure it in 1792, the Bibliothèque nationale tried to get hold of a copy in 1797 and again in 1799, failing despite the assistance of Mulot, who was responsible for imposing French control on the new sister republic east of the Rhine.[120] In 1801 and 1802 the library repeatedly ensured that high-level pressure was put on the University of Mainz to hand over a number of precious books, including the Psalter.[121] Evidently intimidated, they hastened to respond but could not send the Psalter, for they did not know where it was.[122] They apparently believed it had been placed in a local depot by Custine or possibly by Rudler.[123] Otherwise they instantly obeyed, submitting a plaintive request to be allowed to keep at least one early book in Mainz as a reminder of the invention of printing.[124] Fischer, on the other hand, wrote with self-satisfaction to Van Praet about how punctilious he was in executing the library's request and instantly went on to negotiate the sale of some other incunabula which he had somehow acquired.[125]

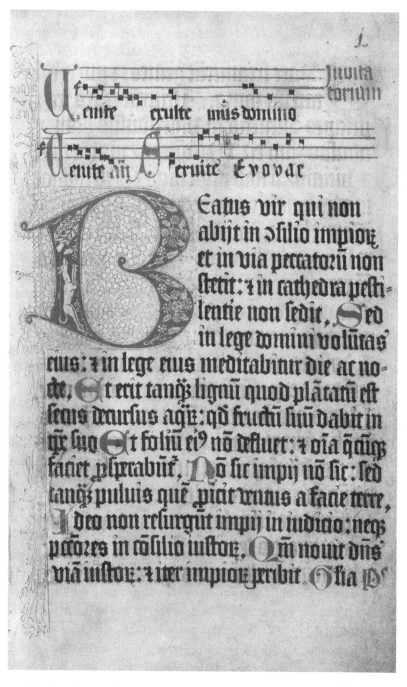

Figure 2.9 *Psalterium*, sig. [a]1 recto, [fol. 1 recto]. [Mainz]: Fust and Schoeffer, 14 August 1457. JRL, 9784.

Another copy of the Psalter was known to exist in the Premonstratensian house at Roth, near Memmingen, having been described by von Heinecken a few decades earlier.[126] Horn wrote to Spencer on 27 February 1798: 'It scarcely began to appear that the great monasteries in Swabia would be fixed upon as a kind of compensation to those Princes who had lost their territories on the west bank of the Rhine when I thought that now or never I should be able to procure the Psalter of 1457 for your Lordship.' On 22 March 1798 he wrote: 'The secularisation of Swabia will make an excellent harvest for collectors of old books.'[127]

Although himself a Benedictine monk, Horn made no attempt to hide his pleasure at the vulnerable position of other Benedictines:

As I did not now doubt that these Messieurs would in case of the dissolution of their monastery be glad to divide a sum of 3,000 florins between them rather than leave the Psalter behind I wrote to them a fortnight ago represented to them the danger they incurred and concluded with repeating my previous offer of 300£.

But the situation was more complicated than this for the monks were not in so much of a panic that they did not bargain: they insisted on 4,000 florins and the librarian wrote to Horn: 'How much pleasure would I not have from this matter, on which we have already worked for many years, were it to end with mutual satisfaction.'[128] The deal had been under discussion at least since 1796.[129]

Although Spencer authorised Horn to spend up to £500 on the 1457 Psalter, in the end the price was 335 louis d'or, that is about £326. The book was sent to Spencer in May 1798.[130] The very same copy headed several lists prepared by the Bibliothèque nationale for the troops to confiscate in these years, and it was on a list drawn up on 26 March 1799 by Capperonnier and Van Praet, who were unaware that the book was already in Spencer's hands.[131] The competition between the First Lord of the Admiralty and the Bibliothèque nationale was being played out in the library of a Swabian monastery; in 1805 Van Praet still had to concede: 'This important edition belongs to the small number which the Imperial Library has been unable to insert among its incomparable riches.'[132]

At the same time George III also acquired a copy of the Psalter. Without using troops to confiscate the property of his subjects, as King of Hanover he ensured that the University of Göttingen gave him a copy by 1801, only later paying an indemnification. Recognising the method, Van Praet wrote approvingly of the 'donation'.[133]

To Horn, the dissolution of monastic houses was a great commercial opportunity, not a disastrous demise of a much-cherished culture: 'Every liberal minded man will allow that the mendicant orders of friars are a nuisance, and that the others are far too numerous.'[134] In his first letter to Spencer, in 1794, he had already referred to the ignorance of monks, mocking them for their superstitious attachment to their Bible.[135] He seems to have been of the view that one is not really entitled to own books if one does not appreciate them in the same way as would a very rich man. The Benedictines of St Emmeram in Regensburg had in their library a single-sheet indulgence, printed in 1454, and Horn did not think them worthy owners of it. He wanted to sell it to Spencer and wrote in 1798:

I am sorry to add on this occasion that I have no hopes of coming into possession of this letter which is on vellum though the Monks have not the least idea of its rarity and scarcely know of their having it. In case of the Librarian being changed I should be very much tempted to cut it out of the book where it is to serve as a blank leaf before the beginning.[136]

But, like their colleagues in Roth, the monks of St Emmeram were not ignorant. Two years later, in 1800, Horn was still negotiating for the indulgence. The monks now asked for 1,000 florins for the indulgence, their copy of the Venetian edition of Pliny from 1469, and Thomas Aquinas printed in 1477.[137] Horn bought the books for the equivalent of £90 or £100 and sold them on for a total of £120, making a mark-up of 20 per cent or at most 22 per cent.[138] We can follow the price of the Pliny which Horn sold to Edwards for £70, nearly exactly the price in 1782 of the de la Vallière copy, £68. This was probably the copy which Edwards sold to Spencer in 1800 for £120, so we see a total mark-up at the point of final sale of some 100 per cent. Having gone through the hands of two dealers, this does not seem unreasonable and is not out of line with the mark-up in our contemporary antiquarian booktrade. It seems all the more reasonable considering the effort and risks involved in getting a book from war-ravaged Germany to the luxury market in London. All-in-all, the monks did not do badly and they certainly cannot be said to have been cheated.

Just as important as monetary value was the nature of the deals done. The monks of St Emmeram did not take cash but exchanged the two items for other books to the equivalent of £90–£100. They got a complete set of the *Philosophical Transactions*, Dugdale's *Monasticon anglicanum*, 'and a few other inferior works', as Horn put it. The following year when Horn sold Spencer yet another, more interesting indulgence,[139] one with a seal still attached, it emerged that he had acquired it in exchange for a

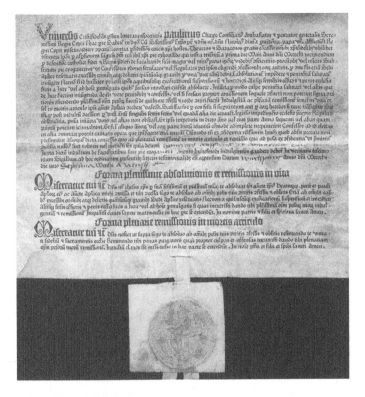

Figure 2.10 *Indulgentia*, [Mainz: 1454–5]. With a seal and a manuscript sale date, 7 March 1455. JRL, 17250.2.

copy of the *Encyclopédie méthodique* which had cost him 600 florins, that is about £54.[140]

The acquisition of the most important English scientific journal, the *Encyclopédie méthodique*, and a major publication of English antiquarianism does not indicate backward, ignorant monks who did not know what they were doing. The changed political situation made it possible for librarians to sell items for which they did not themselves have any use, but which they could market in a place where their value was monetarised. Contact with French revolutionary officials may have increased their awareness that some of the collections were considered valuable by others: this was not the first contact with a world where old books were highly valued in money terms, but it was a very radical exposure to a different valuation of their possessions. The upheavals of the war had ironically also created a new access to the London market. Some of the men in charge of religious houses had their own enlightened priorities and kept a clear eye on what was of intellectual importance to them, catching up with the modern world. The intensified external interest in their old books gave them an opportunity to do this.

A war emergency was not necessary for religious institutions to alienate their property. The Chapter of Hamburg sold books from its library in 1784 and the Chapter of Strängnäs did not even shy away from a public auction.[141] Even in England, the Chapter of Lincoln Cathedral sold three Caxtons to Spencer in 1811, the price suggested to them being £100 'to be laid out in modern books'. Perhaps less interested in modern science than their Swabian counterparts, in the end Lincoln settled for the money.[142] Given the prices fetched by Caxtons in 1811, £100 for three fine copies of his books seems to indicate that the influence and the prestige of the earl had a more negative impact on the ability of the Chapter of Lincoln to obtain the market price than the turmoil of war had on the monks of St Emmeram. Similarly, one of Spencer's spectacular acquisitions from Germany during the Napoleonic wars was a woodcut of St Christopher from 1424, the earliest dated European woodcut. It had first been described by von Heinecken and was of central importance in his discussion of the origin of woodcuts and metal engraving in Europe, which was, as we shall see in Chapter 3, also of great importance for the understanding of the invention of printing.[143] Spencer bought this important document through Horn from the Charterhouse of Buxheim in 1804, after the property was no longer threatened by the French, as it had been transferred from religious to German aristocratic ownership.[144]

The trade makes money out of different priorities; it mediates between different degrees of need but also between different types of need. External duress was not without importance for the monks selling their incunabula to the English luxury market; on the contrary, the war had a significant impact on the willingness, need, and ability of German institutions to sell. But this pressure was only one element in their assessment of their priorities. Even in those extreme circumstances the actions of the institutional owners were also profoundly informed by how the market in rare books could best meet their own intellectual criteria. The selling of old books to Spencer in exchange for useful modern works reveals an understanding of old books surprisingly similar to that which the French state displayed when it gave a collection of modern books in return for the historic collections they confiscated. For instance, the University of Mainz was despoiled of its old books, and in return got a contemporary collection. In his book on the invention of printing Fischer approved:

Mainz can congratulate itself on the solicitude of the government for the restoration of its literary institutions. Our drawing school will acquire new splendour when we have the paintings destined for Mainz by the decree of the consuls, our students can take these grand models for their guides. Our library has been enriched by the Minister of the Interior by nearly 3,000 French volumes.[145]

Although Fischer was exceptional in his extreme desire to please his new masters, modern books may well have been considered an improvement by many professors at the university who had no professional interest in early printing. Although Fischer profited personally from the trade in old books, he was also motivated by his professional concern with palaeontology, for which his Parisian contacts were at least as important as his contacts in the book world.[146] Money was a strong motive, but not the only one: acquiring modern scientific books for his out-dated library was a genuine concern.

The very extensive, twelve-page list of incunabula acquired by the Bibliothèque nationale from a number of libraries in Bavaria, delivered in 1801 to Neveu, the French commissioner, by von Haeffelin, national librarian for Bavaria, is perhaps the most extensive of all the lists of incunabula acquired by the Bibliothèque nationale in this period.[147] But here we are not talking about spoliation: it was, it would appear, part of an amicable exchange, the result of a negotiation suggested to the Bibliothèque nationale by Neveu in September 1800. After an indication from the Minister of the interior, Lucien Bonaparte, that exchange, not spoliation, was the desired policy, Neveu underlined the importance of organising a process which would 'enrich France without impoverishing Germany', where all would derive advantage to the equal glory of French and German artists and men of letters.[148] The stated policy was not essentially different from the individually smaller deals negotiated for buyers in London, whereby institutions got useful modern books in return for incunabula.

Even those who regretted the loss of early books could see a similarity between French spoliations and British purchases. And the purchases were not always judged more favourably. In 1805 the German collector and incunabulist, Zapf, assessed the loss of historic books to Germany:

The spirit of our times has without a doubt opened many doors behind which treasures used to be hidden, and has released them from a jail in which they languished … Germany has lost many of its treasures … They have partly gone to England and partly to Russia. Many travelled to Paris during the recent war, to the National Library, where they are, however, being used.[149]

While the books sold to England and Russia were seen not to be accessible, those which went to Paris had truly been set free from their monastic or aristocratic prisons.

The 1796 sale catalogue of the collection of Kulenkamp, the Göttingen professor, was prefaced by Heyne, the distinguished classicist and University Librarian. The collection had been intended for the University Library, and Heyne deplored that the financial crisis had made the acquisition impossible. The auctioneers were aware that English participation in the sale would increase their profit and the catalogue contains an introductory note, in English, explaining that bids could be placed through the German Circulating Library at Charing Cross in London, which would organise delivery free of charge.[150] There was a significant differential between market prices for rare books in Germany and in England. Even a bid far above normal German price levels would seem cheap in London. Both vendors and buyers could feel they did well if English bidders could take part in a German auction. While Heyne deplored its effects, the auctioneer and the owners accepted and exploited the market. The purchasing power of the rich was legal, but it was as inescapable as the French armies.

The presence of French troops and English dealers gave improved access to a distant world where old books were expensive. Greater contact was often imposed without consent; life under French occupation was marked by arbitrary as well as organised brutality and by the need for local economies to sustain the living costs of the occupying forces. At the same time we should not underestimate the desire of the affected institutions to modernise. During the nineteenth and twentieth centuries men who were increasingly conscious of the German nation only saw monkish ignorance and the cunning greed of foreign dealers, such as Horn and Maugérard – this is how it looked to Heinrich Joachim Jaeck in 1835.[151] The apparent indifference of some religious houses to the books which caused such interest in the luxury markets of London and Paris was, to him, a sign of intellectual stagnation. It seemed inconceivable that some monks had shared the modernising aspirations of the eighteenth century. This understanding of events had no room for the sale of both manuscripts and incunabula from German religious houses to the ducal library in Gotha through the efforts of Maugérard,[152] or the Grand Ducal library in Darmstadt, which acquired books from Fischer, an even sharper, but German, dealer.[153] On the other hand, some recent scholars have argued that German religious houses were in fact centres of antiquarian scholarship, emphasising the work on old printed books which emanated from some monastic houses in the late eighteenth century.[154] The keen interest among some in acquiring new books tends to argue against the former. The willingness of some to sell old books in order to modernise does not exactly argue against the latter view, but it does mean that it requires modification. It might be preferable to see the willingness of some monks to exchange their old books for new, useful ones, as an expression of the disjunction between the view of books as luxury, and an enlightened assessment of books as texts of intellectual importance, where copies of long out-dated works or indulgences were of no significance next to works of modern scholarship.

In one sense Renouard and his Jacobin friends were profoundly wrong about the aristocratic owners of books in the *Ancien Régime*. Trying to construct a new view of the past and the future, Renouard drew up distinctions with great clarity. But he had less need to see similarities. An analysis of the libraries of émigrés has shown that those who rejected or were forced to reject the Revolution did not read books which supported a vanishing world; they too read the politically enlightened and economically improving works of the day.[155] François Furet has said: 'The nobility at Versailles and in the towns read the same books as the educated bourgeois, discussed Descartes and Newton and wept for Manon Lescaut and admired the *Lettres philosophiques* or *La Nouvelle Heloïse*.'[156] Lady Spencer in fact acquired *Manon Lescaut* in 1783, and Spencer too was a man of his own time. He was no religious fanatic, no supporter of unbridled monarchical power. He bought the *Almanach de Gotha*, the much mocked symbol of the fatuousness of aristocracy, but much more numerous and characteristic were his acquisitions of contemporary scientific works, for instance *Les sciences des ingénieurs*, and the publications of the important Bath Agricultural Society. He owned a detailed life of Malesherbes, from 1802, Condorcet on the mathematical method for calculating proportional representation, and indeed Condorcet's complete works from 1804. He bought contemporary history, often highly critical of traditional society. He bought Gibbon's *Decline and Fall*, Necker on religion, Loménie de Brienne's accounts of his financial policies, and Volney's accounts of his travels, full of political significance as well as practical commercial information.[157] In spring and early summer of 1797, while busy conducting war on revolutionary France from the Admiralty, his reading matter was Voltaire, the *Encyclopédie* and Gibbon's memoirs.[158] Like Renouard, perhaps even more, Spencer was immersed in the modern world. His shift from collecting classical texts to collecting incunabula was part of his awareness of the modern world around him. We begin to get an impression of why so many grand collectors of the last quarter of the eighteenth century collected incunabula and other early printed book but no manuscripts, to mention only Loménie de Brienne, Reviczky, d'Elci, Cracherode, Spencer, and George III.

But in another sense Renouard was right. The competition between republicans and aristocrats was not just ideological and military but financial and followed the opportunities created by the changes caused by the French themselves. Before the polarising events of the Revolution, and even long after, ideas which were later to be seen to be contradictory could easily live together in one person. Yet the widely shared apprehension expressed by Zapf, that in contrast to the easy access for all in the Bibliothèque nationale, books sold to England became inaccessible in private collections, is an indication that there was a genuine difference between the two collection strategies. Far from foaming with destructive anger, English visitors used the Bibliothèque nationale with gratitude in the awareness that there was nothing like it at home. In 1802 William Shepherd commented enthusiastically on the generous opening hours, not least for scholars like him, and on the large number of readers, but especially on the friendly reception he met, from his first encounter with the armed guard to the expert guidance which he received from the keeper of manuscripts in the reading room. Henry Redhead Yorke, a more casual visitor, was equally impressed with the friendly and learned reception which Van Praet afforded him, also in 1802.[159] French visitors to London commented, with some satisfaction, on the absence of an institution comparable to the Bibliothèque nationale, for the British Museum was poorly stocked and hard to gain access to, whereas the rich English collections were scattered and private.[160] Being located in remote Northamptonshire, Spencer's vast collection could not be part of the intellectual world of the great metropolises.

The creation of a truly public, national library, with its unprecedented levels of access and assistance and with its strong emphasis on national, public grandeur and public instruction redefined the meaning of grand private collections, which until now had seemed unproblematic. When national collections were opened to the public in capitals across Europe, from Copenhagen in 1793, to Lisbon in 1796,[161] the notion of a private collection could be seen at best to express the outmoded view that enlightenment was a private rather than a public matter. Books evidently did not serve the same ideological and practical purpose in a private, aristocratic collection held in the remote countryside as those in a public, urban collection.

The next chapter will explore how the formulation of incunabula as a coherent category of objects gradually grew out of a number of related but often contradictory attitudes to books. This will enable Chapter 4 to develop further the issues developed here, examining how these approaches to objects from the past, including their ability to flatter aristocratic pride, can be used as a way of understanding tensions between opposing but overlapping views of the function of books and collections in the public and the private spheres.

3 | An object-based discipline emerges: old books, new luxury

The first two chapters explored how views of fifteenth-century books were changing during the last decades of the eighteenth century. To take another chronological perspective we can first turn to Seymour de Ricci's important Sandars lectures of 1929–30. He placed the beginning of the collecting of old printed books, especially incunabula, in the first decades of the eighteenth century with a few English aristocrats, the Duke of Devonshire, the Earl of Pembroke, the Duke of Roxburghe, the Earl of Sunderland, and the first and second Earls of Oxford. Equally important was the Earl of Leicester.[1]

The lasting monument to their collections, now dispersed, is the chronological bibliography of Michel Maittaire which began its complicated history of publication in 1719. Maittaire did not limit himself to incunabula, but his *Annales typographici* provided a point of reference throughout the century for supplements, corrections, and criticism. His importance as the starting point for a century of work on historic books was acknowledged in 1793 by a reviewer of Panzer's even more comprehensive bibliography, and also by Panzer himself, who used a modified version of Maittaire's title Maittaire's title for his own work.[2] In 1789 when Spencer began his collecting career, Maittaire's *Annales* were among the first books of reference which he bought.[3]

The monumental transfer of European cultural goods undertaken by these English aristocrats had a big impact in England but, by its nature, their collecting also had a big impact outside England, in Germany and to a lesser extent in France, and most of all in Italy. The first supplement to Maittaire, published as early as 1722, was an Italian reaction to the purchases made by rich northerners. Orlandi deplored the lack of discrimination of men who collected books printed in those dreadful gothic letters which infected books from 1475 to 1575. He contrasted such ill-advised foreigners with Italians whose scholarly collections were rooted in knowledge of the texts; yet, most especially, he disapproved of those Italians who supplied the foreigners. Simultaneously, he disapproved of the books of which he produced a catalogue, disapproved of their being sold to northern European collectors, and created a catalogue which, in practice, added to their marketability.[4] These uncomfortable inconsistencies point towards a categorisation which is not yet quite in place.

Without diminishing the role of the English noble collectors, it must be pointed out that Orlandi may equally have had in mind the slightly earlier collecting activities for instance of Frederik Rostgaard, who collected in Italy in the late 1690s, or of Prince Eugene of Savoy, whose extensive collection of printed books was well under way by 1713, and which included numerous incunabula.[5] But de Ricci was of course right. Something unprecedented happened to the collecting of old printed books around 1715 and 1725. What I seek to explore is the emergence of incunabula as a distinct category among printed books, to examine that emergence in terms of a process rather than a sudden phenomenon, and to recognise the roles in that distinct categorisation of attitudes to books as text, as objects, and as merchandise.[6] The attitudes of the aristocratic collectors to early printed books were not created by the objects themselves, nor were the aristocrats the first to find value in them. Rather, their monetary value grew out of the intellectual value with which the books could be associated.[7] This chapter will outline a process whereby different intellectual and economic currents gradually came together, forming a new, coherent type of commodity out of books which in terms of their subject matter and their physical appearance are completely heterogeneous. A category was created which encompassed books as diverse as multivolume commentaries on the Bible and manuals on how to store wine, and ranging from small slips of paper to sumptuously produced items of luxury. The chapter will also examine the emergence of a new discipline, largely created outside established institutions, capable of engaging with objects as historical evidence, making them distinguishable, and thus marketable as a new commodity. The markets for luxury in Paris and London are central to the analysis, but they are set in a wider European context. Three types of intellectual activity played prominent roles in this process, philology, antiquarianism, and historiography, bearing in mind that they were often closely related.

Philology comes first. In 1639 John Howell, the London book dealer, sold a copy of Crastonus's Greek lexicon printed in 1499 and promised that if the book was returned within three months, he would buy it back.[8] He must have felt confident that he could sell it or lease it again to another customer. Although it was the Aldine edition, it did not have a high repurchase price: it was not a bibliographical curiosity, but a useful text for a student of Greek. Also in 1639 Lawrence Sadler, another London bookseller, sold a copy of the works of Virgil from 1494 with a similar guarantee. There were plenty of modern editions to be had, but the age of an edition of Virgil was neither a disadvantage nor an advantage: it did not matter.[9] In this respect philologically important texts resembled other academic genres. Sadler sold a biblical manuscript from the first half of the thirteenth century under similar conditions.[10] Two incunabula on Aristotelian philosophy were sold with buy-back agreements by Francis Greene, in business in Cambridge from 1628 to 1635.[11] These books were not sold as incunabula but simply as useful texts, and they were evidently in demand.

Another type of evidence for the continued straightforward use of incunabula as texts is a copy of the Oxford Rufinus edition, later the object of much debate because of its erroneous date of 1468. Thomas Barlow received it as a donation in 1657, and may well have found the early date a curiosity, but his marginal notes demonstrate that he used it as a text for theological studies.[12]

Yet, a historicising approach to incunable editions of classical texts was emerging. In 1653 Philippe Labbé, a Jesuit, published a catalogue of classical manuscripts in the Bibliothèque royale. Books printed before 1501 appear as the ninth of ten appendices. This was not a prominent place, but the reason why they were included at all was that they were often better textually than manuscripts. In a tenth, more miscellaneous appendix Labbé included books printed on vellum, also allegedly for textual reasons: the more expensive medium was proof that their creators had thought that they had an inherent value which merited long-term survival.[13] However that may be, the Jesuit's list of vellum books brings to mind the scorn of the Gallican Gabriel Naudé for men who collected for 'feeble reasons',[14] and this might make one think of Labbé's list of incunabula also in terms of collectability. Yet the *Nova bibliotheca* was no bibliography; it did not provide printers' names, and it is impossible to use it for identifying actual editions. It served the purpose of displaying the magnificence of the Bibliothèque royale, and did not attempt to establish a shared knowledge, whether scholarly or commercial.

By contrast, in 1688, in the preface to his *Scriptorum ecclesiasticorum historia literaria* William Cave wrote: 'Editions of the Holy Fathers are normally the more reliable the older they are.' He hoped for the formation of a large public collection where they would be more easily accessible than in private collections and which could ensure their survival: early patristic editions had been destroyed by the Roman Church, and were now hard to find.[15] This recalls the Protestant philological project of Thomas Bodley and Thomas James from the earlier part of the seventeenth century.[16] However, giving a high status not only to manuscripts but also to the earliest editions of the fathers, Cave argued that the Reformation had had an impact on the process of editing itself. Editions were most valuable if published before 1517: until then the Church of Rome had felt no polemical urge to falsify texts. Of secondary value were books printed before the council of Trent, at which point the Roman Church had begun to corrupt texts systematically.[17] Cave gave several examples of how the Index demanded the excision or alteration of passages in patristic texts.

A special relationship between the Fathers and the Church of England was set out in 1679 by Edward Stillingfleet in a dialogue called *Several Conferences Between a Romish Priest, a Fanatick Chaplain, and a Divine of the Church of England*. They meet at a book auction. The puritan and the priest are scandalised by the prices which the men of the Church of England pay for patristic texts. Anglican devotion to patristic learning is contrasted with a Romish dependence on pious ignorance. Here the importance of the earliest editions of the Fathers to the Church of England is articulated in the context of the religious conflict in the years around the Glorious Revolution. Cave's theme recurred in the union catalogue of manuscripts in England and Ireland, published in 1697, *Catalogi librorum manuscriptorum Angliae et Hiberniae*:

I wish that the errors of the book trade were the only ones to appear in books, whether printed or manuscript, holy or profane … But the Popes have taken great care to contaminate the Councils, Fathers, even the Bible. They have mutilated them, in order for their opinions not to be contradicted, or they have distorted them to establish their dogma. What a scandal![18]

The *Catalogi* included a few early printed books as honorary manuscripts, for their textual importance. In addition, it supplied a list exclusively of books from the beginning of printing, those of John Moore, the Bishop of Ely, the first such list in an English context.[19] In 1653, in his catalogue of classical manuscripts in the Bibliothèque royale Philippe Labbé had included classical printed books with manuscript marginalia written by learned men. The *Catalogi* took the same approach to printed editions of patristic texts, singling out books with manuscript notes by Edward Bernard, one of its authors, as well as by prominent seventeenth-century Dutch and German scholars. In 1699 the Bodleian Library bought a collection of classical texts exactly for the reason given in the *Catalogi*, including some incunabula: they contained manuscript notes by Bernard, and by Dutch and German scholars.[20]

The same North German and Dutch Protestant philological environment had seen an importance in the earliest printed editions of Latin and Greek classical, non-Christian, authors. For instance, in 1688, Daniel Georg Morhof, a professor at Kiel, and in 1704 Burkhard Gotthelf Struve mentioned a number of fifteenth-century editions as well as editions by Aldus Manutius which competed with manuscripts for textual importance.[21] They were not valued for being printed, but for their similarity to manuscripts. Two collectors rooted in this learned environment were Marqvard Gude and Frederik Rostgaard, senior administrators in the Dano-Norwegian-Holsatian monarchy with a social position similar to that of the *noblesse de la robe* in France.[22] Rostgaard studied in Leiden and Paris, and also in Oxford, where contacts with Netherlandish philology were close. His incunabula, all classical texts, were mainly purchased in 1699, while he was in Italy, and found a natural place in his library among his classical manuscripts. His library was similar to those which the Earl of Leicester and the Earl of Sunderland were to form a decade or two later: the early editions of the classics were part of a unified collection, including classical manuscripts, and later, modern, editions of the same texts.[23]

Maittaire also edited a series of classical texts, beginning in 1713. His edition of Virgil from 1715 was based on two undated incunable editions, which he thought might even be the earliest.[24] Both were in the library of the Earl of Sunderland, to whom the edition is dedicated, as was his edition of Catullus, Tibullus, and Propertius. He dedicated his 1721 edition of the *Batrachomyomachia* to the Earl of Leicester, praising him as one of the foremost of a group of noblemen who had brought rare and useful books to England in greater numbers than any had ever done before. In the seventeenth century Etienne Baluze, Colbert's second librarian, had explained that a collection of printed books was suitable for a scholar, whereas the library of a nobleman achieved grandeur through its ancient manuscripts. Learned men would ensure the nobleman's reputation by referring to his manuscripts in their published works.[25] Maittaire gave the same importance to the earliest printed editions of the classical authors, making sure to acknowledge the owners of the books which he had used.

Seen in this light the collections of the early eighteenth-century English aristocrats resembled the grand collections of the seventeenth century. With its different political aims, even the library of the Harleys, rich in manuscripts and charters, is related to the utilitarian collections of the preceding century. What was new was that certain categories of printed books, mainly classical texts, now gained right of entry as honorary manuscripts, neatly expressed by John Bagford, who in 1708 described the Bishop of Ely's 'books of the first printing' singling out 'fine beautiful books printed on Vellum and illuminated, which might pass for Manuscripts'.[26] We are far from the world where books were collected because they were printed, when Alexander Horn, in 1802, could send a luxurious Bible manuscript to Spencer with an apology: 'Though Your Lordship is no collector of manuscripts yet I shall take the liberty of forwarding by the first Chariot de Poste the most beautiful manuscript that ever existed.'[27]

The earliest Harleian incunabula for which we know the dates of acquisition were nearly all editions of the classics and by the early 1720s they were truly expensive in the London market.[28] In 1721 the Earl of Sunderland paid £40 for a 1472 edition of Virgil, printed by Zarotus in Milan, not the first edition, but admittedly rare.[29]

The importance attached to the earliest printed editions of classical texts was thus not from the outset in conflict with the importance attached to the best texts.[30] They were tools for establishing good editions, not in themselves the best editions. While the early texts might be of use for an editor there was no reason for a reader to acquire them. Yet the philological approach contained an element which focused on the age of the publication. To some extent despite itself, it was one of the most important intellectual trends which made early printed books collectable. But with the urge of collectors to have the first, the best, the finest, the most, they were increasingly priced beyond the reach of scholars who had put forward the arguments for their importance. In his novel *The Life of John Buncle*, from 1756, Thomas Amory described the library of the virtuous men at Ulubrae. They realised that 'There is no reason for laying out so much money for the old editions, when in reality the modern ones are better'.[31] Amory's criticism of a now well-established collecting practice reflects how the functional value of early editions and their market price diverged.

But as early printed editions were collected and became available in northern European libraries, together with the relevant manuscripts, a consensus began to emerge that incunable editions were, most often, based on inferior manuscripts. The collections undermined the original intellectual motives for their formation. Being one of the earliest to have privileged access to comprehensive but private collections of early classical editions, Maittaire saw the problem. In a polemic against Pieter Burmann, the Dutch philologist, he accepted that the earliest editions often were poor, but they were, he claimed, faithful reproductions of manuscripts by scholars less inclined to make conjectures than later generations. Consequently he retained their readings except when they were manifestly wrong.[32] To the scorn of, for instance, Bentley, he did not exercise judgement, relied minimally on conjecture, and produced texts which, as we might see it, vacillate between being editions and transcriptions.

In 1715 Maittaire was proud to base his Virgil edition on two early editions which he could not date. For his Virgil edition of 1767, Christian Gottlob Heyne found nothing of value in any of the many fifteenth-century editions which he had seen, and judged that few had been produced with care. In his London edition from 1793, Heyne had not changed his mind about their textual importance, but now acknowledged that incunable editions had a different type of importance for men of culture. This may suggest the influence of Heyne's London publishers, Payne and

Figure 3.1 Juvenalis, *Satyrae*. [Venice: Vindelinus de Spira, 1473]. © British Library Board. C.19.d.4. Bound by Walther for Cracherode *c.* 1792.

Edwards, who made a living from selling incunabula.[33] But in practice he had no use for the insights of collectors.[34] By the end of the eighteenth century, an element in the new valuation of the early editions was their recognition as marketable cultural trophies, while their role as useful texts had waned.

Two sets of evidence reflect this. Even if collectors strove to give an over-all coherent appearance to their book collection, their bindings are rarely uniform but rather articulate a hierarchy among their books, the classics being given the most expensive treatment.[35] While the Bodleian, a university library, did not set out to acquire early classical editions for their symbolic value, the library's treatment of these works shows that their status as objects of luxury competed with their status as intellectual tools, even within a learned institution. If less showy than many of Cracherode's, the elegant and expensive red morocco bindings which the Bodleian Library paid to have put on its newly acquired classical incunabula in the early 1790s were inferior only by two thin gold fillets to those made for the Bibliothèque du roi or for Earl Spencer (Figures 3.1–3.4).

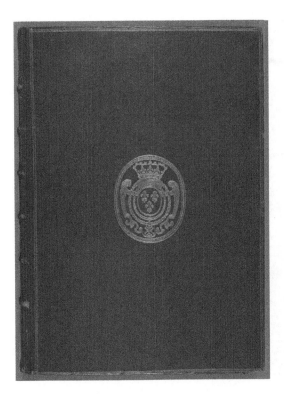

Figure 3.2 *Biblia*. Rome: Sweynheym and Pannartz, 1471. Bound for the Bibliothèque royale. Bodleian, Auct. M 1.10.

Secondly, in his monumental work on Aldus from 1803, Renouard described Aldus's own times as part of the barbarous Middle Ages. This was evident from the unacceptable Latin of the *Hypnerotomachia* paralleled by the pictures which it contained,[36] much inferior in taste to those which had been made for the French sixteenth-century edition, after the restoration of letters had taken effect. Similarly, Aldus's manual of Latin grammar lacked precision and analytical clarity, while his edition of Lucretius was 'excessively rare but of little merit'.[37] Aldus and Paulus Manutius saved the classical texts from intellectual chaos by making them more affordable and accessible. The importance of their classical editions consisted in being the first steps towards the formation of a reading public based on taste, which their material production standards and their design similarly reflected.[38] Philology had contributed to the market value of early printed books but had in the process also contributed to draining them of textual significance. Even Aldus's books now had to be redeemed from their textual shortcomings by their market value, achieved as monuments of human progress.

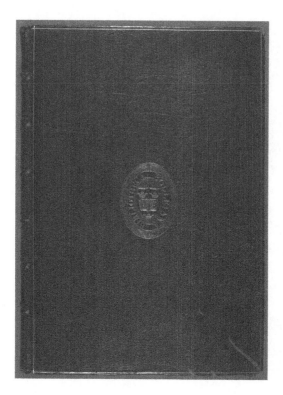

Figure 3.3 Aulus Gellius, *Noctes Atticae*. [Rome]: Sweynheym and Pannartz, 1469. Bound for the Bodleian by Walther or Kalthoeber, *c.* 1790. Bodleian, Auct. L 2.2.

We now turn to the role of antiquarianism in creating the category of incunabula. Antiquarians were interested in ancient objects and physical remains, and were much mocked for it, but they were also predominantly interested in early printed books for their texts, not in their case classical texts, but texts relating to the history and religion of the European nations in the Middle Ages. Yet, unlike students of classical and patristic texts, antiquarians might be interested in the period and the place in which the old books had been produced. In their case, it is hard, and probably wrong, to make a sharp distinction between an interest in the text and in the object.

John Selden provides an early example. He had about 150 incunabula out of a collection of over 7,000 printed books. In order to establish if he acquired his incunabula because they were old objects, they should be examined as part of a wider pattern of retrospective purchases. Selden's incunabula amount to some 4 per cent of his pre-1600 books, all of which can reasonably be considered second-hand purchases.[39] Without knowing how many fifteenth-century books were available among those sold as

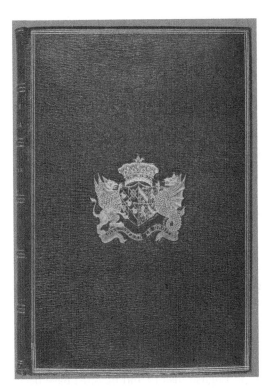

Figure 3.4 Horatius, *Epistolae et carmina*. Ferrara: Carnerius, 1474. Bound by Kalthoeber for Earl Spencer, February 1791. JRL, 3341.

second-hand in the first half of the seventeenth century, this figure is difficult to assess as an expression of a deliberate choice, but it does not in itself provide strong evidence of an interest in the earliest printed books by virtue of their age.

Seen from a textual point of view, most of Selden's incunabula are close to the centre of his professional interests, such as Aegidius Romanus's *De regimine principum* on the extent of monarchical power;[40] Petrus Bertrandi, *Libellus de iurisdictione ecclesiastica* on the extent of ecclesiastical power; the ever-current Thomas Becket affair on relations between Church and state,[41] or the opinion of the University of Paris on the payment of the tithe, a theme on which Selden himself had published.[42] Selden had two incunable editions of Albumasar's *Flores astrologiae*.[43] In his work on the birth of Jesus, he discussed Albumasar's view that the beginning of the Christian era was connected with the revolutions of Saturn.[44] One of his copies of Albumasar was bound in a volume in which all the items relate to astrology, to mathematical calculations of the calendar, and to chronology, the most modern item in the volume being a copy of Selden's own work on the calendar.[45] His incunable Albumasars were a straightforward functional part of his academic library, used as texts and bound with other, modern, texts of a similar nature.

When it comes specifically to Selden's English incunabula, the matter is more complex. Not so long ago it was stated that he 'has the distinction of having been one of the earliest book-buyers to collect Caxtons for what they were – monuments of English typography'.[46] This deserves a closer look. Eleven or twelve books printed by Caxton appear among Selden's some 150 incunabula. This seems both a high number and a high proportion.

Selden's interest in English antiquities was an integral part of his political work. Some of his Caxton editions fall into the category of historical documentation, useful for his contemporary concerns, as do books by other early English printers.[47] Some deal with the relations between the estates which make up the body politic, some relate to theology, and some to the pious life.[48] Only Caxton's translation of a French prose paraphrase of the *Aeneid* seems marginal to Selden's textual interests and it may have been acquired simply because it was bound with an edition of Marsilius of Padua, *The Defence of Peace*, which was at the core of Selden's political concerns.[49] Selden was of course interested in English history and he must have been aware that Caxton was the first English printer; on the other hand, in contrast to the incunabula of the early eighteenth-century collectors, all Selden's incunabula except one can be shown to have been in England before Selden acquired them.[50] Perhaps, if you bought widely in the second-hand market, some books would incidentally be printed by Caxton.[51] While it is possible, it remains to be convincingly argued that Selden chose to buy books specifically because they were by Caxton.

In Richard Smith's posthumous sale catalogue from 1682 a number of books were grouped under the heading 'Caxton'.[52] But one of them, 'Caxton, the first English Printer, his Chronicle of England – Printed 1498', was printed some six years after Caxton's death,[53] and another is dated 1553.[54] Yet these are not errors. The *Recuile of the Histories of Troy* from 1553 features Caxton on the title page as the translator. In fact, nearly all were books in which Caxton had a role as translator or author. This corresponds to Smith's unpublished history of printing, 'Of the First Invention of the Art of Printing', where he discussed Caxton as an author and a translator, not as a printer.[55] Yet Smith was interested in early printing: he donated to Thomas Barlow a fairly late Mainz imprint which he had used in his treatise on printing, and in which he had written a list of early Mainz books.[56]

Selden and Smith are interesting because of the ambiguity of their motives for collecting books which we have come to regard as English incunabula. The incipient nature of this interest is confirmed in the marketplace. Even if Smith and the auctioneers thought that Caxton was of special importance, it is hard to argue that the buyers at his sale thought so too. The Caxtons were bought by several different persons, so the unexceptional prices which they fetched cannot be explained as an absence of interest in the sale as a whole. The most expensive was described as '*Godfrey* of *Bulloigne*, or The siege and conquest of *Jerusalem* (being K. *Edward*'s the *4th.* own book) – 1481'.[57] It was sold for 18s to Henry Mordaunt, second Earl of Peterborough, a fiercely Royalist nobleman who just like Godefrey had fought the infidels, in his case the Berbers around Tangiers. This suggests that he was interested in the book as chivalric romance, a long-standing aristocratic taste in literature. *The Game of Chess*, promoted as 'The first Book which ever was Printed in Engl.' was sold for 3s 2d to Samuel Ravenshaw, the bookseller.[58] The *Mirror of the World* from 1481 (stated to be 1480), which some hundred years later was to fetch over £150, fetched 5s. By comparison you could have bought lot 246, 'Thomas Horton 100 select sermons upon several texts of scripture London' (1679) for 13s 4d, just about the same price, sheet of paper for sheet of paper, as the *Mirror of the World*. Appreciation of Caxton was not yet reflected in the market.[59]

The same ambiguity can be seen in the donation made by Moses Pitt to the Bodleian in 1680. He presented a volume of four Caxtons which, despite their imperfections, is now considered a major treasure; it is one of the few Caxton tract volumes not to have been split up by booksellers or librarians.[60] It had failed to sell at auction, and not as a result of a bad day at the sales: if that had been the case, Pitt, a book dealer, could have kept it in stock and presented it for sale again. There was no market for this volume, but he knew that there would be an interest in it in the Bodleian Library.[61]

Once we get to the founders of the Society of Antiquaries they were without any doubt interested in early printed books, especially early English printing. John Bagford, cobbler, antiquarian, and book dealer, had the important and fascinating role of mediating between two groups which ascribed radically different cultural values to the same objects, famously collecting not only from owners of books but also from shopkeepers who owned not books but wrapping paper. Bagford's role in Hans Sloane's developing interest in early English printing during the first years of the eighteenth century has recently been described.[62] He played an equally important role for other major collectors.

Thomas Hearne, a close antiquarian friend of Bagford's, has been well studied, and it is clear that many of the old books which he owned were of direct textual relevance to his concerns about Church and state, so manifest in his extensive published works. It is equally clear that he was fascinated by samples of early printing. However, in contrast to his approach in his historiographical work, he did not use his books and fragments to make a contribution to a shared knowledge of early printing, often simply relying on Bagford's opinions. At times, he seems so poorly informed about the contemporary state of knowledge that the only explanation seems to be that his interest was both limited and focused on very specific aspects, mainly the introduction of printing into Oxford.[63]

Caxton and other early English printers were by then certainly of antiquarian interest. But this was not enough for the books to become valuable as luxury commodities. In 1721 Caxton's *Golden Legend* cost about £4, much the same price as one might pay for a more recent book useful for antiquarian studies, Dugdale's *Warwickshire*.[64] This is in contrast to the 1472 edition of Virgil, which cost £40 also in 1721.[65] Most of Lord Harley's Caxtons were acquired for him by Humphrey Wanley, his librarian and another of Bagford's friends, but not until the late 1720s, at the sale of the books of the antiquary Thomas Rawlinson.[66] Prices were low. Some incomplete Caxtons fetched no more than their value as paper and prices fell further in the 1740s and 1750s.[67] For most of the century their place in the market was ambiguous. This did not begin to change until the 1770s when George III bought eight Caxtons at the 1773 sale of James West, including the first edition of the *Canterbury Tales* for a stunning £47 16s 6d. One may suspect that the price was also affected by the importance of the author, Chaucer, for most of the other Caxtons sold for about £5 or much less.[68] George III also bought Caxtons at the sale in 1776 of John Ratcliffe, a Bermondsey chandler, book collector, and dealer.[69] It is hard to imagine a more spectacular change in status than this, from Bermondsey to Buckingham House in one day. Again prices were often around £5 and nearly all under £10. As late as 1796 Edwards sold Caxton's *Golden Legend* for £6 6s, and the second edition of the *Canterbury Tales* for £10 10s, whereas, in the same catalogue, he offered the first edition of Sallust for £21.[70]

In contrast to the failed sales of Caxtons around 1730, in 1810 a bookseller asked 5 guineas not for a complete book, but for a fragment of fifty-three leaves missing from Francis Douce's copy of Caxton's edition of the *Golden Legend* from 1483.[71] The market was so established that even smallish fragments were valuable, able to supplement imperfect copies which were now part of a universe so well explored that their individual defects were known,

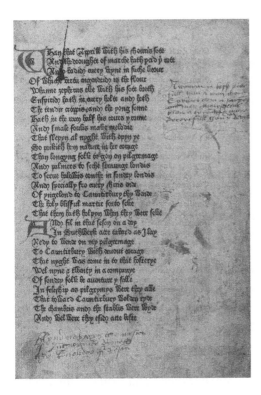

Figure 3.5 Chaucer, *Canterbury Tales*, sig. [a]1 recto, fol. 1 recto.
[Westminster: Caxton, 1476?]. This scruffy book had become fit for a king.
© British Library Board. 167.c.26.

enabling dealers to source the missing part and to place them profitably. With very few exceptions English incunabula, even most Caxton editions, did not reach the price level of first editions of classical texts until the very last years of the 1790s, at which point they took revenge and by the time of the sale of the collection of the Duke of Roxburghe in 1812 often outstripped them in price. Yet the English antiquarian interest in early English books, paralleled in other European countries, was an essential part of the intellectual world which contributed to the construction of the category of incunabula.

Last of these three areas of intellectual activity, we turn to historiography. Stimulated by the celebration of the 200th anniversary of the invention of printing, in 1640, Bernhard von Mallinckrodt wrote the first book devoted entirely to this topic. It was a scholarly work, but also a defence of Mainz as the city where printing was invented against the assertive nationalism of the Low Countries emerging into prosperous independence.[72]

Founded on statements from long after the alleged events, Dutch authors claimed that printing was invented in Haarlem by a Laurens

Coster. In some versions of the story one of his workmen, Gutenberg, was said to have stolen his types. This story proved a fruitful error, or fraud, defended with great tenacity. As each piece of alleged evidence was dismissed by critical scholars, new imaginative attempts at saving the account stimulated more historiographical engagement, not least the publication and interpretation of archival material. Local patriotic or political interest motivated others to assert a claim to a role in the early history of printing. In 1644, Strasbourg joined as a competitor to Mainz, and in the eighteenth century Milanese and Venetian authors sought to displace Subiaco as the first place of printing outside Germany.[73] But none was as stubbornly and as productively promoted as Haarlem.

The book on the origin of printing in Paris by André Chevillier from 1694 began with a general history of printing. Methodologically Chevillier was influenced by Jean Mabillon's *De re diplomatica* from 1681, whose rigorously critical method of dating and assessing documentary evidence was instantly controversial for its ability to overturn established truth.[74] In contrast to historiographers who used history as a repertoire of morally or politically appropriate examples, Chevillier saw himself in the role of a judge assessing witness statements, quoting at length to enable readers to judge for themselves.[75] He called his book both '*historique*' and '*critique*' for a good reason. Yet, he was not without a practical aim: he had been commissioned to document the historical privileges of the Sorbonne against increasing royal control and against a booktrade reluctant to accept the rights of the university. Characteristic is the weight which he gave to the evidence of Johannes Trithemius, the fifteenth-century abbot, who used information provided by people directly involved with Gutenberg but with no bias in his favour. This account had been published from the manuscript as recently as 1690.[76] The Strasbourg account was relatively quickly dismissed. More time was devoted to the writers, nearly all Dutch, who supported the Haarlem theory. Chevillier concluded that none of their statements stood up to scrutiny; they were inconsistent and suffered from the same bias as the alleged authorities which they quoted. Chevillier asked for real, documentary evidence if the theory was to be taken seriously, not just lists of opinions of other authors.[77] His work set high standards for the assessment of archival documentation and remained central during the eighteenth century for academic historiographers of typography. Earl Spencer bought his copy of Chevillier on 16 May 1789.[78]

Maittaire's extensive historical introduction to his *Annales typographici* owed much to Chevillier, as he generously acknowledged. He too rejected the Haarlem thesis, in his view motivated by envy, yet he accepted another account which depended on it. There is an Oxford edition of Rufinus's *Expositio in symbolum apostolorum*, dated 1468, an error for 1478.[79] In 1664, referring to documents allegedly in Lambeth Palace, Richard Atkyns had published an account of a Frederick Corsellis, an under-workman from Coster's printing-house in Haarlem, who had been brought to Oxford by Henry VI where he produced the '1468' *Expositio*.[80] This would have made printing dependent on royal privilege, and that would have benefited Atkyns's own business. In his account of the affair, Adrian Johns has brought out how this challenged the Stationers' Company, especially the booksellers, and how Atkyns's arguments were used by the Oxford authorities in defence of their publishing privileges.[81] Atkyns appeared to have used archival material in exactly the way which had been envisaged by great collectors of state papers. But the documentation was not merely fake: it was non-existent. Atkyns's account had been made available to Maittaire by the Earl of Pembroke, and this may have coloured his attitude to it. It was not the only occasion on which Maittaire let his position as client of a grandee affect his critical judgement. *Decor puellarum*, printed by Nicolaus Jenson, a Frenchman based in Venice, is dated 1461, for 1471. This would have made Venice the earliest place of printing after Mainz. Maittaire acknowledged that the book looked more modern than other books from the early 1460s but concluded that this showed how much faster perfection was achieved by the French than by the German spirit; Laire was justified when he explained Maittaire's credulity by love of his country, or that of his parents, with a slightly condescending tone towards such an unenlightened approach to historiography.[82] But Maittaire's loyalty to his patron, Pembroke, also played a role. It was Pembroke who had given him access to a copy of Jenson's edition of the *Decor puellarum*. Reducing the importance of one of the treasures of one's patron might not be advisable. In his dependence on private libraries, Maittiare illustrates the subservience to aristocratic interest which Condorcet had so criticised and which was one motive behind the creation of public collections of historic books, beyond the control of family interests.

In his *Dissertation Concerning the Origin of Printing in England* from 1735 Conyers Middleton was the first English author to display a critical approach to the history of printing in the tradition of Chevillier. The wider consequences of this were now inescapable. In 1731 Middleton had criticised Daniel Waterland's attempt to present Christianity as rational, in order to refute deism. Middleton argued that by defending the indefensible Waterland undermined Christianity. This might sound like orthodox Augustinianism, but Middleton did not present contradictions in the Bible as a spur to faith. In several details he was close to *Histoire critique du Vieux Testament* from 1672 by Richard Simon, an Oratorian, whose proof that Moses was not the author of the Pentateuch had led him to being ousted from his religious order and his book being banned in Catholic Europe. The English translation was not banned but nor was it welcome to the Church of England. Middleton's first historiographical work had been entirely acceptable to the Protestant world, for it had demonstrated how the ceremonies of the Church of Rome were based on ancient pagan rites, each Romish practice being footnoted with references to classical sources.[83] But when Middleton applied the same approach to the Bible, the reaction was different. He was understood by the Anglican establishment to seek to 'weaken the authority of Moses'.[84] There was some truth to this for he argued that the religious rules of the Pentateuch, far from being revealed first to the Jews, were found earlier in other ancient cultures, not least that of Egypt.[85]

This was the context in which Middleton's approach to the Oxford–Haarlem account was seen by Hearne, a non-juror, believing in divinely instituted monarchy.[86] In Middleton's rejection of Atkyns's royalist fable Hearne recognised the critical spirit which had subjected the Bible to rational examination:

He envys us this glory which no one need wonder at, that considers a much bolder stroke of his lately, which made a great noise, and very deservedly blasted his reputation, which was his book ... to prove that Moses was not an inspired writer.[87]

Not only was Middleton heretical and proposed a view of history based on analysis of facts rather than moral desirability, but in addition his book was cheap, 'a twelve-penny pamphlet'.[88] Views unacceptable in a learned and expensive book were the worse for being promulgated in books affordable to the public at large. Hearne's reaction is a measure of how disconcerting the critical assessment of historical evidence was to contemporaries for whom authority was a cornerstone of society.

Middleton also argued from a physical analysis of the 1478 Rufinus, relying on data from Samuel Palmer's recent history of printing. The date of 1468 could not be correct, as the book had features which were otherwise not known that early. As Middleton summed up: 'But it is strange that a piece so fabulous and carrying such evident marks of forgery could impose upon men so knowing and inquisitive.'[89] The forgery led to the writing of one of the best studies of fifteenth-century printing produced in eighteenth-century England, and one in which the analysis of documents and physical evidence from books were for the first time truly integrated.

The historiographical interest in the chronology of early printing, whether the English debate with its political implications, or the increasingly professional study of the invention of printing, is reflected in the radical change in price attached to a limited number of large folio books which carry the very earliest dates of printing, chiefly the first dated Bible, from 1462. At the death of Colbert in 1683 his copy was valued to the equivalent of £8 16s,[90] whereas Lord Harley bought his in 1724 for £112.[91] The Bodleian purchase of an incomplete copy of volume one in 1750 is a sign that it was established as worthy of collecting, even though this copy was in a rather poor condition, which was amply reflected in its price, £2 10s.[92] The library bought no other incunable until 1784.

Further historiographical interest was stimulated by the tercentenary of the invention of printing, celebrated in 1740. Prosper Marchand's long-planned history of printing, completed to coincide with it, was essentially an assessment of existing literature, summing up the historiographical consensus of the early part of the century.[93] As such his book remained a point of reference for the rest of the century, but the most significant contributions focused on the publication and discussion of archival documents. The so-called Helmasperger instrument stems from a lawsuit of 1455 dealing with the financial relationship between Gutenberg and Johann Fust.[94] It had already been published in 1734, without any comment, in a miscellany of legal documents edited by Heinrich Christian Senckenberg.[95] In 1740 Johann David Köhler, professor in Göttingen, discussed it jointly with other newly published documents relevant to Gutenberg's life in Mainz, and Christian Gottlieb Schwarz, professor in Altdorf, presided over three academic theses in which these documents were examined.[96]

Senckenberg held high public office and his publication of the legal documents was part of his official function. In this he resembled Johann Daniel Schoepflin, a German in French service, who presented a communication to the Académie royale des inscriptions et belles-lettres. Without publishing them, he relied on important documents newly found in Strasbourg archives concerning Gutenberg's time there.[97] He was closely connected with the French court, and was to found a royally sponsored school in 1752 which aimed at educating a political elite in law and history. Schoepflin's works on the history of the lands around the Rhine are models of eighteenth-century legal historiography based on extensive archival research, but not devoid of political motivation, as the connection with the lands on the Rhine makes clear.[98] Like Senckenberg's, Shoepflin's important contributions arose out of a German tradition of historiography undertaken by jurists, integrated into the public administration and supported by university positions.

Historiographical interest in the earliest dated editions created a framework for a new field of collecting, and a very powerful one which facilitated competition and gave intellectual legitimacy to the collectors' urge for the creation of complete collections, the argument which we have seen repeatedly used by the Bibliothèque nationale in the 1790s when asking for fifteenth-century books to be confiscated on its behalf.

The very existence of a variety of starting points for addressing the same body of evidence, here grouped under the three headings of philology, history and antiquarianism, made it possible for diverging methods to meet and to inform one another. This meeting took several forms. The three approaches shared a potential outcome, the creation of a collection, and the market for rare books was therefore an important meeting place for different views.

For things to gain value in the market they must be identifiable as belonging to a class of objects, but they must also be distinguishable within the class. There is no market for an unidentifiable mass of material. In the absence of a single institutionalised discourse about incunabula, different approaches to this differentiation, sometime compatible and sometimes contradictory, were possible.[99]

As Lotte Hellinga has shown, Joseph Smith vacillated between being a trader and a collector. The two first catalogues of his collection, from 1725 and 1737, only contained books from the fifteenth century and gave special emphasis to sumptuous books, not least those distinguished by their hand-painted decoration.[100] His printed books were part of an aristocratic, visual culture, consonant with his role as a prominent art dealer who supplied paintings to northern European noblemen. Indeed, both the collection of manuscripts which he sold to the Earl of Sunderland and his collection of fifteenth-century printed books were described by him as suitable for any prince no matter how grand.[101] The *Decor puellarum*, with an erroneous date of imprint of 1461, was the only item which explicitly related his collection to an interest in chronology and priority. By contrast, Smith's much larger catalogue from 1755 was no longer devoted to incunabula alone. It had an extensive appendix reproducing prefaces mainly to the early editions of the classics, revealing an increasingly philological approach to the value of his books.

It is useful for the trade to have a variety of criteria for establishing financial worth. However, while sumptuousness was never abandoned as a criterion for promotion, Smith's attempt to promote incunabula for their visual impact had limited resonance in the eighteenth century.[102] Painted decoration did not play a significant role in the marketing strategy of dealers, who rather focused on luxurious bindings, which were mainly of a later date and did not reflect the original historical context of the books.

If visual grandeur enabled only a small selection of fifteenth-century books to gain some prominence in the market, many more could become valuable through a focus on books as manufactured objects, evidence of their own history. This implied an approach to early printing similar to that which Mabillon and Montfaucon had used when they sought to establish a chronology of handwriting, as Maugérard put it when he tried to persuade Spencer to employ him to catalogue his incunabula.[103] It was also an advantageous approach for dealers because it provided the trade and collectors with a ready structure for comparing copies of the same edition, once identified, and for promoting your copy as better than other examples of the same edition: it was ideal for enabling and encouraging collectors to compete.[104]

In the London sale of the printed books of Anthony Askew, held in 1775, nearly exclusively early editions of the classics, a few of which were stated to be illuminated, only one book is tentatively ascribed a chronological and geographical place on the basis of its typeface.[105] This is in sharp contrast to the promotional strategy used in 1783 by Guillaume Debure l'aîné for the sale catalogue of the duc de La Vallière. Several of the duke's books had been acquired for him by Debure at the Askew sale, but they were now promoted for different reasons.[106] An interesting example is Debure's focus on the production of Ulrich Zell, one of the earliest printers outside Mainz, until then of next to no value in the market. He wrote:

Zell, Cicero's, *De finibus bonorum et malorum*: First and very rare edition, twenty-seven long lines [as opposed to being in two columns] per page, without date, indication of town or printer, without page numbers and signatures. Until now it has been declared that this book came from the presses of Mainz, because there was thought to be a great conformity of its characters with those of the *De officiis* of Cicero, printed in that town in 1465. Having compared the two editions very carefully, we have established that there is little similarity and that the characters of the *De officiis* are much smaller. On the other hand, they match perfectly the characters used by Ulrich Zell from Hanau, printer in Cologne, for the tracts by St Augustine called *De vita christiana* and *De singularitate clericorum*. Furthermore the two editions are the same format and the lines are of the same length.[107]

On other occasions Debure dated a book on the basis of its type being in a more worn condition than in other dated editions.[108] This ability to fix an object in a chronological relationship to other objects was essential for the creation of the enthusiasm with which the Bibliothèque nationale, Lord Spencer, and many other collectors pursued undated editions in the 1790s, and indeed for creating competition between them.[109] Books, until recently part of an unstructured mass, became identifiable, desirable, and marketable. A hitherto unnoticed document from 1785 in the Archives Modernes of the Bibliothèque nationale de France consists of a list of books from before 1472 which Maugérard offered to the Bibliothèque royale because they would provide material for comparison with undated ones which were or in the future might be in the collection:

Extract from the catalogue of books of Dom Maugérard, Benedictine of Metz, 1785. Note: This extract is made exclusively of the editions with a colophon which are wanting in the Bibliothèque du roi and to serve as model for comparison to identify those without a colophon which are already in the collections or those which may later be acquired.[110]

This is the first instance known to me of books being offered for sale because they could serve to organise other books into a chronological sequence. Incunabula had become self-reinforcing in the marketplace: they were valuable because they had a role in establishing the value of other incunabula. Maugérard formulated an intellectual, market-based reason for the claims made by the librarians of the Bibliothèque nationale some ten years later, that they need more books to be confiscated to complete their collection of books from the earliest years of printing. Incunabula were now acquired in order to support the study of incunabula.

The trend is further documented in volume I of Loménie de Brienne's catalogue, written by Laire and published in 1792, part of a Debure sale catalogue and the first Parisian auction catalogue to be exclusively devoted to incunabula, breaking with the tradition of organising catalogues by subject in which Parisian booksellers took much self-conscious pride.[111] The first London bookseller's catalogue known to me to have a section on incunabula is Edwards's catalogue from 1790, 'Books of great rarity in the infancy of printing', although only the most valuable of the incunabula appear in this section, others being distributed in the 'various classes to which they belong'.[112] The first London auction to consist exclusively of incunabula is from 1799. It probably consisted of books acquired by Maugérard in Germany which were sold at auction for Edwards.

The importance to collectors and to the market of establishing a chronological sequence, within which the objects could be organised, is confirmed by the emergence of fakes. Without a shared understanding of how objects are interpreted it is difficult to achieve a consensus of what is fake and what is genuine. In a period when new ranges of objects were attracting the attention of scholars, collectors, and the market this is particularly acute. In

1797 John Wolcot wrote, under the pseudonym of Peter Pindar, in *Peter's Prophecy*:

But more the world reports (I hope untrue)
That half Sir William's mugs and gods are *new*;
Himself the baker of th'Etrurian ware,
That made our British antiquarians stare;
Nay, that he means ere long to cross the main,
And at his Naples oven sweat again;
And by his late successes render'd bolder,
To bake *new* mugs, and gods some ages *older*.[113]

It was of course a malicious rumour that it was William Hamilton himself who had made his ancient vases but, in the absence of a shared understanding of how to date and interpret these new objects, the satire is not without foundation. It is difficult to classify items correctly which do not belong to a pre-existing category of valuables: Hamilton's vases were not fake, but nor were they Etruscan, as we now know. An analogous uncertainty applied to incunabula, again not entirely without reason. Already in 1734 Hearne had observed:

Mr. [Thomas] Baker some times since told me of a discovery made by Mr. Palmer, of a book printed by Guttenburgh. Mr. Baker hath since received the half sheet, showing it to be a mistake, or rather a cheat. They have long made a trade of counterfeiting medals, and now are beginning with prints, at least with the colophons.[114]

The fake colophon appeared in a book which we now believe to have been printed in 1472 and had been used by Samuel Palmer in his history of printing published in 1733, as an argument in the debate about what exactly Gutenberg had invented, where he had worked, and what Fust and Schoeffer had brought to the invention.[115] Palmer had been taken in by a fraud which was subsequently easy to detect.

The Haarlem theory and its Oxford spin-off were irresistible invitations to fraud. George Smith, based in Amsterdam, was behind several of them. In 1756 he offered to the Sunderland Library a prayer book which was stated to be printed by Coster in 1450. The librarian investigated and the book was not acquired. The most optimistic was perhaps a fake colophon in a copy of Plautus's *Curculio* assigning it to 'Corcellis' in Oxford in 1472, along with a manuscript note 'by de Worde' to the effect that it was Corcellis who had introduced printing to England in 1465.[116] Also in 1756, George Smith offered a copy of Pliny's letters to John Osborne, who advertised it for sale expensively priced at £15 15s because it had a colophon which said 'Oxon.

apud F. Corcellis 1469'.[117] Osborne apparently never saw the book, but it was recognised as a fraud by Meerman. While Smith had been able to cause confusion in the 1750s and 1760s, by 1792 when Spencer had acquired the book the fraud had become an amusing curiosity.[118]

If fraudulent colophons from the 1750s seemed naive by the 1790s, new types of fraud became worthwhile as other books from the fifteenth century gained market value. The new-found interest in single sheet indulgences, some with early manuscript dates, became a cause for concern. In 1815 Spencer feared that single sheets offered to him by Horn were fakes, especially one which Horn said that he had 'forced out of an archive'. Horn's condescending dismissal of his apprehension, claiming that no one in Germany had the skill to undertake such fakery, cannot have been reassuring for a few weeks earlier he had himself referred to a false colophon written by Gotthelf Fischer, university librarian in Mainz and one of Horn's known suppliers, who also worked closely with Franz Joseph Bodmann, the Mainz archivist. He or Bodmann, or both, are known to have produced items with fake contemporary inscriptions along with seals to go with them and to have invented documents relating to the invention of printing.[119] When, on 4 August 1815, Horn wrote that one of his suppliers offered 'an old wax seal of Peter Schoiffer with his arms as usual which a friend of mine had cut off from an insignificant document of his', there was good reason for Spencer to be cautious; and although they were not finally dismissed as fakes until the 1830s, Dibdin already in 1817 expressed grave concern about how some of Bodmann's documents could make sense.[120] A market which is characterised by competition between many dealers and collectors can be a stimulus to fraud, but equally fraud, in association with a high value attached to the genuine objects, can be a stimulus to new types of rigorous analysis.

The ability to analyse objects, and to draw information from physical and visual evidence, was not created within universities nor, in France, by the *hommes de lettres* in their established institutions, who in fact often expressed strong hostility. It was, to a significant extent, created by people marginal to the established institutional approach to history, antiquarians, traders, and craftsmen.[121] However these outsiders were in dialogue with men of more learned backgrounds, mainly historians, and we will now look at aspects of this dialogue, their interaction with the philological understanding of books as texts being reserved for Chapter 4. This diversity of their engagement with the past led to a conflictual meeting of different types of expertise and of different ways of arguing, less likely to take place within disciplines which were cultivated by socially more cohesive groups.

Pierre Simon Fournier published a history of wood engraving including the origins of printing in 1758, followed the next year by a second work on the same topic. He was no scholar, but declared himself the more qualified to discuss the history of printing because he was a type founder. With much self-assurance he challenged both the scholarly establishment and the emerging competing centre of knowledge around the marketplace:

Men like Mallinckrodt, Maittaire, Naudé, Chevillier, Mentel etc., were no doubt very learned in literature, and printing owes to some of them profound and laborious research. But they were not craftsmen. Now, when dealing with the operations and mechanism of a craft which they understood badly, many errors inevitably escaped them; they were neither in a position to notice nor to correct them. La Caille and Prosper Marchand, albeit booksellers, were no less deceived. They have followed the same aberrations as the others, for there is a great difference between the selling of a book and the various processes which make it.[122]

Fournier held that Gutenberg had never proceeded beyond printing with movable wooden type, a phase in the development of printing which most in the first half of the eighteenth century took for granted.[123] The letters on the pages of the Psalter of 1457 were so irregular that it must have had been printed with carved wooden types, while Duranti's *Rationale* of 1459 was the first book to have been printed with cast, movable metal type, an invention which Fournier, like others, held to be Peter Schoeffer's.[124] The Haarlem printers, if they had existed at all, had at most produced blockbooks, a procedure which Fournier, like most others with professional experience of typography, did not recognise as printing.

This went against Schoepflin's theses that printing had begun in Strasbourg with movable wooden type and, despite its calm academic tones, *Vindiciae typographicae* from 1760 was Schoepflin's polemic response to Fournier, although he only deigned to mention him twice. Schoepflin now published the documentary evidence about Gutenberg's years in Strasbourg, to which he had only referred in 1740, notably a document from another of the lawsuits in which Gutenberg had been involved, one concerning an invention which Gutenberg had sought to turn to profit in association with others. Beginning with a carefully crafted definition of printing, Schoepflin ensured that the supposed use of individually carved wooden types constituted the invention; this would, in his view, place it in Strasbourg, and he identified a number of Strasbourg editions which he believed to have been produced with wooden type, notably works by Mentelin and Eggestein produced as late as the 1470s (see Figure 2.7).

Schoepflin's *Vindiciae* reads like a diplomatic effort, seeking to gain advantage by building alliances and avoiding causing offence, except when useful. Arguing from the stronghold of his definition, he promoted his theory as a conciliatory solution, the middle way, granting all a part of the glory.[125] Although he found no evidence in favour of Haarlem he generously granted it a place in the story, because it was laudable of its citizens to be so devoted to the honour of their city. Despite his reliance on documentary evidence he declared his respect for undocumented, traditional views. This was in part a reaction to the polemical tones of Fournier, who had no desire to agree with people simply because they were thought to be authorities, and for whom the claims of Haarlem were 'laughable tales'.[126]

Far from being put in his place by the voice of French official historiography, Fournier took it as a challenge.[127] He dismissed Schoepflin's idea of movable wooden type as technically impossible but, more critically, he believed that it was he, the practising craftsman, not the professor, who had the qualifications to determine when something could be called printing. He usurped the professor's right to the most fundamental academic activity, the classification of the phenomena.

In 1758 François Gando, another type founder, declared that Fournier could not be the true author of his books: type engravers could not argue with the learned. He called on those in authority, the *hommes de lettres* and the ministry, to punish Fournier for his insolent opinion that knowledge does not depend on one's status.[128] Gando felt threatened by Fournier's claims to privileged rights in certain types for setting music, and Fournier's transgression of social boundaries was sufficiently radical for a competitor to hope to exploit an anticipated formal hierarchical reaction for his own commercial gain.

A more authoritative response was published anonymously in 1761, although its author was known to be Friedrich Carl Baer, Protestant professor of theology in Strasbourg.[129] Fournier's audacity in challenging Schoepflin's definition was, in his eyes, an encroachment on academic territory much worse than his historical howlers.[130] For the sake of argument, Baer accepted Fournier's claim that only type founders are qualified to assess the evidence on the origin of printing. 'But I will attack only his logic … and as I sustain that I am as good a logician as he is a capable type founder, I deliver myself to the judgment of the public, and I hope that Monsieur Fournier will not consider it a crime.' And later: 'I defy Monsieur Fournier to contradict it. But to understand it one must know Latin and to attack it one must be a logician. Neither seems to be the strong point of our type founder.'[131] A formal *reductio ad absurdum* led to the conclusion, addressed to the public as the jury, who would agree that: 'Monsieur Fournier would be better off exercising his craft than criticising men of learning; that Monsieur Schoepflin should write books and that Monsieur Fournier should cast letters to print them.'[132]

This debate was followed closely in the *Journal de Trévoux*, where each contribution was carefully reviewed. It described the controversy as part of the ideological conflict between the *Encyclopédie* and those who supported the distinctions of rank: 'It is, so to speak, learning set as a parallel, or even in opposition, to craft.'[133] While deploring Fournier's combative style, which recalled the scholarly controversies of the sixteenth century, undoubtedly inferior to their own enlightened times, it was argued: 'Truth ranks above such considerations.'[134]

There can be a number of reasons why the *Journal de Trévoux* sided with Fournier. It was essentially the learned journal of the Jesuits, and during the years leading up to their dissolution by the king in 1762, their negative reception of Schoepflin must have been in part caused by him being both a prominent Protestant and close to the royal court. But Fournier's other books were also generally positively received in its pages, so this cannot be the whole explanation. And Élie Catherine Fréron, who discussed the controversy in *L'Année litteraire* for 1761, was likewise generally sympathetic to Fournier.[135] It was recognised by all, including Fournier himself, that his participation in a debate as an equal of the most learned men of the kingdom was a departure from social norms.

Fournier was self-consciously part of an incipient interface between the world of learning and the world of crafts and trade. In England this had seen its beginning already in 1678 with Joseph Moxon, type designer and engraver, printer, publisher, and member of the Royal Society, but in France Fournier was a pioneer.[136] He was a contributor to the *Encyclopédie*, and d'Alembert had men like him in mind, when he wrote:

Disdain for the mechanical arts seems to have influenced even their inventors. The names of these benefactors of mankind are nearly always unknown, while the names of their destructors, the conquerors, are known by all. Still, it is perhaps among craftsmen that one must look for the most admirable proof of the wisdom of the human spirit, its patience and its resourcefulness. I grant that most crafts were invented little by little and that it has taken many centuries to bring clocks, to take an example, to the point of perfection where we now see them. But, surely, they are, none the less, sciences.[137]

Conversely it was the ambition of men like Fournier to elevate the mechanical arts to a level of intellectual respectability which led Louis Dutens to assert in 1767 'that the most part of the admirable and useful inventions, in which our age so glories, such as printing, gunpowder, the compass, telescopes, etc were not the acquisitions of genius and philosophy, but mere effects of chance, or the lucky hits of some ignorant artizans'.[138] Fournier was one 'of the class of artisans' among whom Malesherbes, as we heard, found people 'who were capable of holding their own against no matter whom'.[139]

It was a fruitful dialogue. Fournier spurred Schoepflin to publish some of the most important archival materials on Gutenberg ever to have been found, and in the subsequent debate Fournier sought to integrate practical knowledge of book production with an analysis of documents. Even if his conclusions were often wrong, in our view, his procedure was comparable to that of Middleton who integrated documentary analysis and the examination of surviving books. The controversy between the craftsman and the royal historiographer was an unavoidable point of reference for the study of incunabula. Earl Spencer bought his Schoepflin on 10 March and his Fournier on 15 March 1790.[140]

On the other hand, Johann Georg Schelhorn's work on printing from 1761 exemplifies the distance between the academic text-focused historiography of printing and the object focus of Fournier.[141] Following Schoepflin he provided a long list of books which he believed to be printed with individually carved type.[142] After his book had been printed he became aware of Fournier's rejection of the possibility that small letters could be used for printing. Schelhorn came up with a new theory which relied on individually engraved metal type. This idea was thought up to save his argument, in support of Strasbourg, and was to be elaborated a few years later by Meerman, in an extremely well-distributed book, now in an attempt to save the Haarlem account.[143]

In England, in the earliest years of the century, Bagford had attempted to bridge the two roles of dealing in books and undertaking a formal and ambitious historiographical project. His bibliographical expertise was widely acknowledged by his contemporaries, and the failure of his project illustrates how difficult his transcending role was, as do his published works which make manifest his lack of formal education.[144] Samuel Palmer, a printer, was the first Englishman to write a history of printing.[145] But Joseph Ames is the closest English equivalent to Fournier. An ironmonger from Wapping and the author of the catalogue of the medals in the collection of the Earl of Pembroke, Ames published his catalogue of early English printing, *Typographical Antiquities*, in 1749. Becoming a leading member of the Society of Antiquaries, Ames was accepted as a participant, even if an unusual one, in a learned discussion, to a greater degree than Fournier. Yet he was aware of the obstacles imposed by his social position, even within the Society of Antiquaries.[146] Its members did not receive the modest payment which followed membership of the official French bodies of men of letters, and they were chosen without consideration for approval or disapproval from any state authority. In this English context, where inclusion and exclusion were less formally expressed, satire is our indication that Ames was undertaking something unusual for a man of his class. He was gently mocked in *The Inspector*, who visited an ironmonger's in Wapping only to find that the shopkeeper was the secretary of the Society of Antiquaries and away from his counter, at a meeting in Fleet Street.[147] He was mocked much more roughly in *The Grumbler*, in which we find a satirical letter written in the name of the dissatisfied 'wife of a wealthy citizen who having made his plumb, retired from business ... and then joined the antic-queer-ones'.[148] In *The Olio* Francis Grose called Ames 'a very little man of mean aspect and still meaner abilities' who was 'totally ignorant of every language but English, which last he did not speak with the greatest purity' and felt that his history of printing had to have been written by someone with a higher status, namely John Ward, the Gresham professor,[149] exactly the same way Gando claimed that Fournier could not possibly be the author of his books.

Yet, with his lack of linguistic sophistication, it was Ames who in practice solved a problem identified by Maittaire, the Westminster and Christ Church educated editor of classical texts, who in 1719 despaired of identifying unnamed printers of incunabula and even more of dating undated books. This could not be achieved, he found, without a terminology sufficient to distinguish the minute differences between typefaces, and he held out no hope that such a terminology could be created.[150] He proposed, as a nearly unattainable aspiration, the preparation of copper plates reproducing each fount, not as a tool in themselves, but as a first stage towards the creation of a shared language of description:

I wish I knew how to depict in words sufficiently graphic the many shapes of the letters which those printers used for their differences immediately to stand out, distinguishable by clear criteria and for each edition to be assignable to its printer. It would be a task laborious in the extreme to survey each and every fount; to consider the minute drawing of each letter in them, their highest points, the curves of the serifs, the inclines of the strokes and their distances, the fine joints of the lines, in brief the composition of the elements, their appearance and their proportion and to find sufficient variation of expression when describing the incredible variety of typefaces. In such a varied and complex matter I fear that words would fail. It would be an important aid towards expediting this laborious yet useful task, if copper plates were engraved with specimens selected from the various editions of the ancient printers both of alphabets and of whole passages.[151]

The difficulty which was encountered in using the analytical tools developed in universities for creating a systematic approach to describing man-made objects is illustrated by a number of German academic dissertations. Their authors described generic characteristics by which one could recognise a very early printed book from later ones. They were largely a set of features which modern readers would expect to find in books but which were absent from early books: signatures, page numbers, running headings, title pages, etc. These were attempts at classification in an Aristotelian tradition, defining a *genus* through a set of *differentiae*, although differentiation through negative criteria was, strictly speaking, not acceptable.[152] With its aim of creating fixed definitions of classes of items, this approach is eminently unsuited for describing a process of change and equally unsuited for finding a way of identifying individual editions.

By contrast, Ames, the ironmonger who had not been brought up in the tradition of the universities where word-based differentiation was the only reliable criterion for classification, approached the issue practically, by producing type facsimiles. They were numbered, not named, and he provided no verbal description of them. Independent of language-based description, he simply made the means of identification available, publishing a tool for a shared visual assessment of physical objects. Ames's experience with the identification of coins and medals undoubtedly played a role in his approach to establishing identity or difference. Not polemical against a well-defined establishment, but equally aware of the contribution of non-academics, he dedicated his reproduction of Caxton's typefaces to William Caslon, the type designer and founder (Figure 3.6).

The work of Ames may have informed others. The analysis of typefaces was at the centre of Laire's work on Roman typography from 1778, a scholarly work but dedicated by Monaldini, its publisher, to Crevenna, the Amsterdam-based merchant and book collector.[153] This is scholarship working with the marketplace, a fact which undoubtedly was an important reason for Audiffredi's aggressive polemic against Laire, not always justified, and certainly not recognising his pioneering role in dating Roman incunabula. The market-led approach to early printed books was the spur both for Laire and, indirectly, for Audiffredi, whose work, in some contrast to Laire's, displays all the clarity of thought and exposition which results from the combination of a formal education and an enlightened inquisitive mind.

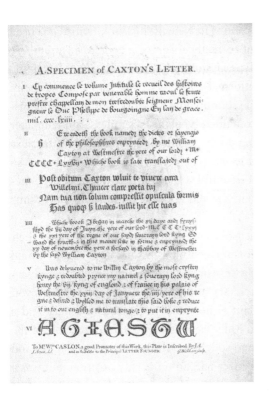

Figure 3.6 A plate reproducing Caxton's type from Ames, *Typographical Antiquities* (1749).

But a more systematic use of facsimiles of typefaces had to wait for the last years of the 1780s, years which again emerge as critical for the formation of incunabula as a coherent body of evidence for a unified discipline. A new generation of German students engaged with the physical objects completely differently from the scholars of the 1740 Gutenberg celebrations. Köhler, the university historian, had not relied on any physical evidence derived from books, although he reproduced four coats of arms relating to the documents which he discussed. Schoepflin, the royal historian, had reproduced a few specimens of types and watermarks, but his arguments rested squarely on the interpretation of documents. Equally the highly academic Audiffredi had relied entirely on verbal descriptions of minute differences between various typefaces.

By contrast, in his work on early printed books in SS Ulrich and Affra in Augsburg published in 1788–9, Placidus Braun produced eight copper plates with alphabets based on sixty different typefaces, and devoted special attention to dating undated editions on this basis.[154] His work was instantly used by other South German librarians. For instance, in his catalogue of the library of the Augustinian canons in Neustift in Tyrol, Franz Gras used Braun's plates for tentatively but correctly assigning a book to a Nuremberg printer.[155] Gras also provided type facsimiles himself and, when describing undated books, he included information on watermarks. Georg Wilhelm Zapf published numerous works, but notably his work on the printing history of Augsburg from 1788 contained typeface facsimiles. Paul Hupfauer also relied on type for grouping books together, but was hesitant because printers from the 1470s began to use typefaces which he thought were so similar that identification was doubtful. He published woodcut type facsimiles, but was quite aware that they did not match the quality of Braun's copper engravings.

The new German book historians were socially different from their predecessors, neither jurists nor university professors. Zapf was, it would appear, Protestant, the son of a craftsman, and had no university education but made a living as a secretary and notary. Christoph Gottlieb von Murr, another leading Protestant writer on printing, was a notary and a customs officer. Both Zapf and Murr were acutely aware of the role of the market in their field of study, and sought to sell their books to English and French consumers of luxury. Panzer had no university position, but was a Protestant vicar. However, in contrast to the nearly exclusively Protestant interest in the 1740s, Gras, Braun, and Hupfauer were Catholic and had functions as archivists or librarians in religious institutions,[156] as was Sebastian Seemiller who in 1787–9 published his catalogue of the fifteenth-century printed books in the university library of Ingolstadt.

The growing Catholic interest in this field, considered part of literary history, was noticed by Protestant scholars. In 1791 Zapf remarked that Catholic religious houses had not previously been allowed to own the reference works which they needed for studying their incunabula, for they were in the main written by Protestants, but these books were now well-regarded in some monasteries.[157] The same view is expressed in a review in the Protestant *Allgemeine Literatur-Zeitung* from 1791 of Gras's catalogue, which was felt to exemplify a Catholic effort to catch up with Protestants,[158] and in the review of Hupfauer's catalogue of incunabula in Beuerberg.[159] In a review of the catalogue of the collection of the Augustinian canons in Rebdorf, Andreas Strauss was particularly commended for his lack of interest in early editions of sermons and of penitential literature, the type of works one might have expected a monk to admire.[160]

Book historians have explored the economic and cultural structures which lay behind the production of South German pirated editions of North German modern books as part of the spread of Enlightenment ideas from Protestant Germany to the Catholic south, creating greater cultural unity across the confessionally divided Germany.[161] The new South German Catholic engagement with incunabula was seen by contemporary Protestant German scholars to perform exactly the same function.

Protestant reviewers of incunable catalogues from Catholic Germany emphasised their innovatory methodological approach, the reproduction of typefaces, and the detailed identification of printers of unassigned books. The method was not uncritically accepted; indeed it seems as if the reviewer in the *Allgemeine Literatur-Zeitung* gradually came to grips with it. In the review of Sebastian Seemiller's catalogue he has a brief sceptical note on the usability of typefaces for this purpose, as he assumed that type founders, then as in his own time, would have formed a separate trade and that they would have worked for more than one printer at a time.[162] In later reviews the anonymous author became more focused and more precise in his criticism: the method was becoming accepted but also more clearly defined. His concern now centred on its applicability to books produced in the 1480s and 1490s, when he felt that typefaces were increasingly likely to be commercially distributed, and he suggested supplementing typographical observations with an examination of woodcuts, based on hand-carved blocks which were not susceptible to multiplication. His increasingly constructive criticism of the use of typefaces reveals a shared methodological universe, which accepted the centrality of the analysis of the physical processes of book production.[163]

The appearance of incunabula as a coherent category constituting a shared field of discourse also achieved a linguistic expression, apparently first in Germany. In classical Latin the word *incunabula* was used as a metaphor for the childhood or origin of anything. Cicero wrote 'In montis patrios et ad incunabula nostra | pergam': 'I will go | into the hills of my fathers and back to the land of my childhood'.[164] In the Renaissance and later, this usage was relatively frequent in titles of learned books: Schrevel's book, from 1647, *Harlemum, sive urbis Harlemensis incunabula* had nothing to do with early printing, but was about the earliest history of the city of Haarlem. The word was used in the same way for instance by Cornelius à Beughem in his catalogue of early books. *Incunabula typographiae*, referred to the childhood of typography, not to the books themselves.

But when Armand-Gaston Camus travelled in Germany in the summer of 1802 he reported on 'incunabula, to use the barbaric expression of these learned lands'.[165] And indeed the word was now used like that in Germany. The title of Seemiller's catalogue from 1787 was *Bibliothecæ academicæ ingolstadiensis incunabula typographica*. Strictly speaking that means 'The typographical cradle of the University Library of Ingolstadt', and it was duly criticised:

The reviewer prefers to applaud the work of the author without beginning with a long quarrel about the usage of the word 'incunabula' for books which appeared in the childhood of printing, which of course is just as wrong as using 'cradles' to mean children in a cradle.[166]

In his 1789 contribution Seemiller had to admit that, strictly speaking, this was true.[167] In 1791 a contributor to Johann Georg Meusel's *Historisch-litterarisch-bibliographisches Magazin* used the word about books, although he knew that it would raise the hackles of some.[168] He felt that it was now in common usage in German. In 1799 Murr still cautiously referred to 'so-called incunabula',[169] but by 1815 the word had spread beyond the sphere of experts, when a German visitor to Paris, ill informed about the Bibliothèque royale, exhorted German librarians to follow its example, to focus on modern books and to abandon their obsession with paltry 'incunabula' which have no value other than coming from a barbarian age.[170] Just as the category had been firmly established, so the name of the category was now in established use, despite the shudders of Latinate outsiders.

What we have witnessed is the success of knowledge about objects and crafts in transforming the approach to early printing and in creating a shared discourse focused on objects relating to something as fundamentally academic as books. This arose from expertise and experience based outside institutions, be they universities or academies. As incunabula became more and more important as merchandise, this discourse found a space of its own in the world of dealers and collectors, private and public.[171]

Importantly, however, the dialogue went both ways, for methods of dealing with physical evidence were also being integrated with documentary evidence which, methodologically, had always been at the centre of attention for academically trained historians. A prominent example of this is von Heinecken. As director of the print collection in Dresden, at the time probably the second largest after the royal collection in Paris, he had become familiar with a vast body of evidence and, being very acquisitive, he had a need to be able to distinguish. A university-educated lawyer and a successful civil servant, he was fully trained to assess evidence and to express his findings in a cogent form, in the tradition of Senckenberg and Schoepflin. In *Idée générale d'une collection complette d'estampes*, his treatise on the history of engraving from 1771, he joined sharp analytical method and clarity of structure with a detailed practical knowledge of the mechanical processes of both metal and wood engraving and the book became one of the most highly respected reference works among eighteenth-century scholars and collectors of prints and early books.

While relatively few collectors were connoisseurs of both antiques and printed books, many collected both books and prints. In France this is exemplified by Louis Jean Gaignat, secretary to Louis XV, and the royal collection, the prints and drawings of which were part of the Bibliothèque du roi, and in England, for instance, by George III, Cracherode, and Francis Douce, whose collections of books and prints have now, unfortunately, all been split up between separate institutions. This dispersal of evidence has tended to obscure the close links between the art market and the market for books, as well as those between discussions of printing and of engraving, although they shared both methodological and some more specific technical issues. Some of these points of cross-over were block books, books produced from wood engravings, which were at the heart of the Haarlem claim to having priority over Mainz; the notion of movable wooden types; and the woodcuts and metalcuts found in early books, which if dated or datable, might settle the debate whether woodcuts and engravings were invented in Italy by Finiguerra or in Germany by unnamed artists, a discussion which mirrors some of the issues around the invention of printing. It was therefore inevitable that von Heinecken addressed themes crucial to historians of typography, book collectors, and dealers, and his work highlights an important point of contact between the study of incunabula, art, and the art market. He was able to dismiss several accounts of the invention of printing which had made assumptions about the development and techniques of wood engraving, modestly saying that he avoided discussing printing as such, not to make as egregious mistakes in their field as historians of printing had in his. For instance he could reject the generally held view that the Psalter from 1457 was printed with movable wooden type. In contrast for instance to Meerman and Schoepflin, but also to Fournier, von Heinecken's arguments were not limited to a superficial consideration of the irregular appearance of the marks on the pages; before reaching any conclusion, he analysed the entire process which would have been required to create a book using wooden type. The theory of engraved wooden types did not take into consideration a number of practical issues, including the financing of a production process. It failed to consider the labour which would have been involved to engrave all the many instance of the same letter required to set up a text page, never mind a whole book; it failed to account for the difficulty in ensuring that the face of each shaft on which each type was engraved was uniform for all instances of the same letter, that the width of all instances of one letter was identical but varied from one letter to another, and that each individual hand-carved type was exactly the same height, not to break the paper. The irregularities which appeared on the page were to him, instead, easily explained by the varying skills and the varying amounts of money available to printers, which might have made them seek solutions which to a modern eye seemed technically unsatisfactory. Able to place his knowledge of physical processes at the heart of his analysis of both books and documents, he found his way systematically through the many suggestions which had been put forward to save the Haarlem and the Strasbourg theories.

As he himself suggested, von Heinecken did not engage with the history of the printing of books, except when it happened to impinge on his theme, but his acceptance of the need to understand in full the physical production processes before he could evaluate his historical evidence was an important part of the intellectual world which enabled bibliographers in subsequent decades, in Germany and elsewhere, to use similar methods to analyse incunabula as they emerged as a coherent class of valuable objects.

In this way the development of the study of incunabula can be seen to have a central place in the wider context of the formation of a new approach to the past which emerged in the eighteenth century. Antiquarians engaged with a different range of sources from academic historiographers, who, with their focus on dynasties, their realms and their wars, were methodologically and thematically equally distant from the philosophical, anthropological history of men like Hobbes, Herder, or Rousseau.[172] Discussing this methodological split between academics and *beaux esprits* in eighteenth-century Germany, Hinrich Seeba has emphasised the importance of the emergence of art history for the paradigm change of eighteenth-century historiography, focusing on the importance of Winckelmann, who in his second phase, when working in Rome, was among the first to bridge the divide.[173]

Von Heinecken displays a similar ability to integrate aesthetic, material observations within an evidence-led chronological framework, enabling objects to be used as historical evidence, while facilitating a shift in historiography. Winckelmann was, originally, of a Protestant German background, like von Heinecken and, like him, closely associated with the palatine court in Dresden, a centre for princely, baroque art collecting. Unlike Winckelmann, von Heinecken, perhaps bound by his academic background, did not use his object-based discipline for developing a wide-ranging theory of the relationship of artistic beauty to social structures. Yet the similarities should not be ignored. Winckelmann's approach enabled a discipline to be created in which art objects were the chief source of information about themselves, not exclusively as objects of beauty, but as objects whose aesthetic expression reflected a specific cultural and political background, that is to say art as part of history. Through von Heinecken's work, we see how the development of the study of incunabula belongs in a wider cultural context, exercising a function similar to that of art-based history, bridging academics and outsiders, creating new methods which enable objects to become reliable pieces of evidence and opening up new ways of approaching and reassessing the past.

On a more modest scale, in England Ralph Willet was able to incorporate a knowledge of how books were in fact physically produced with a sophisticated analysis of documentary evidence. In 1785 he presented to the Society of Antiquaries two magisterial papers refuting the various Haarlem theses, subsequently published as a separate book. He was academically trained but, the owner of plantations in the West Indies, he was also a man of significant independent means and not restrained by the practical, social, and intellectual obligations imposed by a university position. In fact he had not taken his degree when at Oxford, as if he were keen to underline that his position was as independent as that of a nobleman. He also created a vast collection of books. His two contributions to *Archaeologia* are as lucid and logically compelling as the work of Schoepflin, but he joined his analysis of the physical evidence of books with a real knowledge of the whole manufacturing process, from the design of fonts to the printing of the pages. He emphasised how he depended on expertise which only the practice of printing could confer and that he had 'taken great pains' to learn the craft himself. Willett is said to have learned printing in Vienna and he said that 'Martin', probably Robert Martin of Birmingham, had 'instructed me fully in the whole art of letter-founding'.[174] Combining this expertise, highly unusual in a gentleman, with financial independence and clarity of analysis he exploded the Haarlem myth, dismissed the notion of carved wooden types, as von Heinecken had done, and applied the same critical technique to Schelhorn's twist to this theory, which was at the heart of Meerman's attempt to save the Haarlem account. The time would come when people would be embarrassed to have suggested such notions. Reflecting the great value which he associated with manual expertise, he appealed not so much to academics but to Bowyer and Nichols, who had repeated Meerman's view in their preface to their edition from 1776 of Middleton and Meerman, *The Origin of Printing*: being able printers they would have to agree with him 'that Meerman's *fuso-sculpti* are *impossible*'. That of course did not prevent both stories from being told over and over again by later writers.

David McKitterick has drawn a parallel between eighteenth-century attempts to create bibliographical order and the systematisation of the natural world.[175] The wider intellectual importance of the classificatory approach of natural history was evident to Goethe and again we are drawn back to the historical consideration of art. It was when he had bought his copy of Winckelmann that Goethe wrote 'My experience with natural history is repeating itself here.'[176] After reading Winckelmann for a month he realised how essential it was to trace the history of styles 'in their gradual growth and decadence'. 'Any serious student will understand', he wrote, 'that in this field, as in others, judgment is impossible without knowledge of historical development.'[177] Goethe needed a framework for understanding what he saw, and Winckelmann enabled him to let the objects themselves provide the criteria for their own chronological organisation.[178] Quatremère de Quincy was at least as emphatic that it was not Winckelmann's individual results that made his work essential, but his method which had enabled him to make a coherent corpus out of an unstructured mass of debris. Quatremère equally saw that Winckelmann's work was not so much traditional 'historiography' as a chronology.[179] The focus on chronology is found again in the sculpture collection of the national museum of French sculpture created by Alexandre Le Noir, so criticised by Quatremère. Le Noir wrote in 1796 or 1797: 'The monuments here brought together should be understood only as a collection of old models according to the periods to which they belong.'

This might have been said about incunabula, for when it comes to them the bibliographical order became specifically a chronological order based on the date of production of the edition. In 1802, less than a hundred years after Maittaire's lament that the task was impossible, Angelo Maria d'Elci wrote in his first letter to Spencer:

It seems to me that many of those editions without date or name which we call 'doubtful' and to which we have until now not been able to assign either time or printer, begin to be less unknown and less uncertain.[180]

Object-based observations were used in the market to establish the place of the earliest printed books in a chronological sequence, and thereby give them identity, differentiate them, and give them value. While this approach may seem obvious today, it was both methodologically and procedurally new. For instance, if the need for chronology on its own had been the driving force, the earliest books could have been classified according to their date of composition, as were the some 200,000 post-1530 imprints in the sale catalogue of Count Thott from 1789–92. However, it was not this philological and text-based approach to the chronology of books which won the day.

In the same way as the sculptures in the museum created by Le Noir were deliberately detached from their functional context, the focus on chronology of production was part of a decontextualisation of books, but also part of an appropriation of the material so that it could be mastered and controlled. In the Royal Library in Munich, vastly enriched by books from dissolved religious houses, the uprooting of the books was completed by their chronological organisation on the shelves.[181] Ames, Debure, and Maugérard did for early printed books what Winckelmann did for Greek sculpture: they provided collectors with a way of looking at objects so that they were no longer part of an unstructured mass, but each had its place, marketable and eminently collectable. A discipline had grown up which enabled dealers, collectors, and scholars to date and locate books, to differentiate them, and thereby to enable the market to assign value to them, using visual, physical criteria as evidence in a way which was shared and understood, even if they did not always reach agreement. Dealers like Maugérard and Edwards could prosper, in their different ways. Librarians like Laire and Dibdin could find enhanced roles. While librarians in Paris could direct the troops to individual copies, Lord Spencer could direct his agents in distant German provinces, because they shared ways of knowing about objects.

4 | Competing for authority: 'the insolence of English wealth'

In the preceding chapter we looked at three approaches to the past which contributed to making one coherent and marketable category out of otherwise heterogeneous books from the fifteenth century. As they were both distinct and connected, these approaches were also in competition with one another about the interpretation of the books. This challenged a hierarchical distribution of cultural authority because it placed the ability to judge books in the hands of those who had enough money to buy them, disregarding their literary or academic credentials. This chapter examines the ensuing debate as a competition for authority. Although the debate was not essentially about incunabula it was on them that the discussion often focused: this was where divergent approaches to books were being explicitly formulated, where authority was contested by a nascent new discipline, based on objects not on texts.

In the seventeenth century a rare book had most often meant a 'useful' book. This increasingly clashed with a different reality, as people now often collected rare printed books not for practical use but for a wider range of purposes.[1] In the first half of the eighteenth century a number of predominantly Protestant university dissertations sought to give a coherent account of this phenomenon. They did this by asserting 'rarity' as a permanent and unchangeable category.[2] For Christoph August Heumann, for instance, the word *rarus* meant 'few in number', but he did not distinguish consistently between two categories, texts and editions which are hard to find.[3] He provided a number of causes of rarity of books: university dissertations characteristically used analytical tools ultimately derived from Aristotelian physics and metaphysics, designed to identify inevitable outcomes and universally valid categories through differentiation. This tended to provide an explanatory framework seemingly impervious to change. Typical was Johannes Ihre, professor at Uppsala, who struggled to provide an account, simultaneously logically compelling and morally acceptable, of why books disapproved of by the authorities were often the most sought after:

Nowadays the craving for gratification has got to such a point that the more the pious express their disapproval of an author, the more half-learned men desire to have them. In fact, atheistic writings and other books of that ilk are collected and preserved as the chief ornaments of libraries.

These books excite the 'turbulent minds of men' and Ihre only had disapproval to offer as an explanation of why people do not spend their time reading pious books: 'Many prefer reading for pleasure and for fun, rather than to be instructed. That is why we often find that readers make great efforts to seek out amusing books which can unfurl their brows.'[4]

Vacillating between normativity and analysis, explanations of the rarity of books in university dissertations were often contradictory in their own terms. Joachim Ernst Berger's classes of rare books were the result of a theoretical analysis rather than of the reality of collecting. In practice he had to abandon an approach to structuring the world as fundamental as the categorisation by mutually exclusive criteria, and his classes were not species of one genus, to use terminology which would have been familiar to his readers. Nevertheless he sought to retain an important outcome of that approach, namely fixed and unchangeable classes.[5] This type of inconsistency, where systematic approaches come into conflict with reality, reveals a critical point, and it helps us to see the dissertations not as irrelevant academic exercises but as attempts to control change through an assertion of the authority of a group by marginalising deviation from its authorised views as objectively wrong.

It was no professor, but Guillaume François Debure le jeune, the bookseller, who in his *Bibliographie instructive* from 1763 provided a coherent definition of rarity, with a confident indifference to the learned establishment bordering on arrogance. He did not aim his work at the *hommes de lettres* who concerned themselves with whether a book was useful or not.[6] The rarity of a book was solely a function of the market for antiquarian books. In the aggressive controversy which followed its publication, he insisted, in deliberate opposition to alleged permanent causes of rarity, that the value of books was determined by the market, not by their intellectual or textual importance. It was not even scarcity which made a book 'rare'. Some books existed only in a few copies, but had no place in the market; a book was not expensive because it was rare: it was rare because it was expensive. Debure was not so much opposing established cultural values by positing an alternative durable system of values whereby a book's price determined its rarity.[7] It is a necessary function of the marketplace that prices can go down as well as up and it was Debure's insistence on the impermanent nature of value which was new and challenging.

To appreciate the level of confidence which was required of Debure to confront the *hommes de lettres* on their own territory, it is worth recalling the question posed by Alexis de Tocqueville when he identified them as the only group which carried any authority in eighteenth-century France:

How did it come about that, without having high ranks, honours, wealth, responsibility, and power, the *hommes de lettres* became the leading even the only politicians of the day, because only they had an authoritative voice, while others had the power of government?[8]

Aware of the authority of the *hommes de lettres* – their symbolic capital to use one of Bourdieu's terms – Debure was equally aware of the fragility of their position. In anticipation of their disparagement, he mocked their poverty: his critics were envious and would have been ardent collectors, if they could only have afforded to be.[9] Their criticism was a displacement activity to cover up their envy because they had been priced out of their own territory.

In the early twenty-first century it is widely accepted that prices vary rapidly according to attitudes to a commodity, even to those assets which are essential for the stability of our society. The market is understood to work through a seemingly natural process, which social, political, or ethical considerations cannot challenge. In much the same way as a rhetoric of permanent change is used to legitimise power and wealth today, apparent stability was the basis for traditional hierarchical society. E. P. Thompson has described how, in the eighteenth century, there was a 'moral economy' in which high prices for basic goods, such as corn and bread, were perceived as a breach of an unwritten ethical code.[10] Most goods were regulated by the authorities and by guilds; the deviation of a price of a commodity from its perceived real value was given an ethical interpretation, a result of greed. Ethical attitudes to prices extended to all goods and this included books. We saw in Chapter 1 how the greed of publishers and printers was interpreted as the cause for the publication of material which challenged the accepted order of things. In this context it is not so surprising that Debure was provocative when he delighted in the variability of the market. The celebration of the market as the only tribunal which determines value contrasts with the desire for centralised control, for instance as described by Boyer d'Argens who recommended setting up a tribunal to judge with the impartiality of a magistrate what is good and what is bad among both old and recently published books, as a counterweight to *journalistes*.[11]

Unlike the challenge posed by literate soldiers and craftsmen, identified by Malesherbes, we are here not dealing with a conflict caused by members of disempowered parts of society demanding to be heard, but rather with a disjunction between confident social groups, each with their different power bases but both relying on books. It has often been described how, in pre-revolutionary France, *hommes de lettres*, members of institutions set up in the late seventeenth century to ensure stability, themselves became critical of the state, embodying a conflict internal to the Colbertian system of which they were part. Here we are witnessing, in addition, the challenge to the monopoly on authority of the *hommes de lettres*, in part brought about by their own challenge to the system which had created and maintained their position. When the class of *hommes de lettres* no longer spoke on behalf of the governing establishment, as its revolutionary ideas created a growing rift between it and the French state, its own claim to privileged authority was open to challenge, not least from people from the world of commerce who had what the *homme de lettres* lacked, namely money.

Viardot and other scholars have explored how the apparently neutral interest in rarity could be used as a cover for incorporating subversive books.[12] Where others saw the corrupting effects of luxury, Voltaire and the *Encyclopédistes* saw the flourishing of the arts and the sciences.[13] They believed that the condemnation of luxury was an obstacle to the creation of a prosperous society based on the equal right to exercise one's trade. However, when it came to books as objects of luxury, it was the authority of the *hommes de lettres* themselves which was challenged. When Fournier, the type founder, took part in a debate about books from the point of view of a craftsman, he claimed the right for him and men like him to analyse books as objects, but he did not posit a new system of values by which to judge books. The challenge from the marketplace was another matter. Here the reformulation of the social group who could assess books was of much more profound importance, because it was based on a changed set of criteria for the appreciation of books. From the point of view of those in authority, whether as censors or as *hommes de lettres*, texts were not only either good or bad; they were themselves the tools used by those in authority to set out what was good or bad, false or true. If books were to be assessed by the market as part of a range of luxury objects rather than as a means of establishing truth, it implied the abandonment of an important tool of control and also of an important instrument in assuring the position of men of learning.

In his article on 'l'imprimerie' in the *Encyclopédie*, Jaucourt did not engage with printing in a polemical way, but he sought to keep books separate from objects such as statues and paintings, which by their nature existed as unique physical objects and were legitimately part of a luxury market. In contrast, by their nature texts transcended the objects which communicated them, each individual material manifestation being of secondary importance at best, easily replaceable with another essentially equivalent object. He wrote:

The advantage which authors have over these grand masters [of painting and sculpture] derives from our ability to multiply their writings, by printing, renewing for ever the number of copies which one desires, without the value of the copies being inferior to the originals. What would one not pay for a Virgil, a Horace, a Homer, a Cicero, a Plato, an Aristotle, a Pliny if their works were confined in one place or in the hands of one person, as may be the case for a statue, a building, or a painting?[14]

This was the distinction which was rejected by Debure. The *Encyclopédie* celebrated low prices as a benefit created by the invention of printing, while he celebrated the high prices paid by those who saw their rare books as just as much objects as were their paintings or sculptures. Three letters critical of Debure's *Bibliographie* were published in the *Journal de Trévoux* in 1763. Far from hiding the criticism, Debure republished the letters as supplements to his *Bibliographie*, along with his two responses. He reproduced the pages of the *Journal* as they had been published, in decimosexto, a very small format, and with a design and a typeface which were at best functional. This emphasised the contrast with his own elegantly produced octavos, of which he had even announced that he had produced a limited edition of fifty printed in quarto on luxurious paper *'grand papier d'Hollande'*. His catalogue was itself part of the world of luxury objects, created as a collectors' item, and he used this as a visible means of putting the critic in the *Journal de Trévoux* in his place.[15]

Whereas Debure covered a much wider range of collectable books, the debate focused nearly exclusively on books printed in the fifteenth century. At first the anonymous author only gave oblique expression to his disdain for Debure's status as a bookseller. He criticised his clumsy French; nor was his command of Latin as strong as it might have been.[16] An example was his misdating of a book to 1521, although the colophon unambiguously states that it was printed in 1500 on 21 September.[17] The error was not spelled out in grammatical detail for the Latinate reader would understand and Debure fell into the trap and defended a point which was beyond saving. Faced with such irrational behaviour, his critic pulled rank and revealed himself as Barthélemy Mercier, canon regular and librarian of Sainte Géneviève, soon to be the editor of the *Journal de Trévoux*. He now exploited the low level of authority which should be attached to someone of Debure's class. In the index of authors Debure had included the Flemish word for 'printed' and Mercier had much fun with 'Monsieur Ghedruckt'. This error was copied from a catalogue by Martin, the Parisian book dealer, but there was the difference: such howlers mattered little in a mere sale catalogue. Debure, however, had set himself up as a learned man, and had proved himself to be nothing but trade.[18]

Debure did not concede the superiority of Mercier but took pride in having remained in the estate of his fathers and claimed for his trade the exclusive right to assess rare books.[19] At the same time he underlined the social acceptability of his trade by mentioning the names of two of his most distinguished connections, Gaignat, secretary to Louis XV, and the duc de La Vallière. His subject matter was suitable for his status and his trade had given him access to persons who held the highest positions in society, far beyond the reach of Mercier. The understanding of books had become charged with tensions where distinct groups had opposing definitions of what constituted legitimate culture.[20] When Debure published the sale catalogue of the Gaignat collection in 1769 he presented it as a supplement to the *Bibliographie*, finding yet another way of rejecting the distinction between trade and learning.[21] No matter how right Mercier was in detail, and he often was, Debure's bibliography became one of the most cited in the eighteenth century. It was an indispensable tool, acquired for instance by Spencer on 18 January 1791.[22]

In the same year as the Gaignat sale, a Nuremberg bookseller published a catalogue of the collection of Schwarz, the historian who had presided over a number of dissertations marking the tercentenary of the invention of printing.[23] After a few manuscripts, follow three block books, undated books likely to be from the fifteenth century, and finally a chronological series from 1455 to 1697. The two sales, of Schwarz and of Gaignat, illustrate the difference between a market dependent on academic interest and a market where the books were objects for the curious. Many of Schwarz's books, even many of his fifteenth-century books, had no place in Debure's bibliography: he did not aspire to include all incunabula, only those which were rare, that is expensive. The market had its own normative function, even if its normativity was acknowledged to be variable. Debure wrote:

It is necessary to inform the public that if I have sometimes omitted some editions printed before 1500, it is because the majority should not be regarded as very important books.[24]

But even if not all Schwarz's incunabula were collectable in Paris, there was an overlap. In several instances copies of the same editions were sold in the two sales, the ones in Altdorf in their original bindings, the ones in Paris rebound. Prices in Paris were often as much as ten times higher than in

Altdorf, a difference which cannot be explained by the cost of rebinding. The bidders in Altdorf and those in Paris were buying the same books, but simultaneously they were buying completely different objects. The former bought books from the fifteenth century as historical documents, while the latter bought luxury commodities.

Despite the *Encyclopédie*'s separation of books from art objects, this process of change was analogous to one under way in the art market. When the Salon opened in Paris in 1737 a forum was created for a more numerous and diverse audience or customer base, which could give expression to its own, varied aesthetic appreciation of art, a function which had previously been safely in the hands of the Académie royale de peinture et sculpture.[25]

In today's art market, types of objects hitherto neglected may gain prices which exceed those of works which have formed a collectors' canon for the last fifty years. In the eighteenth century such a change questioned contemporary assumptions much more profoundly than they do today. In France, paintings were commissioned by the monarchy and other parts of the establishment and art criticism was therefore a useful vehicle for attacking them: a diversity of standards was in itself subversive. In England there was no institutionalised expression of state-sponsored art until the foundation of the Royal Academy in 1768. Even so, some felt unease at the changeable nature of the taste of a widening public. Hogarth's work on aesthetics from 1753, *The Analysis of Beauty*, had the aim of 'fixing the fluctuating ideas of taste'. Consistent with his satire of modern mores, he sought to identify true stability, whereas Debure claimed a superior right for the instability of the cultural values inherent in a commercial market.

On the eve of the Revolution, in 1789, the Abbé Rive published his blast against the authority of traders and collectors, his famously irascible *La chasse aux bibliographes et antiquaires mal-advisés* (*Hunting Bibliographers and Misled Antiquaries*). There is no room for doubt that Rive was motivated by private grudges. But the way in which they were expressed is significant: a sneer only works if it means something to the audience. Rive had been librarian to the duc de La Vallière, who, it would appear, had found him amusing. But the duchesse de Chatillon, de La Vallière's heir, did not, and Rive lost his post.[26] She commissioned the sale catalogue of the de La Vallière collection from Guillaume Debure l'aîné, in the words of Rive: 'This unfortunate bookseller, whom nature has failed to endow with wisdom, because genius and the God of Riches are rarely in agreement and hardly ever travel along the same road.'[27] If his attacks were most persistent against Guillaume Debure, whom he mocked for his stammer, he was also consistently disparaging of Van Praet, trade, and worse, staff: 'that bookshop boy' who had crossed social boundaries and moved to a position in the Bibliothèque royale, a demonstration of the indecorous results of the erosion of the position of *hommes de lettres*. It was his work on the de La Vallière catalogue which had led to Van Praet's appointment to the Bibliothèque royale in 1784.[28]

Nearly all Rive's examples of misleading dealers and hood-winked collectors focus on incunabula. His very first quarry was Maugérard. Rive deplored the duc de La Vallière's extravagance in wasting luxury bindings on trivial books, incunabula, supplied by the box load by Maugérard. 'This monk', said Rive, had gone into raptures about the high price which a Virgil had fetched, while admitting that its readings were barbarous. In truth, therefore, this edition was not even worth 5 per cent of the price which it fetched.[29] Similarly Rive inveighed against Laire, who had reacted 'with a disgusting enthusiasm' to the price of 3,400 livres (£136), 'its weight in gold', which had been fetched by a copy of a manual of confession.[30] The real value of fifteenth-century books did not derive from the analogy of their unknown type with types from known presses, but from the textual readings of the manuscripts from which they were copied, from the accuracy of the text and for their legibility: 'The age of editions does not make them valuable. It is only bibliomaniacs and traders who are warmed by that notion.'[31]

Rive indirectly confirms Maugérard's role, discussed in the previous chapter, in establishing the main criterion for the value of a fifteenth-century book through an engagement with them as objects which were chiefly recognised through their place within a chronological sequence, not least through type recognition. For instance Rive discussed Pius II's *Bulla retractationum*, ascribed to Zell and thought to be printed in 1468.[32] The duc de La Vallière had bought it for 6 livres, but at his sale it fetched 410 livres, the equivalent of £16 8s, an increase in price of about 6,730 per cent. It was of no textual value, as there were numerous later, more correct and more legible editions. It was in other words, essentially a *bouquin*, a trivial book, despite its price.[33]

Like Adamoli, the Lyon collector who listed market prices as well as the intellectual value of his books expressed in monetary terms, and like the 1725 sale catalogue of Cisternay Du Fay which indicated two prices, 'sale value' and 'real value',[34] Rive sought to create a system of values independent of the pricing mechanism of the market, a parallel, imagined value system where, nonetheless, the intellectual importance of books was monetarised, with an element of contradiction which recalls the inconsistency of the academic theses on rarity. His *Chasse* constitutes a global rejection of the ability of the market to assess the value of books, of the commoditisation of books in an emerging consumer culture. His criticism was aimed at all participants in the trade, buyers as well as dealers. Noble lords who collected books as if they were mere objects were part of the same activity as booksellers; this helps explain Rive's ambiguous attitude to the collecting strategy of the duc de La Vallière which has been noted by Dominique Coq.[35] Noblemen might believe that they were knowledgeable, but they were led astray by their librarians and their suppliers, who depended financially on their bad collecting habits. The market way of assessing the value of a book was a vicious circle and noble collectors ended up as 'poor victims of charlatanry':

> Do books deserve praise because a lord with no or only a very middling bibliographic knowledge, is duped by charlatans into buying some bibliographic objects? Are lords not rather to be deplored when they want to get involved with all sorts of knowledge, without any professional education?[36]

This sort of book was suitable only in collections of certain people who could offer them asylum, despite their inherent worthlessness, namely the 'great public libraries', by which he must refer to the Bibliothèque du roi. There they could be of use for the study of the chronology of typography.[37] So not unlike Louis de Jaucourt in the *Encyclopèdie*,[38] Rive felt that such books might be of some worth but only in a public context, and that this should make them exempt from the workings of the marketplace. A man should have the library which is appropriate for his standing.

As a man of letters, Rive fended off all newcomers, the moneyed customers and their exploitative, sycophantic associates in the trade, united in the market against the norms which ought to govern the understanding of books. By his definition those who had proper authority to assess the value of books, their inherent importance, on behalf of society at large were those men who some thirty years earlier had been at the receiving end of the mockery of Guillaume Debure, le jeune. Like Boyer d'Argens before him, he proposed the creation of a royally sanctioned pre-publication censorship with the power to prohibit bibliographical error from publication and simultaneously protect the privilege of truly learned men to engage with bibliography:

> Would it not be a good idea for the literary superintendency to ban the too free and superficial reception which journalists give to bibliographical works? Without the intervention of such a police, the profession of journalists will remain a base commercial occupation.[39]

Jean Viardot has made the acute suggestion that Rive, a former professor of philosophy, sought to organise the chaos of collecting into a coherent science.[40] His book does not, however, achieve this ambition and his discussion took place on the terms set by men like Debure and Maugérard: he dealt with typefaces, names of printers, and dates of unidentified fifteenth-century books. He had at least as great an insight into this as the men whom he criticised for focusing on such trivialities, but he undermined his own central proposition, that the only important aspect of a book was the quality of its text. If Rive failed to present a compelling case for his own cultural values it is in no small part because he relied on the same methods to confront the same problems as did those whom he attacked. Two groups with distinct sets of cultural values dealt with the same objects, but the emerging method for interpreting the books was only compatible with the aims of one of them. Despite his claims, Rive did not profoundly contest the nature of the market-based engagement with the books. No matter how much he protested, he too was part of the bibliographical and commercial world where rare books were primarily objects.

Rive wrote as the French grand bibliophily of the *Ancien Régime* reached its zenith, but these were also the last years before the Revolution when points of view were vociferously if not always sharply drawn up. Unsurprisingly, we do not find English equivalents of the French polemics, just as we do not find the state-sponsored institutions which both controlled and promoted literary activity. Sporadic use of libel laws, even if draconian and controversial, did not require the formalised structures which the French academies and the institutions of censorship jointly provided. Although the absence of systematic and institutionalised repression meant that reactions were quite different, this does not imply that there was no controversy about the changing status of books. The printed book was a politically, religiously, and ethically important tool: even if not censored before publication, books were nevertheless important in their ability to support or to undermine Church and state.

In his *Actes and Monuments* John Foxe had in 1570 explained to English Protestants their origins and their relation to the Roman Church. In 1704 a book of extracts appeared, *The Benefit and Invention of Printing by John Fox*. It repeated the Protestant certainty that the invention of printing was part of a divine plan for the promotion of truth:

The first and the best were for the bishop of *Rome* by the benefit of printing to learn and know the truth. If he will not, let him understand that *printing* is not set up for nought ... That as nothing made the Pope strong in time past, but lack of knowledge ... So contrariwise now nothing doth debilitate ... his papacy so much as reading, preaching, knowledge and judgment; that is to say The Fruit of Printing.[41]

The matter was a live issue not least because of the disputed legitimacy of the Protestant succession to the throne. On one level the Protestant view of printing was suited to the emerging, modern world: we have seen French Enlightenment philosophers take it up and reformulate it. Yet Protestant and Catholic dogmas were equally drawn into question by critical studies of the Bible and the fathers, and Protestant authorities also felt undermined when printed books were assessed by criteria other than those established by an appointed, trained hierarchy. Equally deplorable was the amassment of books which threatened to outnumber and outweigh those which were truly needed. *A Tower Conference* is set in the Tower of London during the imprisonment of Robert Harley, the first Earl of Oxford. Most of it is a dialogue between Robert Walpole and the earl. But it opens with a dialogue between the earl and John Bagford, his bookseller:

Earl. I am already overstockt with *Arabick* and *Coptick* books; I think 'tis high time to furnish my self with some *English* and *Latin*. Pray have you ever a *Directory* and an *Amsterdam Bible*.

Mr B. Yes my Lord – Shall I bring your Lordship a sett of the *Classicks* with them?

Earl. *There is now a small Affair depending between the Parliament and me, as soon as that's over, you and I will talk about* Virgil *and* Horace.

Mr B. When shall I wait on your Lordship?

Earl. Send me the *Bible* and *Directory*, and I shall be glad to see you at the *Park*, a month hence.[42]

The dialogue gives the reader a measure of the mortal danger of the earl by showing how his library of pagan authors had become a pointless luxury when all that mattered were the Bible and a guide to salvation, such as Richardson's *Christian Directory, or a Certain … Guide to Heaven; the One Thing Needful*.

Nor was the rejection of superfluous books confined to religious discourse. Seneca was a rich source for advice against luxury of all kinds, including books: 'Having many books is a distraction. You cannot read as many books as you can own; it is enough to have as many as you can read.'[43] His rejection of books as luxury was an integral part of Stoic ethics so often aligned with a Christian rhetoric of a pious renunciation of worldly goods.[44] The Christian rejection of all but the tools necessary for salvation happily coincides with a philosophical rejection of books as luxury. The secular, ethical equivalent to the religious assessment of the function of books is well known from Pope's *Epistle to the Right Honourable Richard Earl of Burlington*, published in 1731. In an echo of the satirical remark of La Bruyére's *Characters* from

1688,[45] who described the library of a collector as a tannery, Pope mocked a noble collector:

His *Study*? With what Authors is it stor'd?
In Books, not Authors, curious is my Lord;
To all their *dated Backs* he turns you round,
These *Aldus* printed, those *Du Sueil* had *Bound*.
Lo some are *Vellom*, and the rest as good
For all his Lordship knows, but they are *Wood*.
For *Lock* or *Milton* 'tis in vain to look,
These Shelves admit not any Modern book.[46]

There were in other words expectations of behaviours associated with books which were different from the behaviour associated with objects. The changed status of books as luxury merchandise was presented as an ethical issue, but it was given an aesthetic expression, by rejecting their reification as inappropriate, silly, and ridiculous behaviour.

The same aestheticised approach to the ethical issues which applied to religious books could by analogy apply to the classics. Edward Harwood's *View of the Various Editions of the Greek and Roman Classics* was first published in 1775, a successful work with many subsequent editions. Unlike the massive and scholarly *Bibliotheca graeca* and *Bibliotheca latina* by Albert Fabricius, Harwood's *View* was essentially a collectors' guide. Yet he was not entirely at ease with the marketplace. The collecting of the classics was a socially highly specific activity, especially the first editions from the fifteenth century and the editions of Aldus and Estienne. It required the status associated with substantial property. You would expose yourself to ridicule if your fortune was inappropriately small for a collection which denoted grandeur. You would be equally ridiculous if you could not read the books. A collection of the classics required the skills which were acquired through a formal academic education. On the other hand, it was appropriate for kings and princes to collect them, even if they could not read them. The same held true for the aristocracy, but not for newly ennobled men, only those who were illustrious by birth.[47]

Harwood had to set out the social criteria for collecting because they were being transgressed all around him. A lord might well find himself in a society where he would be judged not as a lord, nor by his possessions, but on the basis of his knowledge. In 1763, on his first grand tour, the young Lord Palmerston, the father of the prime minister, visited Voltaire and engaged in discussions with German philosophers. Not surprisingly, this was an intimidating experience for the young man. He commented: 'Notwithstanding their attention and commendation, I could not help feeling sometimes mortified at my own ignorance and thinking that there is a kind of superiority which books give one better than horses.'[48]

Twenty years later Count Reviczky addressed the same situation, but very differently. He performed the highest functions of state as the emperor's envoy to London. He knew Latin, Greek, and Hebrew better than many a man of letters. He knew the main western European languages and, exceptionally, English. He had Arabic, and translated a Turkish military manual into French and Persian poetry into well-formed Latin odes.[49] He allowed his learning to be given formal expression in these works, densely annotated with classical and contemporary references. By contrast, in the catalogue of his library he made a display of his learning by taking careful steps to disguise it. His catalogue was published pseudonymously, under the name of 'Periergus Deltophilus', although it was of course known that it was his. The pseudonym is a learned conceit;[50] but far from underlining how his collection was based on profound learning, he distanced himself from *gens des lettres*. In the preface to one of the supplements to his catalogue, he used a topos of modesty but, as so often happens, not to express modesty. He collected beautiful copies of first editions of the classics, but it might have been any other type of object, and he concluded with a self-confidently self-deprecatory reference to the famous put-down of collectors from La Bruyére's *Caractères*:

Men are only too happy to have some folly which gives them pleasurable amusement, and which charms their boredom away. It fills the void which is always felt amongst their more important occupations, and diverts them from passions which are often more dangerous: ambition and cupidity. What matter is it how one obtains this benefit, if it is chasing butterflies, gathering sea-shells, gambling or completing one's collection of authors? I would suggest, Sir, that you should come and see my books in their present state, but I am justified in fearing that when you have seen them you will pass a judgment similar to that of La Bruyére.[51]

As we shall see in Chapter 5, Reviczky's wish to distance himself from men of learning had a big impact on how he treated his books. But the reification which he celebrated also meant that he could not stay detached from a world where status had a very different function.

Focusing on the language of bibliophile appreciation, rather than bibliographic description, Yann Sordet has analysed the emergence in booksellers' catalogues of a language about books, dependent on a shared activity.[52] The shared terminology defined the group from which it emanated. Sordet's starting point was a provincial collector. For collectors based in a commercial

Figure 4.1 The Reverend Clayton Mordaunt Cracherode, a plate facing p. 327 in Dibdin's *Bibliographical Decameron*, vol. III, where it is said to be based on a portrait commissioned by Earl Spencer.

metropolis the community of language had a physical manifestation, not least in the bookshop.

As part of a daily routine, Cracherode met other collectors in bookshops visiting first Peter Elmsley's then Thomas Payne's.[53] There they had a shared space despite their differences. For instance here Cracherode, known for his hostility to any challenge to the established order, regularly met Richard Payne Knight who was considered a Jacobin.[54]

Grand collectors joined with booksellers in placing books in a sphere where price was the chief criterion for value, where money increasingly competed with position for importance. The Spencer papers do not contain any bills for early books or for books on bibliography and early printing until May 1789,[55] an indication that his interest was not formed by reading, but was aroused by conversation. Dibdin tells how, sitting in the back room of Peter Elmsley's shop, Cracherode overheard Earl Spencer placing his order at his first visit to the shop. Cracherode predicted that the young man would one day become a first-rate collector, although his order was

Figure 4.2 Earl Spencer with his sisters, by Angelica Kauffmann, 1771. An aristocrat of fashion could buy his own books in same bookshop as the bourgeois Cracherode. From the Collection at Althorp.

'restricted to merely useful and popular works, without any express directions as to bindings or large paper copies'.[56]

Spencer did his own shopping for books, and he was not the only aristocrat to do so. In June 1789 he and Count Reviczky met in Edwards's bookshop. This was where the idea arose that Reviczky might sell his library to the earl.[57] Spencer's diaries reveal that, like Cracherode, he made daily visits to the two or three up-market London bookshops. Even when his function as First Lord of the Admiralty was most demanding, he made weekly morning visits to the shops, when in London, and often even when at his suburban villa in Wimbledon. For instance:

Tues. Jan 23 [1798] B[reakfast] Adm[iralty] / Homer / Office/ Walked out / Mr Cracherode / Edwards's / Leigh's / Payne's / Office Dinner Adm[iralty]. Lav[inia]. Ld Pembroke / Play Bluebeard / Office / Cice[ro] Orat[or] / S[upper] Adm[iralty].[58]

In an earlier generation there would have been no respectable, specialist bookshop where an earl could meet a count or where gentlemen could sit in the back room and exchange views on their recent acquisitions. Sixty years before, Lord Harley had relied on men of an infinitely lower class, John Bagford or Humphrey Wanley, to source his books from suppliers who often conceived of the books completely differently from the collector. When sellers and buyers do not share an understanding of the merchandise, collectors depended on men who can cross such boundaries. Operating in both worlds was not an option for grandees; they relied on others to move in the world of retailers who bought books for scrap paper. Even in the 1780s incunabula were sourced from people who used them as wrapping paper. Laire reported in 1786 that he had hoped to acquire a collection of sermons printed in Cologne but 'three months ago the grocer had bought the books which the ignorant monks had set aside'.[59] But by the end of the century, there were specialist book dealers with shops at fashionable addresses where members of the highest nobility could shop, just as they might when they bought works of art.

The ability of old books to be two different kinds of merchandise, scrap paper or a luxury good, highlights two different sets of cultural values which can be attached to them, but it also brings to our attention the society within which book collectors operated. Their world coexisted with a world of penury where nothing was wasted and everything had to be turned to practical use, if only a small amount of money to scrape a living. In 1789 a Copenhagen newspaper informed its readers that following a practice already common in Hamburg and in Holland, the auctioneers would charge for the catalogue of the collection of Count Thott, its price being set just above its value as scrap paper. The newspaper condemned paupers as greedy villains who abused the catalogues by treating them as raw materials. It was impossible for paper to be available for free without being appropriated by people who had more basic needs than book collectors. The construction of old books as scraps or as treasure is not, in the first instance, due to a difference of perceptions but reflects an actual social difference. In the market the two spheres met, which necessitated the erection of a financial barrier to allow the luxury market to function. The need to separate the two worlds reinforces our understanding of why a collection of books, often physically unremarkable, could function as a mark of status.[60]

By the end of the century, one collector notable for his absence from the bibliophile circles was George III. Edward Edwards was undoubtedly correct when he suggested, in 1859, that the king's collection was largely the independent responsibility of Barnard, who worked though George Nicol, the dealer.[61] The king could not be part of a society evolving around the bookshops and the auction houses, where like-minded men formed friendships around shopping. It is symptomatic that he is hardly mentioned in Dibdin's works of book collectors' gossip, nor in the nine volumes of John Nichols's *Literary Anecdotes* from 1812 to 1815. Furthermore, whereas Spencer and other collectors constantly referred to one another in their correspondence, forming a pan-European network, George III does not feature here either. His absence even from their correspondence underlines the importance of the community created around the trade and the shops.

This constitutes a striking parallel to the changing status of antique sculpture in fourteenth- and fifteenth-century Italy. As late as the fourteenth century, there was a limited market and that only for complete figurative sculpture. The rest was of so little interest that it was sold as raw material for lime burners. There were no specialist dealers and collectors had to rely on agents to search in an unstructured market. But during the fifteenth and sixteenth centuries increasing ranges of material became marketable and specialist dealers emerged who had achieved a new status which meant that the collectors themselves could deal directly with them.[62]

As the commodity in which they dealt achieved recognition, so did some of the most successful booksellers. Van Praet moved from being a shop boy to being a revered keeper of printed books in the Bibliothèque nationale. Writing his learned catalogues in French and Latin as well as in English, in which he confidently ascribed unassigned books to printers on the basis of their typeface and gave approximate dates for undated ones, James Edwards became integrated into the learned world. A French abbé wrote to Francis Douce concerning Edwards's visit to Paris in 1800, describing him as an amateur famous throughout the Europe of letters.[63] He even dined with a member of the aristocracy, if only a recently created baron,[64] and was to retire to the country living off a private income like a gentleman, with his own collection of valuable historic printed books.[65] The status of dealers in old books had changed as dramatically as the status of the books themselves.

But this structural indifference to class distinctions was not necessarily shared by those who participated in the market and, far from being free of conflict, the shared space of selling and buying created tensions because people from different classes met in ways where well understood and established rules governing their interaction were no longer valid. Francis Douce, as so often, went straight to the point:

At this present time owing to the Pitt system the real gentlemen of the Kingdom are supplanted and exchanged for certain tradesmen who without education or any real taste or feeling for learning or the fine arts set up for connoisseurs and collectors.

Thus we have a banker collecting books, pictures and Etruscan vases[66] (here I except the elegant author of the pleasures of memory [Samuel Rogers] in whose company I always find real pleasure). We have a dentist, an ironmonger and a grocer collecting coins and medals of all kinds.[67] A banker's clerk – *proof* prints of all kinds,[68] a shoe-maker – *large paper* books,[69] a glazier – prints and books of prints, a gunsmith – illuminated manuscripts.[70]

Items of intellectual importance, the preserve of gentlemen of letters, had become meaningful and collectable to an emergent class of people, although they lacked both education and taste. And Douce was forced to interact with them. The same awareness of an unfortunate social mix was revealed when Spencer asked the Earl of Pembroke for the loan of a book. Pembroke grandly pointed out that he was the guardian of an inherited library in which he did not take an excessive interest. The contrast with Spencer, who had to buy his own books, was left understood. Pembroke did not want to turn down a request from a peer, but he was apprehensive about Spencer's intercourse with men of a lower order. As a condition he demanded that Spencer kept the book well away from the disreputable company which he kept: 'your fraternity of book collectors or their associates'.[71] Douce was, on the other hand, more than happy when he could reveal that expertise no longer was to be found among his least favourite class, the clergy, who had to defer to the trade in order to understand their own books: 'An instance of modern book knowledge in the clergy. The Chapter of Ely sent for Triphook from London to make a catalogue of their library. They can scarcely under-stand the title of a book that is not English.'[72]

A danger of meeting in the marketplace was that one might end up being regarded as trade oneself. To avoid this embarrassment, collectors could exchange gifts.[73] The exchange of duplicates or even of leaves of books between collectors fell into this category. But exactly because the giving of gifts did not involve money, it could be difficult to deny a gift to someone of a higher standing, without seeming to reduce oneself to the level of trade. For instance, when the earl saw Douce's 'very fine and perfect copy of a Lyndewode by Wynkyn de Worde' he said … [to Douce] 'Aye this is some-thing'; Douce found this 'somewhat indecorous', but it was enough to make it clear that a gift was desired.[74]

In 1810 Douce gave Spencer some leaves from his incomplete copy of Caxton's edition of the *Golden Legend*, in order to make the earl's copy less incomplete, complaining that the leaves had been crudely extracted from his book.[75] Decorum had made it difficult to turn down a request from so eminent a person. The market was affected by status and Douce evidently

Figure 4.3 The old book room, Althorp, 1892. From an album in the John Rylands Library.

resented it that he could not refuse, feeling that the earl exploited his standing to receive more than he gave. In his notebooks Douce had little good to
say about Spencer.

For others it was welcome when hierarchy intruded on the marketplace.
A non-financial reward for a donation could be more valued than money.
The earl had admired a copy of Livy at the vicarage of Flower (Flore) in
Northamptonshire and expressed a wish to possess it. The vicar allowed the
earl to set his own price, avoiding all suspicions of behaving like a dealer.
For Mr and Mrs Morrice an invitation to Althorp was a more sought-after
reward than money.[76]

Similarly Cracherode enthusiastically yielded to the desires of Spencer,
although this must be seen in the context of the two men being as close
to being friends as a commoner and an earl could be. Spencer had given
Cracherode a duplicate copy of the first edition of Musaeus; in return
Cracherode allowed him to extract leaves from his superior copy of the first
edition of Homer, not one 'but as many leaves in the two volumes as may
in any degree suit your purpose'.[77] The still splendid Cracherode copy of

Homer shows the rather sad and confusing signs of leaves lost and of others inserted from an inferior copy.

If not carefully managed, exchanging was dangerously close to trading. Joseph Banks turned down a book given to him by Spencer in exchange: it was too valuable and he could not accept it: 'Conscience which makes cowards of us all tells me that I cannot consistently with the ideas I have hitherto entertained of propriety receive a greater value in return without entering myself upon the Roll of Dealers and Chapmen.'[78]

D'Elci, the Florentine nobleman, was also scornful of booksellers.[79] Spencer was at a higher point in the hierarchy, as d'Elci did not fail to point out, for instance in a floridly submissive letter which must have made the rather measured Spencer cringe.[80] It was more important for d'Elci that it was understood that he was not a dealer. Their correspondence opened in 1802 with a gift from d'Elci, Henry VIII's *Assertio septem sacramentorum*, printed by Pynson in 1521, a copy on vellum and illuminated, possibly in part recently. This was a sophisticated move which sought to place the relationship between two noblemen outside the marketplace.[81] The present also summarised d'Elci's conservative and hierarchical views which have been described as 'devotion to the throne and the altar'.[82]

D'Elci frequently proposed exchanging duplicates with Spencer, but a closer reading of their correspondence reveals that d'Elci got nearer to trading than his sense of propriety would allow him to admit. In contrast to Banks, he openly sought to ensure that exchanges were not to his financial disadvantage, carefully assessing the market price for each proposed item. He deployed at least two strategies to avoid the embarrassment of being seen to be selling, although it must have been perfectly obvious to Spencer that this was what was going on. A deal could be mediated through a bookseller. It is no coincidence that d'Elci's correspondence with Spencer began when James Payne, the young English dealer, was in Vienna.[83] There was an advantage to Payne in bringing the two men together and for a short period he was the intermediary who sheltered d'Elci from being seen to trade. Thus d'Elci proposed an exchange of books which involved a copy of Statius's *Thebaid* which he presented as his property, but the exchange of duplicates depended on Spencer purchasing Statius from Payne, and a subsequent letter reveals that d'Elci had never seen the copy of the *Thebaid*.[84] Had the book been d'Elci's we would have witnessed an exchange of objects between the two noblemen, only indirectly involving money. In fact, it would seem that it had been procured by d'Elci for Payne to sell to Spencer.[85] Bluntly put, in this case d'Elci acted as Payne's runner.

Another way of softening the embarrassment of negotiating over the price, used by d'Elci as well as by dealers, was to present oneself as mediating between the purchaser and a reluctant vendor, with no apparent aim of making a profit for oneself. This made hard negotiation for a price much less awkward. This approach was used by Gotthelf Fischer, the disreputable Mainz professor and librarian who profiteered from the trade in books during the Napoleonic wars. When dealing with Van Praet he made use of Giuseppe Podozzi, a fictional collector who, with no embarrassment, could be made to reject the prices proposed by Van Praet and to threaten to sell his books in London, Mannheim, or Gotha.[86] The same use of a third party was made by Payne in his dealings with Van Praet and d'Elci wrote over a protracted period to Spencer about an unnamed owner in Prague who allegedly demanded £100 for Pius II's Bull for the crusade against the Turks, in German.[87] The truth was made evident in a letter to Spencer from Alexander Horn whom d'Elci had begun to use as his intermediary with English collectors. In 1811 d'Elci's need for money may have been greater, perhaps because of the effects of the war,[88] and in 1813 Horn facilitated d'Elci's offer of the Bull as one of three books for 100 louis d'or, or £96: 'I beg leave, however, to observe that … they are to be paid en espèces sonnantes.'[89]

D'Elci was not reduced to trading by the emergency situation of the early nineteenth century. Even in 1790, long before he began his correspondence with Spencer, he had sold books to him.[90] D'Elci took great pains to disguise it, but not least in the turbulent Italian market, he was a conduit of books for the English market, much like Maugérard in Germany.[91] Whereas Maugérard was a dealer who half-heartedly sought to masquerade as a collector with limited and short-lived success, d'Elci really was a collector, and a notable one at that. Nevertheless, no matter how much he saw himself as an aristocrat unsullied by contemporary mores, he was deeply involved with a trade which he professed to despise. By trading with the earl, he increased his collection much more than he could have done if he had only swapped duplicates acquired without any subsequent deal in mind. D'Elci's need to keep up an appearance highlights some realities which the marketplace had made inescapable, both the degree to which incunabula had become a commodity and the extent to which the trade was a source of social discomfort.

The market inevitably obscured the distinction between collector and dealer. This was also the case for Giacomo Filippo Durazzo, who in the 1770s bought and sold, exploiting the enthusiasm for fifteenth-century first editions to promote his own more textually focused interest, and all the while deploring the role of the trade.[92]

At a much lower social level we see something analogous in the trading behaviour of John Ratcliffe, a chandler in Bermondsey, book collector and evidently dealer, like Bagford before him, mediating between the waste-paper trade and the rare books trade. In this way he was able to form the largest Caxton collection of the eighteenth century, dispersed at his sale in 1776.[93] According to Nichols, every Thursday morning he invited collectors of books and prints for chocolate and coffee. He whetted the appetite of his guests, or customers, by showing them his recent acquisitions. But often he already had another copy of the same book which he could subsequently offer, the customer being primed to pay a high price.[94] He camouflaged the process of buying and selling and, by turning a straightforward sale into a personal relationship, he softened its harsh commerciality both for him and for his customers. But he also mixed two spheres which decorum required should be kept apart.

It was as shocking to Francis Douce as it was to the Earl of Pembroke that men met in ways which transgressed the rules which should govern their behaviour and ensure their separation. His unease at the mixture of social forms is summed up in his account of an unusual dinner party, which confounded the distinction between commerce and conviviality:

In 1811 a gentleman of my acquaintance of very small fortune invited a large party to a dinner that was most adapted to the purse of a nobleman … All this is very foolish. But what followed is more extraordinary. After dinner a large parcel of his books are brought on the table and put up to auction among the guests, the proprietor putting them in at a certain price. In this way many or most of them were disposed of and in this way the owner probably got more than indemnity for his dinner.

The gentleman infringed against decent behaviour in two ways. He gave a party which was too luxurious for a gentleman of his modest means, but he also used a private dinner as an occasion for dealing. At least Ratcliffe had kept a decorous pretence of a distinction between chocolate mornings and business transactions.

Douce was put out because he felt his own position as a gentleman to be precarious, socially and financially. This was a large part of the reason why he supported the French Revolution. We saw his unhappiness with gentlemanly pursuits being undertaken by tradesmen but, like so many others, he felt that the increasing tax burden to finance the war, imposed by the ruling aristocracy, was becoming unbearable for landed gentry, as was inflation for the middle classes who relied on investment income. His disapproval of the transgression of accepted norms was directed as much against people above him in the hierarchy as against those below him. Money made some people believe they were higher in the hierarchy than they were, but it also made others behave as if they were lower. The market seemed to confuse socially important distinctions. Just as we saw that the *hommes de lettres* in France had their authority questioned or even usurped, in England Douce could feel that his position as a gentleman and the authority which he derived from his knowledge and education, his social capital, were undermined by an alliance of aristocracy, money, and trade. He wrote:

The love of laying out money in a variety of articles, especially among the collectors of objects of virtù, contributes greatly to put them on a level with those of whom they make such purchases and render them ardent lovers of money. For my own part I can conscientiously say I have never felt this impulsion, nor was ever guilty of this weakness, except in my own defence in a very few instances. I never saw a man so completely under the influence of this passion as Lord N, and in a negoti-ation which I had with him for some articles, I was compelled to treat with him as I would have with Mssrs M. Y. or T. During the treaty, which was a stubborn one, he manifested some degree of peevishness but on its conclusion, he relaxed into the utmost civility and opened all his treasure to my inspection.[95]

Douce felt that the nobleman was demeaned, but he also felt demeaned himself, having been treated as trade. After the deal Douce was shown the nobleman's collections, so it was Douce who had brought him some items for which he wanted money. His criticism of the nobleman also reveals his discomfort at his own monetary interest in their interaction.

In 1815 Douce summarised his view of what had happened to cultural property in Europe during the preceding two and a half decades:

The monuments of art which had been taken in successive wars of Napoleon … are in danger of being dispersed. These had been taken, in great measure, from people either incompetent or indisposed to use them properly and were, in their new situ-ation, about to be rendered of general interest to society. Paris is a more central repository than any other place for these monuments of the old world … Of what use were the treasures of the Vatican locked up as they were from all rational use? At Vienna it was little better and in Spain worse. France itself during the whole of its convoluted state during the last 20 years has to lament the losses it has sustained by the immense quantity of fine articles bought up, amidst its pecuniary distress by other nations, particularly the barbarous Russians who are still semi-Tartars.

Already do the English agents for the arts &c. talk of the purchases they mean to make of the Pope and others to whom restoration is to be made. So much for the virtuous and honest use of English wealth. We have already the plunder of Egypt without any compensation to the Turks from whom the French have taken them. This is robbing the robbers without making restitution. Where this cannot be done our money does the rest. A Boccaccio has lately been sold in this country to a mad collector of books who never reads them for £2200! Another was heard of at Milan and an opulent lord who had failed in the competition for the first sent an express to the owner of the latter, thinking that his insolent and indelicate offer of a large sum would ensure him the possession of the rare article. To his great mortification and to the honour of the Milanese proprietor the latter indignantly rejected the proposition and would not even permit the book to be seen. A proper and wholesome correction for the insolence of English wealth.[96]

The man described as mad was the Marquess of Blandford, later the fifth Duke of Marlborough. Mocking him for collecting books which he never read was a conventional and, as it happens, not entirely fair attack, as Douce's own correspondence shows, but it recalls Rive's disdain for aristocrats entering the field of men of learning.[97] The attack on the 'opulent lord', Earl Spencer, the underbidder, was more radical. His monetary attitude to books led him to indelicate behaviour in dealing with the Milanese proprietor, evidently a real gentleman, with the gratifying outcome of 'a proper and wholesome correction'.[98]

The book in question was one of the relatively small number of incunabula in the sale of the Duke of Roxburghe in 1812,[99] the first edition, by Valdarfer of Boccaccio's *Decameron*. The status of incunabula is evident when comparing the price of £2,260 for this visually unprepossessing printed book with the price of £685 15s which Blandford paid two years later for the Bedford Hours, now one of the most treasured illuminated manuscripts in the British Library, while the *Decameron*, of which the British Library now also has a copy, attracts little attention.[100]

The collecting of early printed books was now part of conspicuous consumption: the sale and the prices were in all the papers, both in London and in the provinces.[101] Most reports included a little anecdote of civilities exchanged between Earl Spencer and the Marquess of Blandford, presenting an auction of old books as an elegant event where the highest nobility could be seen in public to display their wealth, their sophistication, and their status. *The Times*, however, omitted the anecdote:

Yesterday a competition took place at the sale of the Roxburghe Library, for the Decameron of Boccaccio, a single volume in small folio, printed in the year 1471; it was knocked down to the Marquis of Blandford for 2260£. We can only say that it is a lamentably erroneous way of indicating the love of learning, to give immense prices for rare or old editions, which do not even possess equal means of infusing knowledge with the modern and common ones. It would be a better testimony of a correct taste, to study useful, than to purchase scarce books.[102]

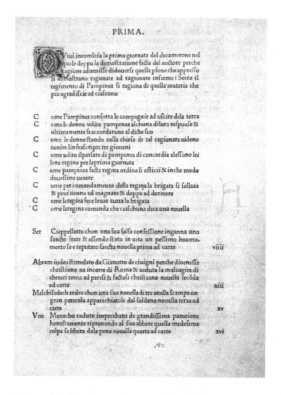

Figure 4.4 Boccaccio, *Decamerone*. [Venice]: Valdarfer, 1471. Sig. [a]1 recto. JRL, 17659. Bought by the Marquess of Blandford in 1812 for £2,260.

In comparison, nobody seemed to mind when Charles Fox, the politician, sold two of his racehorses for £2,330 each, including Chanticleer, evidently named after the story of Chanticleer and the Fox in Chaucer's *Nun's Priest's Tale*.[103] It was not the sum itself which gave offence, but the continued existence of opposing values attached to the same objects. If you were in Oxford in 1798 and really were interested in Aulus Gellius, you did not have to pay £58 16s as the Bodleian did a few years earlier, for an edition with an inferior text. You could buy Gronovius's highly respectable edition from 1706 for 11s and get a book which was 'very neat and gilt'. If you were in York you might have to stump up 18s for the same edition.[104]

The most expensive modern book listed in the *London Catalogue of Books* for 1799 was 'Lavater's Physiognomy, 3 vols large paper', a heavily illustrated book which would cost £27, otherwise you would have to buy many volumes to approach such levels of expense. Eighteen volumes of the 'Encylopædia Britannica in quarto' cost £22 10s. 'Statutes at large, by Runnington, 13 vols, quarto' cost £17 5s or, if you bought them on large paper, £22 5s.[105] One of the most expensive books of the whole century

Figure 4.5 The Bedford Hours. © British Library Board. Add. MS 18850, fol. 15 verso. Bought by the Marquess of Blandford in 1814 for £685 15s.

was de Caylus's *Recueil des peintures antiques* from 1757 which would set you back nearly £54, but for which you would have got, in three volumes, one of the most stunning luxury hand-coloured books ever produced.[106] When you pay £60 for an indulgence, as Spencer did in 1802, it is not for its value as a book; far from being a multi-volume set, and far from being produced to the highest standards of luxury, it was a piece of utilitarian printing on one side of a scrap of skin to ensure its spiritually important durability. Not only have these prices parted ways with the traditional way in which books were priced, by their bulk, as Arnold Hunt has pointed out.[107] They have left the range of the book market behind completely.

In the Stoic/Christian tradition, *The Times* objected to the amounts spent on the books at the Roxburghe sales, but the prices show us that they were not expensive books: they had become a different class of objects which had a completely different function and meaning from the one which *The Times* felt that books had or, more properly, that books ought to have. The criticism of this approach to books is in contrast to the quiet approbation afforded by *The Times* to Spencer in 1793, when it was felt that his collection reflected a proper engagement with literature.[108]

Douce highlighted the private nature of pre-revolutionary collections, in opposition to the new public one created in Paris, and he saw that the removal of these useful objects from the public went hand in hand with their transformation into a luxury commodity. After Reviczky had sold his collection to Spencer he continued to collect but now on Spencer's behalf, gradually handing over his connections in the trade to Spencer. Yet there was one point where the two men disagreed. Reviczky had assumed that his collection would stay in the metropolis and be available to scholarship, and he had been promised permanent access to it for himself. Ideally, he had hoped to see his collection in a public library to secure its permanence, avoiding the dispersal which would have been inevitable if it had passed into the hands of some 'idiot heir'.[109] But Spencer had another view. He moved the collection to Althorp, in the inaccessible countryside where he wanted to integrate it with his family's other treasures. His attachment to his family's rural background was alien to the imperial count who, although Hungarian, was born and bred in Vienna. Spencer's draft answer to Reviczky's letter of regret addressed the importance of the books only in terms of their importance to Spencer himself:

The only thing in which I fear I must continue to differ with you is the place where the Library is to be; I am myself so thoroughly wedded to a country life, and my heart so fixed at Althorp that (to reverse a quotation from scripture) I cannot help saying that where the heart is there should the treasure be also.

Both men were aware of the cultural divide. Spencer's rejection was firm, and he sought to soften the blow only by expressing the unrealistic hope that the removal of the library to Althorp would make Reviczky a more frequent guest there. Reviczky couched his position in his characteristic, charmingly ironic phrases, and warned the earl against his quaint and dangerous interest in the hunt, recommending instead the peaceful reading of his vellum copies of Gratius and Oppianus on hunting with dogs.[110]

The acquisitions made by British collectors were widely perceived to be withdrawn from the republic of letters and hidden in private houses. This was in contrast to the republican collections in Paris where the Bibliothèque nationale was famously accessible to the public, as were, increasingly, royal collections elsewhere in Europe. This private nature of British collections was a theme much developed by the French. Quatremère de Quincy had written *Considérations morales* by 1796 in response to the creation of the big public museums in Paris which first grew out of the Revolution. Here objects were gathered together and displayed, removed from the context of the repugnant oppressive past which they had originally been made to glorify, now placed in a chronological order to show the progress of mankind. Quatremère de Quincy did not object to public access or ownership but he deplored that artistic productions were deprived of their context. Consequently he took even more exception to the private collections which were being created in England. Being dispersed in far-flung rural houses, artistic productions exported to England were even more deprived of context; additionally they were even less accessible than they had previously been:

After Italy, no country is richer in antiquities than England … And what is the result? Riches are scattered in all castles. We have to travel hundreds of leagues through all counties to see these partial collections. I know nothing less useful for Europe, and even for the arts in England themselves, than the objects of this nature possessed by England.[111]

This attitude gained some currency among scholars; for instance in 1805 a German traveller could express the view that sculpture kept in English country houses might as well never have been excavated.[112] We have seen how Zapf, the German incunable scholar, also in 1805 compared books sold to England and Russia with the looted books which were accessible to all in the Bibliothèque nationale, and how Lévis in 1802 compared the public riches of French collections with the poverty of the British Museum's library, noting that in Britain 'all riches in these categories are private'.[113]

The books of grand English collectors could exercise their function as symbols of wealth and status by being in the public eye, even when not seen. While the monument to the collections formed by the noblemen of the early eighteenth century was Maittaire's catalogue, the monument to the collections of the grandees of the late eighteenth century and the early nineteenth century was the work of Thomas Frognall Dibdin, whose importance should not be obscured, as Munby has warned, by the 'elephantine facetiousness' of his prose.[114]

The *Bibliographical Decameron*, published at the author's expense, and distributed by the leading antiquarian booksellers of London, G. and W. Nicol, Payne and Foss, Evans, John and Arthur Arch, and Robert Triphook, displays the symbiosis between market and collector.[115] Dibdin presented to the public the competitive collecting of books as an activity which was essentially social, as against reading, which was essentially private. He focused on conversations between men of a desirable class, whose lives centred on old books, not least on their acquisition, and whose status made real association with them unattainable.

Figure 4.6 Portrait of Dibdin, a plate facing the title page, inserted into Thomas Grenville's copy of Dibdin's *Bibliomania*, 1811 (BL, G. G.29,30).

In several of Dibdin's works each person has a code name: collecting is an activity for the initiated. Yet they were not too difficult to decipher, so that many could feel that they had a privileged insight into an unattainable world. The objects, removed from the public, became symbols of the immense distance between the rich collectors and those who might buy books for reading, but the strategy of exclusion sought to make the reader desire to belong. Dibdin cited prices incessantly and gushed over the luxurious aspects of individual objects; he showed no restraint, least of all with his name-dropping anecdotes which gave the objects extra social meaning. Sometimes the books sound like celebrities of our time, famous in a circular way for having been owned by famous people who then gained fame from having owned them, exactly the attitude which had been denounced by Rive. Dibdin gave a literary form to the private chit-chat of the auction rooms and the bookshops, and to the graciously granted tour of the private collection.

The glamorous life around the collections of rare books and the trade is presented to the public for admiration, and also for emulation. Any man

Figure 4.7 *Un tournoi*, by Pierre Révoil, 1812. Musée des Beaux-Arts de Lyon. © Lyon MBA/Photo Alain Basset. Painted in the year when Dibdin described competition in the marketplace as an aristocratic activity equivalent to jousting.

with money could create something for himself which was, if not similar, at least analogous. This was important for the trade, and also for the social function of the books to persist. For the aspirant participant in this society Dibdin provided not so much bibliographical knowledge but assistance with the important ability to maintain a conversation about books. Even his copious hard information is presented as gossip, including his information on prices, somewhat relentless if taken at face value as part of a conversation, but essential for the world of competitive collecting which he presented. His enthusiastic ecphrases of the admired objects conjure up an impression of a cultured and prosperous world, the books being an essential tool for the public display of wealth and accomplishment.

More than anybody else, Dibdin shows that events had created an element of truth in the view of Renouard and his Jacobin colleagues, that grand lords collected their books for reasons which were ideologically opposed to the republican quest for freedom and equality. In his extensive description of the grandest of bibliophile events, the sale of the Roxburghe collection of 1812, Dibdin glorified the marketplace in a laboriously sustained metaphor: it was the modern equivalent of the jousting field, that most aristocratic of meeting places. The market for luxurious books was a place for the public display, no longer of greed or profligacy, but of valorous aristocratic virtues, the weapons being not lances but money. His description conveys to an aspirant readership that buying luxury books was an aristocratic pastime in which one could engage to make a display of one's wealth and sophistication, an encouragement for others to emulate Blandford and Spencer, for instance through the formation in other spheres of bibliophile clubs similar to the grand Roxburghe Club which Dibdin himself ensured was founded. For instance, in 1815 and 1816 fifteen gentlemen met in the shop of William Ford, in Manchester, to present to one another 'a paper upon something rare, or a meritorious publication, which should be read to the Society and afterwards transmitted to the *Editor of the Manchester Herald*.'[116] The Manchester gentlemen followed the pattern of the grandees of the Roxburghe Club, indulging their pursuits in full co-operation with the commercial world.

The report of the Roxburghe sale in *The Times* shows that the question of authority cannot be said to have been settled, but participants in the market had grown to be completely indifferent to the assessment of the books as texts, tools useful for the promotion of learning. When it came to rare books, authority lay with the market and its agents, dealers, auctioneers, and collectors of luxury, and for them the books were primarily things. By other ideological means, the reification of rare books was as complete for Spencer and Blandford as it was for the revolutionaries. The consequences for the books themselves of this transformation will be the theme of the next chapter.

5 | Commemorating and obliterating the past: 'old books, very displeasing to the eye'

Often considered a component of national heritage, libraries, archives, and museums have more recently been described by administrators and funding bodies as 'memory institutions'.[1] But memories are intensely personal, not institutional. Commemoration, on the other hand, is typically a public rather than a private act and it often has a wider political or social purpose. For a historical analysis it is useful both to understand why the two are linked and to attempt to differentiate between them. Shared memories tie families or groups of friends together. Commemoration can seek to attach the emotions of shared memories to selected events of which we have no personal memory, and in that way it can use the powerful ability of shared memory to define who belongs to a group and who does not. Associating emotions with a commemorated past blurs the distinction between knowledge and taking sides. Commemoration comes close to expressing approval of an event or of a specific attitude to it. By not commemorating, one can indicate indifference or outright disapproval. The political significance of both implies that, for a historian analysing people's ways of dealing with the past, commemoration and oblivion are equally meaningful.[2]

In the preceding chapters, I examined some ways of gaining an insight into the understanding of the past which are behind the formation of historic collections. The wish to commemorate or not to commemorate has had a significant impact on what has been collected but it has also influenced how objects were treated. The past is not parcelled up according to the interests of posterity, and in the surviving objects the desirable and the undesirable are intimately associated.

This chapter will look at the process of collecting itself and will explore how books were made to conform so that they could reflect both what collectors valued of the past and what collectors did not care to commemorate or, sometimes, even positively wished to consign to oblivion. It will look first at the bindings of books, then at the way the leaves of the book were treated, then their decoration, and finally at attempts to make items more complete than history had left them. To end, it will outline some aspects of the wider cultural background which motivated the physical modification of the books.

Any act of collecting detaches objects from a previous context and inevitably inserts them into a new one. Here they gain new meaning both as individual objects and as part of a collection. The collector can have a wide range of motives. It was a source of pride to Cracherode that he owned books which had previously belonged to Jean Grolier, the French sixteenth-century collector.[3] This was an ambition understood by other collectors and Cracherode could gain in stature among his peers by associating himself with objects which had previously been owned by a person to whom prestige was attached. The books no longer had the same function as they did in Grolier's own collection: they now served to enhance Cracherode's position by memorialising Grolier: they had become Groliers. At the same time, Cracherode's lack of interest in most other past owners of his books is an indication of a differentiation: he attached special importance to some past cultural contexts and no importance to others. The lack of perceived importance can sometimes approach outright hostility, a positive rejection of the culture from which the books emerged, as we saw with the French revolutionary rejection of signs of noble ownership.

To understand how this differentiation had an impact, it is important to remember that incunabula bought and sold in the eighteenth century were as much part of eighteenth-century book culture as any other book. Thomas Cogan's satirical novel *John Buncle, Junior, Gentleman* from 1776–8 can help with establishing a context for eighteenth-century incunabula. Cogan presented his book as a sequel to *The Life of John Buncle, Esq.* by Thomas Amory. But Junior was not merely 'Esquire', as was his father; he was a 'gentleman' and he sought recognition for his family's recent social progress. He believed that writing a book of profound thoughts would be just the right way to achieve this. The novel relates the process of this book's own transformation from thoughts to object, as Buncle learns that in smart society books do not serve the purpose of conveying thoughts. He wants his book to be cheap so that many can afford to read it, but his publisher knows better:

Men of letters (quoth he) are so few in number, that they cannot reasonably expect particular attention should be paid them ... but for the public at large it is the most kindly tax imaginable. It pleases everybody. First as to the author; I have already hinted it is a happy and certain method of making a few thoughts *valuable* ... Again it is more gratifying to the pride of the reader. He sets himself down before a pompous quarto or folio, with all the dignity of a professor. Or if he condescends to dip into these duodecimos, he lolls upon the sopha. With his toothpick in his hand, he has the satisfaction to find that, even in his indolent moments, he can soon become a very *voluminous* reader. And sir, it is infinitely more to *our advantage*.

Why, sir, expensive editions secure the custom of those, who though they complain everything is dear, will purchase nothing that is cheap. And the number of such, in this metropolis, is so very considerable that were they readers, nine parts out of ten, would enquire the price of a book, exclaim against it as exorbitant, pay the money, and look with contempt upon an edition they might have had for one third of the value. And finally, these superb impressions are sure to draw the attention of most of your nobility and gentry; who collect books as they collect pictures, or keep mistresses – not from the great pleasure they take in either, but merely as articles of state.

Eventually Buncle realised that he stood a better chance of gaining immortality through one of his everyday possessions: his horse-whip. 'At that illustrious period, when posterity shall have the same reverence for us, their ancestors, as we entertain for ours!' – then his horse-whip will be a treasured monument of the past, and future antiquarians will write learned dissertations about it.[4]

The satire reflects the economics of the booktrade; in contrast to the situation which was to emerge in the nineteenth century with the maturing of the mass market, expensive books were overall more important for the trade than cheaper books: books were part of the luxury market and therefore could not sell if they were not priced as luxuries. Yet the satire asserts the values attached to the opposite attitude. Cogan's own belief in the importance of books as a means of communication of ideas and knowledge was reaffirmed in his travel book *The Rhine, or a Journey from Utrecht to Francfort*, in which he celebrated the invention of printing as a shield against tyranny, as we saw in Chapter 1.

It was essential for Cogan's satire that the thoughts of John Buncle only deserved to achieve value as a reified commodity for frivolous customers. It was not an intellectual achievement demeaned by an uncomprehending public, but a pointless text elevated by the market to the realm of luxury. This is paralleled by incunabula. Old books were affected by the same consumer expectations and the same market forces, and they had to conform in order to become 'articles of state', a viable alternative to keeping mistresses. But it was a problem with fifteenth-century books that few of them lived up to eighteenth-century expectations, as George Mason wrote to Spencer: 'Many of my copies of old books look'd miserable till Roger Payne took them in hand and have now a very decent appearance.'[5]

The process of detachment from past contexts and of reinsertion into new ones is radically manifested in the removal of historic bindings from old books. On the one hand, we should not underestimate the importance of a long-standing tradition whereby a wealthy owner decided to express the values which he attached to his books by rebinding them. When collectors had their incunabula rebound and had their coats of arms placed on the covers of the books, they were in one sense continuing a long tradition. On the other hand, we should not take such a radical transformation of the objects as self-evident or natural, just because we are used to it. Even if it was merely to impose an elegant uniform appearance on their books, this was a way for the owner to give visual expression to his ownership and mastery of the books. Uniformity was prized for what it meant, or at least for what it would have meant if it had not been imposed.

Uniformity is in fact rather rare: few collectors bound their books in entirely uniform bindings. What they sought was to make their books present a visually cohesive appearance which spoke of the value which was attached to them. The Bodleian Library was typical when, in 1790 and 1791, it used different types of bindings to differentiate levels of value and importance.

Henri Grégoire described a hierarchy of bindings when he explained how noble collectors had lavished expensive morocco bindings on books which promoted the values of the *Ancien Régime*, whereas texts which had been important for the formation of revolutionary thought had found refuge from censorship in humble parchment bindings, 'the sans-culottes of libraries'.[6] Grégoire's assertion has to be taken with a good pinch of salt, but he makes the point forcefully enough that bindings reflect the value which their owners attach to their books. Bindings were expensive and owners spent money on them because they placed a value on the difference between the significance of the book in its old binding and the significance of the rebound book.

The duc de La Vallière put expensive bindings on incunabula supplied by Maugérard, books which Rive considered cheap and nasty.[7] Rive was not opposed to rebinding nor to luxury, but these bindings indicated that the duke did not share his assessment of the value of books. The difference in how they understood value undermined Rive's status as the duke's paid authority.

Lavishly rebound, Lord Spencer's copy of an old Latin grammar is no longer easy to associate with a fifteenth-century classroom and the teaching of pre-humanist Latin. It claimed a place in a luxury collection of the early nineteenth century. It did not, in the first instance, become valuable because of its binding, but was given a valuable binding because it was considered to have a status which it did not itself adequately display. Rebinding integrated it into an aesthetic which made visible the value which was attached to it, and only then could it reflect the grandeur of its owner.

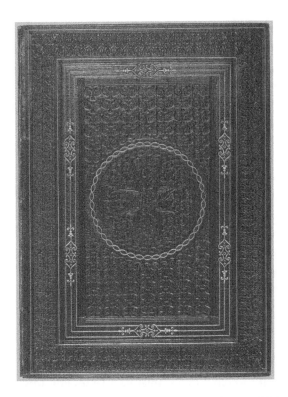

Figure 5.1 *Grammatica rhythmica*. Mainz: [Fust and Schoeffer], 1466. Bound for Spencer by Hering. JRL, 17265.

When the monks of Roth sold their 1457 Psalter to Spencer in 1798, it was bound in pigskin, presumably over wooden boards, had metal furniture, and contained supplementary manuscript vellum leaves, all now gone. The librarian at Roth described it:

In addition I must note that our Psalter is a thickish, heavy folio, partly because of the brass on the covers, partly because of the supplement. Because the Psalter fifty years ago was still in use by the young canons for the canonical hours, psalms and hymns written on parchment nearly as strong as the Psalter, and bound in pigskin. But this supplement can easily be separated if you require the Psalter unbound. For the rest the Psalter is in good condition, except for one leaf from which something has been torn off, but this is only to be taken as an indication of its great age.[8]

Spencer had the Psalter bound in mauve velvet over cardboard, with yellow cloth pastedowns and endleaves, thickly varnished to enhance their gloss, now displaying with sad, didactic clarity the structural and material inadequacies of early nineteenth-century bindings. The function of the Psalter as a religious text was of no concern to Spencer.

It changes the nature of the decision to rebind and to integrate a historic object into a new contemporary aesthetic if it was undertaken in an awareness of the value of at least some bindings as historical evidence. Towards the end of the eighteenth century this could increasingly be the case as can be seen from the connotations of a phrase like 'original bindings' used in sale catalogues. 'Original' or 'old' could mean 'old but not bad', rather than 'old and therefore desirable'. When, in 1790, Benjamin White described a copy of Isocrates printed in London in 1749 as 'very neat, in the original binding', it is hard to believe that he suggested that a book would be collectable for the historic importance of a forty-year old binding.[9] Here the word is probably closer in meaning to the phrases 'elegantly bound, good as new' or 'very neat, old binding' which were used by John Cuthell in his catalogue of 1800 to refer to books printed in 1763 and 1778.[10] In his catalogue of 1739 Thomas Osborne on occasion referred to books as being in their 'original binding'. Most often this was not given great emphasis, and seems merely descriptive, but on occasion it seems part of a promotional statement. A book printed in 1606 was described as 'very fair, gilt on the leaves, and in the fine original old binding, worked on the sides with gold'; in this context the old binding was worth promoting, but because it was lavish, not so much because it was old.[11] In a similar vein James Edwards's catalogue of the *Bibliotheca parisiana*, from 1791, contains numerous references to 'original bindings'. The statements were integral parts of descriptions of excellent condition and were given typographical prominence.[12] All the bindings thus designated were originally made to be luxurious and are featured as analogous to modern luxury bindings by Derôme; it is not easy to be sure that he valued any binding for its age; yet an 'original' fifteenth-century binding had a place in Edwards's repertoire of features which he could use for promotional purposes. On the other hand, George Wagstaff undoubtedly suggested that an old binding merited attention for its own sake for instance when, in his winter catalogue for 1774, he described an 'original binding' as 'curiously stampt'.[13] Similarly, in 1770 Richard Dymott mentioned in a positive context an original binding on an incunable, probably a binding made for Koberger, the Nuremberg printer and publisher.[14]

Yann Sordet has provided information and analyses of relevance far beyond the attitudes of Pierre Adamoli, the eighteenth-century Lyonnais collector on whom he focused. Although Adamoli shared the common distaste for the gothic aesthetics of the fifteenth century, he rebound his books with reluctance and on occasion even retained parts of fifteenth-century bindings as documentation for posterity. While he was enthusiastic about the hand-painted historiated initials in his incunabula, Adamoli regretted

Figure 5.2 *Anthologia graeca*, ed. Janus Lascaris. Florence: de Alopa, 1494. © British Library Board. IB.28002. The binding on Cracherode's copy of this edition is similar to the one which Reviczky had removed from his.

their printed equivalents, which 'lapsed into the dreadful gothic' which dominated printing until the 1530s.[15] Adamoli was provincial and a man of learning. His collection did not have the ambitions of an Earl Spencer, a Count Reviczky, or a duc de La Vallière. This may have left him more space for an interest in the historic appearance of the books.

It is possible to give some concrete examples which help us assess the impact of the awareness and knowledge of the potential significance of bindings as historic evidence. In the 1791 catalogue of the incunabula of Loménie de Brienne, Laire described two copies of the Gutenberg Bible.[16] One was in a fifteenth-century binding which conveyed information on the earliest owner of the volume, which Laire carefully recorded. But when the Bible was bought by the Bodleian Library, it had been rebound, by Derôme, in full awareness of the historic evidence which was being destroyed.

A similar attitude could have an impact on books which had bindings which were very expensive from the outset. Reviczky acquired his copy of the *Anthologia graeca* in 1785 for 1,000 livres, about £40. According to Née de la Rochelle's description in the catalogue from which Reviczky bought it, its binding made it 'obvious that this book was eminently suitable for a young prince who loved letters, and that this was a worthy present to give him'.[17] This is a type of binding which Anthony Hobson has described as integral to Janus Lascaris's desire to give the books which he produced the appearance of ancient classical manuscripts.[18] In full knowledge of its importance Reviczky had the binding replaced with one of red morocco with pea-green lining.[19] Late fifteenth-century views of luxury and of the ancient world were of no interest to Reviczky, just as the fifteenth-century view of the Psalter was of no concern to Spencer.

In 1799 Sotheby's sold a collection of books, probably on behalf of Edwards, the bookseller. The collection was billed as being 'In the Finest Preservation and in the Original Monastic Bindings'. This was not only the first London auction devoted exclusively to incunabula; it is also the earliest auction known to me which uses the historical nature of the bindings as a sales pitch. While the 'original bindings' which were mentioned in the *Bibliotheca parisiana* sale catalogue were all luxurious, there is no reason to believe that the bindings on these books would have been so. Many of the books can be associated with the Franciscan house of St Anna in Bamberg. The few St Anna books surviving in old bindings known to me, none from this sale, have good, solid, but very plain monastic bindings (see Figure 5.3).[20] As suggested in Chapter 2, it is highly likely that this collection of books was put together by Maugérard.[21] Again we find Maugérard closely involved in events which give a market value to fifteenth-century books as fifteenth-century objects. In London, by the late 1790s, there was enough of a shared understanding of the interest which could attach even to unspectacular bindings for their historic and cultural context to be used for promotional purposes. The low prices fetched at the sale are an indication that the trade was ahead of collectors in attaching value to historical features.

Francis Douce thought that the provenance was of sufficient interest to note on his copy of the catalogue 'from a monastic house in Bamberg'. Yet he saw to it that his purchases were rebound, cheaply, which suggests that it was getting rid of the old bindings, the act of oblivion, which was important to him, not the new bindings which he had made.[22]

George III too bought extensively at the 1799 sale.[23] None of his purchases is still 'in the original monastic binding'. All were rebound in the Buckingham House bindery, and again not in very luxurious bindings.[24] Different as they were, both Douce and George III obliterated evidence revealed by the bindings about the original function of the books, not least because in many cases texts which had been together since their earliest days were split up. The

Figure 5.3 Bartholomaeus de Chaimis, *Confessionale*. [Nuremberg], 1480. A book from St Anna in Bamberg, still in its fifteenth-century binding. Paris, BnF, Rés. D.67967.

function they had had was not a cause for commemoration, for Franciscan monks were not the height of fashion. As we heard, Horn, a Benedictine, put it in 1802 in a letter to Spencer: 'Every liberal minded man will allow that the mendicant orders of friars are a nuisance.'[25]

The current state of his incunabula and the many bills especially from Kalthoeber but also from other binders, show that Spencer too consistently had his incunabula rebound, at least if they were in fifteenth-century bindings.[26] About three months after the Sotheby's sale, on 9 August 1799, Maugérard wrote to Spencer:

I come back to the History of Daniel, for which your Excellency offers me 1000 francs. You will yourself, sir, judge that it seems that one should not break the binding of this volume to separate them from the others which are bound together. One of these is the *Biblia pauperum* also by Pfister and the other is the History of Antichrist. This has persuaded me to keep the volume as it is or to sell it as a unity. So if your Excellency wishes to keep the volume as it is, you will be kind enough to pay me 1800 francs for it.[27]

Figure 5.4 The breakfast room at Althorp in 1892. From an album in the John Rylands Library. Even at Althorp, where no architectural setting was built for the library, medieval books were out of place if they looked medieval.

Spencer was informed about the importance of keeping the items in the original binding; he was even given a financial indication of the importance; yet he had the volume split up and rebound. Monkish books were not articles of state, to use the phrase of John Buncle, Junior.

It is probably not by chance that several of the persons who attached importance to early bindings were members of the booktrade. As explorers of the landscape they were confronted with the books in their earlier context. It was by seeing items together that Maugérard had been able to establish the identity and thereby the value of some of the most important items with which he had dealt. In their search for points of special interest which might add value to the items in which they traded, dealers could identify historic bindings as potential features of value. This does not mean that they approached this cynically. James Edwards, the bookseller, had in his private collection books which were notable for their original bindings. Men of the booktrade shared the values of their customers but they also formed them, and they gave them an expression which we can recognise in their catalogues or in their commercial correspondence.

It has been suggested that Spencer had a respect for early bindings, but the example which has been quoted to support this relates to a book which was in the possession of James Edwards.[28] Dibdin occasionally voiced regret for the loss of an original binding, for instance on the *Anthologia graeca* mentioned above: 'The reader cannot but regret with the present noble owner of it, that the original exterior has been exchanged with a modern and less appropriate binding.'[29] However, this turns out not to be a lament for the lost original structure but a criticism of the taste of the recent but no-longer fashionable binding, with its pea-green lining, and appropriateness and taste was fully restored when Spencer had the modern binding replaced within another even more modern one. In his *Bibliographical Decameron* from 1817, Dibdin frequently attacked Derôme, the luxury binders of the now fading eighteenth-century fashion. When he visited the Imperial Library in Vienna in 1821 he saw a Valdarfer edition from 1471 in its original binding, and suggested to the librarian that it would be more appropriate if it were rebound in morocco and gold tooled, by Charles Lewis.[30] Getting rid of an old binding was what Dibdin preferred, but it had to be replaced with a fashionable one, not with one which would have been fashionable a few decades earlier. Derôme was out of fashion as was the much admired Kalthoeber, now described as clumsy. Several times Dibdin placed the responsibility on Reviczky for the poor taste of Kalthoeber bindings on Spencer's books, but Kalthoeber's invoices to Spencer tell another story. Dibdin's hostility to certain modern bindings does not fundamentally reveal an appreciation of the historic bindings which they replaced but is rather to be explained by a change of taste: late eighteenth-century bindings were no longer smart.

The same attitudes can be documented in the Bibliothèque nationale. As a supplier to Van Praet, Gotthelf Fischer was aware of the incompatibility of a fine condition with an original binding. When he offered a number of books from the collection of the fictitious Podozzi he wrote: 'They are in superb condition … except for the German ones which are still in their wooden bindings.'[31] Only two copies survive of the four biblical stories printed by Pfister in Bamberg, of which Spencer acquired and dismembered one. The other was acquired by the Bibliothèque nationale, also in 1799 for 1,500 francs, half-way between the 1,800 francs which Maugérard asked for and the 1,000 francs which Spencer offered for his copy. This is a good indication that there was a shared market with a fairly predictable price level for this sort of item, and that even under extraordinary circumstances the French state and the English aristocrat acted on an equal footing in the market.[32] A paper was read on it to the Institut national by Camus, a politically important member of the Assemblée nationale. Van Praet was not a member of the Institut and it must have been a major occasion for him when a paper read there focused on one of his acquisitions. And that is not all: Camus's paper to the Institut was formally presented to the Conseil des Cinq-cents, as far as I know the only book to achieve such high-level political recognition.[33] Camus's description of the original binding was an important part of his argument to prove that this volume was the one discovered first in 1792, not the one which had been offered in 1795 to Van Praet by Maugérard. Yet Van Praet had the book rebound in blue morocco, signed by Bozérian jeune. Like Spencer, Van Praet did not consider the old binding worthy of its new context, although its importance had been drawn to his attention.

The same fate befell the unique copy of another book printed in Bamberg, the volume of Boner's *Fables*. It was looted from Wolfenbüttel and transferred to the Bibliothèque impériale in 1807, still in its late medieval binding, as noted by Van Praet when he received it. It was instantly rebound and this humble volume truly became an article of state.[34] Confiscated by Stendhal and rebound with Napoleon's imperial eagle stamped on its covers, this medieval book was reconfigured to enable it to play its role in the new European political order.

This was the book which caused most pain to Van Praet when he very reluctantly assisted the campaigns of restitution which were undertaken in 1814 and 1815 as part of the peace agreement.[35] He complained in general about having to return books with new morocco bindings which had cost so much money, feeling that rebinding had immensely enhanced their value. This view was shared by those who were later to reclaim these literary treasures. When in 1816 Emperius wrote in a Braunschweig newspaper about the return of this book to Wolfenbüttel, he mentioned how crude its illustrations were, how exaggerated its estimated value of 20,000 francs (about £800), and how it had been splendidly rebound in Paris.[36]

Rebinding had in fact been expensive. In the bid for funds for year VIII [1799–1800] the Bibliothèque nationale asked for 6,600 francs, about £260, for rebinding printed books confiscated abroad. Many were in old wooden board: 'The majority are those which come from our conquests in Germany and Italy, and while infinitely precious, they have arrived to us in a deplorable state.'[37] The cost of rebinding confiscated books from one year can be contextualised by comparing it with the total expenditure on binding in the British Museum which in the 1790s averaged just under £61.[38] On the other hand, the proposed expenditure of the Bibliothèque nationale was approximately half of Spencer's actual expenditure on binding: two of his annual bookbinding bills for 1799–1800 add up to £512.[39] This provides us with a

Figure 5.5 Detail of an 'Etruscan' vase, 1813, by Percier, painting by Beranger. Museé nationale de céramique de Sèvres, MNC 1823. © RMN/Martine Beck-Coppola. On 27 July 1798 Italian war booty entered Paris in triumph. Books were given their place of honour between two of the most celebrated sculptures, the Laocoön and the Cnidian Venus.

practical measure of how important it was for old associations to be obliterated before the books could take on their new functions.

When it came to works of art there was a debate about the effect which it had on our understanding when they were moved into the newly created public museums and became objects of luxury. Quatremère de Quincy wrote in 1815, here in the English translation from 1821:

The public unconsciously derive this view of art from the awkward way in which works of art are esteemed by those who watch over their preservation. There are cares and attentions shewn to these productions more dangerous even than neglect: such are those which are lavished on them when, in transforming them into objects of luxury and curiosity, they are shut up for the sake of preserving them, from every useful application which rendered them of value, and when they are made to exchange their power to captivate the mind for the inferior purpose of pleasing the eye and flattering the senses.[40]

The same cultural forces worked on historic books, interfering directly in their physical structure and turning them into objects of luxury. The view that books in old wooden boards were in a poor state is analogous to the view that confiscated paintings were better off in Paris because they had been kept in a deplorable state by the previous owners, drawing on and simultaneously reinforcing the perception that the confiscations were justified by the greater ability of the French to look after the historic objects than their original owners.[41] But although historic books were changing category from book to luxury, they did not have a spokesman as eloquent as Quatremère, who could set out the importance of the original context for our understanding of them. Their restoration and their transformation were not subject to the intense public scrutiny of, for instance, the restoration of Raphael's *Madonna of Foligno*, where the Institut national instructed a group of leading scientists to produce an independent report on the restoration methods of the Louvre.[42]

The lack of reaction to the transformation of books contrasts with the outrage that met the proposed changes to the physical structure of books during the Terror, which after thermidor was described as vandalism. This difference of reaction helps us to gain another view of meanings attached to bindings. The demand made by the Convention nationale in 1793 for aristocratic and royal insignia to be removed from books made their ideological function explicit as never before. An accepted expression of ownership, and for aristocrats specifically of their aristocratic ownership, was transformed into an act which had political meaning, a small part of the profound changes to traditional, hierarchical society, whereby all that had previously been accepted as natural and unchangeable was revealed as a specific historic creation, subject to public debate and ripe for change.

In his campaign against the destruction of books, Romme identified a shared perception among those who had used feudal insignia and those who sought to destroy them, that they ascribed meaning to them over and above the meaning of the text with which they were associated. Destroying a useful text because its physical manifestation carried a fleur-de-lys put the destroyers on the same level of superstition as those whom they wanted to supersede and made them comparable to the religious fanatics who had destroyed the library in Alexandria.[43]

A missal printed in 1481, now in the Bodleian Library, seems to have been affected, not by the decree, but by a similar attitude.[44] It is in an eighteenth-century velvet binding from which extensive decorative metal furniture has been removed. It would appear that it was not fifteenth-century but eighteenth-century insignia which were removed from this historic book. The state of this book reflects a conflict over the ownership of the past between two eighteenth-century owners, not between fifteenth- and eighteenth-century views of the world. When fifteenth-century objects were modified, it was not simply because the Middle Ages were rejected, but rather because the Middle Ages had an eighteenth-century meaning which was rejected.[45] On the cover of volume I is written: 'Constitution. L'an 3', and on volume II: 'Droits de l'homme'. This date is confirmed inside volume II by an extract from the Declaration of the Rights of Man from the Constitution of 1795, well after the threatened official destruction had been officially repudiated and branded as 'vandalism'. The removal of the metal decoration and the writing of the new inscriptions are statements of the subordination of the rules of the Church to those of the secular world, an act of desacralisation. If we think of it as profanation we use a word from the religious sphere which still depends on the view that there is more to a book than its text, a spiritual status which can be sullied by inappropriate treatment, just as it can be enhanced by physical aggrandisement.

Renouard, the vociferous opponent of the proposal to have the books of the Bibliothèque nationale rebound, created an extensive collection of Aldines of his own. His copies were nearly all rebound. His progressive views cannot be doubted: for him Aldus was part of the human progress, which gained its full expression in his own times. The old bindings did not fit that view of Aldus.

The period of 'vandalism' has a recognised place in French historiography, reflecting the continued role of the Revolution in contemporary French political discourse. The destruction of the past, decreed but never enacted, now

Figure 5.6 *Missale Parisiense*. [Paris]: Du Pré and Huym, 22 Sept. 1481. Bodleian, Auct. 6Q 3.24,25.

seems outrageous. But something very similar was in fact implemented on a vast scale by collectors, including those who actively fought the Revolution. In this respect, Renouard, the persons who modified the Bodleian Missal, the French 'vandals', and Spencer all had a similar understanding of the function of the ancient book. With different aims they engaged in similar processes of cultural appropriation, detaching books from their original context, obliterating their past, and inserting them into new – competing – interpretative environments. The destruction instigated by men like Grenville and Spencer has a different historiographical importance and their collection methods have been less polemically identified as deliberately destructive, and certainly not condemned as an ethical outrage.[46] But their rejection of the past was not only more thoroughgoing, it was as full of meaning as the aborted revolutionary rejection: the original appearance of the books, with its strong visual reminder of the fifteenth century, was not part of that which they sought to preserve and commemorate.

As discussed in Chapter 3, one of the earliest stimuli for collecting early editions of the classics was the presence of marginal notes. In 1699 the Bodleian Library bought fifteenth-century books for their manuscript notes. A high proportion of the Roman classical editions acquired by the Earl of Sunderland around 1720 still display their marginal notes. They have also been much less pressed and hammered to look smooth and modern than books rebound in the last decades of the century. For the Earl of Sunderland the presence of marginal notes did not diminish the importance of his books.[47] As late as 1785 the Askew sale consisted mainly of printed books with manuscript notes by learned men, many of which were bought by a learned institution, the University Library in Cambridge.

When the same types of object were to display the values which a grand, late eighteenth-century owner might attach to his books, notes were far from being an advantage. In the preface to his catalogue Count Reviczky distanced himself from the ambitions of learned collectors both ostentatiously and self-mockingly:

Although my name ends in '–us' I am not learned, nor is it likely that I ever will be. I have not chased collated copies, with manuscript marginal notes, much vaunted by certain men of learning, and grandly announced in certain catalogues: 'a copy collated with three Vatican, two Palatine manuscripts, four from the Medici library' etc., or 'A book with notes in the hand of Salmasius, Vossius, Scaliger', etc. However worthy these copies are and however useful for editors of ancient authors, they are still scruffy old books, where the little space left by worms is covered in ink of different colours, in a manner very displeasing to the eye, which makes them look like manuals of mumbo jumbo.[48]

If the books did not look the way they ought to, collectors, and not only Reviczky, set out to change them. In September 1789, having just sold his library, Reviczky continued to collect, now on Spencer's behalf. He acquired a copy of Urbanus Bellunensis's Greek grammar printed by Aldus and agreed with Spencer that it should be sent to Kalthoeber to be sorted out: the first ten leaves needed restoring and the notes could be got rid off.[49] Kalthoeber did his best, and charged 12s for binding the book and 4s 6d for washing it, although he did not entirely manage to get rid of the marginal notes.[50]

Giacomo Filippo Durazzo, who felt that he operated in an environment where standards were set by the Parisian luxury market, asked for his incunabula to be washed and cleaned up so that they would as beautiful as if they were new.[51] Their age counted against them.

Although it probably did not itself spend money on washing out marginal notes, the Bodleian Library bought books in the same environment. Information which to a later generation was to be highly important had been knowingly destroyed, when, for instance, a copy of a book printed in

Subiaco, the first place in Italy where printing was exercised, was washed, obliterating an ownership inscription showing that the book had remained in the ownership of the monastery in Subiaco, probably until the mid eighteenth century.[52] One of the Bodleian copies of Bembo's *De Aetna* printed by Aldus Manutius in 1496 is in an English binding, probably from 1801 which celebrates Aldus, having the Aldine anchor stamped in gold on both covers.[53] It was thoroughly washed but one can still, just, detect that it once contained marginal notes. Curt Bühler has shown that the manuscript corrections were made in Aldus's workshop but the ones contained in the Bodleian copy are gone for ever.[54]

In Chapter 4 we followed the struggle between collectors, the trade, and scholars about who were authoritative when it came to old books. This conflict is here given a physical manifestation. The book as a tool in a scholarly endeavour was not part of what late eighteenth-century collectors sought to preserve and commemorate. They actively disliked the signs that their books had ever been useful and took considerable trouble to purge them of all signs that this had ever been the case. They changed the books so that they would fit their own expectations.

Washing was soon not enough, for in the late eighteenth century new expectations of paper were created. Here the interaction between historic books and contemporary visual expectations is borne out not only by the books themselves. In his poetic history of the progress of printing from 1786, Pierre Didot devoted more space to the new English invention of wove paper than to any other technical innovation.[55] It meant serious competition to French paper-makers who soon sought to make their own *papier-vélin*. In 1803, in his *Annales de l'imprimerie des Alde*, in a discussion of the paper in Aldus's octavo editions of the classics, Renouard commented on the uniformly clear appearance of printer's ink. This led on to a discussion of contemporary paper over several pages in which he worried about the ability of French paper-makers to compete with the high quality and uniformity of the paper made by Whatman.[56] He described the craze which had made a talisman of wove paper, the only thing which rendered a book estimable.[57] Market forces worked in favour of wove paper, even when it was of a low quality despite its smooth appearance: it was cheaper to make very white paper with less glue; it was flabby and it subjected the printers' material to less wear, but it could not withstand any degree of use. The demand for smooth uniformity above durability exerted a downwards pressure on the quality of paper. The competition enhanced the importance of paper and the expectations formed for modern books were soon transferred to old ones: incunabula had to co-exist in a market where commercial pressures had a strong impact on how paper was made and prepared.

In 1774 Carl Wilhelm Scheele, the Swedish chemist, discovered dephlogisticated muriatic acid. Claude Louis Berthollet used it for making oxygenous muriatic acid, called *eau de Javel* after the district then outside Paris where it was made.[58] By 1790, sodium hypochlorite, or household bleach as we now call it, was in use in paper-making in Britain.[59] And soon it was also used to ensure that old paper could have a place in the luxury market of the late eighteenth century. It was washed, bleached, and sized to compete with the showy modern paper which fascinated collectors and in which French and British paper-makers competed for pre-eminence. An article in the *Whitehall Evening Post* described, in October 1794, how muriatic acid was used for bleaching old paper and prints. It concluded: 'The paper acquires a degree of whiteness it never before possessed.' The newspaper reported that muriatic acid would not remove grease stains but you could get rid of them by next bathing the paper in caustic alkali.[60] All modern techniques were applied to bring paper up to contemporary expectations and that was the aim. As it said in an 1815 sale catalogue of a book from 1465: 'The paper is so white that one might take it for a book which has just been printed.'[61]

In 1798 Clement Archer wrote on the many excellent uses of muriatic acid. He was a physician who promoted the practical application of chemistry; he was a member of the Bath Agricultural Society, the publications of which Spencer regularly acquired.[62] Books were not Archer's field, but he knew why the new chemical was used by book people:

13th [use]. It discharges the colour of writing-ink, which is composed of a decoction of an astringent vegetable and vitriolated iron; but it rather strengthens printer's ink, which is made of oil and lamp black. In consequence of this last property it is of great use in cleaning old prints and in rendering old printed papers legible; for it almost instantaneously whitens the paper and blackens the ink.[63]

In February 1791 Reviczky saw Spencer's copy of the Horace edition from Ferrara at Kalthoeber's.[64] It was in a frail state and had to be handled delicately.[65] Even worse was Spencer's copy of Servius, printed in Rome around 1470 by Ulrich Han.[66] It was in such a state that it could hardly be touched without being damaged. Reviczky wrote:

Books washed as this one seems to have been, and God knows how, last quite some time if they stay closed, but as soon as air reaches them, they turn brittle and the leaves become fragile. I have prohibited the binder from putting it in a press and even to touch it except for applying morocco on the spine.[67]

But it was not only God who knew how this happened. For instance Spencer had himself commissioned Edward Jeffrey to bleach a book for him.[68] An invoice details the papers acquired in which the eighty-eight leaves of Cicero's *De officiis*, should be wrapped so they could be handled while they were immersed in 'acqua forte'. With the subsequent washing and sizing of the paper it cost 1s per page. The whole intervention on this book alone cost Spencer the substantial sum of £6 11s. This was not just any book: judging by the number of leaves it was a copy of either the 1465 or 1466 Mainz edition of the *De officiis*, one of the first classical texts to be printed.[69] There is no copy on paper recorded among Spencer's books, perhaps an indication that the volume did not survive.[70]

As Reviczky indicated, people knew that perhaps it was not such a good idea to bathe old books in bleach, but the short-term result was often excellent. In 1819 Lord Spencer went to Florence and saw for the first time d'Elci's books, by then donated to the Bibliotheca Laurenziana. The two men were never on really cordial terms, and Spencer seized the opportunity to inform d'Elci that his books demonstrated how treatment with *eau forte* means that they end up falling to pieces. In reply d'Elci wrote that he had long known this and got rid of those of his books which had been treated like that and subsequently used another method. This is not entirely unlikely. Among the papers of Van Praet there is a recipe for a new method for bleaching papers, probably not much better for paper in the long term.[71] It was also a none too subtle hint that some of the copies which Spencer had received in exchange from him were the very books which had been damaged.[72] The current state of many of d'Elci's books suggests that either he was not telling the whole truth or that his other method for bleaching was equally damaging.

Cracherode too was an avid bleacher of his newly acquired luxury books, the desire for brilliant white paper overriding his learned aspirations. The bleaching was not always entirely successful, so we can sometimes easily see that that there used to be extensive notes in many of his books, but we can also see the long-term damage caused to the paper which no longer has the intended whiteness. Although Cracherode claimed that he acquired his books for their textual worth, in contrast to the Bodleian Library, he was more interested in the elegant presentation of his books than in the information which he could derive from the notes.[73]

When the leaves of books had been washed or bleached they could also be resized. A paper slip, probably from a bookseller, pasted into the Bodleian copy of Lucian's *Vera historia* from 1475 announces 'in the orig. boarded cover, carefully washed and sized. c[ollated] and p[erfect]'.[74] The paper was thus made thicker and more sumptuous, and books produced with entirely

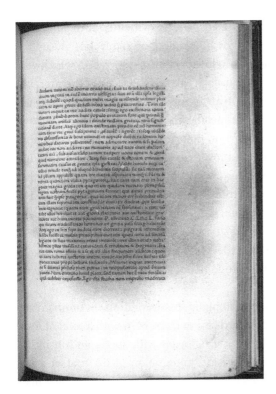

Figure 5.7 Cicero, *De oratore*. Rome: Han, 5 Dec. 1468. © British Library Board. C.19.d.11. The effect of the bleaching now shows the opposite of the desired effect.

different aspirations were modified to match the aesthetic expectations of luxury books of the late eighteenth century. This treatment emphasises how old book had become objects which needed modification to be acceptable and how they now resembled art objects. Statues were repolished and rubbed down to meet the taste of collectors and, according to Feijfer, they were treated with saltpetre and hydrochloric acid.[75] If it was indeed used, the analogy with the treatment of paper is remarkable, as hydrochloric acid became widely available when its commercial manufacture was made possible in 1791 by the French chemist Nicholas Leblanc.

A third way of making incunabula conform to eighteenth-century aesthetics was the painting of new decoration, perhaps the most radical imposition of contemporary visual values within the covers of the books. A number of the books in the library of George III come from the library of Joseph Smith, who was resident in Venice for many years. A few of these have had decoration added in the first half of the eighteenth century. His copy of Dante from Florence, 1481, has an elaborate architectural border, lifting the volume into the world of a classicising aesthetic appreciated in the eighteenth century. This decorated page is evidently an eighteenth-century piece of work, executed by 1724, and probably not meant to deceive about its age; yet it broadly follows a style of decoration which was found in fifteenth-century northern Italy, the blank spaces of the margins being used to present the text within an architectural framework. Whether the artist who made this page had a specific fifteenth-century book in front of him when creating this page or not, he produced a reinterpretation of a fifteenth-century style which had resonances in the eighteenth-century appreciation of classical architecture.[76] Two major projects to create illuminated choir books are known from Padua, in each case fifteen massive choir books being illuminated from 1727 and 1758–65.[77] Neither project resembles the work found in Smith's incunabula, but the second commission in particular indicates that, at least for very grand enterprises, skills were available in the Veneto to produce book decoration in a variety of styles and to a high standard.

A very much more dramatic example is the decoration in Smith's copy of the edition of Livy by Vindelinus de Spira from 1470 with a total of four full pages with elaborate architectural fantasies with spolia and insignia, executed by 1737 for Smith, as the close integration of his coat of arms makes clear (Figure 5.8).[78] Lotte Hellinga has suggested that the artist may be Antonio Visentini, with whom Smith had close connections as an art dealer.[79] Although he may have seen examples of fifteenth-century architectural decoration, this work is far from the Renaissance architectural title page. An eighteenth-century view of the ancient world has obliterated the historic period in which the book was produced and the fifteenth-century attempt to produce a classical appearance which it originally presented.

Several incunabula from Cracherode's collection, bequeathed to the British Museum in 1799, also have modern decoration. Cracherode's copy of Aulus Gellius, printed in Rome in 1469, has a full border with portraits imitating cameos of Pythagoras, Homer, Herodes Atticus, and Aulus Gellius himself. Confined by the space provided by the fifteenth-century printer, it is in some respects reminiscent of fifteenth-century decoration where cameo portraits were used, but all is reinterpreted in an eighteenth-century style, with dainty bouquets of flowers tied together with red ribbon (Figure 5.9). His copy of Suetonius printed in Rome in 1470 is decorated in a broadly similar style: portraits of twelve emperors are displayed with mythical beasts, victories, and putti in a grotesque border. At the foot of the page flanked by the portraits of Caesar and Augustus, is an ambitious narrative painting (Figure 5.10). Its colours have not stood the test of time, especially the silver which is now heavily oxidised, but the two men standing in

Figure 5.8 Livius, *Historiae Romanae decades*. [Venice]: Vindelinus de Spira, 1470.
© British Library Board. C.6.d.1–3. Livy's warlike imperial themes, articulated in an
exuberant eighteenth-century theatrical idiom.

a small boat, rowed by two others, apparently with the serried ranks of an
army on land, probably depict the dramatic scene of the naval battle at the
lighthouse of Alexandria just before Caesar dived into the sea to swim to
safety, having jumped into a boat to rescue his men.

Most striking is perhaps his copy of the *Scriptores de re rustica* printed
in Venice in 1472 (Figure 5.11). Here are no concessions to any fifteenth-
century approach to decoration: a Ceres, with the rosy-cheeked charms of
an eighteenth-century shepherdess, a pair of courting doves, an eagle, and a
Roman harvest scene. Cato's severe manual on estate management has been
turned into an eighteenth-century pastoral idyll.

Equally eighteenth-century in aspiration is the decoration on his copy of
the *Ad Herennium* from 1470 acquired by Cracherode in 1797 (Figure 5.12).
The first page has a whole-page border on a gold background, the inner
margin has a Greek-key border recalling the classicising decoration typically
used on eighteenth-century bindings. The other three margins have a scroll-
ing foliate and floral motif which takes on an appearance wholly alien to the

Figure 5.9 Aulus Gellius, *Noctes Atticae*. Rome: [Sweynheym and Pannartz], 1469. © British Library Board. IB.17118; acquired by Cracherode in 1798.

fifteenth century. This is no attempt to create a fifteenth-century foliate decoration, but a successful use of a motif much loved in the second half of the eighteenth century, used for instance in Spencer House (Figure 5.13).

Several of Cracherode's incunabula with modern decoration were acquired in the last years of the 1790s, but he acquired a copy of Ammianus Marcellinus as early as 1783,[80] and several were acquired in the intervening years. The presence of seven incunabula with modern decoration in his collection acquired at different dates may suggest that Cracherode himself was responsible for commissioning the decoration.

D'Elci frequently used decoration to transform his fifteenth-century editions of the classics into eighteenth-century objects. An exception is his copy of the *Scriptores de re rustica* which has a copy of the fifteenth-century decoration found in Spencer's copy of Sallust from 1474.[81] His Tibullus and Catullus from 1472 no longer looks like a book from the fifteenth century but the decoration certainly recalls the ancient world, as seen from an eighteenth-century viewpoint.[82] The only concession to the fifteenth-century style is the *trompe-l'œil* of a torn, stained, and crumpled-up scrap of paper which contains the 'Life' of Catullus. The grotesque

Figure 5.10 Suetonius, *Vitae XII Caesarum*. Rome: [Johannes Philippus de Lignamine], 1470. © British Library Board. IB.17366; acquired by Cracherode in 1797.

style, inspired in the sixteenth century by the discovery of Nero's *Domus aurea*, gained renewed interest with the discovery of Herculaneum. The decoration of Raphael's *Loggie* in the Vatican was well known, and gained further prominence when it was restored around 1770 by Christoph Unterberger, who was likewise responsible for the Herculanean and Raphaelite grotesque decoration of the Museum Clementinum in the Vatican and in the Hermitage in St Petersburg.[83] This was a fashionable antique style, also recalling the highly acceptable style of Raphael, but not the less accomplished preceding age. Spencer House, as it happens, provides one of the earliest examples Europe-wide of this style in interior decoration, from 1766, followed, in Britain, by Osterley Park, Syon House, and many others.

D'Elci's copy of Homer from 1488 has a full-page representation of a scene from the *Odyssey*, based on an illustration in Winckelmann.[84] His copy of Curtius Rufus is decorated with a full-page miniature based on Charles Le Brun's painting of Alexander at the Tent of Darius, painted for Versailles about 1660, also known in the form of engravings, for instance by Gerard Edelinck, and much admired by Italian eighteenth-century painters

Figure 5.11 *Scriptores rei rusticae*. Venice: Jenson, 1472. © British Library Board. IB.19658. Acquired by Cracherode in 1797.

in the grand style, although the miniature in d'Elci's copy follows Le Brun rather than the reworkings by Trevisani or Batoni.[85]

The books which I know to have been provided with eighteenth-century illuminations are all early editions of the classics, and less frequently of the Italian vernacular classics, Dante and Petrarch, and they were all in the possession of collectors who primarily focused on classical texts.[86] They were books to which great cultural significance was attached by their new owners, but books which failed to live up to the expectations made of them. To be worthy of the classical culture which they represented, they had to undergo a complete physical transformation which obliterated the period in which they had been produced.[87]

Adamoli, the Lyonnais collector, had letters supplied in some of his incunabula in a style very close to that of the fifteenth century. He wrote:

In 1761 I had added to this copy, initial letters painted in red and blue, perfectly imitating the gothic style, the spaces having been left blank. The work was done by a young assistant of Detournes, the booksellers, a very skilful and intelligent young man.[88]

5.12   5.13

Figure 5.12 Cicero, *Rhetorica ad Herennium*. [Venice: Jenson, 1470] © British Library Board. IB.19607(1); acquired by Cracherode in 1797.

Figure 5.13 Pilaster from James Stuart's painted room in Spencer House, completed 1766. © Spencer House. Photograph by Mark Fiennes.

Both the skills and the historical sensitivity to supply historically plausible imitations were available for these grand collectors to adopt but they chose to do otherwise. Adamoli's modest but successful attempt to imitate a very plain fifteenth-century style encourages us to see the modern decoration also in the context of attempts to create a complete copy, supplying initials in the same way as one might supply a missing page from another copy. When George Mason asked for permission to borrow Spencer's copy of the *Speculum Chrisitani* which 'has all the initials added with a pen' he gave as his motivation 'that I may have the initials transcribed into my copy'. He wanted to make his book complete, including initials which looked the part.[89] This can be considered a sort of restoration, similar to the way in which collectors completed, 'made good', their incomplete objects through a fusion with other, historically separate objects. Collectors do this to our day.

Figure 5.14 Quintus Curtius Rufus, *Historiae Alexandri Magni*. [Rome]: Lauer, [not after January 1472]. Florence, Biblioteca Laurenziana, d'Elci 1034.

In 1810 Spencer was allowed to extract some leaves from Douce's incomplete copy of Caxton's edition of the *Legenda aurea* to make the earl's copy less incomplete. Douce complained that his copy was treated roughly but the integrity of the earl's copy was not felt to be compromised in any way.[90] From a modern bibliographer's point of view, the production history of the *Legenda aurea* is particularly complex and is made so much more difficult to disentangle by such merging of historically separate items.[91]

Acting for George III, Nicol bought two copies of the same edition of Cato at auction in 1799. He paid the same price for both, £2 5s. Only one copy is now in the King's Library, while the other later found its way into Grenville's collection.[92] The king's copy has been completed with two leaves from the Grenville copy along with some further leaves, presumably because they were deemed to be of better quality. In return the leaves displaced from the king's copy are now found in Grenville's.[93] As the king's copy had slightly wider margins than Grenville's, the inserted leaves had to be extended; this is now very noticeable, for the paper used for the extension no longer matches the colour of the old leaves, as it presumably once did.[94] Grenville's copy was washed, bleached, and rebound 'out of the original boards', as Grenville noted, and its edges were gilt. As a result his copy now looks much more luxurious than the king's.

This process of completing books by moving leaves from one copy to another did not only make up for accidental damage done to the objects during their long existence. It regularised the output of fifteenth-century printers and made them seem more like books produced in the eighteenth century. For instance, as David McKitterick has discussed, it was not uncommon for copies of fifteenth-century editions to be issued with leaves supplied in manuscript, reflecting the early printers' practical solutions to irregularities in their work processes.[95] At de La Vallière's sale a copy of the first edition of Boccaccio's *Genealogiae deorum* was described as containing some manuscript pages. When the Bodleian Library bought it, it had been through the hands of Crevenna and Renouard and the manuscript pages had been replaced with printed pages from another copy.[96] The object has lost its original completeness and now conformed to a type of completeness which it probably did not have from the outset; it has been modified to fit eighteenth-century expectations of a complete book.

Instead of pages from another copy, a book could be completed by the insertion of facsimiles. Owners wanting a complete text had long had manuscript copies made of missing pages. Making a facsimile which looks old is a different matter. The dividing line between completing and faking is sometimes deliberately crossed, and on occasion it can be hard to be certain whether a page is a facsimile.[97] A detectable, but remarkable instance is found in Cracherode's copy of the *Anthologia graeca*. At a certain point it would seem that page 2 was mutilated to remove a decorated border: leaf 3 shows the marks of the knife which removed it, and it is probable that all of page 1 was removed. Two facsimile pages have been made to replace them and they are made to such a degree of similarity with the printed page that it seems evident that they were intended to deceive any but the most sceptical observer.[98]

Some copies of this book were issued without a concluding letter written by Lascaris. The copy owned by Grenville was originally one of those. However, when he bought it those leaves had been supplied by leaves in manuscript facsimile which since then have been replaced with printed leaves from another copy.[99] While Cracherode's copy acquired manuscript facsimiles of leaves which would have been there when the book was issued, Grenville's copy has become 'more complete' than when it was issued by the publisher.

It was not only dealers who would seek to make books complete in this way. D'Elci wrote to Spencer and asked him for an exact copy made on transparent paper of a page from the first edition of Florus,[100] and in the

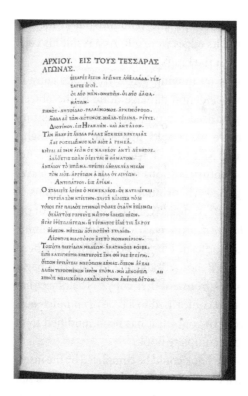

Figure 5.15 *Anthologia graeca Planudea*. Florence: Laurentius de Alopa, 1494. A leaf in manuscript facsimile. Cracherode's copy. © British Library Board. IB.28002.

1790s Durazzo wrote to Giuseppe Molini and Eusebio Della Lena asking them to find him Aldine pages with only the Aldine anchor on it so that he could make type facsimiles to take the place of title pages missing in his own books.[101] But the trade must have been a frequent source. Dibdin describes how Chardin, the Jacobin bookseller who had worked for Beckford, supplied deceptively convincing manuscript facsimile pages:

He has a great passion for making his Alduses perfect by means of *manuscript*; and I must say, that, supposing this plan to be a good one, he has carried it into execution in a surprisingly perfect manner: for you can scarcely, by candle-light, detect the difference between what is printed and what is executed with a pen … How any scribe can be sufficiently paid for such toil is to me inconceivable: and how it can answer the purpose of any bookseller so to complete his copies, is also equally unaccountable: for be it known, that good M. Chardin leaves you to make the discovery of the MS. portion; and when you have made it, he innocently subjoins 'Oui, Monsieur, n'est il pas beau?'[102]

Dibdin wondered about the financial viability of this. Elsewhere he has indicated that it cost Spencer about £50 to have twelve facsimile pages made

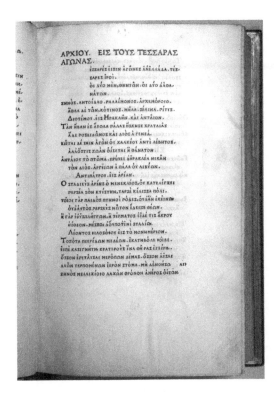

Figure 5.16 *Anthologia graeca Planudea*. Florence: Laurentius de Alopa, 1494. The corresponding printed leaf. © British Library Board. G.8482.

for his copy of the *Morte d'Artur*, that is £4 3s 4d per page, adding about 15 per cent to the purchase price of £320.[103] Books had to be very expensive for this to be worthwhile.

The technical procedures of modification were special to books, but they mirror the approach to other historic objects. Grand tourists were often ridiculed for the fragments of ancient stones which they brought back with them. Undoubtedly they were sometimes cheated, and were sold bits which would have been worthless to more discerning collectors. But the ridicule also indicates a conflict of values which needed resolution. The eighteenth-century tourist in Rome was confronted with a collecting culture where even a small fragment could be valued, although in their original state they were not suitable for their new status.

Christian Gottlob Heyne explained why in 1779: 'As the way in which antiques are used largely is to adorn palaces, villas and hall, it is evident that no statue, bust, or other elevated piece of work can be an object pleasing to the eye, if in a mutilated state.'[104] Heyne's view was confirmed by Francis Russell, the Marquess of Tavistock, who said that he would not give one

Figure 5.17 Alexander the Great, Paris, Musée du Louvre, No. d'entrée LL11 (no. usuel Ma 46). © RMN

guinea for 'the finest torso ever discovered'. He wanted them complete, or completed. Thomas Jenkins, the English artist, art merchant, and excavator based in Rome, said about Gavin Hamilton, a more scrupulous colleague, that he 'did not understand the taste of the English virtuosi who had no value for statues without heads'.[105] As Miranda Marvyn puts it, collectors treated ancient sculptors much as they treated modern ones: they made demands of them.[106] Much the same held true for books. Collectors wanted the best copies, discarding books as duplicates when better copies became available, merging them with one another, and ruthlessly modifying them to make them match the expectations which were now made of them.

A statue of Alexander the Great, now in the Louvre is made up of two separate antique sculptures, the head, much restored, definitely from a statue of Alexander the Great, and the body, more restored, probably from another Alexander statue, assembled for Cardinal Albani, probably by Bartolomeo Cavaceppi.[107] An extreme example of a made-up state is the Diana statue which used to belong to Henry Blundell at Ince Hall, which has now been shown to have been made up of 127 fragments.[108] The Spencer copy of the

Golden Legend, with pages inserted from Douce's copy of the books, is as much a creation of the early nineteenth century as the Alexander statue is a creation of the mid eighteenth century. If we now deplore this, we have to consider what would have happened to them if they had not been made collectable. However, it is worth noting that we still accept completed books as being fifteenth-century objects, whereas Alexander is now relegated from the Louvre's collection of antiques only to emerge for specialist displays of eighteenth-century taste.

The collection of Alessandro Albani, cardinal and nephew of Clement XI, is perhaps especially well known in Britain as the source for a large part of the drawings acquired by George III. His collection of antique statues was important for Winckelmann and also for Cavaceppi, the sculptor and restorer. While he detailed how statues which did not need any modern work were more valuable in the marketplace, Cavaceppi drew a distinction not between modernity and originality but between the appropriate and the inappropriate. It was not wrong to supply significant parts of a statue, and it was not a matter of dishonesty, but an error of taste to turn a fragment of a muse into a statue of a consul or the fragment of a slave into a statue of Prince Paris,[109] while it might be acceptable to transform a Discoboulos into a Dying Gaul.[110] The subject of debate was whether the supplied material was suitable or not.[111] Appropriateness was not always felt to be observed when sculptures were modified; nor was it when it came to books. Dibdin criticised Kalthoeber's bindings not for being historically alien to the books but for being inappropriate and in poor taste. Rive's objection to the duc de La Vallière's luxurious rebinding of textually unimportant incunabula should be understood as a reflection of the same attitude. It was wrong not because it offended against historicity but because it offended against a Horatian aesthetic principle of decorum, which saw the combination of objects with different status as offensive and laughable. But Rive's view of the status of books had been overtaken by the values established in the marketplace.

Antique sculpture was, most often, being restored to look antique, at least in the eyes of the eighteenth-century owner. Yet there were also unacceptable aspects of ancient aesthetics. The standard mutilation of male genitalia sometimes involved a more comprehensive rejection of classical representation of sexuality. Henry Blundell bought from Townley a sculpture of a hermaphrodite breast-feeding three babies. He reacted to it exactly as Reviczky did to learned marginal notes which made books 'very displeasing to the eye'. Blundell said in his catalogue of 1809: 'The figure was unnatural and very disgusting to the sight; but by means of a little castration and cutting away the little brats, it became a Sleeping Venus and as pleasing as any in this collection.'[112] Blundell was not alone in being hor-rid to hermaphrodites. In 1670 the duc de Mazarin had done nearly the same to his hermaphrodite who became the Genius of Eternal Repose.[113] Sensuously subversive hermaphrodites did not conform to the expectations of the noble ancient world, so they were made to conform, just as fifteenth-century books were transformed to fit into the modern world, their earlier meaning being obliterated.

Collectors of ancient sculpture often sought to integrate them into an eighteenth-century aesthetic scheme. This was normally an eighteenth-century view of ancient aesthetics. What we see, for instance, in Adam's Syon House is a collection of originally disparate sculptures, some modern, some modern copies, and some ancient pieces, brought together in a clas-sicising environment. Considered as ancient art they are meaningless if we follow Quatremére de Quincy in thinking that individual works of art only have a meaning in their original context. Yet they are meaningful in that they form a coherent and often compelling eighteenth-century expression of the contemporary function of the ancient world. Ancient statuary is part of an eighteenth-century country house, a space which was created to visu-alise a view of the ancient world. The sculptures speak to the viewer about the relation of their new owners to the world of Rome and Athens.

Similarly, a collector might create a visually compelling unity out of dis-parate books, binding them uniformly and inserting them into a shared architectural universe. Yet the similarity of approach ascribes a different meaning to the historic printed books. Often they are integrated into a clas-sicising whole, jointly with statues, illustrating the point made by Joseph Spence in 1747 when writing his successful guide to classical sculpture for an audience more familiar with the ancient world from the surviving texts.[114] In the now destroyed library building at Merly in Dorset, Ralph Willett created a sumptuous pictorial representation of the progress of mankind.[115] Despite Willett's extraordinary expertise in printing and his detailed examination of the circumstances surrounding its invention, the grandeur of his library did not celebrate the fifteenth century but the mod-ern result of human progress. The historic books were inserted into a purely eighteenth-century aesthetic, which referred to the long-term civilising effect of books, but had no reference whatsoever to the cultural world from which they emerged.

The rejection of the fifteenth-century appearance of the fifteenth-century books goes hand in hand with the low regard for the culture from which they emerged. While historians and increasingly collectors were inter-ested in the invention of printing, there was not much appreciation of the texts. We saw the main textual interest had been focused on editions of the classics and to a lesser extent the fathers of the Church, but they had not lived in the deplorable gothic period of the fifteenth century nor were the fifteenth-century editions of their works valued for their fifteenth-century background. And even their textual importance was waning.

For Protestants, the special place in the history of mankind of the invention of printing became problematic. It was all very well for an anonymous Protestant essayist to write in 1752:

The Noble art of printing found
No sooner, but it Rome did wound
And ever since with nimble ray,
Spread knowledge to a perfect day.[116]

When one looked more closely, the early printers did nothing of the kind. In 1766 Samuel Pegge wrote:

William Caxton who first introduced printing into England has, no doubt, been instrumental in preserving many things which otherwise would have been lost. But the misfortune was that he was but an illiterate man, and of small judgement, by which means he printed nothing but mean and frivolous things ... whereas had he been a scholar and had made a better choice of the works that were to pass his press, it is probable many excellent performances now lost, would have been secured to us, especially if he had recourse to some of the more antient pieces; but as it is, Caxton's works are valuable for little else than being early performance in the Art of Printing, and as wrought off by him.[117]

Nor were their works impressive from an enlightened point of view. Gibbon put Caxton's production firmly in its historic context, emphasising how his choice of trivial texts was a reflection of his contemporary society:

In the choice of his authors, that liberal and industrious artist was reduced to comply with the vicious taste of his readers; to gratify the nobles with treatises on heraldry, hawking, and the Game of Chess, and to amuse the popular credulity with romances of fabulous knights, and legends of more fabulous saints.[118]

For Gibbon, medieval historians were potentially source material, but even the historiographical works produced by Caxton indicate the intellectual paucity of his period. Such attitudes were widespread even among men who, unlike Este and Gibbon, engaged seriously with early printed books. A luminary of eighteenth-century incunable studies, the Protestant Schelhorn said about an incunable, in a book dedicated to Cardinal Passionei:

This book is worthy of being preserved in libraries, although it is completely useless. How can you prove more clearly how ugly and Thersites-like things were in the days which preceded the fortunate restoration of good letters and the associated correction of the Church, than from writings of this sort, in which rubbish and nonsense, horridly expressed, stuff each and every page?[119]

Renouard has no more sympathy for the substance of the books produced in the fifteenth century. They were mainly scholastic, legal, or mystic, by which he meant theological. One of Aldus's editions is described as of no interest because it belonged to a class of books which no one reads and which were rightly, ignored, but yet highly desirable in the eyes of collectors because of their exceeding rarity.[120]

The fifteenth century was generally agreed to have been the low point before the revival of letters, intellectually as well as aesthetically.[121] Remarkably, it is in the most comprehensive eighteenth-century bibliography of incunabula, in which the Enlightenment and the Protestant rejection of the Dark Ages combine to form the strongest possible rejection of the intrinsic worth of the production of the earliest printers. Panzer published the first part of his complex bibliography in 1788 and completed it in 1803. His prefaces are rhetorically highly charged, although his Latin is at best inelegant. In the preface to the volume from 1793 he wrote, here in a somewhat compressed translation:

One must make allowance for those who were skilled in this new art, because of the spirit of their times; so nobody should be surprised that the beginning of this art was so well matched to this very spirit that only a few more refined productions appeared, especially ancient ones, as if floating in a vast maelstrom. They could barely find themselves a space among the serried ranks of sermons, legends, missals, lectionaries, the laws of both secular and spiritual monarchs, and scholastic exercises of Thomists and Scotists. Nevertheless, it was something of a stroke of good fortune that the divine art concentrated on this one thing in the beginning: bringing to light the productions of learned ignorance. Once they had been published, it offered a much desired opportunity to reject them so that they could henceforth be committed to perpetual darkness … As the shape of learning has changed, darkness has happily been overcome, and the earliest examples of printing, especially those which reveal the lamentably barbarous condition which carries the inappropriate name of learning, came to be completely disregarded or at the most to lie about in monastic libraries exposed to the sport of cockroaches and book-worms. This is a well deserved fate if you look at the subject matter of most of them, but it is to be regretted if you are interested in the art, for the beginning of which they constitute the source material … Although it took centuries, it is not surprising therefore that, finally, certain learned men assessed the matter fairly and were aroused as if from a sleep to give serious thought to restoring glory to the art to which letters and their progress owe all … With the indefatigable effort of their work it seemed that from that time the study of the history of letters took on a new appearance … and treasures which were hitherto hidden in libraries were again brought out into the view of nearly everybody, and a fair price was established for them.[122]

Panzer deploys some arguments which had long been used by historians of printing, also at the beginning of the century by Maittaire in his *Annales typographici*. But he used them differently. Maittaire and Panzer alluded indirectly to the same passage from Virgil but in order to make two significantly different points:

A few of the men's weapons, paintings, and treasures of Troy
Appeared scattered swimming in a vast maelstrom.

For Maittaire the shipwrecked treasures of Troy were the classical texts surviving through the maelstrom of the Dark Ages into the age of printing.[123] For Panzer it was the few good texts produced by the early printers that swam in a maelstrom of ignorant printed books. Not only were medieval texts irrelevant to his times; they had always been inherently worthless. The function of printing had been to demonstrate their pointlessness. Panzer undoubtedly came to this theme from a Protestant background, but unlike Maittaire, for instance, he did not engage in theological polemics. Seeing publication as part of a process which would establish the truth through human agency, Panzer has moved far from the Protestant view that the invention of printing was a providential tool which would put an end to the diffusion of error. It has become subordinate to the Enlightenment view that it was a tool of emancipation from all irrational belief, because it enabled the readers themselves to discard published nonsense.

It is remarkable how close his views are to those of, for instance, Hubert Pascal Ameilhon who recommended that one should get rid of 'old commentaries on the Bible, outdated editions of the Fathers of the Church, old sermon collections in French and Latin, treatises of scholastic theology, ascetic or mystic works, polemic writing on the Jansenist affairs, mostly relegated to barns at the mercy of rats and mice'.[124] Panzer's polemic was aimed not so much at the past as at his present. His rejection of the Middle Ages and its institutions was a way of rejecting those parts of his own contemporary world which he could see as still embodying those dark unenlightened ideas. In their own environment incunabula would meet a well-merited destruction, for there they were texts not merchandise. By being removed from this environment, the books could acquire a modern, progressive meaning and gain a fair price in the marketplace. Reification and commoditisation and, inevitably, modification, were the salvation of incunabula from themselves, and from destruction.

While in exile in England Abbé Barruel published his history of Jacobinism in 1797–8, which explained the Revolution as a conspiracy by secret societies, an explanatory model which would make it possible to dream of reverting to the old order without having to reconsider more profound conditions which might have caused its collapse. In a chapter entitled 'De l'impiété et de l'anarchie' he attacked a south German Masonic group, the Perfektibilisten, led by Adam Weishaupt, a former Jesuit, who believed, according to Barruel, that it was a virtuous act to steal books from monastic libraries where they served no purpose and to make them accessible and useful. Barruel quoted Weishaupt as having said of the books of the Carmelites: 'All those things will be much more useful for us, for what use do those buffoons make of their books?'[125] Here Barruel found the background for the 'Jacobin' spoliation of collections.

In fact, as we have seen such views were widely current. While the celebration of printing had deep Protestant roots, the rejection of the Middle Ages was not confined to Protestants. Denise Bloch has described the attitude of Baluze, the librarian of Colbert, who collected manuscripts from religious houses. Neglected by the monks and open to theft, they were not worthy repositories, and if resistance was met he found that a little contribution made a big difference. It could be difficult to say no.[126] Charles de Brosses described how Cardinal Passionei acquired rare books for his collection, with a disdain for monks which equalled that of any Protestant:

The Cardinal has often busied himself in Germany, where he ferrets around in the convents of the monks, and, whether they want to or not, makes them give him quantities of curious books and rare editions. He seasons it all with lavish compliments; he can do the Italian comedy all right. They have no notion of how to turn down His Excellency Monsignor the Nuntius, whose thanks always precede the offers of the objects for which he in the end pays – with a grave blessing.[127]

In 1745, in the wake of the enthusiasm generated by the anniversary of 1740, Giuseppe Antonio Sassi published a book in which he set out to prove that printing was practised in Milan from 1465, before anywhere else in Italy. His aim was patriotic, yet his assessment of the texts produced in Milan was not enthusiastic. He did not wish to hide from his readers that they were useless and inept.[128] Thomists and Scotists were not much more in vogue among eighteenth-century Catholic hommes de lettres than among their Protestant equivalents.

Rive's caustic remarks can stand as emblematic for the opinion of many men of letters in the Catholic world: 'There is no depot which is more insecure and risky that those which one has been daft enough to create in the secular, monastic or religious communities.'[129] Conversely, we have seen German monks eager to exchange their useless medieval books for the *Philosophical Transactions*. Even they preferred modern progress to the medieval past with which their critics associated them.

Textually the incunabula were the last gasp of the intellectually poverty-stricken period preceding the modern period, before the rebirth of letters in the sixteenth century. They were valuable despite themselves, and despite the intellectual world in which they were produced. Monastic collections were rejected as suitable places for early printed books because they were seen as contemporary remains of the past, both symbolic and real manifestations of those things in the present which needed to be overcome, the part of contemporary life not yet touched by the light of the human spirit.

The famous Italian paintings newly displayed in the Louvre sometimes failed to satisfy a public whose expectations were formed by the immaculate state of the modern prints of the originals and raised by the high status attached to the objects.[130] Similarly eighteenth-century visitors to Rome often found the reality disappointing compared with what eighteenth-century depictions of the ruins had made them to hope to see.[131] If genuine historic objects had the ability to disappoint an audience accustomed to eighteenth-century standards to the extent that neither fashionable sixteenth-century painters nor even antiquity itself lived up to expectations, we should not be surprised that books from the grimly gothic fifteenth century had to conform before they were acceptable and that the monkish appearance of fifteenth-century books needed to be changed, in order for them to assume the contemporary cultural and commercial function which was expected of them. The monkish origins of these work was, at best, not given sufficient worth to withstand the pressure to conform to the requirements of the enlightened eighteenth-century and often they were explicitly rejected. The physical evidence of the fifteenth-century intellectual context of fifteenth-century books was the collateral victim in the creation of an eighteenth-century commemoration and celebration of the achievements and future aspirations of the eighteenth century. What elegant or modern man, noble or Jacobin, wanted to be surrounded by a collection of dowdy old books, very displeasing to the eye?

6 | Conclusion

In 1793 the Reverend Charles Este toured down the Rhine, having ensured a publishing contract for his travel account. He visited Mainz and, although he knew little about it, wrote at length about the invention of printing.

Till the year ninety-seven [1497] there was no Latin classic in England … All the rest of the books printed in England, till the opening of the fifteenth century, were little more than the publication of disgrace, both as to power and will! That the country was dark, and wished to continue so, and that there were no organs for any sounds but those of childhood and inanity, cant and horse-play, chivalry and superstition! – Such barren absurdities as the Siege of Rhodes, and the Golden Legend, St Catherine and St Elizabeth, The Historyes of Troy, King Blanchardyne and Queen Eglantyne his wife, the Ladder of Perfection, Coat Armour, and the Golden Fleece.[1]

Este's readers might not have known all the details about these books, but many would have recognised that these barren absurdities were increasingly canonical and belonged to a genre collected by members of the highest aristocracy. This enabled Este to convey a political message, as other visitors to Mainz had done before him:

In the ignorance and vulgarity of the people who directed such objects for the press, the Dutchess of Burgundy and the Princess Margaret &c, there might perhaps seem some apology at the time, but how will our first printers, Caxton, Penson, and De Worde, answer to their contemporaries and to themselves, for such cruel inculcation of ill, such a wreck of consequences from opportunity and art?

The contemporary implications would have been unmistakable to any reader in 1795, when the account was published. While Gibbon had excused Caxton because he had been compelled to be subservient to the norms of his day, Este saw it differently.[2] Caxton's patrons might be excused, for what would you expect of aristocrats except ignorance and vulgarity? But a printer should have known better. This view made sense when measured against the economic environment of publishing in Este's time, when authors and publishers could increasingly make money without depending on patronage, as Este's own publishing contract shows. The intellectual and economic slavery of those who allowed themselves to be dependent on

noble protectors was a theme explored to great effect by French revolutionaries. For instance in 1794, year III of the Republic, when Dupuis dedicated
his learned work on the origins of religion to his wife, it was a self-conscious
assertion of those bourgeois virtues which Caxton had betrayed, a declaration of freedom from aristocratic tyranny under which dedications were
fawning expressions of indigent dependence.[3]

Condemning Caxton's acceptance of his place in aristocratic culture, Este
rejected a contemporary political culture dominated by an ignorant and
vulgar nobility, who used patronage to perpetuate its grip on power. It was
evident to Este that a medieval revival challenged his modernising interpretation of history and his view of the new canonical texts brings him close
to Renouard and his Jacobin friends, who found, in 1793, that book collections in the hands of aristocrats posed a danger to society because their
owners appropriated the past for their reactionary political purpose. The
aristocratic culture of collecting the past, their interest in barren books, had
become a political act which was in opposition to Este's own interpretation
of the needs of the present.

Francis Douce held views similar to Este's; if anything, he was more radical. Yet he collected the books which Este thought barren. From Este's list
Douce only owned *The Siege of Rhodes* and the *Golden Legend*, but he had
eight different editions of the latter, and there is little doubt that he would
have acquired the others, if he had been able to.

While he left his collection of medieval objects to a friend, he bequeathed
his medieval manuscripts, incunabula, chapbooks, playing cards, prints,
and drawings to the Bodleian Library, along with an extensive modern
working library. His collection of prints has subsequently been transferred
to the Ashmolean Museum.[4] Detached from its intellectual context, Douce's
collection of books might be seen as part of the medieval revival, which so
often associated an interest in pre-Reformation liturgy and devotion with
attempts at restoring medieval hierarchical structures.[5] Yet Douce was anti-
monarchical and it was with dismay that he noted already in the 1790s that
opposition to organised religion, just like expressions of republican sympa-
thies, had come to be considered subversive:

During the years 1796, 1797, 1798, 1799 (and it is just now impossible to calcu-
late how many more will be added to the list) it was almost a crime to speak in
favour of a republican form of government, as if there were something monstrous
in the thing itself, because France had become a republic and nearly threatened the
destruction of those monarchical governments that had wantonly and insidiously
made war upon her with the sole view of restoring the antient tyrannical regime
for the purpose of screening and supporting their own enormities. So the Roman

Catholic religion and the Pope himself got into high repute, because the French had subverted both, and had they warred against the Devil himself, no doubt it would have been equally fashionable to have admired and protected his infernal majesty.[6]

Not limiting himself to the traditional English hostility to the Roman Catholic Church, Douce understood all links between state and Church as manipulative and hypocritical attempts at control:

As a proof of how little reality there is in national religion it is worth remarking that a very short time after the abdication of Napoleon Bonaparte and the restoration of the Bourbons many of the dignified clergy of England became solicitors for the interest of the Roman Catholic religion in France. During the reign of Napoleon the church of Rome had lost half its original members who either abandoned religion (that is a professed or formal one) altogether or adopted the reformed one. It was contended that with such a defection and even preponderance, the new government was in jeopardy. This develops the real connection between church and state. At home the established church was persecuting the Irish and English Catholics.[7]

Despite his extensive collection of printed and manuscript Books of Hours of the Virgin, Douce had no more patience with the re-emerging Marian piety, the devotional aspect of medieval religion, than with formal liturgical or theological manifestations of religion. Far from diminishing, Douce's distaste grew as the neo-religious movements of the nineteenth century gained strength, both in England and in France.[8] Around 1824 he wrote:

It will scarcely be credited by posterity that at this time a professor of divinity at Cambridge (one Hollingworth) lectured on the subject whether the virgin Mary remained a virgin after the birth of Christ. This I had from … an auditor at the lecture which would have suited the times of Thomas Aquinas and father Sanchez.[9]

The Middle Ages were not a lost world of innocent piety, but an age of fear generated by a deliberate inculcation of ignorance. The irrational fear of death was a theme which engaged Douce and was one of the reasons why he was especially interested in representations of the Dance of Death, which he collected avidly and explored in one his early publications. He wrote:

In the dark ages of monkish bigotry and superstition, the deluded people, terrified into a belief that the fear of death was acceptable to the great Author of their existence, had placed one of their principal gratifications in contemplating it amidst ideas the most horrid and disgusting; and the frequent descriptions of mortality in all its shapes amongst their writers.[10]

He suggested that images reminding the populace of imminent death and the horrors of an afterlife of punishment were part of a cynical manipulation 'invented by the clergy, for the purpose of at once amusing and keeping the people in ignorance'.[11]

Douce's medieval books, images, and objects were tools for his exploration of popular life in all its irrationality, of which religion was one aspect. They served the same purpose as his collection of chapbooks and broadsides. Douce collected Books of Hours and liturgical books largely because of their illustrations of popular life and popular belief. His attitude was captured by Jonas Edwards who, on his return from Paris in 1814, offered Douce a Book of Hours 'with borders on every page representing sports, buffooneries, country employs etc etc', 'amusements, games etc etc etc.' He was convinced that Douce would be interested, and not for aesthetic reasons for 'the paintings are not fine'.[12] Medieval art was pictorial evidence of the past and this requires no aesthetic appreciation,[13] in the same way as Douce's religious texts do not indicate a positive assessment of religion. Douce was no precursor for the new appreciation of painting from before the sixteenth century nor for the incipient aesthetic appreciation of pre-sixteenth-century illumination and illustration, which began to be in evidence in the 1830s as Douce entered the last years of his life.[14] His collection of religious images was part of his investigation of a manifestation of an irrational phenomenon which required a rational explanation.

His interest in saints and Books of Hours was of the same nature as his interest in fairies and devils – the beliefs of a deluded populace.[15] His copy of an incunable edition of Augustine's *De civitate dei* did not inspire him to contemplate the afterlife; it was instead the source for a picture of an interesting fool.[16] Understanding popular culture was an aim in itself for Douce, who referred to 'the culpable indifference of historical writers to private manners, and more especially to the recreations of the common people'.[17] In a much less theoretical way, Douce, like Condorcet, proposed a view of history which was not determined by the acts of the great, of rulers and their dynasties.

Douce's view of the role of incunabula in the exploration of human history is astonishingly close to the attitude which was expressed in the introductory note to Maugérard's sale of his stock/collection in 1792 as he was preparing to leave revolutionary France. The preface defines a place for incunabula in a world devoted to radical change: whether the author (probably not Maugérard) believed in his approach or not, this was what was most likely to make them attractive or at least acceptable:

Notification. The list which we present to the public consists of books which are less important for that which they contain than for their age, for some predate the invention of printing; others date from the birth of this art. Three centuries, and especially the last three years, have brought such important changes to the way in which people in France think and to the matter which they study that the greater part of the books printed by our first printers have become totally alien.[18]

Strangely for a sale catalogue, as it seems at first, the preface talks down the books, giving examples of their inanity. For instance, it singles out two lots, *De laudibus virginis Mariae* in which is discussed the range of options for the physical arrangements for the Annunciation, and one where the building materials for Mary's throne are discussed, while she is compared to an elephant.[19] The intellectual worthlessness of incunabula being established, their real value is revealed:

We know that if, one day, one will undertake to write the history of the French, rather than the history of the kings of France, it cannot be done properly without knowledge of that which engaged the French, and the only way to know this is through the books composed in the period of which one writes the history; in them one will find the cause for their enslavement, their minds having been degraded by being weighed down with inanities.[20]

In the same way, Douce's interest in a history of the beliefs and manners of the people must not be misunderstood for sympathy or agreement. He saw a similarity between medieval religion and pious belief in saints, indeed all external expressions of religion, with the most extravagantly ridiculous superstitions of his own day, discussing past and contemporary quackery in terms very similar to those which he used about religion.[21] If documenting irrationality was part of a process to understand its causes in order finally to overcome it, then it is entirely consistent that the irrationality of his contemporaries had no more appeal to Douce than religion. Easily annoyed, he was often exasperated by the behaviour of the common people of his own day:[22]

The boys of the present day, but chiefly among the lower classes, are a set of silly faced, whistling, mischievous blackguards. Every urchin you meet with stuns you with his life-screaming which he thinks is musick, and an imitation of the military fife, to which indeed it is not much inferior.

Douce's recurrent criticism of Spencer and Blandford, idle noble owners who reduced their books to objects of luxury, is another manifestation of his impatience with behaviour which he perceived to be irrational. He summed up his view of aristocratic luxury in 1793: 'Where there are numerous palaces, there will be numerous prisons; the progress of luxury is but the progress of vice.'[23] Not surprisingly his own collection was very different from theirs. As against Spencer, who became interested in incunabula as monuments of typography, Douce seems to have had little interest in books for being incunabula, a category founded on their reification. Analogously, the two men had very different attitudes to manuscripts. While Spencer owned some, he decidedly did not focus his collecting activity on manuscripts; this was a characteristic which he shared with many grand English collectors of the period. We have seen how this attitude was reflected in the market, where early printed books were much more expensive that manuscripts. Douce, on the other hand, bought medieval illuminated manuscripts, against the fashionable trends of the market.

While Earl Spencer sought to complete his books by inserting leaves from other copies, a process which suited his intellectual purposes, Douce cut images out of his books, which suited his. He did this with total disregard for bibliographical completeness or for textual integrity, and indeed for rarity. For instance he cut out images from his copy of a *Plenary* from 1489. Neither its great rarity nor its original binding held him back.[24] He detached a remarkable mid-fifteenth-century metal-cut of the Crucifixion, which had been sewn into the extremely rare *Canon missae* at the time of its production in 1458.[25] We have already seen in Chapter 5 how he replaced late medieval monastic bindings with plain contemporary ones. He had no interest in the integrity of books as medieval objects.

The elucidation of popular life, in part through pictures, was not only a theme of rational merit in its own right; it also had a more traditional antiquarian function, providing assistance with understanding texts which, incidentally, referred to popular habits. Douce's study of ancient manners, of clowns and fools, and of card games helped the understanding of obscure passages in Shakespeare[26] and other old English authors. George Hibbert sought Douce's advice on what the word 'rannette' referred to in Caxton, 'when speaking of the disguise which Vertumnus wore when personating an old woman as he made his approaches to Pomona'. By way of answer Douce sent him a drawing of a piece of headgear based on an illustration in one of his books.[27] Douce also sought to use medieval images for the antiquarian purpose of establishing a chronology for the history of dress to eliminate anachronisms in pictorial, theatrical, or written representations of the past.[28] Not unlike Aby Warburg's *Bilderatlas*, created a century later, the scrapbooks were a working tool for organising and reorganising material to make sense within a new interpretative context. If Spencer and Cracherode reinterpreted entire volumes by uprooting them, Douce did something analogous with individual leaves and images. His extraction of illustrations from their context and his creation of scrapbooks can be seen as a paper equivalent to the museum created by Lenoir of sculptures removed from their aristocratic or religious contexts to be placed in chronological order as an assemblage of models dressed according to their times.[29]

But Este and Douce fought in vain against the revival of the Middle Ages. Samuel Roffey Maitland was librarian to the Archbishop of Canterbury. His very influential book from 1844, *The Dark Ages*, was the work of a professional historian far removed from attempts to re-enact medieval society; yet it was an apology for the Middle Ages in which he sought to minimise the importance of the invention of printing. He deployed a number of arguments, some of which have merit beyond their polemical context; for instance his observation that the destruction of monastic libraries had deprived historians of the means of assessing the quantity of cheaper productions of the manuscript period. He accepted the position of printing as part of the modern world but, concentrating on arguments put forward by the least sophisticated of his opponents, he argued against the impact of printing on the prices of books. More profoundly, he denied that printing represented a significant change in the course of the history of mankind. He did this by establishing a hierarchy of texts: works which had been canonical and which had been found in most medieval libraries were, essentially, of greater importance than works which had not had this institutional recognition:

> We come, I think, fairly to the idea that, although the *power of multiplication* at work in the Dark Ages was infinitely below that which now exists, and even the whole *actual produce* of the two periods not to be compared, yet as it regards those books which were considered as the standard works in sacred and secular literature, the difference was not so *extreme* as may have been supposed.[30]

Breaking with the historiographical requirement which he made of others, to see a phenomenon in its own historical context, Maitland sought to underplay the importance of fifteenth-century printing by pointing out that its output was insignificant compared with nineteenth-century printing. This was undoubtedly true. By 1830 the rapid change in printing technology had already become so obvious that it could find expression in fictional form, in a dialogue between the past and the present represented by two inanimate objects, an old-fashioned wooden press and a mechanical press.[31] The same changes were described the following year, in 1831, in a bureaucratic report by Firmin-Didot who, like his contemporary Karl Marx, worried about the emergence of a capitalism which was as monopolistic as the monarchical monopolies which had only recently been abolished. Firmin-Didot saw that technological innovations were a threat to the structure of the printing trade. Lithography had deprived small printers of jobs, especially ephemera for commercial use, and the invention of stereotype had deprived them of the business of reprints. Even more important was the level of investment now required. While an old wooden press might cost some 500–800 francs, or £20–£32, a printer would have to find serious capital, 20,000–25,000 francs, or £800–£1,000, to acquire a modern mechanical press. This tended to concentrate the trade in the hands of a few large companies.[32]

The invention of printing was no longer part of modernity, but it could still be seen as the beginning of the liberation of mankind from feudal oppression and Gutenberg could be seen as a role-model for nineteenth-century innovators. In Britain, both Caxton and Gutenberg appeared along with the likes of Newton and Mungo Park as models for budding entrepreneurs in William and Robert Chambers's *Exemplary and Instructive Biography for the Study of Youth* in 1836, the publication timed for the Christmas market. 'A more acceptable gift to youth we cannot at this moment recollect and the price brings it within the reach of almost everyone', wrote a reviewer in the *Caledonian Mercury*.[33] In France, an article by Lamartine on Gutenberg published in the journal *Civilisateur*, was immediately re-edited in the series *Bibliothèque des Chemins de fer* in 1853, a suitable biography to celebrate the modern invention of the railways, and in the 1890s one of the two telephone exchanges in Paris was called 'Gutenberg', the telephonists' repetition of his name reinforcing the association of the old and the new revolutions in communication.[34]

The parallel anti-modern view of printing as the deplorable cause of a non-hierarchical society is found repeatedly in the nineteenth century among medievalising writers. It was expressed with characteristically unpleasant force by Ruskin in one of his most popular volumes of criticism, *St Mark's Rest*:

Then comes printing, and universal gabble of fools ... and so at last Modern Science and Political Economy; and the reign of St. Petroleum instead of St. Peter. Out of which God only knows what is to come next; but He *does* know, whatever the Jew swindlers and apothecaries' 'prentices think about it.[35]

But the invention of printing could now also find a place in the nostalgia for the vanished medieval world because its techniques and working methods were no longer recognisable in contemporary printing practice. The two views are seamlessly joined by Charles Knight in his biography of Caxton published in 1844 in the series Knight's Weekly Volume for All Readers, priced at 1s. Knight was yet another Englishman to use a visit to

Mainz to make a political point. In 1837 the burghers of Mainz had erected a statue to Gutenberg; no expense was spared: it was commissioned from Thorvaldsen, the greatest living sculptor, yet its inauguration was no royal unveiling but a popular festival. On their way down the Rhine, Knight and his travel companions met a German noblewoman:

> She gave us an elaborate account of the fashionable dullness of the baths of Baden and Nassau, and … told us by all means to avoid Mentz during the following week as all kinds of low people would be there, to make a great fuss about a printer who had been dead two or three hundred years.[36]

This tale of an ignorant woman of the idle classes illustrates how popular celebration of Gutenberg provided opportunities for bourgeois opposition to aristocratic rule and Knight described the festival as a popular event celebrating the achievement of a man whose life was useful. This was a theme dear to Knight, whose last chapter on Caxton was called 'Work to the end'.[37] Here he described how Caxton was on familiar, nearly equal, terms with his workforce, fellow craftsmen not exploited factory workers. This was all pure imagination, but important for the image which Knight wanted to project of a society where human decency could co-exist with technical innovation, an alternative to modern industrial society with its exploited, poverty-stricken, and potentially rebellious workforce. Knight had invented for Caxton those bourgeois virtues which Este had castigated him for not possessing. Although they were not, admittedly, the higher virtues of a man assisting society towards improvement, Caxton had become an example of the honest, hardworking, pre-industrial artisan. Knight's biography of Caxton can be seen as a historical counterpart to his 'Days at the factories' column, in his *Penny Magazine of the Society for the Diffusion of Useful Knowledge*, where he sought to calm revolutionary fervour by promoting a better equilibrium between factory-owners and their workers so as to lessen tensions between the rich and the poor classes of society.[38]

With such a range of medievalising reasons for reassessing late medieval printed books we might have expected to see a reappraisal of early printed books as medieval objects and a reappraisal of texts which reflect the spiritual life of the Middle Ages, but this is not convincingly brought out by the evidence, and we begin to see why: even when it was possible to set printing within a medieval world it was most often used in a progressive political context. The invention itself, its economic structures, and its long-term consequences could all be celebrated, but in this context there was little room for admiration for the texts which were produced. The Religious Tract Society put on a brave face, but it was an effort:

The 'Histories of Troy' would have no attraction for the reader in the present age; but far different was it in the days of Caxton; while the earliest work that issued from his press cannot but be regarded with lively interest, as the first sheaf of an extensive harvest, into which multitudes in after days have thrust in the sickle.[39]

In Chapter 4 we encountered Dibdin who in the first decades of the nineteenth century presented collecting as a socially exclusive activity, associated with medieval aristocratic values, an early sign of the medieval revival. Similarly, when Brunet, the French book dealer, looked back at the early years of the century and examined what had happened in the market for rare books, one of the greatest changes was the reappraisal of the past of the aristocracy: 'Never was there such a demand for books on the art of heraldry and the history of noble families as after the nobility of France, spoiled of its ancient privileges, preserves of its past only memories, titles, and blazons.'[40] The change can be illustrated by Douce's contrasting view, from before 1812: 'Heraldry the pursuit of vain and empty minds is altogether contemptible and unworthy of the name of science.'[41]

But the nineteenth century also saw a sharp reduction in the aristocratic fashion for collecting historic books, a shift away from the cultural values which are often associated with the grand tour. Brunet emphasised the importance of public institutions for the rare books trade and described the decline of the status of book collectors in a striking way, linking the decline of large, universal collections with bourgeois life in Paris, where people lived in flats: a collector was now lucky to have a study with room for 3,000 books.[42]

The same shift was identified by Dibdin who, never missing a publishing opportunity, in 1832 published his *Bibliophobia* on the disappearance of grand book collectors. Here he recorded how he discussed the sad state of affairs with Bulkeley Bandinel, Bodley's Librarian, who, as Dibdin saw it, was now the only significant buyer of rare books.

Dibdin and Brunet had observed the movements in the market correctly. Although the Bodleian expenditure never reached the heights of the first big bang of 1789–90, not even when the expenditure is adjusted for inflation and deflation, more is hidden behind the bare information on acquisition expenditure which was presented in Figure I.2 in the Introduction. In the 1790s the Bodleian Library bought fashionable classical texts, and it had acquired relatively few books at high prices. In the nineteenth century, between, say, 1830 and 1860, the Bodleian Library bought many more incunabula but their average price was relatively low.[43]

In the 1850s W. H. Smith's railway stalls classified a book as 'cheap' if it was priced at 2s 6d.[44] Although many cost much more, numerous incunabula

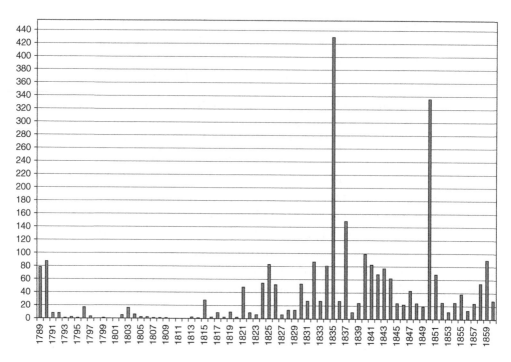

Figure 6.1 The annual number of incunable volumes purchased by the Bodleian 1789–1861.

bought by the Bodleian could be classified as cheap even compared with modern books marketed by the emerging mass retailers. For instance, a little guide to the spiritual life by Cherubino da Spoleto is the sort of text which one might expect to have gained more recognition in the marketplace now that medieval devotion had become fashionable; yet a copy was acquired in 1851 for 1s 6d.[45] The first edition of an important ecclesiological text by Augustine was bought in 1835 for 2s.[46] These were small books, but some very substantial incunabula fetched similar prices; for instance an edition of Ficino's commentary on Plato was bought in 1854 for 2s.[47] Where we have the opportunity to compare the development of prices for individual copies of books, the evidence even suggests that often collectors in an age keen on the religiosity of the Middle Ages were prepared to pay even less for medieval devout texts than a generation which had been hostile to it.[48] Price developments provide no evidence of any market interest in most medieval works, whether law, theology, sermons, or devotion.

Even if the medieval revival did not bring about an appreciation of medieval texts, one might expect that the interest in medieval aesthetics would have had a significant impact. But prices indicate a similar absence of a broadly based interest in medieval aesthetics as expressed by late medieval books. Overwhelmed by its own extensive acquisitions, the Bodleian Library quite often bought two copies of the same edition. Aristotle's *Nicomachean Ethics* printed by Mentelin in or before 1469 was bought in 1840 for £12 12s, a considerable sum of money. It was in a French late eighteenth-century gold-tooled blue morocco binding by Bozérian le jeune. The result is a tidy eighteenth-century book. In contrast, in 1854, the Bodleian bought for £3 4s another copy of the same edition, still in its late fifteenth-century French binding. A book tidied-up in the eighteenth century cost four times as much as one which still reflected medieval aesthetics.[49]

Downward pressure on prices may have been created by the availability in the market of a large number of books sold by institutions which had ended up with numerous duplicates after the massive centralisation of collections during and after the Napoleonic wars. The sales of duplicates from the Royal Library in Munich were by far the most important of these. Yet there is evidence that the greater availability had less of an impact than a general lack of interest in the type of book which was on offer. In contrast to the books which had been shipped laboriously and dangerously to London in the 1790s in order to maximise profits, in the mid nineteenth century incunabula often cost more when bought direct from the Royal Library in Munich than when they were bought in London. For instance, a canon law text relating to confessions by Astesanus de Ast, in an edition by Mentelin from before 1473, was a type of book which one might assume would have gained importance in the climate of the neo-religious revival. In 1837 Bandinel bought for 5s at auction in London a fine copy which has contemporary decoration – lovely in our eyes –including drawings of those grotesque faces which were well established as part of the repertoire of neo-medieval architecture: by 1825 all gothic mouldings or ornaments could be bought wholesale, as Kenneth Clark has pointed out.[50] But it had no identifiable impact on the price of the book. In the same year a visually much less attractive copy was bought direct from Munich for £2 8s, that is nearly ten times as much.[51]

Whatever motivated the Bodleian Library, the prices which it paid demonstrate that books with medieval texts printed in the fifteenth century were, more widely, not valued in the market. It was against market trends that the Bodleian bought late medieval books. One explanation could have been that the Bodleian was exceptional in having a medievalising approach to its limited purchases, Oxford being so central to the English medieval revival. But we find the same pattern of acquisitions in another great British institution which emerged as a buyer in the 1840s, the British Museum, which had no such links and which was soon to exceed the Bodleian in this field.[52]

The British Museum library was radically different from the Bibliothèque nationale and from other European national libraries in the nineteenth century which had grown out of royal collections. Founded in 1757 as a national and public institution, it was neither a tool of government nor intended to express the grandeur of the monarch. This independence came at a price: it lacked continuous political support and funds. Not least compared with the French Bibliothèque royale/nationale and the Imperial Library in Vienna, its engagement with the eighteenth-century book market had been patchy: while it depended largely on donations for its growth, its purchases were in the main financed from the sale of duplicates. When in the 1830s it was benchmarked against other European libraries, it was found that the top three were Paris, Munich, and Copenhagen, while the museum was only seventh in size, despite the donation in 1828 of George III's large library.[53]

In the turbulent decades of the 1820s and 1830s, the British Museum came under political attack from radical reformers. Far from being a national library it was seen as an embodiment of aristocratic indolence and privilege. Avowedly Jacobin, Cobbett considered the museum 'a place intended only for the amusement of the curious and the rich'. *Hansard* reported his comments in the House of Commons:

If the aristocracy wanted the Museum as a lounging place, let them pay for it … Sixteen thousand pounds granted for the support of such a place, were £16,000 thrown away – given for the amusement of loungers who paid little or nothing towards the taxes from which this £16,000 was taken. Ten thousand out of this £16,000 was paid away in salaries. He should like to have a list of the salaried persons: he should like to know who they were; he should like, above all things, to see whether they were not some dependents of Government – some of the aristocratic fry.[54]

In 1830 Nicholas Harris Nicolas criticised the selection of the trustees of the museum. They included 'one duke, three marquesses, four earls, and four barons, and two members of parliament!' None had been chosen on intellectual merit: 'In England … this distinction, like all other honors is exclusively reserved for rank; and affords another to the many proofs which might be adduced, of the contemptuous neglect with which genius is treated by the British government.'[55] He sarcastically observed that it was evidently the case that 'knowledge is in the gift of the crown, and that in all branches it co-exists with the rank of peer and privy counsellor'.

A parliamentary select committee set up to inquire into the affairs of the museum in 1836 was influenced by these radical views. Antonio Panizzi, the Italian bourgeois revolutionary in exile, had recently been appointed to the museum's staff, and exploited this opportunity to promote profound change. In his evidence to the select committee he famously stated:

I want a poor student to have the same means of indulging his learned curiosity, of following his rational pursuits, of consulting the same authorities, of fathoming the most intricate inquiry as the richest man in the kingdom, as far as books go, and I contend that the Government is bound to give him the most liberal and unlimited assistance in this respect.[56]

He articulated the museum's function in opposition to inaccessible private collections, which gave the rich privileged access to 'rational pursuits'. His ambitions for the library of the British Museum may be compared with those of the newly created National Gallery, which provided access to paintings to a section of the population which could never hope to own them, and he presented this as a national duty, which the British government had failed to meet: while private persons had made donations, the nation had done nothing for the collection.

In 1832, Robert Peel was reported in *Hansard* arguing for the financing of a permanent building for the National Gallery, in the hope that Britain could finally catch up with other European nations, showing much the same political sentiments as Panizzi:

In the present times of political excitement, the exacerbation of angry and unsocial feelings might be much softened by the effects which the fine arts had ever produced upon the minds of men. Of all expenditure, that like the present, was the most adequate to confer advantage on those classes which had but little leisure to enjoy the most refined species of pleasure. The rich might have their own pictures, but those who had to obtain their bread by their labour, could not hope for such an enjoyment.[57]

A select committee inquiring into the National Gallery in 1853 was informed that Prince Albert held that 'the endeavour should not be merely to form a collection of pictures by good masters, such as a private gentleman might wish to possess, but to afford the best means of instruction and education in the art to those who wish to study it scientifically in its history and progress'.[58] Panizzi's aims were very similar. The museum library of the age of reform was to become a public, state-funded alternative to the private libraries of the rich, to ensure equal access to information and knowledge. Proposing the formation of other public libraries where a greater emphasis could be placed on common books, Panizzi's acquisition policy placed a special emphasis on old, rare, and expensive books, for they were the ones to which the general public could not easily afford access.[59] Incunabula, 'scientifically' studied with the newly developed methodology focusing on 'history and progress', fitted this aim eminently. Although it was not until much later in the century that the museum followed the model of the Royal Library in Munich of organising its incunabula chronologically, their systematic acquisition was one aspect of Panizzi's aim to create an institution which would enable the general public to have the advantages previously reserved for aristocrats.

With their extensive purchases of fifteenth-century books the Bodleian Library and the British Museum participated neither in a positive re-evaluation of the Middle Ages nor in the later nineteenth-century redefinition of the Renaissance which was to include the fifteenth century.[60] It was an eighteenth-century intellectual background which informed their collecting. If grandees no longer collected fifteenth-century books comprehensively, the conceptual framework which had formed their collections was adopted by those great public institutions which we now see as so characteristic of the nineteenth century. Eighteenth-century ideologies and methodologies enabled them to achieve the nineteenth-century aim of providing public and national access to books in the didactic and chronological context of progress. This helps explain why these two prominent libraries began collecting unfashionable late medieval books long before, for instance, the National Gallery turned its attention to fifteenth-century paintings, and why they continued to do so in the absence of any widespread medievalising interest in fifteenth-century books, even when, in the world of visual aesthetics, the century before Raphael became the most fashionable of all.[61] The eighteenth-century redefinition of incunabula as historical objects was a significant factor in the shift from the private collecting of historic books to the public and institutional safeguarding of the past, reflecting new attitudes to the relationship between state, nation, and people.

As an epilogue, we can cast a brief eye on how incunabula fared in their new institutional homes. The eighteenth-century reification of the fifteenth-century book, acceptable only when dissociated from its deplorable content, continued to be profoundly formative. The object-focused discipline which it had engendered was maintained and developed but, as libraries and museums increasingly grew apart, it was isolated within libraries and, although their origins had been so close, it grew to be distinct from art history, based in museums and in university departments. This growing away from the methodological background shared with art history, towards a method perceived to be objective and scientific, can be seen in several countries.

In the rapidly industrialising Germany the study of the invention of printing, and consequently the study of incunabula, were reshaped as part of the celebration of the modern country, recently unified as a new nation state. As ever a German symbol, Gutenberg was now an example for the men who led the economic expansion; relying on their scientific innovations, engineering expertise, and business acumen the new Germany could compete with the old colonial powers. An instance is the way in which Gutenberg was quoted as a liberator of the German spirit, a civilian precursor for General Scharnhorst who had liberated the Germans of Alsace and Lorraine from French oppression.[62]

The *Gesamtkatalog der Wiegendrucke*, a Prussian cultural flagship project begun in 1904, was promoted by Friedrich Theodor Althoff. His greatest achievement was the imposition of an uncompromisingly central control on all German universities which, in his capable hands, led to a dramatic enhancement of standards. The same combination of national ambition and central control is recognisable in his grand project to create one world-wide catalogue of incunabula, to which all future catalogues in Germany and abroad were to be merely preparatory listings. The technical focus of the institutionalised, centralised, and national German study of incunabula was so exclusive that it eventually led to sharp criticism.[63] This is not surprising, as its lack of interest in the texts contained in the books which it described presented a profound intellectual contrast to the burgeoning textual studies in the universities of Catholic Germany. A papacy deprived of its secular powers had sought to support a revival of medieval religion and philosophy, especially Thomism, as an alternative to the scientific studies which it associated with the threat posed by the emerging democratic, liberal, secular states, most famously in *Aeterni patris*, the papal encyclical bull of 1879.[64] In Germany the success of the neo-scholastic revival can be illustrated by *Archiv für Litteratur- und Kirchengeschichte des Mittelalters*, begun in Munich in 1884, one of the earliest of the many scholastic periodicals which began in these years, and by such an outstanding student of medieval philosophy as Martin Grabmann, who began publishing shortly after the *Gesamtkatalog* issued its first volume. The technical and progressive focus of incunabulists could seem irrelevant to students working with the texts contained in the books.

On the other hand, religious opposition to the secular state was one of the motivating factors behind the French national catalogue of incunabula, which was funded privately by Marie Pellechet, and never completed as it lacked the backing of state finance which was required for such a long-term project. Her place in the ultramontane world is depressingly confirmed by the hate-mail campaign which she sought to organise against those who used their palaeographical skills to prove the innocence of Dreyfus, sharing the anti-Semitism which, in France as in Italy, was so integral to the Catholic rejection of the secular state.[65]

In contrast to the ultramontane rejection of modernity, natural science was at the heart of the study of incunabula in England. It was associated with the most revolutionising of scientific theories, that of the development of the species. Henry Bradshaw, based in Darwin's Cambridge, suggested a taxonomy of printing types as if they had developed through natural generation and selection.[66] In this context it became important to distinguish the material study of incunabula from the aesthetic, dilettante tradition with which it had shared its origins.[67] The classificatory and chronological ambitions of the late nineteenth-century approach to fifteenth-century books sought to detach incunable studies from all traces of subjectivity, while late nineteenth-century art history was still as close to the art market as ever.

The study of incunabula in England was equally associated with the socialist utopian dream of recovering a lost medieval paradise where manual work had been admired and respected, in contrast to the dehumanised life associated with factory production of poor-quality objects for mass consumption. Robert Proctor, fiercely anti-monarchical, was deeply influenced by William Morris's utopian socialism and his arts and crafts aesthetics, and was the leading force behind the creation of the British Museum's catalogue of incunabula, strictly organised according to production history and the deployment of printing materials, rather than by authors and theirs texts, which were treated as sketchily by the early incunabulists in the British Museum as they were in Berlin. Diverse as they were, these three projects all had the same overall aim and used the same methodological approach, albeit with some practical variations.

Prices for incunabula were to rise again in the twentieth century, undoubtedly in no small part because of their prestigious association with such grand national research projects. But for most of the nineteenth century prices indicate that incunabula were no longer a contested cultural field which could shape and express contemporary political issues; widely different political views could find expression through the now thoroughly institutionalised engagement with their history. The young Renouard, the firebrand denouncing private and aristocratic domination of the past, had won; incunabula had found their place as objects, if not as books, in the public domain, in institutions where the past and its interpretation could be both promoted and controlled.

Notes

Introduction

1 The graphs relating to purchases made by the Bodleian Library are based on my examination of the bills from 1613 to 1900 and on Bodleian Library, *Catalogue of Books Purchased*. Information on individual purchases was published in Bod-inc.

2 With one exception, Bodleian, Auct. M 1.3, a defective copy of the 1462 Bible, bought in 1750 for £2 10s.

3 I have used the composite price index of O'Donoghue, Goulding, and Allen, 'Consumer price inflation since 1750'. For a discussion of the methodology and its validity see Officer, 'What were the UK earnings rate and consumer price index?'

4 Philip, *Bodleian Library*; also Philip, 'The background to the Bodleian purchases of incunabula 1789–90'.

5 Bodleian, Auct. 4Q 1.3.

6 Chateaubriand, *Mémoires d'outre-tombe*, I, book 6, chapter 1 and Book 10, chapter 5: 6s a month for lodgings and 1s for a basic dinner.

7 In a letter to Earl Spencer, 6 November 1792, BL, Ms. Add. 76068, James Payne referred to a copy at Althorp. This is confirmed by Alexander Horn, 29 June 1798, BL, Ms. Add. 75964, who knew that he could not sell Spencer a copy.

8 Bodleian, Arch. B b.10,11.

9 *Psalterium*. [Mainz]: Fust and Schoeffer, 14 Aug. 1457.

10 *1789 Le patrimoine libéré*, item 35, entry signed by Dominique Coq.

1 Enlightenment ideas and revolutionary practice

1 Adam Philippe, comte de Custine. For his occupation of Mainz, see Blanning, *Reform and Revolution in Mainz*, pp. 274–302.

2 BnF, A.m., boite 270. A copy of a letter sent to his minister by René Desaulnays, keeper of printed books from 1775 to1793: 'Permettez moi de me rappeler à votre souvenir, et de vous prier d'avoir la bonté d'informer le Général Custines [*sic*], qui marche sur Mayence, qu'il se trouve dans la Bibliothèque du Chapitre de la Métropole, un exemplaire du premier livre imprimé avec date, dont je joins ici le titre. C'est le fameux psautier de Mayence, de 1457 in fol. Il lui serait aisé de se le procurer, ou se le faire donner. Le volume en entrant dans la Bibliothèque nationale, y compléterait notre collection des premières éditions de cette ville,

qui a été le berceau de l'imprimerie. Accueillez avec vos anciennes bontés pour moi, ma demande. Desaunnays [*sic*], garde de la Bibliothèque nationale. A la Bibliothèque nationale. Le 22 octobre, l'an 1 de la République française.' The recipient may have been Jean Roland de La Platière, minister of the interior from 10 August 1792 to 14 March 1793, under whom the Library belonged, or, less likely, Lebrun-Tondu, the foreign minister.

3 Custine failed to confiscate the Psalter which had apparently disappeared. This was not because Desaulnays's request was ignored. Sorel, *L'Europe et la révolution française*, III, p. 155, quotes a letter from Lebrun-Tondu to Custine dated 20 October 1792, without indicating his source, suggesting that he should take the opportunity to enrich the Bibliothèque nationale.

4 The confiscation of cultural property by French revolutionary and Napoleonic troops is well known. Still valuable is Müntz, 'Les annexions de collections d'art ou de bibliothèques'. The revolutionary period is dealt with in his two last contributions. The celebration of the bicentenary of the Revolution occasioned a number of valuable studies, among those specifically on books notably *Le patrimoine libéré*. Perhaps the best joint overview of the confiscations of books from both Italy and Germany is Hobson, 'Appropriations from foreign libraries'; on Italy, Zorzi, 'Les saisies napoléoniennes en Italie'.

5 Savoy, *Patrimoine annexé*, I, p. 21 emphasises continuity with pre-revolutionary expertise, in an outstanding study of the confiscation of all types of cultural property from German lands.

6 Capperonnier was at the Bibliothèque royale from 1789. Van Praet was appointed by Desaulnays in 1784. See Varry, 'Joseph Van Praet'.

7 See Chambon, 'Le rôle de l'Abbé Leblond', at pp. 68–9.

8 A good summary is in Seckel, 'La Bibliothèque nationale et les dépôts littéraires'.

9 BnF, A.m., boite 270, contains a list nearly exclusively of contemporary useful books, signed by Keil on 11 ventôse An V [1 March 1797]. For revolutionary dates I have used Renouard's *Manuel* from 1822.

10 BnF, A.m., boite 270, a letter from the ministry of the interior [Pierre Bénezech], fifth division, dated 3 ventôse An V [21 February 1797]. On Keil's confiscations see especially Savoy, *Patrimoine annexé*, I, pp. 51–2; and Ursula Baurmeister, in *1789 Le patrimoine libéré*, nos 43–54, at pp. 88–91.

11 BnF, A.m., boite 270: 'Le citoyen Van-Praet est prié de faire sans retard une note. 1e Des ouvrages allemands et anglais non-complets de la bibliothèque nationale 2° Des ouvrages anglais, allemands, italiens et latins, dont il serait utile d'enrichir la bibliothèque nationale 3° Des livres rares tant par rapport à l'époque où ils ont été imprimés que par rapport au petit nombre d'exemplaires qui en existent – qui ne se trouvent pas à la bibl. nat. Keil. Paris le 23 fructidor l'an 4.' (Citizen Van Praet is asked without delay to make a note 1. Of German and English works, incomplete in the National Library 2. Of English, German, Italian, and Latin works, which would usefully enrich the National Library 3. Books which

are rare either because of the period of their printing or the small number of existing copies – which are not in the Nat. Lib. Keil. Paris 9 September 1796.)

12 BnF, A.m., boite 55, pp. 39–40, records a letter from 'Bénezech, Ministre de l'intérieur' (from 3 November 1795 to 15 July 1797), and 'Ginguené, directeur général de l'instruction publique'. The library was instructed not to select duplicates from the books confiscated from émigrés and religious institutions, noting for instance that Shakespeare had been selected ten times, Pope eleven, Voltaire nine, sometimes in old editions. On pp. 44–7 is the record of Capperonnier's answer, dated 3 brumaire An IV [25 October 1795]. Bénezech must have written before taking office. The passage quoted here: 'Qu'il nous soit permis d'exprimer un regret à cet égard, c'est d'avoir rencontré des obstacles dans l'exécution d'un projet qui fut formé dès le commencement de la Révolution et auquel n'ont cessé d'applaudir plusieurs gens de lettres célèbres. Ce projet avait pour but de rassembler dans la Bibliothèque nationale la collection la plus complète possible de livres en tous genres et en toutes langues, et d'y recueillir le plus d'éditions diverses de ces mêmes livres, et profitant d'une occasion unique et telle qu'aucun gouvernement de l'Europe n'avait encore rencontrée.'

13 BnF, A.m., boite 270, 'Ch.s Coquebers': 'Livres étrangers de minéralogie dont les conservateurs de la bibliothèque nationale sont invités à enrichir le dépôt qui leur est confié.' (Foreign books on mineralogy by which the curators of the national library are encouraged to enrich the collection with which they are entrusted.) On Coquebert see Laboulais-Lesage, *Lectures et pratiques de l'espace*.

14 BnF, A.m., boite 267: 'État des différentes listes des livres imprimés manquants à la Bibliothèque nationale, qui ont été envoyées au ministre de l'intérieur [probably during the ministry of Jean Antoine Chaptal, minister from 21 January 1801 to 8 August 1804], en l'an IX et en l'an X: … An X: On met aujourd'hui sous les yeux du ministres [*sic*], les états suivants:

1	État des livres à faire venir d'Allemagne	20942 [*c.* £838]
2	------- d'Italie	5518 [*c.* £220]
3	------- de Hollande	1131 [*c.* £45]
4	------- d'Espagne	513 [*c.* £20]
5	------- de Russie	6179 [*c.* £247]
6	------- d'Angleterre	88000 [*c.* £3520]
7	État des livres imprimés à faire relier	72,744 [*c.* £2,909]
8	Somme provisoire pour les livres manuscrits à faire relier	12,000 [*c.* £480]
	Somme totale	298288 [should be: 207027; *c.* £8,279]

15 BnF, A.m., boite 270 contains extensive lists of modern books to be acquired from England, which must be the documentation for the funding bid from 1802, not lists of candidates for spoliation. The lists of books from 1793–7 were based on the *Analytical Review*, while the most recent ones, until May 1802, were based on the *Monthly Review* and on catalogues from 'White', presumably Benjamin and John White.

16 BnF, A.m., boite 267, a letter signed by Capperonnier and Van Praet and addressed to the Ministre de l'intérieur [Nicolas-Louis François de Neufchâteau]: 'Nous avons l'honneur de vous mettre sous les yeux une liste de livres précieux qui se trouvent dans plusieurs bibliothèques d'Allemagne, et dont la plupart manquent à la Bibliothèque nationale, où la suite des éditions du quinzième siècle est déjà très considérable. Ces raretés typographiques serviraient à y remplir des lacunes. Nous les recommandons, Citoyen ministre, au vif intérêt que vous prenez à notre établissement, et à votre amour pour tout ce qui tient à la gloire de la nation et au bien de l'instruction publique. Nous vous prions en conséquence de vouloir bien donner les ordres nécessaires, pour qu'à mesure que nos armés pénétreront en Allemagne, ces Monuments de l'art de l'imprimerie deviennent aussi des monuments de nos victoires. Salut et respect. Capperonnier, Van Praet. Paris le 11 germinal An VII.'

17 BnF, A.m., boite 270: 'Le plus intéressant livre qui existe, puisque c'est le premier de tous. Nota: rien ne doit être épargné pour assurer à la République la possession de cette importante édition à la quelle on sacrifie volontiers toutes les autres éditions dans la présente liste.' In a list in boite 267 it is described as 'premier livre imprimé avec date; édition de la plus grande rareté et sans prix' (the first dated printed book; an edition of the greatest rarity and beyond price).

18 Turrecremata, *Meditationes*. Rome: Han, 1467; 'édition de la plus grande rareté et le seul exemplaire connu.'

19 Wuerdtwein, *Bibliotheca moguntina*, p. 55. The librarians could also have known this copy from Gercken, *Reisen*, III, p. 38.

20 Heinecken, *Idée générale d'une collection complette d'estampes*, pp. 269–70.

21 Strauss, *Opera rariora* and Gras, *Verzeichniss typographischer Denkmäler*. See BnF, A.m., boite 270, 'Catalogue de la foire de Francfort 1793' and 'Foire de S Michel 1793' annotated with dates when orders were placed respectively 'Demandé 1ᵉ jan 1793' and 'Demandé le [blank] ventôse an 2' [i.e. between 19 February and 21 March 1793]. On the confiscation of Hupfauer, *Druckstücke aus dem XV. Jahrhunderte*, see Baurmeister in *Le patrimoine libéré*, no. 43, and p. 91.

22 BnF, A.m., boite 270 contains a draft of the first list dated 5 germinal An VII [25 March 1799] and a draft of a longer list, of thirty-five sheets, dated 24 messidor An VIII [13 July 1800], in part copied from the earlier list, but augmented.

23 BnF, A.m., boite 270, a letter from Neveu to Capperonnier dated 4 vendémiaire An IX [27 September 1800].

24 Savoy, *Patrimoine annexé*, I, p. 52.

25 Thus BnF, A.m., boite 270, a letter from Capperonnier to the minister of the interior (Chaptal) dated 'Paris, le 27 prairial an 9' [16 June 1801] 'Le Muséum central des arts a remis le 16 du présent mois à la Bibliothèque nationale une petite caisse arrivée de Strasbourg, et contenant quelques livres précieuses et rares, imprimés dans le XVe siècle. Ces livres dont vous trouvez ci joint l'état que j'en ai fait dresser, proviennent de la Bibliothèque publique de Nuremberg, et sont dus aux recherches du Citoyen Neveu, commissaire du gouvernement en Allemagne pour les sciences et les arts, qui avait déjà bien mérité de notre bibliothèque d'autres monuments littéraires imprimés dans le XVe siècle qu'il y avait envoyée.' (On the 16th of this month the Central Museum of Art sent to the National Library a small chest, received from Strasbourg, with some precious and rare books printed in the fifteenth century. I have had an inventory of these books drawn up, attached. The books are from the public library in Nuremberg and are due to the searches of citizen Neveu, commissioner of the government in Germany for science and arts, who has already previously provided excellent service to our library with other monuments of literature printed in the fifteenth century which he has sent.) The list is elsewhere in the same boite. 'Livres provenant de la Bibliothèque publique de Nuremberg et envoyés a la bibliothèque nationale par le citoyen Neveu' dated 16 prairial An IX. (Books from the public library of Nuremberg and sent to the national library by citizen Neveu, 5 June 1801.)

26 For instance BnF, A.m., boite 270, a list of 196 books from the Imperial Library in Vienna, all but three being incunabula. Denon signed for their receipt in Vienna on 25 July 1809, countersigned by Józef Maksymilian Ossoliński, 'Conseiller Intime, Préfet de la Bibliothèque', and Franz Sensel, 'conservateur de la Bibliothèque', although they did not hand over the books willingly. See also Mosel, *Geschichte*, pp. 222–4.

27 Thus BnF, A.m., boite 270, a note on books from the Vatican, presumably from 1796, 'Première liste. Bibliothèque du Vatican. 77 articles. On en a trouvé 72. Ceux non trouvés sont les no. 28, 31, 61, 76 et 77'. (First list. Vatican Library; 77 items; 72 found; not found are nos 28, 31, 61, 76 and 77.)

28 In BnF, A.m., boite 270, letter from the minister of the interior [Bénezech], 9 germinal An V [29 March 1797] followed by an extensive correspondence, because the ministry could not field the staff required to be present for the opening of the boxes. The letter recording that they had been sent to Paris is dated 11 ventôse An V [1 March 1797], signed by Keil.

29 *Correspondance de Napoléon Ier*, III, p. 51, Articles secrets faisant suite et partie du traité de paix conclu entre la république française et celle de Venise, Milan, 27 floréal an V (16 mai 1797), article 5: 'La République de Venise remettra enfin aux commissaires à ce destinés vingt tableaux et cinq cents manuscrits, au choix du général en chef'. On the Italian confiscations see Dupuigrenet, 'Les trésors d'Italie'.

30 Monge, 'commissaire de la République en Italie' from May 1796. His work was facilitated by a list prepared at the Bibliothèque nationale, 20 thermidor An V [7 August 1797].

31 On 21 October 1795 the Comité d'instruction publique adopted Lenoir's project to create 'Un musée historique et chronologique où l'on retrouvera les âges et la sculpture dans les salles particulières, en donnant à chacune le caractère, la physionomie exacte du siècle qu'elle représente' (a historical and chronological museum where one finds in separate rooms the periods and their sculptures, giving each the precise character and physiognomy of the era which they represent). See Baczko, 'Vandalisme', p. 910, who regards this as the formal end to 'vandalism'.

32 See Roche, 'La police du livre'.

33 La Caille, *Histoire de l'imprimerie*, p. 1: 'Si les ignorans regardent l'imprimerie sans l'admirer, c'est qu'ils la voient sans la connoistre: les sçavants en ont toujours jugé tout autrement; et ils ont estimé avec raison, que depuis près de trois siècles que cette merveille s'est fait voir dans l'Europe, l'esprit humain n'avoit jamais rien inventé de plus heureux, ni de plus utile pour l'instruction des hommes.'

34 As an example Mirabeau, *Sur la liberté de la presse* who, with a reference to Milton's *Areopagitica*, contrasted the free trade and the free press in England with a regime of privileges and controls in France.

35 Formey, *Principes élémentaires des belles-lettres*, for instance p. 229, principle number 788: 'Depuis ce temps là l'avidité du gain a introduit une assez grande décadence dans l'exercice de cette profession, dont les libraires disposent à leur gré et relativement au bien de leur commerce, plutôt qu'à celui du public.' Formey, *Elementary Principles of the Belles-Lettres*, pp. 220–1: 'Since that time the avidity of gain has occasion'd a great decay in the exercise of this profession, which the Booksellers dispose of at will and relatively to the welfare of their trade rather than the good of the public.' See also Häseler, 'Formey et Crousaz'.

36 Bollioud de Mermet, *De la bibliomanie*, pp. 52 and 55: 'C'est une question encore indécise, que de savoir si l'invention de l'imprimerie a plus contribué aux progrès des lettres et à la perfection de la morale, qu'elle ne leur a nui. Ce n'est pas ici le lieu de l'examiner ni de la résoudre: tout ce qu'on peut dire est que le nombre des livres est immense, et que celui des bons livres est très-petit … De ce mélange informe et monstrueux des productions frivoles et téméraires que le génie humain enfante dans ses égarement, qu'en reste-t-il autre chose à un lecteur avide et inconsidéré, qu'un amas confus d'idées biens moins propres à enrichir son esprit, qu'à troubler, ou à corrompre son imagination.'

37 On Laire, later librarian to cardinal Loménie de Brienne, see Vernus, *Une vie dans l'univers du livre* and also Charon, 'Un amateur russe', at pp. 216–21. I am grateful to Annie Charon for several suggestions concerning Laire.

38 Laire, *Specimen historicum typographiae romanae*, pp. v–vii: 'Auctor lectori. Nullum sane inventum arte typographica praestantius, nullum generi humano optabilius accidere umquam potuit. In memoriam revocemus tristissima illa tempora in quibus universa doctrina fugitivis verbis, scriptisque facile perituris continebatur; tum incertum illum atque labilem cogitemus litterarum statum qui olim obtinebant. Quam lento sane gradu et quot et quantis viarum difficultatibus

atque periculis ad remotissimas, barbarasque nationes scientiarum lumina propagari opportuit! … Haec typographicae artis commoda nemo negabit nisi in silvis educatus et scientiarum hostis imperitissimus. Verum quidem est, nec satis omnium lacrimis deplorandum, utilissimas quasque res in detrimentum et perniciem vergere. Sed quid inde? Tollendus quidem est abusus, sed usus religiose servandus; rejecta enim hac regula, societatem omnem in pejus ruere jam necessum esset, et maxima vitae humanae emolumenta exsulare satius foret; quod quam stultum et perniciosum sit, nemo non videt. Quae cum ita sint, praeclarissimae artis ortum, atque progressum scrutari abs re non erit.'

39 Laire, *Specimen historicum typographiae romanae*, pp. 12–15: 'Sicque per gradus et quasi pedetentim ad remotissimas quoque gentes, Africam, Americam, apud Indos ac Japponenses feliciter pervenit ars utilissima magno scientiarum et universae societatis commodo, atque emolumento. Sincerum gerant typographi erga artem suam amorem, ac scientiam hanc sua auctoritate protegant, suisque tueantur beneficiis principes et veri litterarum amatores; tuncque hanc artem ab iis, quibus maculatur atque deturpatur vitiis et abusibus, brevi tempore liberatam atque repurgatam pro humani generis bono laeti intuebimur.'

40 See the complaint from the Ministry of the Interior that the Bibliothèque nationale took too many editions of Pope from libraries confiscated from émigrés, above note 12.

41 d'Alembert, 'Discours préliminaire', p. iii: 'La communication des idées est le principe et le soutien de cette union, et demande nécessairement l'invention des signes; telle est l'origine de la formation des sociétés avec la quelle les langues ont dû naitre.' (The communication of ideas is the principle and foundation for this union and requires the invention of signs; this is the origin of the formation of societies, with which languages had to come into being.) And p. xx: 'Aussi fallut-il au genre humain, pour sortir de la barbarie, une de ces révolutions qui font prendre à la terre une face nouvelle; l'empire grec est détruit, sa ruine fait refluer en Europe le peu de connoissance qui restoient encore au monde; l'invention de l'imprimerie, la protection de Médicis et de François I raniment les esprits et la lumière renaît de toutes parts.' (To leave behind barbarism mankind needed one of those revolutions which give the world a new face; the Greek empire fell and its ruin caused the few remains of knowledge to flow to Europe; the invention of printing, the patronage of the Medici and of François I revitalised the sprits and light was everywhere rekindled.)

42 See again Roche, 'La police du livre'.

43 Roche, 'La censure'.

44 Published in Malesherbes, *Les 'Remontrances'*, with an excellent introduction by Elisabeth Badinter. Also Malesherbes, *Mémoires sur la librairie*, 1994, with a preface by Chartier. In Badinter's and Chartier's context it was Malesherbes's understanding of the actual function of publishing in the eighteenth century which was of central importance. Chartier, *Les origines culturelles de la Révolution française*, p. 69, mentions Malesherbes in the context of his important

contribution to the discussion of the cultural origins of the Revolution. I seek to keep my discussion distinct from this discussion of causality, while focusing on both continuity and rupture of thinking about the past during the last part of the eighteenth century.

45 Malesherbes, *Les 'Remontrances'*, p. 273: 'L'art de l'imprimerie a donc donné à l'écriture la même publicité qu'avait la parole dans le premier âge, au milieu des assemblées de la nation. Mais il a fallu plusieurs siècles pour que la découverte de cet art fît tout son effet sur les hommes. Il a fallu que la nation entière ait pris le goût et l'habitude de s'instruire par la lecture, et qu'il se soit formé assez de gens habiles dans l'art d'écrire pour prêter leur ministère à tout le public, et tenir lieu de ceux qui, doués d'une éloquence naturelle, se faisaient entendre de nos pères dans le champ de Mars ou dans plaids publics.'

46 Malesherbes, *Mémoires sur la librairie*, 1809. The intellectual complexity of Malesherbes's memoir is reflected in its publishing history; suppressed in 1788 it was not published until 1809, when it served to support Napoleonic restrictions on the freedom of the press. It was published again in 1814, now as ammunition against attempts by the restored monarchy to reimpose censorship. See Birn, 'Malesherbes and the call for a free press'.

47 Malesherbes, *Mémoire sur la librairie*, 1809, p. 269: 'Nous avons vu, depuis quelques années, des gens du monde, des militaires, qui n'avaient jamais couru la carrière des lettres et jamais étudié la science des lois, se charger eux-mêmes de la défense d'une cause qui les intéressait … Dans le peuple même, dans la classe des artisans dont presque aucun ne savait lire dans le siècle passé, il s'est trouvé des talents littéraires dont on a été surpris … Ne regardons plus le peuple, dans notre siècle, du même œil qu'on le considérait dans les siècles passés. Je ne prétends pas dire que tous les individus de la nation soient des gens instruits; mais je dis qu'il n'y a pas une classe d'hommes ni un coin de province où il ne se trouve des gens qui ont une façon de penser à eux, et qui sont capables de l'exposer et de la soutenir contre qui que soit. C'est le heureux effet de l'art de l'imprimerie. Il n'y a que trois siècles et demi que cet art existe; ce n'est pas trop de temps pour avoir fait acquérir, aux nations entières, cette instruction dont il est temps de recueillir les fruits.'

48 Darnton, *The Great Cat Massacre*, especially pp. 148–50.

49 Le Roy Ladurie, 'De la crise ultime à la vraie croissance', pp. 529–36 drew attention to the emerging literacy among the rural poor and to the fears of Voltaire and Rousseau that it raised unrealistic expectations among the poor.

50 Schandeler, *Les interprétations de Condorcet*, p. 15, sees reading the *Esquisse* after the terror as an attempt to regain the ability to see the Revolution in an optimistic light.

51 In 1775 Condorcet dedicated to Malesherbes a 'Mémoire … sur le moyen de rendre utiles les académies de province'. See Baxmann, *Wissen, Kunst und Gesellschaft in der Theorie Condorcets*, p. 61.

52 Baxmann, *Wissen, Kunst und Gesellschaft in der Theorie Condorcets*, especially pp. 133–44, discusses the growth of communication as key to Condorcet's view of historical change. Belhoste, 'Condorcet, les arts utiles et leur enseignement', explores Condorcet's proposal to reform the École des ponts et chaussées as an expression of the importance of communication in his thought.

53 Condorcet, *Vie de M. Turgot*, especially at pp. 11 and 215. Turgot, *Tableau philosophique* here from *Oeuvres de Turgot*, I, pp. 214–34, at p. 232.

54 Hesse, *Publishing and Cultural Politics*, pp. 102–8, associates Condorcet's view that knowledge is based in an objectively shared world with his hostility to the private ownership of ideas.

55 Here from Condorcet, *Esquisse*, 1988, p. 187–8: 'Les lumières sont devenues l'objet d'un commerce actif, universel.'

56 Coutel's and Kintzler's introduction to their edition of Condorcet, *Cinq mémoires sur l'instruction publique*, includes a discussion of the relationship between *instruction* and *éducation*.

57 See Minois, *Censure et culture*, pp. 244–5, also for the quote from Réguis, unidentified, but presumably from his *La voix du pasteur* from 1773. Also Chartier, Julia, and Compère, *L'éducation en France*, p. 40. On the suppression of the Jesuits and the management of schools see Bailey, 'The French clergy and the removal of Jesuits from secondary schools'.

58 On Condorcet's opposition to slavery see William, 'New constructions of equality'.

59 Volney, *Leçons d'histoire*, p. 58: 'Telle est la puissance de l'imprimerie, telle est son influence sur la civilisation, c'est-à-dire sur le développement de toutes les facultés de l'homme dans le sens le plus utile à la société, que l'époque de son invention divise en deux systèmes distincts et divers, l'état politique et moral des peuples antérieurs et des peuples postérieurs à elle, ainsi que de leurs historiens; et son existence caractérise à tel point les lumières, que pour se informer si un peuple est policé ou barbare, l'on peut se réduire à demander: A-t-il l'usage de l'imprimerie? A-t-il la liberté de la presse?' The translation is from Volney, *Lectures on History* from 1800. On Volney's relationship with Condorcet see Jorbet's introduction, to Volney, *L'École normale de l'an III*, pp. 42–3.

60 Volney, *Leçons d'histoire*, pp. 66–7.

61 Jondot, *Observations critiques*, pp. 8–9: 'Une vérité trop répandue se perd, ou au moins n'a plus que le mérite d'une tradition. *Le cercle des lecteurs était très-étroit*; oui, mais aussi les remarques étaient plus sages, l'esprit d'observation plus juste et la critique plus saine. Malheur au pays, où le plus grand nombre s'avise de vouloir raisonner et prononcer! Où le foyer des lumières est le plus resserré, c'est là qu'il est plus ardent; c'est là qu'il éclaire d'une manière plus uniforme. C'est le feu sacré de Vesta: il est immortel.' And p. 16: 'Quelles sont donc les avantages dus à l'art de l'imprimerie? Ou sont donc les *facultés de l'homme, développées dans le sens le plus utile à la société*? Je vois dans cette société beaucoup moins de vertus, beaucoup moins de morale, beaucoup moins de religion qu'autrefois.

Je vois, au contraire, la discorde s'agiter avec plus de fureur. Sans l'invention de l'imprimerie, les erreurs de Luther, de Muncer, de Calvin et Zuingle ne se fussent pas propagées avec autant de rapidité, et n'eussent pas allumé partout le feu de la guerre civile.'

62 For instance Robelot, *De l'influence de la réformation de Luther*, from 1822.

63 Villers, *Essai sur l'esprit et l'influence de la réformation*. The notes to the English translation from 1804, Villers, *An Essay on the Spirit and Influence of the Reformation*, were the first major work of James Mill. Another nearly identical translation, ascribed to B. Lambert, was published in London in 1805.

64 B—de, *Reflections on the Causes and Probable Consequences of the Late Revolution*, p. 29: 'The invention of printing has diffused knowledge more generally than it could possibly have been in earlier periods of the world. That information, of which mankind were then in possession, could by no means be so easily acquired by every individual as at present. The idea of representation, that happy expedient by which freedom is perpetuated in modern times, was not formerly understood. By this invention, a whole community may concur in framing the law by which it is governed, without being endangered by those tumults and commotions what are inseparable from large assemblies.' And p. 133: 'It was most undoubtedly owing to the invention of printing and the freedom of the press, that any alteration ever took place in the abuses, whether of government or religion. Establish this privilege, in its full extent, in the most despotic government in Europe, and it will soon produce the most decisive effects upon the condition of the people. The press is the grand engine by which the corruption of magistrates is restrained, and the encroachments of despotism controlled and overawed. Its liberty, therefore, is one of the greatest advantages which a nation can enjoy; it seems absolutely necessary to the diffusion of that knowledge upon which freedom depends. The effects of this privilege, among the ancients, must have been greatly limited, from their ignorance of the art of printing.'

65 Eaton, *The Pernicious Effects of the Art of Printing*, pp. 3, 8, and 9.

66 Holbach, *Théologie portative*, p. 136: 'Imprimerie. Invention diabolique et digne de l'Ante-Christ; elle devroit être proscrite de tout pays Chrétien. Les fidèles n'ont pas besoin de livres, un chapelet leur suffit. Pour bien faire on ne devrait imprimer que le bréviaire et le *Pédagogue chrétien*.' (Printing. Invention of the devil and worthy of Antichrist. It should be banned in all Christian countries. The faithful have no need for books, a rosary will do. It would be quite enough to print the Breviary and the *Christian Teacher*.) This is a reference to Outreman, *Le pédagogue chrétien*.

67 Lewis, *The Life of Mayster Wyllyam Caxton*, in the preface.

68 Paine, *The Age of Reason. Part the Second*, p. 74.

69 Cogan, *The Rhine*, II, letters 39–42, pp. 140–213, on the invention of printing.

70 'Imprimerie', in *Encyclopédie*, VIII, p. 609. The article, signed D. J., is by Jaucourt.

71 For a survey of the luxury debate in France and Britain see Hont, 'The early Enlightenment debate on commerce and luxury'.

2 Aristocratic aspirations and the wartime market

1 Douglas, *Diaries*, I, pp. 264–5, 23 October 1798. Bentley, 'The bookseller as diplomat', at p. 484, took 'the national library' to mean the British Museum, but this was how the Bibliothèque nationale was generally referred to; see e.g. *The Times*, 26 November 1793, in note 14 below. The British Museum had not by 1798 received any spoils of war.

2 The British Museum might be thought suitable for comparison with the Bibliothèque nationale, but it had limited funds, bought very few books, and hardly any material of this kind. See also Chapter 5, note 38.

3 Talleyrand, 'Rapport sur l'instruction publique', p. 141: 'Ce sont les ratures nombreuses d'un ouvrage qui ne doivent plus importuner les yeux quand l'ouvrage est fini.' And p. 143: 'Or c'est évidemment du sein des bibliothèques que doit sortir le moyen d'en accélérer la destruction.' See also Sacquin, 'Bibliothèque royale et utopie'.

4 Sénac de Meilhan, *L'émigré*, lettre LXXXVI: 'Le président de Longueil au marquis de Saint-Alban.' This attitude is consonant with Sénac de Meilhan's *Considérations sur les richesses et le luxe*.

5 See Hesse, 'Economic upheavals in publishing', p. 90.

6 Brunet, *Manuel du libraire*, 5th edn, I, p. xxvi.

7 Eaton, *Politics for the People*, pp. 126–30, in his spoof 'Catalogue raisonné', here p. 128.

8 Blechet, 'Le vandalisme à la Bibliothèque du roi/nationale sous la Révolution': decree of 4 August 1792 against papers which had heraldic and chivalric connections; the first burning of genealogical documents 19 June 1793, followed by papers relating to the clergy on 7 August. According to Blechet, p. 275, no binding in the BnF is known to have suffered.

9 *1789 Le patrimoine libéré*, 'Introduction', p. 17.

10 Renouard, *Observations de quelques patriotes*, pp. 11–12: 'Depuis trois années le féroce et astucieux Pitt, l'immonde Catherine, et tous les capitalistes de l'Europe, profitant de l'avantage prodigieux qu'ils trouvent sur les changes, travaillent sans relâche à nous priver de nos morceaux les plus précieux. Ils n'y ont déjà que trop réussi: de nombreux émissaires achètent ici tout ce qu'ils croient devoir plaire à leurs maîtres: et cette sourde guerre qu'ils font à la France littéraire, n'est pas moins active que celle qu'ils dirigent de la manière la plus atroce contre notre liberté … Combien le jaloux orgueil des Anglais seroit satisfait, seroit régalé, qu'on me passe ce mot, si une main ignorante et sacrilège portoit le désordre et la dégradation dans notre bibliothèque nationale, dans ce monument unique qu'ils ne peuvent contempler sans palpiter d'envie et de rage et qu'ils seroient charmés de voir détruire ou bouleverser.' Note: 'J'ai vu de mes propres yeux des Anglais sortir de la bibliothèque nationale furieux et désespérés; ils étoient comme accablés sous le poids des belles choses en tout genre qu'on s'étoit empressé de leur faire voir, et leur œil morne et farouche sembloit appeler la destruction sur cet admirable

monument.' This was followed by Renouard, *Au comité d'instruction publique*, 23 October 1793. Renouard described the undertaking in a note on his own copies of the publications (printed on vellum!); see Renouard, *Catalogue*, IV, pp. 199–200. His account is silent on the arguments deployed, probably so as not to remind post-Restoration readers of his radical past. On Russian acquisitions of French books see Somov, 'Les aristocrates russes acheteurs de livres en France pendant la Révolution', and Charon, 'Un amateur russe'.

11 Romme, 'Rapport au nom du comité d'instruction publique', here pp. 661–2: 'Pour honorer l'industrie française dans les pays étrangers, nos artistes caractérisaient leurs productions par la fleur de lys … C'est aussi la conduite des lâches oppresseurs du peuple anglais à notre égard; ils veulent devenir les tyrans de la France; les talents, l'industrie des Français, les richesses immenses et précieuses qui composent nos bibliothèques et nos collections de tout genre excitent leur convoitise et ils mettent en œuvre tous les moyens que l'astuce et l'hypocrisie peuvent leur suggérer pour poursuivre leurs desseins perfides; ce qu'ils ne peuvent enlever ils veulent le détruire, mais les Français veillent, ils veillent pour défendre leur liberté, leurs lois, leur territoire et tout ce qui peut, dans les arts, dans les terres et les sciences, assurer à la France, sur ses lâches ennemis, la supériorité qu'elle a toujours eue.' (Our craftsmen marked their products with the fleur-de-lys to give honour abroad to French industry … It is the conduct against us of the cowardly oppressors of the people of England: they seek to become the tyrants of France too; the skills, the industry of the French, the vast and valuable riches of our libraries and our collections of all materials incite their covetousness, and they use all means at the disposal of their cunning hypocrisy to meet their perfidious aim; what they cannot take away, they wish to destroy; but the French are vigilant, vigilant in the defence of their freedom, their laws, their territory, and all which can secure for France its eternal superiority over its cowardly enemies, in art, land, and science.)

12 Grégoire, *Rapport sur la bibliographie*, p. 11: 'La politique de nos ennemis fut toujours de nous enlever tout ce qu'ils pourroient, de détruire ce qu'ils ne pourroient enlever; en un mot, de commettre et de faire commettre des crimes pour avoir le plaisir de nous les imputer en nous traitant de barbares qui refusoient un asyle aux arts.'

13 Grégoire, *Rapport sur la bibliographie*, p. 2: 'Les objets scientifiques appartenans à la nation, proviennent des dépôts qu'elle possédait avant la révolution, des ci-devant châteaux du tyran, de la suppression des corporations ecclésiastiques, judiciaires, académies, des émigrés et des suppliciés … Des objets rares et précieux avoient été accumulé ou plutôt accaparés, pour servir l'ambition des familles ci-devant nobles.'

14 Reported by *The Times*, 26 November 1793: 'In the sitting [of the National Convention] of the 14th Chaumette denounced Madame Montausier for having erected the play house in the Rue de la loi for the sole purpose of setting fire to the National Library, for which she received a large sum of money from the

English, and 50,000 crowns from the ci-devant Queen. Hébert said that madame Montausier had offered him a box to keep him silent respecting this matter. It has in consequence been determined that she shall be arrested as a suspected person.'

15 Leniaud, 'Sur quelques délires parisiens', p. 252 describes conspiracy theories about counter-revolutionary plots as Leninist *ante litteram*. For another deployment of this conspiracy theory see Gentil-Brasseur, 'Le livre saisi en Picardie', p. 50 note 3. From the opposite position, the entire Revolution was explained as a conspiracy by Barruel, *Mémoires pour servir à l'histoire du Jacobinisme*.

16 On monarchical attempts to control the history of France, see Baker, 'Controlling French history'.

17 Romme, 'Rapport au nom du comité d'instruction publique', at p. 663: 'Une grande lutte est ouverte entre les peuples et les rois. Nos bibliothèques fourmillent de traits qui attestent leur scélératesse. L'histoire qui flatte le plus leur orgueil n'en est pas moins l'histoire de leurs crimes.'

18 Charlemagne, *Section de Brutus, ci-devant de Molière*. 'Brutus' was the district between rue Poissonnière, boulevard Poissonnière, rue Montmartre, roughly rue Léopold Bellan, and rue des Petits Carreaux.

19 Chardin, *Section de Brutus. Discours prononcé*, 28 February 1794.

20 He was arrested at some point after 9 thermidor, freed 3 December 1794, arrested again 25 May 1795, and freed without acquittal 10 June 1795.

21 See Pommier, 'Discours iconoclaste'. On the new public museums, see the works of Dominique Poulot, for instance, *Surveiller et s'instruire*. Bianchi, 'Le "Vandalisme révolutionnaire"' reformulates the dichotomy between iconoclasm and the cultural programme of the Revolution, seeing 'vandalism' as a term used by the post-thermidor regime and therefore not an appropriate analytical term, but in itself part of the phenomenon which requires analysis. This distinction is especially relevant for understanding why a group of Jacobins promoted the protection of historical monuments.

22 Rabaut, *Rapport … sur l'établissement d'un Muséum national d'antiques*, p. 3: 'pour le perfectionnement de ses manufactures et l'accroissement de ses revenus.'

23 See Chapter 5.

24 Camus, *Rapport … sur l'édition de Virgile*.

25 See Crisman-Campbell, 'L'Angleterre et la mode en Europe au XVIIIe siècle', p. 51.

26 Morris, *Diary*, I, p. 31.

27 The market was international. Debure bought extensively at the sale of Anthony Askew's rare books (1775) (*Bibliotheca askeviana … librorum rarissimorum*), not least incunabula for the duc de La Vallière, at whose sale in 1783 especially Payne and Elmsley were very active, although they bought no incunabula, an interest which had not yet reached the English market. I am grateful to Dominique Coq who showed me his database of the de La Vallière sale.

28 See Connell, *Portrait of a Whig Peer*; the visit in 1791 at pp. 215–47; for 1792 at pp. 262–6.

29 BL, Add. MS 76067, 5 April 1792: 'I have drawn upon your Lordship for £75.1 for the books bought at Mirabeau's Sale. I am afraid that the exchange will never be again so low as 15.' Also 12 April 1792 (date of Parisian post stamp): 'I have drawn a second Bill on your Lordship which amounts to £144.5 for which I rec'd of Mr Perregaux five thousand five hundred and fifty Livres, which is pretty near the sum bought for at Loménie's. Most people think it very doubtful if ever the exchange is lower.' BL, Add. MS 76068, 9 November 1792: 'The exchange rate has risen to 19 ½ which including commission makes it 20.' According to James Payne's figures, in April the rate was 1 franc to 0.634s rather than the standard 1 to 0.8s.

30 Laire, *Index librorum*.

31 Envoy of the Holy Roman Empire to the Court of St James from 16 June 1786 to 10 November 1790; see *General Evening Post*, 17 June 1786 and *White Hall Evening Post*, 13 November 1790. He remained in London for some time after; see *St James's Chronicle*, 10 February 1791. His first letter to Spencer from Vienna is dated 23 July 1791. BL, Add. MS 76016. Here Vienna, 17 March 1792. Della Lena, a former bookseller in Venice, was rector of the Theresianum in Vienna, but continued to trade; his extensive correspondence with Spencer is BL, Add. MS 76007.

32 The Bibliothèque nationale spent 39,615 livres 6 sous [some £1,585] on 557 incunabula, its largest single acquisition, another indication of their new cultural importance for the national institution.

33 See Charon, 'Un amateur russe', p. 219, note 20 with a reference to Spencer's letter of acknowledgement dated 15 December 1791, now in the archives of the Bibliothèque municipale of Besançon.

34 See the annotated copies of Laire, *Index librorum*, pp. 5–11, no. 6, BnF, Us. Réserve Collect.I/Lom; and BL, G.379, bought in by Debure at 2,499.19 francs, that is £100, using the standard rate of 24 francs to the pound; and Bod-inc B-237(1) for the price paid in pounds for Arch. B b.10,11.

35 Douglas, *Diaries*, I, pp. 264–5, entry for 23 October 1798.

36 Maugérard, *Notice de livres rares*, lot 4. 'Aelii Donati opusculum de octo partis orationis. Grand in 4°. Marginal note in BnF Q8240: '520 mylord Spencer acheté par Payne'; that is £20 16s according to the normal exchange rate, or £16 9s, according to the rate used by James Payne in April 1792.

37 Edwards, *Bibliotheca parisiana* and *Bibliotheca elegantissima parisina*. Reviczky had heard from Edwards that the owner was a 'M. Paris de Monmartel', who had outbid Reviczky several times at sale of the duc de La Vallière. For M. Paris, see Rau, 'Bibliotheca Parisina', and the note in the provenance index of Bod-inc, but his identity remains uncertain and, in any case, the sale included items from several French sources. BL, Add. MS 76016, letter from Reviczky to Spencer, 31 July 1790: 'Edwards vient d'arriver de Paris … Il a négocié la vente des livres

choisis de M. Paris de Monmartel, qui arriveront bientôt ici, et donc le catalogue s'imprime actuellement à Paris. La vente se fera sur le compte du propriétaire. Ce Paris de Monmartel est précisément celui qui m'a emporté plusieurs articles à la vente du duc de La Vallière.' On the duc de La Vallière see especially Coq, 'Le parangon' and La Vallière, *Catalogue des livres*.

38 According to Douglas, *Diaries*, I, pp. 264–5, entry for 23 October 1801.

39 He had £600 a year in landed property and £100,000 in the three-percents. See Cracherode, 'Obituary' at p. 354, col. 2.

40 Edwards, *Bibliotheca parisiana*, lot 167, now BL, IA.39009. Le Camus de Limare, *Catalogue de livres rares*, lot 1151, for livres 750, that is about £30. Davis, 'Portrait of a bibliophile', at p. 495 confused the lot number with the price.

41 Bodleian, MS Douce d.20, item 39, 1 January 1791.

42 Renouard, *Catalogue*, IV, pp. 269–70. In fact Renouard's relations with Spencer were relatively close. He had been in touch with Spencer already before May 1813, in an undated letter asking him to ensure free passage on landing in Dartmond[!], although there was no passport when he arrived at Dartmouth 6 May. See his undated letter and that of 6 May 1813 in BL, Add. MS 76014.

43 Reviczky may have been known to Spencer through William Jones, his tutor, who had been in contact with Reviczky, a fellow orientalist, since 1768. See Jones, *The Works*, I, p. 76.

44 BL, Add. MS 76016. The first letter from Reviczky to Spencer, 25 June 1789, set out the conditions. Add. MS 76066, contains letters from Spencer's solicitor, J. A. Garth, 18 July 1789, 22 July 1789, and 26 August 1789 on how to get round the ban on foreigners receiving rent from land. The issue is discussed by Reviczky, Add. MS 76016, 15 July 1789, and 11 August 1789. Implementation is confirmed by Add. MS 76299, fol. 181, a receipt, 2 October 1789, for £150 for one quarter, signed 'Count Reviczky'. Lister, 'The formation of the Althorp Library', states that the collection was bought in 1790 for a down payment of £1,000 and an annuity of £600, paid quarterly; this may derive from BL, Add. MS 78010, p. 3, a list of books at Althorp from 1875 where a down payment of £1,000 is reported as hearsay.

45 Reviczky died aged 56 years old. Assuming that the collection was valued at £10,000 Spencer would have paid over the odds if Reviczky had lived until he was 74.

46 I am grateful to Anthony Hobson for suggesting that Spencer's wealth should be contextualised by his debt. See Wasson, *Whig Renaissance*, p. 16 for Spencer's annual income and expenditure and *ODNB* for Spencer's debt at his death.

47 Spencer, *The Spencer Family*, pp. 170–1.

48 See BL, Add. MS 76082, letter from Cracherode sent posthumously, received 6 April 1799, containing a cancelled debtor's note from Spencer, 22 October 1798.

49 *Elgin Marbles*, p. 95. The statue is now in the Getty Museum where the eighteenth-century restoration was removed in the 1970s, only to be reinstated

in the 1990s. J. Podany, 'Restoring what wasn't there' and Shtrum, 'LACMA's classical sculpture collection reconsidered', at p. 198.

50 According to Richard Payne Knight's statement in *Elgin Marbles*, at pp. 94–9, here p. 99: 'You valued Lord Lansdowne's Marbles? – Yes –. What value did you put on the Hercules? – £1000; it cost Lord Lansdowne £600 at Rome.' On this statue and its restoration under Townley's supervision, see Howard, 'Some eighteenth-century restorations', at pp. 333–4.

51 Robbins, 'Morice, Humphry'.

52 Bodleian, Auct. N 5.6.

53 Bodleian, Auct. L 2.2. Edwards, *Bibliotheca pinelliana*, lot 11215. By contrast a manuscript of the same text contemporary with the printed book was sold also at the Pinelli sale, lot 12849, for £5 5s; now BL, Burney MS 176.

54 Michaelis, *Ancient Marbles in Great Britain*, p. 613 no. 52 and Raeder, *Die antiken Skulpturen in Petworth House*, no. 24, pp. 93–7 and Plate 40, 1.

55 BL, Add. MS 76299, fol. 418: A bill 'Frankfort a/M a 16 October 1794' from Hans Max and Hans Peter Gagel. He bought 3 'aumes' [1 Frankfurt Ohm = 143.419 litres] of 1726 Hochheim at £55 per Ohm and 2 Ohm Johannisberg 1783 at £36 per Ohm, paying £6 for the unusual shipping route via Hamburg, in all £244. Grenville bought 1 Ohm Hochheim 1726 and 1 Ohm Johannisberg 1783, paying £2 16s extra for the emergency transport route, in all £93 16s.

56 Henderson, *History of Ancient and Modern Wines*, pp. 92–130, on appreciation of Rhenish wine; p. 221 for his assessment that 1726, 1748, 1766, 1779, and 1783 were the five best years of the eighteenth century, the 1783 Johannisberger being the most superior.

57 Bodleian, Auct. L 1.8, 9.

58 While a luxury item, it was not top of the range. Prices charged by Lépine for supplying clocks to the court of Versailles between 1767 and 1777 ranged from 650 francs (£26) to 20,000 francs (£800), the majority being just above 2,000 francs (£80); see Chapiro, *Jean-Antoine Lépine*, pp. 223–5.

59 Reviczky, *Bibliotheca graeca et latina*. The title page says: 'exceptis tantum asceticis et theologicis Patrum nuncupatorum scriptis' (excluding only ascetic and theological works of those who are called Fathers).

60 Bodleian, Auct. 4Q 1.7,8. See Laire, *Index librorum*, p. 343 [*recte* 243] no. 19. The book fetched 120 francs at the sale. The price paid by the Bodleian, £3, corresponds to an exchange rate of 1 franc to 0.5s, while the normal rate of 0.8s was used to convert the price for the Gutenberg Bible bought at the same sale.

61 Bodleian, Auct. 7Q inf. 2.8. Edwards, *Bibliotheca pinelliana*, lot 5547, bought for £4 6s. It contains 140 leaves = 0.6s per leaf. Bodleian, Auct. L 2.2. *Bibliotheca pinelliana*, lot 11215, for £58 16s. It contains 162 leaves = 7.26s per leaf. This was not a one-off irregularity in the marketplace: many more examples can be identified in Bod-inc.

62 On the relative status associated with these bindings see Jensen, 'Heinrich Walther'.

63 The prices are from copies bought by Thott; see Bentzen, 'Lord Harley og Grev Thott', p. 323, referring to Copenhagen, Royal Library, Inc. 1315; and p. 294, referring to Copenhagen, Royal Library, Inc. 1314. Compare Bodleian, Auct. L 3.9 and Bodleian, Auct. 7Q 2.17.

64 To give but a few examples from BL, Add. MS 76299, fol. 47: Notes from 'Inspruck publick library' on an edition of Cicero's *De officiis*; fol. 122: 'in biblioteca S. Marci de Florentia', all classical texts; fol. 126: 'Nota de alcune prime edizioni dei classici latini che mancano alla Magliabechiana'; fols 143–4: 'Editiones principes extantes apud equitem d'Elci Mediolanensis' [all editions of the classics]; fol. 145: 'Note des livres qui manquent dans la superbe bibliothèque de son excellence Milord Spencer'; all classics except for 'Psalt. Graece. Char rubris et […] 4o Ven. 1486'.

65 BL, Add. MS 76299, fol. 189, a bill from B. White and son, 9 May 1789, which includes incunabula, the most expensive being 'Valerius Maximus editio princeps 1471 £26.5.0'. BL, Add. MS 76299, fol. 190, a bill from J[ames?] Payne settled 16 May 1789, including 'Typographical antiquities' bought 24 April for £4.

66 BL, Add. MS 76299, fol. 210, bill from Thomas Payne (1719–99), receipted 29 March 1790. Fol. 214, bill from James Edwards, receipted 30 March 1790: 'Schellhorn Amoenitates £1 7s; Meerman Origines typogr. £1 1s.'; 'Schoeffelini Vind. Typogr. 7s. 6d.'; 'Fry's Specimens of types 10s. 6d.'; 'Fournier, Origines de l'imprimerie 12s.'.

67 Fol. 253, a bill from Elmsley, receipted 18 January 1791 including, 'Debure 7 vol. 4° L[arge]. P[aper]. mor[occo] [and] Gaignat 2 vol. 4°. L. P. mor. £9.9.0' and 'Catalogue de La Vallière 6 vol. 8°. L. P. £2.2s.'.

68 Thus BL, Add. MS 76299, fol. 388, a bill from Trattner, receipted Vienna, 22 August 1794, including 'Panzer Annales Typographici, 2 tomi, 15 [fl]'; 'Murr Memorabilia Bibliothecae Norinbergae 3 Tom 7.30'; 'Braun Notitia 6 Tom. 11. 45'; 'Denis Buchdrucker Geschichte 6.0; – Suffragia 0.15; – Buecherkunde 2.Hft 6.30'; 'Zapf Annales Typographici 1.1 – Bibliotheca 0.38; – Augsburg Buchdrucker Geschichte 6.0; – Buchdruckergeschichte von Schwaben 1.30; – ditto Mainz 1.15'. On Trattner, the ennobled Viennese bookseller, see Lehmstedt, '"Ein Strohm der alles überschwemmet"'. A bill from Aloys Blumauer, 10 September 1794, including 'De origine typographiae lipsiensis 4to. 3'; 'Seemüller Incunabula typographia 4 fasciculi 4to. 5.15'; 'Braun Notitia historico litteraria 4 voll in 5 p. 4to 9.3'.

69 Bodleian, MS Douce d.20, letter to Francis Douce from James Edwards, Vienna, 15 August 1796: 'There would be indeed useful people if they had the same advantages in Germany that are to be found in our Metropolis, but as that is by no means the case their works are rather a mass than a whole – If you can read German I shall shew you a work of Mr Breitkopff (a bookseller of Leipcic) upon the origin of playing cards, paper and engraving in wood. Heineken speaks frequently of this bookseller and I had promised myself a high gratification in his acquaintance – unfortunately he died about 2 years ago.'

70 Already in 1789 he had bought, apparently with little enthusiasm, a few incunabula of relevance for biblical studies, from Herman Treschow, vicar in Copenhagen and biblical scholar. BL, Add. MS 76066, letters from Treschow, 24 November 1789 and 6 April 1790. Treschow presented himself as a scholar, using it as an excuse for presenting an inappropriate financial instrument for settling the bill. In fact he was regularly involved with dealing; see Ilsøe, *Biblioteker til salg*, p. 218 and Birkelund, 'Det Thottske bibliotek', p. 91.

71 BL, Add. MS 76300, fol. 491: 'Bought of [Thomas] Payne from 23 July 1796 to 27 March 1797', including '17 December 1796, Albertus Magnus printed by Mechelin £10.10.0'. Albertus Magnus, *Liber aggregationis*. London: de Machlinia, [about 1483]. See Dibdin, *Bibliotheca spenceriana*, IV, pp. 392–3.

72 Dibdin, *Bibliotheca spenceriana*, IV, p. 373, the Mason sale in 1799, lot 155.

73 See Renouard, *Catalogue*, III, pp. 126–7.

74 A note by Spencer on a letter from Horn, 13 February 1806, stating that he was prepared to spend £60.

75 BnF, A.m., boite 270, draft note from Capperonnier to the commissaire, 17 brumaire An IX [8 November 1800]: 'Mais il y a un entre autres articles qu'elle contient un capital que je recommande tout particulièrement à vos recherches. C'est l'ouvrage du cardinal Torquemade (1467) qui existe dans la Bibliothèque publique de Nuremberg et s'il était possible de le procurer qu'en offrant pour 2000 francs de livres de échange au [choix?] du possesseur ou une bible de Mayence de 1462 sur vélin 2 vol infolio, ne hésitez point de conclure le marché.' (But among the items which it possesses, there is one chief one which I especially entrust to your searches. That is the work of Cardinal Torquemada from 1467, in the public library of Nuremberg. If it were only possible to acquire it by offering books in exchange to the value of £80 or a Mainz 1462 Bible on vellum, do not hesitate to strike a deal.) This willingness to pay antedates Neveu's Nuremberg confiscations, 6 March 1801; see a list of twelve incunabula reproduced in Savoy, *Patrimoine annexé*, II, pp. 339–40.

76 BL, Add. MS 75964, letters of 1 June 1798 and 30 August 1800, referring to Chappe, *Indulgentia*. [Mainz: Printer of 31-line indulgence and 36-line Bible, 1454–5]. This copy, with the manuscript date of its sale 13 April 1455, is now in the Pierpont Morgan Library. BL, Add. MS 75964, letters 6 September, 20 September, and 2 October 1800 refer to the sale of an indulgence with the printed date of 1454, presumably JRL, 17250.1. BL, Add. MS 75964, 9 January 1801: 'I take the liberty of mentioning on this occasion that I have purchased a beautiful copy of the litterae indulgentiarum of the same date as that of your Lordship but in better condition and with the original seal hanging to it. As this circumstance adds to the authenticity I mention it herewith first to your lordship, though I do not believe that this will be of much importance as to make it appear in your eyes 20£ more worth than the other.' BL, Add. MS 75964, letter from Alexander Horn, 22 October 1801: 'I am happy to learn by your Lordship's last kind letter that you have thought proper to take the second

Litterae indulgentiarum for which according to your direction I sent a draft for 60£ to Sir. Bt Herries. By this your Lordship becomes the sole possessor of the only known copies and the value of your inestimable collection is greatly enhanced.'

77 Basing his work on papers then still owned by the family, Buzy, *Dom Maugérard*, defensive of Maugérard, omits information on his trade in books. I have been unable to locate the family papers. Although dealing mainly with manuscripts sold to the library in Gotha, Traube's *Jean-Baptiste Maugérard* was received in an atmosphere of Franco-German hostility. A depressing correspondence between Traube and Delisle is in BnF, A.m., boite 271. The best overview of the activities of Maugérard is Savoy, *Patrimoine annexé*, I, pp. 89–113.

78 Based on a letter from Meerman of 1770 this was said by Jacobs, 'Zur Kentniss Maugérards', pp. 159–60 to be the copy later belonging to Grenville. Certain physical features make this unlikely.

79 Vernus, *Une vie dans l'univers du livre*, pp. 80–4.

80 Maugérard, *Notice de livres rares*.

81 On the non-book items which he exported, see Bardiès-Fronty and Wagner, 'Retour à Metz', pp. 110–12.

82 For his appointment see BnF, A.m., boite 271, letter, 27 thermidor An X [15 August 1802]. Letter to the Minister of the interior (Chaptal) signed by Capperonnier. BL, Add. MS 76014, an undated letter to Spencer, received 15 October 1800, the preceding letter being dated '2 Aout 1800' from Erfurt: 'Les affaires ecclésiastiques de France étant pacifiés je pense y retourner (à Metz) après que j'aurais reçu la caisse que j'attends de la complaisance de Mr Edwards; je serais fort aisé Mgr si la je pouvais vous servir en quelque chose. Je ne perdrai pas de vue les petits Zel que votre excellence m'a demandé.' (French ecclesiastical matters having settled, I plan to return to Metz, when I receive the box which I expect at the convenience of Mr Edwards; I would be very pleased if I could assist your Lordship in any way. I will not lose sight of the little Zell editions which your Excellency has asked for.) On this phase of Maugérard's life see Savoy, 'Codicoloque, incunabuliste et rabatteur', and her account in Savoy, *Patrimoine annexé*, pp. 89–113.

83 BL, Add. MS 76014, Maugérard, Erfurt, 12 January 1797.

84 BL, Add. MS 76014, Maugérard, Erfurt, 2 May 1797.

85 JRL, 9375. BL, Add. MS 76014, Maugérard, Erfurt, 8 August 1797 and the invoice included with a box of books sent to 'Mr Fraser, chargé d'affaire de sa majesté britannique à Hambourg', 7 August 1797. The assumption that Horn sold this to Spencer was first made by Schottenloher, 'Beiträge zur Geschiche der Inkunabelkunde in Franken', p. 68.

86 Steiner, 'Eine ganz neue Entdeckung' and Langer, 'Noch etwas die älteste Buchdrukergeschichte von Bamberg betreffend'.

87 Maugérard was critical of Panzer. British Library, Althorp Papers, Add. MS 76014, letter dated 8 August 1797, Erfurt: 'Depuis longtemps je suis en relation

avec Panzer ministre Luthérien à Nuremberg. L'année dernière je l'ai connu plus particulièrement, car pendant deux mois j'ai passés tous les jours deux heures avec lui. C'est un homme très aimable, mais je n'ai trouvé en lui que des connoissances très ordinaires de nos premiers imprimeurs. Le fond que son ouvrage ajoute à ce que Mettaire avoit fait, n'est tiré que de quelques catalogues bien ou mal fait qu'il copie. Lorsque j'ai voulu savoir de lui par la pourquoi il attribuoit tel ou tel livre à Eggestein ou à Mentelin, par exemple cette bible et autres éditions telle que le Sénèque … il n'a pu que me citer l'autorité de vieux catalogues.' (I have long been in touch with Panzer … Last year I got to know him better, because for two months I spent two hours a day with him. He is a very worthy man, but I have found him to have a middling knowledge of the early printers. What he adds to Maittaire is all drawn from catalogues, which he copies, good or bad. When I have sought to know why he attributes a book to Eggestein or Mentelin … he can but quote the authority of old catalogues.)

88 BL, Add. MS 76014, Maugérard, 8 August 1797: 'Nous n'avons pas encore une bonne bibliographie car Panzer a copié les fautes des autres comme je le lui ai dit (mais il travaille pour nourrir sa famille) et votre excellence est, je crois, la seule personne, qui à un zèle plein de lumière joigne les facultés pécuniaires pour faire cette dépense, et dans l'impression de son catalogue, avec des planches gravés des quelques lignes de tous les imprimeurs [in the margin: 'pour faire connaitre leurs types'], éclairer l'âge présent et à venir sur l'art de l'imprimerie et les imprimeurs que nous ne connoissons pas encore. Je sais que les gravures de ce catalogue couteroient et occasionneroient des avances, mais il est très certain que cette bibliographie, qui ne pourroit être contrefaite, rendroit très promptement beaucoup d'argent, et que le monde lettré en rendroit à votre Excellence les mêmes autours de grâces qu'il rendra toujours à Mabillon et Montfaucon pour l'écriture des différents âges. La Duchesse de Chatillon a payé les frais du catalogue du Duc de La Vallière, son père, et après la rentrée des frais, il s'est trouvés 18000 livres de bénéfice qu'elle a abandonné à De Bure, outre son salaire. Pardonnez-moi Monseigneur cette réflexion, mais il me semble qu'il soit glorieux à un grand seigneur de faire ce riche présents au public.'

89 'Si j'avois le tems j'aurais aimé à vous faire quelques questions pour m'éclairer sur deux ou trois points de votre lettre, mais je me bornerais à présent à vous remercier des renseignements qu'elle contient me proposant d'écrire par une autre occasion plus en détail sur ces sujets.' Dated 'à l'Amirauté à Londres 25 Aout 1797'.

90 Spencer was informed of the victory on 12 October; see *General Evening Post*, 12 October 1797.

91 BL, Add. MS 76014, copy of a letter from Spencer to Maugérard, 17 October 1797. 'Je crois vous avoir déjà dit que la raison pourquoi je n'ai pas pris votre exemplaire de la bible Allemande dite de 1462 est que je la possède déjà. J'observe que M. Braun dans son livre intitulé "Notitia librorum ante anno 1489 impressorum in bibliotheca monasterii SS Ulrici et Afrae" attribua cette Bible à Eggestein; elle est effectivement dans un différent caractère de celui ou de Fust

ou de Mentelin; je serais charmé d'apprendre pour quelle raison vous croyez qu'elle est indubitablement de ce dernier? ... Je n'ai pas le loisir à présent de poursuivre plus loin le sujet de cette lettre, mais j'espère tantôt de pouvoir vous écrire un peu plus au long et je serai charmé de profiter de vos connaissances pour corriger et ajouter aux observations que la comparaison de nos livres vis à vis l'un de l'autre et dés différens auteurs qui ont écrit sur ce sujet me mettent quelques fois à partir de faire.' (I think I already told you that I did not buy your copy of the German Bible from 1462 because I already have it. I note that in his book *Notitia librorum ante anno 1489 impressorum* Braun assigned this bible to Eggestein. It is in fact in a type different from his, Fust's and Mentelin's. I would be delighted to learn why you believe that it is certainly by the last named? ... I do not now have the time to pursue the topic of this letter, but I hope soon to be able to write to you at greater length and would be delighted to benefit from your expertise to correct and add to the observations which the comparison of our books and those of various authors who have written this matter, some times prompt me to make.) Maugérard's answer does not survive. See note 68 above for Spencer's acquisition of Braun, *Notitia historico-litteraria*.

92 Rive, *Chasse*, took a dim view of aristocrats who laid claim to knowledge. See Chapter 4, p. 114. Spencer owned a copy of Rive's book, JRL, 17038, and would undoubtedly have known this view of aristocratic pretensions.

93 BL, Add. MS 76014, 12 October 1797. Also BL, Add. MS 76014, letter received 15 October 1800, referred to in note 82 above.

94 Letters of 6 November and 8 December 1798.

95 Sotheby, *Catalogue of a Valuable Collection of Books Printed in the Fifteenth Century*, sold 15 June 1799. The catalogue provides detailed identification of printers by their typefaces, by now frequent in France; Anthony Hobson has suggested that Edwards was the only bookseller in London capable of this.

96 BL, Add. MS 76014, Erfurt, 3 November 1799: 'Outre mes démarches pour vous procurer des raretés dont j'ai eu l'honneur de vous parler dans ma dernière, j'avois deux amis intelligens l'un à Trèves l'autre à Augsbourg qui s'étoient chargés de ces recherches; mais celui d'Augsbourg vient de m'écrire qu'il lui est impossible de rien trouver parce que la crainte de la guerre a fait tout cacher et emporter; l'autre de Trèves m'a écrit qu'il avoit trouvé plusieures choses, puis en termes énigmatiques il me dit qu'il lui est impossible de s'exposer à me rien envoyer ni à rien faire pour moi dans le temps présent parce qu'ils sont tellement sous le joug de la terreur qu'il seroit bientôt déclaré "suspect et déporté". Un autre m'avoit envoyé une bonne caisse de ces objets qu'il m'a écrit être arrivée à Coblenz pour y attendre leur moment de pouvoir passer le Rhin; mais ayant été déclaré suspect pour cet envoi, il n'a eu que le temps de se sauver pour ne pas être envoyé à la Guiane; je ne sais ou il est. Malheureusement je ne sais chez qui est cette caisse que j'ai payée. J'ai tout bien de croire qu'elle est saisie au passage du Rhin.'

97 Bodleian, MS Douce c.8, fol. 1, draft letter, 3 May 1786, to a recipient, who must be Daniel Schmidt in Basel. MS Douce d.20, item 9, a letter from Schmidt,

18 May 1786 suggesting various complex ways of transferring books and money. MS Douce c.8, fol. 2, a draft letter to Schmidt, 25 June 1788, where Douce finally found a way, and enclosed a note for 2 louis and 6 livres for postage.

98 See Blanning, *French Revolution in Germany*, especially pp. 141–8, on the effect of the trade barrier down the Rhine.

99 For a failed attempt by Spencer to use Thomas Jenkins, the art dealer established in Rome, see BL, Add. MS 76068, letter from Jenkins, 14 May 1793. Jenkins was evidently unfamiliar with books. Where he failed in extracting specific books from Santa Maria del Popolo, d'Elci later succeeded.

100 Bodleian, MS Douce d.20. In accordance with the armistice of Bologna, 23 June 1796, French commissioners were sent to Rome to select items for Paris, including 500 manuscripts. See Müntz, 'Les annexions de collections d'art ou de bibliothèques', 1896 instalment, p. 484.

101 BL, Add. MS 76077, Turin, 22 February 1797.

102 Beloe, *The Sexagenarian*, II, pp. 278–9 on the 'exotic bookseller'.

103 *The Times*, 7 April 1807: 'Among the other treasures which have been purloined from Italy since its revolutionary degradation, may be mentioned the Chinese manuscripts, which formed a very curious article in the Library of the Vatican. They have found their way into this country, and are now upon sale; but although they are in a certain degree, objects of curiosity, they will not, we should imagine from the universal ignorance of their language among us, become objects of research.'

104 See Michaelis, *Ancient Marbles in Great Britain*, p. 334. The extent of British trade in spoliated cultural commodities in this period has never been systematically examined.

105 This journey to Paris is set out in Bentley, 'The bookseller as diplomat'. Edwards's Livorno connection was presumably Giuseppe Molini; see Pasta, 'Tra Firenze, Napoli e l'Europa'.

106 Historical Manuscripts Commission, *Report on the Manuscripts of J. B. Fortescue*, VI, pp. 289–93.

107 Bodleian, MS Douce d.20, letter from Edwards, Vienna, 5 August 1796.

108 BnF, MS Fr. Nouv. acq. 3230, contains several letters from James Payne to Van Praet.

109 The meeting with Maugérard is described by James Payne in a letter to Van Praet, Vienna, 28 September 1800, in error for 1802. BnF, MS Fr. Nouv. acq. 3230, fol. 200.

110 MS Fr. Nouv. acq. 3230, fol. 200, Vienna, 28 September 1800 [in error for 1802]: 'I had some dealings with your friend Maugérard. I found him very dear but thanks for your advice as I made him reduce his prices – I was much pleas'd with Mr Ortolani; he is an accomplished gentleman.' Ortolani had been appointed to assist Van Praet, and possibly to keep an eye on him. See BnF, A.m., boite 271, leaf 758, a letter from Capperonnier, 27 thermidor An X [27 August 1802] to the Minister of the interior (Chaptal).

111 MS Fr. Nouv. acq. 3230, fols 152–3, letter from Maugérard, Metz, 18 fructidor An X (5 September 1802): 'Ce jour dernier est arrive M. Ortolani avec le très aimable Mr Payne qui nous a quitté tout a coup vendredi soir après avoir fait lui même le prix de plusieurs de mes vieux livres qui lui ont plu. C'était assez qu'il fut votre ami pour que les prix me plussent.'

112 Specifically he requested a copy of 'St Augustin de arte predicandi by Mentel'; probably the edition from [Strasbourg]: Mentelin, [not after 1466], another book much coveted in this period. Cracherode acquired his copy in 1797, now BL, IB.510; on the special reasons for this interest in Mentelin see Chapter 3.

113 MS Fr. Nouv. acq. 3230, fols 152–3, letter from Maugérard, Metz, 18 fructidor An X (5 September 1802): 'Comme Mr Payne m'a dit que vous avez plusieurs livres in duplo tant anciens que modernes, vous me donnerez des uns ou des autres ce que vous estimerez juste, ou de l'argent.'

114 BnF, A.m., boite 271, letter 8 from Capperonnier to Maugérard, 8 ventôse An XI [27 February 1803], fols 70–3, at fol. 71: 'Nous vous exhortons à l'avenir, lorsque vous rencontrerez quelques ouvrages précieuse à vendre, de nous en donner avis et de nous en marquer le prix avant d'entrer en marché.' (In future when you find precious works for sale, we encourage you to inform us, indicating the price, before beginning to trade.) Also a letter from Capperonnier to Maugérard, 18 vendémiaire An XII [11 October 1803]. BnF, A.m., boite 271, fols 84–8 at fol. 85, where Capperonnier's exasperation is evident: 'Nous voilà donc vos débiteurs d'une somme de 1863 francs pour les divers articles relatés dans votre première lettre du 23 fructidor.' (So here we then find ourselves owing you the sum of 1863 francs for various items mentioned in your letter of 10 September.)

115 MS Fr. Nouv. acq. 3230, fols 50–1, letter to Van Praet from Fischer, Mainz, 22 ventôse An X [13 March 1802]: 'Est ce que Mr Payne n'est plus à Paris? Je lui ai envoyé des livres qu'il avait demandé. Et je suis dans l'embarras de ne point savoir s'il les a reçu.' (Is Mr Payne no longer in Paris? I have sent him some books which he ordered, and I am in the awkward position of not knowing if he has received them.)

116 MS Fr. Nouv. acq. 3230, fol. 204, from James Payne to Van Praet, Florence, 8 April 1803: 'My dear Sir, I received your kind letter of December on my arrival here a few days since. I assure you Lord Spencer is highly delighted with the idea of possessing a copy of the Gr. Rithmica 1468.' Now JRL, 15.

117 MS Fr. Nouv. acq. 3230, fol.141, from William Henry Lyttleton, Althorp, 30 December 1817. Van Praet had offered Spencer a vellum copy of Aldus Manutius's Aristotle, in exchange for Pliny, Rome, 1470, on vellum. On fols 142–3 a draft of Van Praet's reply, 13 January 1818: 'Ce fut en 1803 que eut lieu par l'intermédiaire de feu M. Payne, la proposition de l'échange, dont vous me faites l'honneur de me parler … A cette époque nous pouvions prendre sur nous de faire un tel arrangement, mais aujourd'hui il ne nous est plus possible.'

118 On Payne's imprisonment and treatment see Lawrence's account from 1810, *A Picture of Verdun*, pp. 221–6; Renouard, *Catalogue*, IV, p. 92: 'Le moribond se soulève et dit: "Quand on veut un César de 1469, on ne dîne pas." Et il mourut deux heures après.'

119 Horn also supplied directly to George III. Letters from Horn are pasted into several items in George III's collection. Only one is dated, 18 March 1815; perhaps he turned to George III especially after his relationship with Spencer diminished; see BL, C.1.a.25, C.1.a.26, C.1.a.27, C.9.a.13, C.8.a.4 (dated), and C.11.a.9.

120 Mulot was former librarian of St Victor. His activities in Mainz are documented by public speeches on the inauguration of French administrative structures, for instance Mulot, *Discours prononcé à Mayence*, of 19 February 1798, or on key revolutionary events, such as Mulot, *Discours sur le serment de haine à la royauté* of 21 January 1799. His role as assistant to Rudler is mentioned by Blanning, *The French Revolution in Germany*, p. 275.

121 BnF, A.m., boite 270, draft of a letter, 4 floréal An IX [24 April 1801] to the Minister of the interior (Chaptal), with references to two letters from Mulot, 8 pluviôse and 21 ventôse year 6 [27 January 1798 and 11 March 1798] which stated that the 1457 Psalter had been confiscated and was on its way to the Bibliothèque nationale: 'Cependant désirant que ces richesses littéraires trop long temps restées en dépôt à Mayence parviennent enfin à leur destination nous nous adressons à vous, citoyen ministre, et nous vous prions de vouloir bien écrire au commissaire général des départements du Rhin pour avoir à cet égard les renseignements les plus précis.' (However, desiring that these literary treasures, which have for too long remained in the depot at Mainz finally reach their destination, we write to you, citizen minister, asking you to write to the Commissioner General of the Departments of the Rhine to obtain the most precise information on this matter.)

122 The copy said to have belonged to the Elector is still not located, and may have been confused with a copy which seems to have been in the church of St Jakob in Mainz until 1802, finally acquired by the Bibliothèque impériale in 1813. For the nineteenth-century view see Schaab, *Die Geschichte der Erfindung der Buchdruckerkunst*, I, pp. 345–8; also de Ricci, *Catalogue raisonné*, p. 53, nos 54.5 and 54.8.

123 Rudler was in charge of the French reorganisation of the republic on the west bank of the Rhine from 1797; see Rowe, *From Reich to State*, p. 59.

124 Bibliothèque nationale de France, MS. Fr. Nouv. Acq. 3230, fol. 38: 'Quoique nous ne pouvons que vous assurer, que le dépôt dont vous parlez dans votre lettre au Citoyen Fischer, bibliothécaire, qui nous l'a communiqué, fut fait sans que nous en avions la moindre notice, que même la réquisition des livres en question cessât, lorsque nous donnions les preuves légitimes au Cit. Roudler, alors commissaire du gouvernement, de ce que le général Custine et le Cit. Haerlin (de Thionville) représentant du peuple avait déjà tiré les ouvrages les

plus précieux pour la Bibliothèque nationale, tels que le Psautier de 1457, la Bible sans date en deux volumes et une édition des offices sur vélin imprimée à Venise, nous nous impressions cependant de satisfaire aux désires de la Bibliothèque nationale en autorisant le Citoyen Fischer, bibliothécaire, de vous envoyer sans le moindre délai la belle édition des épitres de Cicéron imprimée par Jenson à Venice. Nous vous prions de nous laisser l'édition de Bechtermüntze que, quoiqu' incomplète, conserve à Mayence, au vrai berceau de l'art de l'imprimerie, le souvenir de Gutenberg, dont elle n'a plus d'autre monument.' (In your letter to Citizen Fischer, the University Librarian, who has sent it on to us, you write of a depot. We can only assure you that it was created without our knowledge and that the requisitioning of the books in question ceased when we had given formal evidence to Citizen Rudler, then government commissioner, that General Custine and Citizen Haerlin, of Thionville, representative of the people, had already selected the most precious works for the Bibliothèque nationale, such as the Psalter of 1457, the undated Bible in two volumes, and an edition of the Offices printed on vellum in Venice. However we hasten to satisfy the desires of the Bibliothèque nationale, authorising Citizen Fischer, librarian, to send without delay the handsome edition of Cicero's letters printed by Jenson in Venice. We ask you to leave us the edition of Bechtermüntze, which even if incomplete, preserves in Mainz, the true cradle of the art of printing, the memory of Gutenberg, of whom we have no longer any other monument.)

125 Gotthelf Fischer sent Cicero, *Epistolae*, now BnF Rés. Velins 1149, on 6 germinal An X [27 March 1802], writing obsequiously: 'Vous voyez, mon très cher Vanpraet, que nous sommes très exacte.' (You see, my dear Van Praet, how punctilious I am.) In the same letter he began negotiating privately with Van Praet over the sale of some other early Mainz imprints, a negotiation continued in a letter of 28 germinal An X [18 April 1802]. In *1789 Le patrimoine libéré*, no. 73, pp. 118–19, Dupuigrenet refers to this book as a donation.

126 Heinecken, *Idée générale d'une collection complète d'estampes*, pp. 269–70.

127 BL, Add. MS 75964.

128 'Wie würde es mich freuen, wenn die Sache, woran wir schon mehreren Jahren arbeiten endlich zu beiderseitigen Vergnügen sich endigte.' The letter from the librarian of Roth is enclosed with Horn's letter to Spencer.

129 BL, Add. MS 75964, 7 April 1796: 'I had some time ago a letter from Mr Edwards desiring me to give £300 for the Psalter of 1457. I suppose it is for your Lordship but have had no answer.' Although it was Edwards who had commissioned him to get the Psalter for Spencer, Horn attempted to cut him out. This sharp practice also emerges from a note on the outside of the letter of 27 February 1798: 'I must beg that Edwards may not be informed.' On 15 July 1797 he wrote that he had discovered a superb collection of classics 'which in all probability on the first day of August will be at my disposal ...' 'They have already engaged with someone unknown to me in a negotiation.' This was

presumably Edwards for the letter continues: 'There is only one thing which I must beg of your Lordship viz not to mention this offer to Edwards as it might perhaps hurt him, we being on very good terms. I would send the whole to him in case [it does not s]uit you.' (The lacuna was caused when the seal was broken.) Spencer annotated the letter, declining, and recommended sending the books to Edwards.

130 JRL, 9784. See BL, Add. MS 75964, letter from Horn, 27 February 1798, annotated in Spencer's hand 'Authorising him to purchase the book for £500 or a little more provided it does not exceed 4000 florins'. On 16 April 1798 Horn announced a price of 4000 florins (363 ½ louis), but on 26 April he wrote that he paid 335 louis in gold, asking for payment in pounds in five different bills. On 12 May 1798 he sent the book to Spencer via Mr Fraser, the British chargé d'affaires in Hamburg.

131 BnF, A.m., boite 270, an extensive list beginning: 'Remis au Citoyen Legrand [probably Claude Juste Alexandre Legrand, commander of the French troops on the east bank of the Rhine in 1799], 5 germinal. An VII [26 March 1799]. Bibliothèque du Monastère de Roth dans le voisinage de Memmingen. 1ᵉʳ livre imprimé avec date de la plus grande rareté et sans prix. Imprimé sur vélin Psalmorum Codex. 1457 in fol …' (Sent to Citizen Legrand. Library of the Monastery of Roth near Memmingen. The first dated printed book of the greatest rarity and priceless. Printed on vellum. Psalmorum Codex. 1457, folio …).

132 Van Praet, *Essai du catalogue des livres imprimés sur vélin*, p. 1.

133 For the date *ante quem*, Horn wrote to Spencer, 9 January 1801: 'As his majesty is in possession of the Psalter of Götting 1457 I have written to Mr Barnard.' Van Praet, *Essai du catalogue des livres imprimés sur vélin*, p. 7.

134 BL, Add. MS75965, 8 March 1802.

135 BL, Add. MS 75964, Ratisbone, October 15 1794: 'The Bible which I mentioned to your Lordship is the same with that is described by Audifredi[!], page 73 but such is the ignorance of the present possessors that they have given me leave to strip their library of the Cicero of 1465, the Decretum Gratiani etc for a trifle, and will not part with their Bible for no[!] sum in the world. They even tell me they have a tradition that their Bible is more worthy than their Monastery.'

136 BL, Add. MS 75964, 1 June 1798. This is the copy mentioned in note 76, with a date of sale of 13 April 1455.

137 £100 according to Horn, but probably closer to £90.

138 BL, Add. MS 75964, 30 August 1800: 'They desisted however from this sum [1,000 florins] on condition of my procuring for them the following equivalent, viz. Philosophical Transactions complete, Monasticon anglicanum by Dugdale and a few other inferior works. The litterae your Lordship had for £50 and Edwards the Pliny for 70£ sterling so that the whole difference in my favour amounted to 20£ sterling.' This implies that the cost of the modern books was about £100.

139 Now JRL, 17250.2.

140 BL, Add. MS 75964, 9 January 1801, referred to above, note 76: 'I take the liberty of mentioning on this occasion that I have purchased a beautiful copy of the litterae indulgentiarum … I gave the Encyclopédie methodique for it, which cost me 600 florins without carriage. As his majesty is in possession of the Psalter of Götting 1457 I have written to Mr Barnard and have given him the refusal of it after your Lordship.' Also BL, Add. MS 75964, letter 22 October 1801; quoted in note 76 above. The *Encyclopédie méthodique* was also part of a deal with the University of Ingolstadt, see BL, Add. MS 75964, 6 November 1800: 'Since my last, I wrote to the University of Ingolstadt, which is now translated to Landshut. And offered them for 5 classics and the Horae virginis, a complete copy of the Encyclopedie méthodique par ordre des matières and I am happy to say they caught the bait so that it now only depends on the Electoral commission and as the latter formerly decided in my favour but was opposed by the university I flatter myself with being soon able to send your Lordship the long desired book.'

141 Ilsøe, *Biblioteker til salg*, p. 26.

142 BL, Add. MS 76107–8, letters to Spencer from Edwards, 3 May 1811 and 20 September 1811. The final price does not emerge from the correspondence. £100 was proposed for Jacobus de Cessolis, *The Play of Chess* [Bruges: Caxton], 31 March 1474. JRL, 14387. Edwards was initially hesitant about asking for the two others to be included in the sale, but evidently met little resistance from the chapter, so Spencer also acquired JRL, 15392 and JRL, 15391.

143 Heinecken, *Idée générale d'une collection complette d'estampes*, pp. 250 ff. While mainly interested in the development of an aesthetic appreciation of fifteenth-century visual art, Parshall and Schoch also analyse von Heinecken's historiographical achievements well in 'Early woodcuts and the reception of the primitive'.

144 BL, Add. MS 75965. The sale was first mentioned on 19 September 1803, and the woodcut was finally sent to Spencer on 17 November 1804. Spencer paid £50 for it and the manuscript in the bindings of which it is still a pastedown, the 'Laus Virginis', dated 1417, from Bohemia. JRL, 17249 (the woodcut).

145 Fischer, *Essai sur les monumens typographiques*, p. 9: 'Mayence a déjà à se louer de la sollicitude du Gouvernement pour la restauration de ses instructions [corrected in manuscript to 'institutions'] littéraires … Notre école de dessein va acquérir un nouvel éclat, quand nous posséderons les tableaux destinés pour Mayence par l'arrêté des consuls, et que nos élèves pourront se guider sur ces grand modèles … Notre bibliothèque a été enrichi par le ministre de l'intérieur de près de 3000 volumes français.' Fischer's French is not always very correct. Camus, *Voyage*, p. 167, similarly explained that the library of Liège had lost its historic treasures but, now it was French, its empty shelves should be replenished with modern works.

146 Fischer, *Das Nationalmuseum der Naturgeschichte zu Paris*. Fischer subsequently had an important career in Russia and the biography from 1956

by Büttner, *Fischer von Waldheim*, is a panegyric, reflecting relations between East Germany and the USSR.

147 BnF, A.m., boite 270, a list ending: 'Je certifie que le catalogue ci-dessus contenant douze pages désigne fidèlement le nombre et la qualité des livres et manuscrits que j'ai délivrés au citoyen Neveu commissaire du gouvernement français. Haeffelin, Evêque de Chersonese, Bibliothécaire en chef.' (I certify that the appended catalogue of 12 pages indicates correctly the number and quality of books and manuscripts [1 ms] which I have given over to citizen Neveu, commissioner of the French Government.) Von Haeffelin was bishop *in partibus* of Chersonesos, cardinal from 1817.

148 BnF, A.m., boite 270, letter from Neveu, Munich, 4 vendémiaire An IX. [27 Septembre 1800], addressed to staff of the Bibliothèque nationale: 'D'ailleurs étant autorisé par le Ministre de l'intérieur à proposer des échanges qui enrichiront la France et n'appauvriront pas l'Allemagne, sans négliger le soin d'augmenter nos richesses, pour le moment je m'attache à vous ménager pour l'avenir les moyens d'obtenir par la voie des échanges ce qui peut être tiré de ce pays, et j'en ai fait gouter le projet au gouvernement de Bavière et à Mr le évêque Effelin, bibliothécaire général de la Bavière et garde des médailles. Tous y trouvent un avantage égal pour la gloire des artistes et des savants allemands et français. Et je ne doute pas que la confiance étant bien établie entre les deux nations vous ne puissiez obtenir les objets que vous demanderez à Mr Effelin et que vous savez exister en Allemagne, comme ils tirèrent de France ce qui manque à ses bibliothèques. Ce moyen qui n'a besoin pour devenir efficace que d'une correspondance réciproque concilie les intérêts de la science, ceux de l'économie des fonds, et ceux aussi des principes de gouvernement adoptés par le premier consul et le ministre de l'intérieur.' (Furthermore, the minister of the interior has authorised me to propose exchanges which enrich France and do not impoverish Germany, while recognising the need to increase our treasure. Currently I therefore endeavour to put in place a future scheme of obtaining by exchange that which can be extracted from that country. I have suggested the project to the Bavarian government and to Bishop Haeffelin, Librarian General of Bavaria and Keeper of Medals. All find that it offers equal advantages for French and German artists and scholars. Trust being established between the two nations, I have no doubt that you may obtain the items that you require from Mr Haeffelin which you know to exist in Germany, just as they will extract from France books which are not in their libraries. The implementation of this scheme only requires a joint correspondence to align scientific interests, those of collection management, and the governmental guidelines as laid down by the first consul and the minister of the interior).

149 Zapf, *Ueber eine alte und höchst seltene Ausgabe von des Joannis de Turrecremata Explanatio*, pp. 10–11: 'Der jetzige Geist unsers Zeitalters öffnet ohne Zweifel die bisher verschlossenen Thüren zu den noch verborgenen Schätzen, und erlöst sie aus der Gefangenschaft, in der sie eine lange Reihe von Jahren, ja

Jahrhunderten möchte ich sagen, geschmachtet haben. Und wie viele können in diesem langen Zeitraum aus Unwissenheit, Nachlässigkeit … unsern Augen entrissen worden seyn! Teutschland hat durch mehrere Reisende und durch andere dazu aufgestellte Kundschafter, viele ihrer Schätze verloren, die theils nach Engelland und theils nach Russland gewandert sind, und viele wanderten während dem leztern Krieg in die Nationalbibliothek in Paris, wo sie aber nich unbenutzt bleiben.'

150 The Bodleian Library's marked-up copy of the catalogue indicates that twenty-five books, seventeen of which were incunable editions of the classics, were acquired at this sale, confirmed by Bodleian Library, *Catalogue of Books Purchased* (1796). The Bodleian did not use the German Circulating Libary for the 1796 summary of expenditure specifies costs for transport and customs.

151 Jaeck, *Vollständige Beschreibung der öffentlichen Bibliothek zu Bamberg*, pp. xv–xvi: 'Horn war, bis zum Sturze Napoleon's zugleich der gefährlichste Spion, öfters geraume Zeit hier, wie Maugérard, welcher nach seinen Briefen an Van Praet … vom Herbste 1795 bis zum Frühlinge 1796 ununterbrochen hier verweilte. Zuverlässig war dieser damals im Besitze vieler ersten Drucke, auch mehreren von Bamberg, welche die Bettelmönche gegen unbedeutende Bücher ihm so lieber abtraten, als ihre Vorsteher aus Mangel an Kenntniss der Literär-Geschichte diese nutzlosen Alterthümer gegen die fruchtreichen Exegeten sehr vortheilhaft abgegeben zu haben wähnten.' (A most dangerous spy until the fall of Napoleon, Horn was often here for considerable periods, just like Maugérard who, according to his letters to Van Praet, was here continuously from autumn 1795 to spring 1796. Apparently he possessed several first impressions, including several from Bamberg, which the mendicant friars ceded to him in return for insignificant books, the more willingly because their leader, in his ignorance of literary history, held it advantageous to exchange pointless antiquities for useful commentaries.)

152 Traube, *Jean-Baptiste Maugérard*, pp. 302–87, on the manuscripts sold to Gotha; part II, Ehwald, *Besonderer Teil*, in Traube, at pp. 374–6, for the incunabula sold to the Duke of Gotha in 1795. Unlike his dealings with France, Maugérard's deals with Herzog Ernst are seen as ethically uncomplicated in modern German literature. Thus Schaab, 'Universitäts- und Forschungsbibliothek Erfurt/Gotha', p. 293.

153 Fischer's dealings with the Bibliothèque nationale have not hitherto been noticed. For his deals with the Grand Duke of Hesse, see Knaus, 'Fischer von Waldheim'.

154 Römer, '"Lediglich ein Bücherwust ohne vollständige Ordnung"', p. 398 note 4, on religious houses as centres of learning, unjustly vilified by Protestant visitors.

155 Desplat, 'Bibliothèques privées mises sous séquestre'.

156 Furet, *La Révolution française*, p. 130.

157 Prévost, *Histoire du Chevalier des Grieux, et de Manon Lescaut* (À Londres [but really Paris?], 1782), in the series Bibliothèque amusante; the copy is now JRL,

8433, signed 'Lavinia Althorp 1783'; Étienne, *La Vie de … Malesherbes*, JRL, 14380; Condorcet, *Essai sur l'application de l'analyse à la probabilité*, JRL, 550; Condorcet, *Œuvres*; JRL, 13098; Volney, *Voyage*; JRL, 13989.

158   His diaries contain formulaic entries, meticulously recording what he read. For instance on Saturday 14 May he read in the *Encyclopédie*; on Sunday 15 May and the following days he read Cicero, *Orator*, and Voltaire. He read Gibbon's *Memoirs* most days in this period. See BL, Add. MS 76320, covering 21 April 1796–28 June 1797.

159   Shepherd, *Paris in Eighteen Hundred and Two*, pp. 65–7. His visit was on 26 June 1802. Yorke, *Letters from Paris 1802*, II, letter 31, pp. 134–5. Edwards, *Memoirs of Libraries*, II, p. 274 recorded that the convention of 25 vendémiaire An IV (17 October 1795) decreed that the Library should be open to students (*aux travailleurs*) for four hours daily nine days every *décade* (the revolutionary ten-day week) and additionally for three days every *décade* for general visitors.

160   Lévis, *Angleterre*, p. 201: 'Note that this English Library, incomplete and poor, is the only national one, compared with the quarters of Paris which have superb ones, to which access is never denied. As for collections of paintings and statues, England, as a nation, has nothing to compare with the French gallery, which contains the most precious paintings known, where one admires the masterpieces of all great sculptors from Praxiteles to Canova. Unlike France she can offer antiquaries no cabinet of medals and cameos, nor natural historians long series of minerals, shells, and all species of animals from the entire world; the multitudes of trees, shrubs, useful or interesting plants, skilfully maintained in their exile. All riches in these categories are private.'

161   On the Royal Library in Copenhagen, Ilsøe, *På papir, pergament og palmeblade*, p. 99. On Lisbon public library, Domingos, 'A caminho da Real Biblioteca Pública da Corte'.

3 An object-based discipline emerges

1   William Cavendish, second Duke of Devonshire, Thomas Herbert, eighth Earl of Pembroke, John Ker, first Duke of Roxburghe, Charles Spencer, third Earl of Sunderland, and Robert Harley and his son Edward, first and second Earls of Oxford. Thomas Coke, first Earl of Leicester.

2   Panzer, *Annales typographici*, review, in *Allgemeine Literatur-Zeitung*, col. 539: 'Er [Maittaire] was der Erste, der ein solches Werk lieferte, und andere Gelehrte dadurch aufweckte, die noch vorhandenen ältesten gedruckten Bücher, welche vorher wenig geachtet wurden und in den Bibliotheken in Staube begraben lagen, sorgfältiger auszusuchen und zu beschreiben. Fast in allen europäischen Ländern traten gelehrte Männer auf, welche durch ihre Schriften die Maittairischen Verzeichnisse der ältesten gedruckten Bücher verbesserten und vermehrten.' ([Maittaire] was the first to produce such a work and inspired other learned men more carefully to locate and describe still existing early books, previously buried

in the dust of libraries. In nearly all European countries learned men appeared who improved and supplemented Maittaire's list of the oldest printed books with their own writings.)

3 BL, Add. MS 76299, fols 205–8, a bill from Elmsley receipted 21 December 1789: 'Maittaire, Annales Typograph. 7 vols. 4to NB vol. wanting £6.6.s'; and fol. 210, a bill from Thomas Payne, receipted 29 March 1790, including £8 8s for 'Maittaire, *Annales typographici* 9 vols'. It was clearly not easy to get a complete set.

4 Orlandi, *Origine e progressi*, pp. 1–3: 'La nuova dilettazione, il quale ha acceso in molti un' ardente desio di andare in traccia di libri antichi delle prime edizioni, con i quali hanno qualificato molte belle librarie, particolarmente nelle parti oltramontane, giunta qui tra noi … hà susciato altresì il prurito a molti dei nostri Italiani di provedersi delle medesime edizioni, ma con modo, e genio diverso. Alcuni soggetti eruditi ne hanno fatto buona raccolta perchè hanno compreso, che quelle prime edizioni sono le più sicure, le più legitime … Altri … senza pensare alla singolarità degli autori, e degl' impressori più rinomati, o alla qualità dei caratteri più eleganti, in vedere in faccia, o nel fine dei libri quel tanto celebrato millesimo del MCCCC. hanno con poco gusto riempito le scanzie, e studii loro d'autori ordinarii, e di libri in carattere gottico, o mezzo gottico, che … ammorbò il mondo letterario … dall' anno 1475 all' anno 1575. Altri se ne proveggono alla giornata, per farne trafico, e vendite, con poco decoro, e con meno riputazione delle buone arti, spogliandone le pubbliche librarie; le case private, e l'Italia tutta, per mandarli nei paesi oltramontani, ove forsi più, che nei nostri, fiorisce la gloria delle più scientifiche cognizioni.' (A new interest has lit an ardent desire in many to hunt for ancient first editions, which now adorn many beautiful libraries, especially in Northern Europe. Now in our country … it has stimulated many of us Italians to acquire such editions, but with a different, moderate attitude. Some learned men have made good collections understanding that first editions are the most reliable, the most legitimate … Others, paying no attention to the characteristics of the authors or the best printers … seeing at the front or back of the books the famous MCCCC, have filled their rooms uncritically … with works of common authors, and with books in gothic or semi-gothic type, which … infected the world of letters from 1475 to 1575. Others acquire them daily, dealing in them with little honour … plundering public libraries, private houses, and all Italy, to send them to Northern Europe, where the glory of scientific understanding is perhaps more flourishing.)

5 See Mazal, *Bibliotheca eugeniana*; Hamann, 'Prinz Eugen als Bibliophile'; *ÖNB-Ink*, I, introduction, p. xx.

6 Pointing to the continuity of collecting by socially less eminent men, Hellinga, *Caxton in Focus*, pp. 27–8, contested the view that the early, aristocratic, interest in incunabula rapidly waned.

7 I disagree with Swift, 'The formation of the library of Charles Spencer', esp. p. 4, who found that scholars had always bought early editions of the classics and that the changed interest originated with aristocratic collectors.

8 See Oates, 'Booksellers' guarantees': 'At the returne of this Booke a quarter of yeare after the date hereof I am to repay 3s 6d. John Howell.' CUL, Oates 2181.

9 'At the returne of this booke I am to repay 5s. Laurence Sadler the 16th of October 1635.' CUL, Oates 2144.

10 In addition to the printed books mentioned by Oates, Sadler sold BL, Burney MS 3, a Bible now dated between *c.* 1240 and 1253, promising: 'At the returne of this booke I am to repay 1£ 6s. Lawrence Sadler'. It appears that old books were of importance for his business; see BL, Stowe MS. 378, Gratian's *Decretum* and BL, Add. MS 53710, both sold by Sadler to Sir Rower Twysden in 1629 for 20s. Twysden also owned BL, Burney MS 3.

11 CUL, Oates 1949: 'I will give agayne for this booke 3s. 6d. ffrancis Greene.' And CUL, Oates 754: 'I doe promise to allowe for this Booke at any tyme 11s in Bookes, Francis Greene.'

12 Bodleian, Arch. G e.7(1).

13 Labbé, *Nova bibliotheca MSS librorum*, appendix 9, 'Veterum editionum ante annum Christi MD breviarium' (Summary of editions from before 1500), pp. 331–58. Appendix 10, p. 358. It seems that the French devotion to books printed on vellum has a French, not an English origin, as suggested by Viardot, in his seminal article 'Naissance de la bibliophilie', p. 282.

14 Naudé, *Advis pour dresser une bibliothèque*, especially pp. 112–13.

15 Cave, *Scriptorum ecclesiasticorum historia literaria*, prolegomena, sect. V, pp. xiii–xiv. Cave knew the catalogue of Philippe Labbé and he had just seen Beughem, *Incunabula typographiae*, also published in 1688.

16 Philip, *Bodleian Library*, p. 15. I disagree with Philip's view, however, that this was a project promoted by a more Protestant Thomas James against the will of a more irenic Thomas Bodley.

17 The theme is not confined to England. Cf. *Scaligerana, Thuana, Perroniana*, from 1740, in the section of 'Pithoeana', p. 496: 'Tous les pères impriméz à Rome ne valent rien, mais sont corrompus. Tout ce que font imprimer les Jésuites est corrompu. Les Huguenots commencent à en faire de même. Les livres de Bâle sont bons et entiers.' (All patristic editions from Rome are corrupted and no good. All Jesuit editions are corrupted. The Huguenots are beginning to do the same. Basel editions are good and complete.)

18 *Catalogi librorum manuscriptorum*, I, sig. ** verso: 'Optandum esset interea, ut soli librariorum errores in codicibus comparerent, editis vel manuscriptis, sacris aut profanis. Sed concilia, patres, imo sacram scripturam studiose contaminarunt Pontificii, sive mutilantes, ne suis opinionibus adversarentur; sive distorquentes, ut sua dogmata eorum autoritate stabilirent. Improbitas sane summa!'

19 *Catalogi librorum manuscriptorum*, I, sig. *** recto: 'Libri impressi, manuscriptis intermisti, non sunt adeo multi; ... Alii qui, quamvis impressi sint, sunt tamen sive propter raritatem, sive ob aliam causam aliquam instar manuscriptorum habiti et manuscriptis connumerati ... Alii, qui fuerant Rev. Episcopi Norvicensis, aut

D. Isaaci Vossii aut D. Edwardi Bernardi fuerant cum manuscriptis collati vel antiquitus editi et raro prostantes adeo pluris aestimandi.' (A smaller number of printed books are listed among the manuscripts … Some may be considered as manuscripts and be listed among them either because they are rare or for some other reason, although they are printed. Others, previously belonging to the Bishop of Norwich, Isaac Vossius, or Edward Bernard, have been collated with manuscripts or are old and hard to find and therefore more valuable.) On the books of the Bishop of Ely, II, pp. 379–83: 'librorum nonnullorum sub artis typographicae primordia, vel temporibus ab eius inventione haud ita remotis impresssorum … indicem placuit subiungere. Pauci quoque accedunt codices quorum characteres ac rudiores typorum formae istius artis infantiam redolent, licet anni quibus editi fuerint minime signentur.' (We decided to add … a list of books from the beginning of printing or from not long after … There are also some books whose crude typefaces suggest the infancy of this art, although they carry no year.) The Ely list was the model for the list in Thoresby, *Ducatus leodiensis*, p. 544 in 1715.

20 On the authorship of the *Catalogi* see Ramsay, 'Libraries for antiquaries and heralds', p. 142.

21 Morhof, *Polyhistor*, pp. 64–5: 'Tertium a veris illis manuscriptis codicibus locum occupant illi libri qui primum e manuscriptis emendatis antiquioribus a peritissimis typographis curantibus viris doctis sunt editi, qui magnam proinde fidem in variis lectionibus decidendis et emendationibus corruptorum locorum habent.' (In third place after true manuscripts come books published from good, ancient manuscripts under the guidance of learned printers, and which consequently are very reliable in deciding among variant readings and amending corruptions.) Only one of the printers was from the fifteenth century. Struve, *Introductio ad notitiam rei litterariae*, p. 221: 'Notandum quod antiquissimae editiones romanae, venetae et praecipue Aldinae, manuscriptorum fere fidem habeant. Ita Plinius Romae 1470 … Silius Italicus Romae 1471 editus, cum manuscriptis fere certant, quia ex collatione manuscriptorum antiquissimorum editi.' (Note that ancient Roman, Venetian and especially Aldine editions are nearly as important as manuscripts. Thus Pliny, Rome, 1470 … Silius Italicus Rome 1471, nearly compete with manuscripts because they were published using very ancient manuscripts.)

22 Gude, *Bibliotheca … instructissima*. Unlike Larsen, *Frederik Rostgaard*, p. 134, I do not believe that his incunabula were simply chosen according to availability. See, e.g., Copenhagen, The Royal Library, Inc. 2001, 2456, 2492, and 3308.

23 See Swift, 'The formation of the library of Charles Spencer', especially the assessment of the library pp. 283–4. Swift also shows that Sunderland mainly acquired books in England until about 1711 and did not acquire from Italian sources until 1718 or 1719.

24 Vergilius, *Opera* (1715), dedication to Sunderland, sig. A4 verso: 'Acceptis a te nuper duobus impressis Virgilii codicibus antiquissimis et (quantum hactenus

scire licuit) primis, nemo occurrit in cuius clientelam hunc poetarum principem jam in publicum prodeuntem possim magis meriti jure tradere quam tuam cuius ope adornatus est.' (Recently I received from you two ancient printed editions of Virgil, as far as we know the first, and my publication of the first among poets owes more to your patronage, by whose munificence it is prepared, than to anybody else.) The dedication is followed by a detailed description of the two editions and a list of readings based on them.

25 Bloch, 'La bibliothèque de Colbert', p. 161.

26 Bagford, 'An account of several libraries', p. 177: 'Books of the first printing, as that printed at *Mentz* in 1640 [!], and many others printed since in other places before 1500. Those of the first printing in *England* at *Oxford* in 1469. *St. Albans, Westminster* by *Caxton, Winkin de Worde, Pynson,* &c, the greatest number in *England,* and other fine beautiful books printed on vellum and illuminated, which might pass for manuscripts, as the fine *Pliny* and *Livy* in 2 vols. both on vellum.' I am grateful to Giles Mandelbrote who drew this work to my attention.

27 BL, Add. MS 75965, from Horn to Spencer, 22 October 1802, he continued: 'It is a Bible on vellum fol written in 1389 with more than 300 miniature paintings inlaid as it were with beaten gold. You may take it at any price or not take it; at least it shall not fall into the hands of the privileged robbers.'

28 Wanley, *Diary,* Introduction, p. lxi; for further references see the index.

29 Wanley, *Diary,* 4 December 1721.

30 The importance of 'the earliest' as against 'the best' for the development of bibliomania was pointed out by Hunt, 'Private libraries', p. 438.

31 Amory, *The Life of John Buncle,* pp. 343–4.

32 Maittaire, *Epistolaris de antiquis Quintiliani editionibus dissertatio,* p. 29: 'nam iis temporibus correctores, quantumvis eruditi ... codices manuscriptos ... sequi superstitiose maluerunt, quam criticae ... audacius indulgere ... In eam igitur ... opinionem adducor, ut librorum in lucem primum edendorum primaria (quantum fieri potest) lectio, modo non fuerit omnino vitiosa, in textu retineatur, si dubia aut confusa et corrupta appareat, rejiciatur utcunque ad marginem, aut variantium lectionum catalogum et si manifeste sit mendosa, eliminetur.' (For very learned editors ... then followed manuscripts religiously instead of indulging in daring conjectures ... This makes me believe that, unless completely wrong, readings from the earliest editions should be given primacy in the text, as far as possible; if they seem doubtful, uncertain, or corrupt, they should be relegated to the margins or to the list of variants, and eliminated if manifestly wrong.)

33 Vergilius, *Opera* (1767), p. lx: 'Ex tanto editionum saeculi XV. vulgatarum numero vix tres aut quatuor a viris doctis critica cum cura et subtilitate excusse sunt; unde fit ut nec satis exploratum sit, quid ex nonnullis earum utilitatis et fructus ad Virgilium exspectari possit, nec accurate definiri possit, quae ex iis inter principes et ex membranis descriptas habendae sint, aut quae reliquarum

familias duxerint. Quantum tamen adhuc curatiore opera ac studio perspicere potui, a venetis ab initio inde Virgiliana lectio fuit constituta. Nam conveniunt fere inter se ad eandem lectionem propagandam Venetae 1486. 1495. 1499. 1501. 1509. Idem de editionibus 1489, 1486, 1480, 1475 suspicor.' (Out of the many fifteenth-century editions barely three or four were published critically by learned men and printed with care; therefore it is uncertain what fruitful outcome for Virgil can be expected from them; nor can it be established precisely which should be considered the first, based on manuscripts, or are heads of families of books. As far as I have been able to work out so far, the text of Virgil was first fixed by the Venetians. For Venice 1486, 1495, 1499, 1501, 1509 all give the same text. I suspect the same is true of 1489, 1486, 1480 and 1475.) Vergilius, *Opera* (1793), I, p. lxxvii: 'Et honestum studium quis neget poni in rei typographicae incunabulis et incrementis cognoscendis?' (And who can deny that the origin and development of printing is a respectable area of study?)

34 Vergilius, *Opera* (1793), I, p. lxxxi: 'Nuper iterum multis de hac editione egit Crevenna ... nullo cum fructo ad te, qui indolem libri et usum criticum volebas resciscere.' (Crevenna recently wrote extensively on this edition ... but pointlessly for understanding its nature and critical value). On a similarly assessment, see Crevenna, *Catalogue raisonné*, review in *Critical Review*, p. 467: 'A complete, learned, and systematical knowledge, and a critical estimate of the intrinsic merit and value of books, is not to be expected from a mere dilettante.'

35 See Jensen, 'Heinrich Walther'.

36 Franciscus Columna, *Hypnerotomachia Poliphili*. Venice: Aldus Manutius, Dec. 1499.

37 Renouard, *Annales* (1803), II, p. 7: 'Sans doute la Grammaire d'Alde n'a ni la précision, ni l'ordre analytique des meilleurs de nos livres élémentaires modernes, mais les Dumarsais, les Condillac, les grands hommes de Port-Royal n'avoient point encore paru; et en ce point, comme en typographie, Alde a le mérite incontestable d'avoir, presque le premier, travaillé, assez bien pour mettre ceux qui sont venus après lui en état de faire beaucoup mieux encore.' (Admittedly Aldus's grammar has neither the precision nor the analytical structure of modern elementary books, but men like Dumarsais, Condillac, and the grand men of Port-Royal had not yet appeared and, as with printing, Aldus has the undoubted honour, as almost the first, of having worked so well that those who followed could do even better.) On Lucretius, II, p. 32.

38 Renouard, *Annales* (1803), II, p. 11: 'Et ce qui doit être remarqué, c'est le goût éclairé qui dirigea ses choix. Les imprimeurs ses confrères, soit de Vénice, soit des autres villes, entraînés par le goût du siècle, ou sacrifiant à diverses convenances, sur-tout d'intérêt, n'imprimèrent presque que des ouvrages de scholastique, des livres mystiques ou de jurisprudence et fort peu de bons ouvrages de littérature ou d'ancienne philosophie. Il étoit réservé au génie d'Alde de changer la direction des idées, de donner une impulsion nouvelle à l'imprimerie, qui

dès-lors reproduisit dans toute l'Europe beaucoup moins de ce fatras scholastique.' (Remarkable is the enlightened taste which directed their decisions. In Venice or elsewhere, their colleagues almost only printed scholastic, mystic [i.e. religious], or legal works, and very little good literature or ancient philosophy, led by the taste of their times, or yielding to practical, mainly financial, considerations. It was reserved for the genius of Aldus to change the direction of ideas, and to give new impetus to printing, which from then on, all over Europe, reproduced much less of that scholastic hotchpotch.) And vol. II, Préface, p. v: 'Ils [Aldus and Paulus] dévouèrent leur vie entière à tirer les écrivains anciens du chaos où huit siècles les avoient plongés. Non contens de les arracher à la destruction, ils voulurent les rendre d'un usage universel, et s'appliquèrent à les reproduire sous des formes qui, rendant leur acquisition moins dispendieuse, les missent à la portée d'un plus grande nombre de lecteurs' (They devoted their entire lives to saving ancient authors from the chaos into which eight centuries had plunged them. Not content with snatching them from destruction, they wished to make them universally useful and applied themselves to reproducing them in a way which made them less expensive and brought them within reach of a greater number of readers.) On the production standards, see for instance II, p. 19: 'Tout étoit bon dans ces livres' (All was good in these books [the classical editions in octavo]).

39 This is based on an analysis of the Selden collection using the Bodleian Library's pre-1920 catalogue on CD-rom, which can no longer be consulted; see Jensen, 'Bodleian Library'.

40 Bodleian, AA 127(2) Th. Seld. Cf. Selden, *Briefe Discourse Concerning the Power of the Peeres and Commons*.

41 See Bodleian, 4° T 1 Th. Seld.

42 Bodleian, 4° A 20(1) Th. Seld. Cf. Selden, *Historie of tithes*.

43 Two copies of Albumasar, *Flores* appear in Bodleian, MS Selden supra 111, fol. 39ʳ: 'Flores Albumasaris 4°'; and fol. 92ᵛ: 'Albumazar Flores Astrolog'. Cf. Bodleian, BB 17(3) Art. Seld. and 4° A 31(1) Art. Seld.

44 Selden, Θεάνθρωπος, p. 54.

45 Selden, *De anno civili … dissertatio*.

46 Rogers, *Bodleian Library*, p. 121.

47 For instance Bodleian, S. Seld. d.4 and S. Seld. d.7. In this respect Selden's collection is similar to the French libraries of great noblemen like Colbert and Séguier. See Bloch, 'La bibliothèque de Colbert', especially p. 158, and Nexon, 'La bibliothèque du chancelier Séguier'.

48 Bodleian, S. Seld. d.13; S. Seld. d.5; S. Seld. d.6; S. Seld. d.11(2); S. Seld. d.8(1); S. Seld. d.8(2); Auct. QQ sup. 1.15; S. Seld. d.11(1); S. Seld. d.10.

49 Bodleian, S. Seld. d.14.

50 Selden may of course yet have acquired it from an English source.

51 On some of Selden's second-hand purchases see Sparrow, 'Earlier owners of books in John Selden's library'.

52 Smith, *Bibliotheca smithiana* (1682), pp. 274–5. On Smith's sale see also Birrell, 'Books and buyers', pp. 55–8, and p. 58 on the Earl of Peterborough, 'a cavalier in the grand romantic tradition'.

53 Lot 83.

54 Lot 87: 'Recuile of the Histories of *Troy*, of the destruction thereof etc – *London* 1553'.

55 BL, Sloane MS 722. The section on English printing in Cave, 'Richard Smyth', pp. 48–56. Before him Bale, *Illustrium Maioris Britanniae scriptorum … summarium*, sig. Fff. iv recto–verso, fol. 208, had considered Caxton primarily as an author.

56 Bodleian, Auct. 1Q 5.15.

57 Lot 94, *Godefrey of Boloyne*. Westminster: Caxton, 1481.

58 Cessolis, *The Play of Chess*. [Bruges: Caxton], 1474.

59 De Ricci, *English Collectors*, p. 32, noted the low prices for Caxtons at the sale of Francis Bernard in 1698.

60 Bodleian, Auct. QQ sup. 1.21.

61 I see this differently from the author of *Wonderful Things*, no. 28, who finds it not surprising that Pitt 'should have given such an important volume' to the Bodleian Library. An indication that there was an interest in the Bodleian Library in early Oxford printing may be gauged from entries in two of the Bodleian Library's manuscript catalogues of Selden's collection which mention Caxton as one of the few printers to merit this distinction. These catalogues were drawn up in the library not by or for Selden. See for example Bodleian, MS Broxbourne 84.10, p. 19: 'Caxton. Chessplay', relating to Bodleian, S. Seld. d.6.

62 Nixon, Goldfinch, and Hellinga, 'Formation of the collection of English incunabula', pp. 71–2.

63 Hearne, *Remarks and Collections*, I, p. 73, 14 Nov. 1705: 'Amongst Dr. Barlow's books is Expositio S. Jeronimi (or rather Ruffini) in Symbolum apostolorum printed at Oxon. in 1468, 3 [*sic*] years after Printing began at Mentz.' The 1459 Psalter was by then well known, and a description of the Vienna copy of the 1457 Psalter had been published. On the other hand Hearne ascribed a fragment of an Oxford imprint to Caxton; Bodleian, Arch. G d.36. It is hard not to agree with Piggott, 'Antiquarian studies', p. 761, that when Hearne's 'antiquarian rather than historical contributions are sought they reveal a limited and pedantic mind'.

64 Hearne, *Reliquiae*, II, p. 461, 26 May 1721: 'Mr John Murray of London being in Oxford he told me last night … that he hath got Caxton's Aurea Legenda, and that it cost him above four pounds … He told me that he gave 3 Guineas for Dugdale's Warwickshire.'

65 Wanley, *Diary*, entry for 4 December 1721.

66 In the introduction to Wanley, *Diary*, p. lxiii, C. E. and Ruth Wright say that there is no Caxton in Wanley's 1717 catalogue, that they were probably acquired in the late 1720s, perhaps largely from Thomas Rawlinson's sales, and that Edward Harley wrote to Hearne, 25 December 1731: 'I have a great number of

books printed by Caxton, and in very good condition, except a very few. I think the number is forty-two.' See also Nixon, Goldfinch, and Hellinga, 'Formation of the collection of English incunabula', p. 75.

67 Wanley, *Diary*, 19 April 1722, ascribed a fall in prices to the death of the Earl of Sunderland. Hearne, *Reliquiae*, II, p. 490, 22 April 1723, ascribed it to the death of Thomas Rawlinson; see Nixon, Goldfinch, and Hellinga, 'Formation of the collection of English incunabula', p. 76 on Osborne's gradual reduction by 75per cent of the Harleian Caxtons in the 1730s.

68 Paterson, *Bibliotheca westiana*. BL, 270.k.7 has manuscript notes of prices. Nearly all fetched low prices, but a few were expensive, notably in the history section; see p. 209, lot 4090, *The recuyell of the histories of Troye*, sold to Nicol for £32 11s.

69 Ratcliffe, *Bibliotheca ratcliffiana*. BL, 822.d.6(1) has manuscript notes of prices.

70 Edwards, *Catalogue of books in all languages*, lots 13 and 59.

71 Note in Bodleian, Douce 270: 'Mr. Uphill a bookseller brought to me another portion of this identical volume long after I had rebound it, containing from fo: XLIV to fo: LXXXXVII, those leaves being here deficient ... As 5 guineas were asked I did not think it worth while to take it as the volume would have still remained imperfect.'

72 For a summary see Glomski, '*Incunabula Typographiae*'.

73 Mentel, *Brevis excursus* and *De vera typographiae origine paraenesis*. Sassi, *Historia literario-typographica mediolanensis*; Paitoni, *Venezia*.

74 Mabillon, *De re diplomatica libri VI*.

75 Chevillier, *L'origine de l'imprimerie de Paris*, sig. aiii recto: 'J'ai considéré que le lecteur d'un nouveau livre en devient le juge. Les juges ne doivent rien croire que ce qu'ils voyent prouvé dans les procédures ... Dans un siècle d'érudition, comme celui où nous sommes, et qui a l'abondance des livres, personne ne doit être crû sur sa simple parole ... Les passages mis devant les yeux lèvent toute difficulté: celui qui les lit en tire lui-même les conséquences.' (It is my opinion that the reader of a new book should be its judge. Judges should believe nothing except what is proved in the procedures ... In an age of erudition, as is ours, with a plenitude of books, nobody should be believed simply on his word ... The quoted passages avoid all complications: the reader can draw his own conclusions.)

76 Trithemius, *Tomus I [–II] Annalium hirsaugiensium*, II, p. 421.

77 Chevillier, *L'origine de l'imprimerie de Paris*, p. 20: 'Qu'on dise où sont toutes ces éditions? en quelle Bibliothèque on les garde; qui sont les possesseurs de ces rares fruits d'imprimerie; si la datte de l'année y est expressément marquée et en quels termes les imprimeurs s'en explique?' (Please, tell us where all these editions are? In which library? Who owns these rare products of printing? Whether the date of printing is explicitly stated and how the printer makes himself known?)

78 BL, Add. MS 76299, fols 205–8, bill from Peter Elmsley receipted 21 December 1789: '16 May. Chevillier hist. de l'imprimerie 4to £9.6.'

79 For the most recent account of the dating see Hellinga, *BMC Part XI*, p. 234.

80 Atkyns, *The Original and Growth of Printing*. See also Hellinga, *Caxton in Focus*, pp. 21–2.

81 Johns, *The Nature of the Book*, p. 343.

82 Laire, *Specimen historicum typographiae romanae*, p. 34: 'partim amore patriae deceptus' (in part misled by a love of his country).

83 Middleton, *Letter from Rome*.

84 Pearce, *Reply to the Letter to Dr. Waterland*.

85 Middleton, *Letter to Dr. Waterland*, especially pp. 28–38 on Egyptian beliefs and practices.

86 See Dussinger, 'Middleton'.

87 Hearne, *Reliquiae*, II, pp. 860–1, 3 March 1735.

88 The antiquarian Hearne is here found on the 'ancient' side of the ancient/modern debate. For a good account of the ethical aims of the 'ancient' approach to historiography see Levine, *Battle of the Books*.

89 Middleton, *Dissertation Concerning the Origin of Printing in England*, p. 3, on the credence given to the story by Maittaire and Palmer and 'one Bagford, an industrious man, who had published *Proposals for an History of Printing*, and whose manuscript papers were communicated to me by my worthy and learned friend Mr Baker: But it is strange that a piece so fabulous and carrying such evident marks of forgery, could impose upon men so knowing and inquisitive'.

90 3005 livres; see Bloch, 'La bibliothèque de Colbert', p. 165.

91 Hearne, *Reliquiae*, II, p. 535, 10 May 1724: 'Yesterday I saw in Oxford my friend, Mr Richard Graves, of Mickleton in Gloucestershire, who told me that Mr James Woodman, a London bookseller, is going to reprint Caxton's Chronicle. He also told me that the Latin Bible printed in Fol. at Menz, 1462, was sold in the sale of the Count de Brienne's library, carrying on at London by the said Woodman, for 112 libs. being bought by my lord Harley, and that other books (the library being extraordinary curious) bring vast prizes. The said Bible is in two vols., vellum, and is noted in the catalogue to be the first Bible ever printed.' For the Amsterdam sale of Charron de Méars, in 1722, where a copy fetched 1200 florins, see Swift, 'The formation of the library of Charles Spencer', p. 40. Following the standard exchange rate, this is about £113, although the rate used by Sunderland's dealer makes it £120 (cf. Swift, p. ix).

92 Bodleian, Auct. M 1.3.

93 Berkvens-Stevelinck, 'Un cabinet de livres européen', p. 17, underlines the importance of books on the invention of printing in Marchand's library.

94 Digital facsimile at Staats- und Universitäts-Bibliothek Göttingen.

95 Senckenberg, *Selecta iuris … anecdota*, I, section three: 'Manipulus documentorum res francofurtenses et viciniam illustrantium', pp. 269–77.

96 Köhler, *Hochverdiente und aus bewährten Urkunden wohlbeglaubte Ehren-Rettung Johann Guttenbergs*. Schwarz, *Primaria quaedam documenta de origine typographiae [pars prima]*, an analysis mainly of the Helmasperger instrument.

Schwarz, *Primaria quaedam documenta de origine typographiae [pars altera]*, a description of two undated Latin bibles, and of dated colophons in Mainz imprints. Schwarz, *Primaria quaedam documenta de origine typographiae [pars tertia]*, a discussion of the textual meaning of verses in Gregorius IX, *Decretales*. Mainz: Schoeffer, 23 Nov. 1473.

97 Schoepflin, 'Dissertation sur l'origine de l'imprimerie'.

98 Grell, 'J.-D. Schoepflin', p. 255; also Voss, *Universität, Geschichtswissenschaft und Diplomatie*.

99 I wish to acknowledge the approach to eighteenth-century orientalists of Irwin, *For Lust of Knowing*.

100 See Hellinga, 'The *Bibliotheca smithiana*'. See also Griffiths, 'The prints and drawings in the library of Consul Joseph Smith'.

101 In his letter to Gibson, Sunderland's dealer, dated Venice 11 October 1720, BL, Lansdowne MS 841, fol. 98: 'all finely miniatured & fitt for a Monarch', quoted from Swift, 'The formation of the library of Charles Spencer', p. 44. In Smith, *Catalogus librorum rarissimorum* (1737), at the end: 'Pretiotissima haec librorum collectio, cuiusvis magni principis bibliotheca dignissima, constat voluminibus CCXLVIII', exactly the same phrase being used in the 1725 catalogue, only the number of books being smaller.

102 On the general lack of interest in illumination, at least until the 1780s, see Munby, *Connoisseurs*, esp. pp. 17–21. Judging from subsequent acquisition patterns, illuminations were not an important selection criterion for George III, who acquired Smith's collection in 1762.

103 BL, Add. MS 76014, to Spencer from Maugérard, Erfurt, 8 August 1797, quoted in note 85, Chapter 2.

104 McKitterick, 'Bibliography, bibliophily and the organization of knowledge', pp. 47–8 used the dedication of Maittaire's work on the Estienne family as an illustration of the commercial interest in promoting knowledge of books. Already in 1708 Bagford, 'An account of several libraries', p. 182, pointed out how the trade contributed to the knowledge of connoisseurs. In these two cases the role of dealers consisted in revealing the extent of the literary universe, rather than in developing tools for the identification of objects.

105 *Bibliotheca askeviana librorum rarissimorum*, lot 3373, an edition of Valerius Maximus, probably the one which is now ascribed to Mentelin in Strasbourg and dated 'not after 1470', here ascribed to Mainz: Schoeffer, 1471, on the basis of the similarity of its type with an edition which is dated and located as such.

106 The sale catalogue was widely distributed, sold at various places in London, Paris, and Amsterdam. Debure was a frequent buyer; see the auctioneer's annotated copy, now BL, S.C.Sotheby.6*(3). In his database of the de La Vallière sale Dominique Coq identifies a number of books from the Askew collection.

107 La Vallière, *Catalogue des livres*, lot no. 2258: 'M. T. Ciceronis de Finibus Bonorum et Malorum libri V. *Editio antiquissima (Coloniae, per Olricum Zel de Hanau, circa 1467)*: in 4. Gothique. [Cicero, *De finibus* (Cologne: Zell, about

1470).] Maroquin rouge. Première et très rare édition, exécutée à longues lignes au nombre de 27 sur les pages qui sont entières, sans date, indication de ville, et d'imprimeur, chiffres, réclames et signatures. Elle a été annoncée jusqu'à ce jour comme sortie des presses de Mayence, parce qu'on a cru y voir une grande conformité de ses caractères avec ceux des Offices de Cicéron, imprimés en cette ville en 1465 [Cicero, *De officiis*. (Mainz): Fust and Schoeffer, 1465]. Après avoir comparé très attentivement l'une & l'autre édition, nous pouvons assurer que les caractères ont très peu de rapports entr'eux, & que ceux des Offices de Cicéron sont beaucoup plus petits; mais qu'ils ressemblent parfaitement à ceux avec les quels Zel de Hanau, Imprimeur de Cologne, a exécuté en 1467 les traités de St. Augustin intitulés: *De vita Christiana & de singularitate Clericorum*, annoncés ci-devant, no. 475 [Augustinus, *De vita christiana*. (Cologne): Zell, 1467]. D'ailleurs l'une & l'autre édition sont de même format, et ont une même justification de pages'.

108 They compare lot no. 756, Henricus Arnoldi, *De modo perveniendi ad veram Dei et proximi dilectionem* [Basel: Wenssler, not after 1 Dec. 1472], which they date to about 1475, with Augustinus, *De civitate dei*. Basel: Wenssler, 1479. They note that the type face is more worn in the latter: 'le caractère est plus usé dans ce dernier ouvrage'. *BMC* regards them as being in two different fonts but acknowledges that the dating is open to challenge.

109 See for instance the competition for a copy of Cicero, *De officiis* [Cologne: Zell, about 1465]. BL, Add. MS 75964, Horn to Spencer, 6 July 1801. Also BL, Add. MS 76014, Maugérard to Spencer, received 15 October 1800, quoted in Chapter 2, note 82.

110 BnF, A.m., carton 270: 'Extrait du catalogue des livres de Dom Maugirard [*sic*] religieux bénédictin à Metz 1785. Nota. Cet extrait a été fait uniquement pour les éditions avec suscription qui manquent à la Bibliothèque du Roi et que l'aurait important d'y faire entrer, pour servir de modèle et de comparaison pour reconnaitre ceux qui y sont déjà sans souscription, ou ceux qui peuvent y entrer par la suite'. The list contains only books dated before 1472, a number stated to be from about 1472, and two block books.

111 Also Dominique Varry, 'Quand l'incunable paraît', on the first Lyon sale catalogue to list incunabula separately, from 1791.

112 Edwards, *Catalogue of a select collection of ancient and modern books*, p. 1 and p. 9: 'For other books of the 15th century see the various classes to which they belong'.

113 Wolcot, *Poetical Works of Peter Pindar*, p. 509.

114 Hearne, *Reliquiae*, II, p. 849, 20 November 1734.

115 A copy of Gregorius I, *Moralia*. [Basel: Ruppel, about 1472] belonging to the Earl of Pembroke: 'Praesens hoc Opus factum est per Johan. Guttenbergium apud Argentinam Anno Millesimo ccclviij', according to Palmer, *General History of Printing*, pp. 299–300. A copy in the BnF has a forged purchase date of 1468, and the copy in the BL has a forged date of 1470. See Scholderer,

'The beginnings of printing at Basel', pp. 192–3. The former certainly existed in the eighteenth century; see Laire, *Index librorum*, lot 35, p. 39. Another eighteenth-century faked colophon dates Livius, *Historiae Romanae decades*. [Venice]: Vindelinus de Spira, 1470, to 1469, to establish it as the first edition. See *Lakelands Library*, lot 1905; as recorded in *ISTC*.

116 Munby, 'Jacob Bryant', p. 196. See Oates, 'The "Costerian" *Liber precum*'. For Smith's fakes see Verwey, 'Frederik Corcellis', and Snoek, 'George Smith'. I am grateful to Jan Snoek for discussing Smith's forgeries with me.

117 Osborne, *Catalogue of the Libraries of the Following Eminent and Learned Persons*, I, no. 1345: '*Plinii secundi epistolarum liber primus*. Exemplar elegans, literis initial. colorat. corico turcic., fol. deaurat. lineis rubris & auro elegans ornat. 15£ 15s. Oxon. apud F. Corcellis 1469.'

118 BL, Add. MS 76016, Reviczky to Spencer, 21 July 1792: 'Les Epitres de Pline avec la fausse date de 1469 sont un morceau très curieux, et c'est le même exemplaire au sujet du quel il y a un assez long article chez Meerman part 2, pag. 16, où il est marqué qu'à la faveur de cette fraude il a été vendu 15 guinées. Il y est dit aussi que c'est une édition de Deventer chez Pfafraet sans date et qu'un anglais à Amsterdam nommé George Smith a si bien contrefait la souscription.' (The Letters of Pliny with the forged date is a very curious item; this was the copy on which Meerman wrote at length, part 2, p. 16, noting that this fraud fetched 15 guineas. It is also said that it is an undated Deventer edition by Pfafraet, and that it was a George Smith, an Englishman in Amsterdam, who forged the colophon so well.) Also Dibdin, *Bibliotheca spenceriana*, II, pp. 271–2, no. 373 and III, pp. 411–14, no. 727.

119 BL, Add. MS 75965, 18 June 1815, where Horn relates his 'discovery' of a forgery by Fischer in the colophon of an almanac which he had sold to the Grand Duke of Hesse. BL, Add. MS 75965, from Horn to Spencer, Wiesbaden, 4 August 1815: 'I could not help laughing when your lordship mentioned your apprehension about counterfeits of the Menz press. The Germans are not so industrious as the Italians are in the fabrication of ancient coins. Besides there are not ten connoisseurs in Germany and even those ten have not one fourth of the necessary bibliographical knowledge and if they had, how could they dispose of their counterfeits with any prospect of advantage ... The most extraordinary trifle which I lately got is a certificate, similar to yours pro regno Cypri 1455, of the indulgences granted by Leo 10th ... and likewise an old wax seal of Peter Schoiffer with his arms as usual, which a friend of mine had cut off from an insignificant document of his.' On 29 August 1816 he wrote 'A friend of mine took it out of his archives'. Now JRL, 17254. This might point towards collaboration with Bodmann, on whom see Knaus, 'Bodmann und Maugérard'.

120 Fischer, *Beschreibung einiger typographischen Seltenheiten*, pp. 42–7, quoted a document from 1459 allegedly transcribed by Bodmann, mentioning that it had four seals attached. Dibdin, *The Bibliographical Decameron*, I, p. 305,

note. Whether Fischer, Bodmann, or both, were responsible, Schaab, *Die Geschichte der Erfindung der Buchdruckerkunst*, I, pp. 32–43 showed that this document never existed. Although his attempts to discredit all documents about Gutenberg are risible, the documents invented or falsified by Fischer or Bodmann are conveniently listed in Hessels, *Gutenberg Fiction*, pp. 169–71. See also Schmidt-Künsemüller, 'Gotthelf Fischer'.

121 Jarausch, 'Institutionalisation of history', explores why some of the most important persons reassessing the past in eighteenth-century Germany came from outside the academic establishment, including Herder and Winckelmann, enabling the historiographical engagement with other aspects of the past than dynasties and their realms.

122 Fournier, *Dissertation*, pp. 4–5: 'Les Mallinckrot, les Maittaire, les Naudé, les Chevillier, les Mentel et autres étoient sans doute des gens très-savans dans les belles-lettres, et l'imprimerie est redevable à quelques-uns d'eux de profondes et laborieuses recherches, mais ils n'etoient point artistes. Or, en traitant d'un art dont ils connoissoient peu les opérations et le méchanisme, il a dû nécessairement leur échapper beaucoup de fautes, qu'ils n'ont pas été en état de sentir ni de corriger. La Caille et Prosper Marchand, quoique libraires, ne se sont pas moins trompés; ils ont suivi les mêmes erremens que les autres, parce qu'il y a loin de la vente d'un livre aux diverses opérations qui servent à le faire.'

123 Although Fournier himself declared that no one had suggested this before, it was widely found, for instance in La Caille and, importantly for a wider diffusion, in Maittaire, *Annales typographici*, I, p. 9.

124 'Liber 1mus omnium typis Moguntinis novo artificii genere jam ad umbilicum perductis impressus' (The first book printed with the Mainz type, with the new craft now brought to perfection) was still given as the reason for the acquisition of the Bodleian copy, Auct. 4Q 1.3. See Bodleian Library, *Catalogue of Books Purchased, 1796*, p. 2.

125 Schoepflin, *Vindiciae*, p. 11: 'Persistendum in medio. Solutilium inventor typorum cuiuscunque hi indolis sint, artis typographiae est verus inventor.' (Let us take the middle position. He who invented movable types, whatever their nature, is the true inventor of the art.)

126 Fournier, *De l'origine*, p. 126: 'Ce n'est qu'après que cet art a été exercé pendant plus que 130 ans … que l'on vient revendiquer cette invention pour en donner la gloire à Harlem, et cela sur de contes de vieillards, sur des preuves équivoques, sur des historiettes ridicules, et sur des contradictions marquées.' (It is only in the last 130 years that claim has been laid to this invention in order to give glory to Haarlem, based on tall stories, contradictory proofs, laughable tales and patent contradictions.)

127 Fournier, *Observations*.

128 Gando, *Lettre*, p. 5: 'Je ne relèverai pas la note (pag. 6 de la dissertation) dans la quelle il avance que pour qui sçait graver et fondre les caractères, l'impression

n'est point difficile, et que ce n'est pas le titre qui fait la science, ni le bonnet de docteur. C'est aux sages supérieurs, c'est au Ministère public à punir les écarts indécens d'une imagination si vagabonde.' (I shall not highlight the note (p. 6) where he proposes that 'for a man who can engrave and cast characters, printing is easy, and that it is not the title which makes knowledge nor the hood of the doctor'. It is our wise superiors, it is the public ministry which should punish the indecent deviations of such an errant imagination.'

129 Baer, *Lettre sur l'origine de l'imprimerie*. On Baer see des Essarts, *Siècles littéraires*, I.

130 For instance a statement which might imply that he thought that Saracens, Moors, and iconoclasts had sacked Rome after the Goths.

131 Baer, *Lettre sur l'origine de l'imprimerie*, p. 5: 'Mais comme je ne veux attaquer principalement que sur sa logique, et que je prétends être pour le moins aussi bon logicien qu'il est habile fondeur, je m'en rapporterai au jugement du public; et j'espère que M. Fournier ne m'en fera pas un crime.' And pp. 26–7: 'Pour décider ce procès le public n'a qu'à lire la définition de la typographie que M. Schoepflin a mise à la tête des son livre; je défie M. Fournier d'y trouver à redire. Mais pour le comprendre, il faut sçavoir le Latin; pour l'attaquer il faut être logicien; et l'un et l'autre ne paroissent pas être le fort de notre fondeur. Quant à la logique nous en trouverons une preuve dans le sujet même.' The *reductio* is based on an inconsistent use of the word *typographie*. Baer had a university formation, including the rite of initiation, the academic disputation, in his case on logic. See Baer, *Dissertatio logica*.

132 Baer, *Lettre sur l'origine*, p. 43: 'Vous conviendrez, avec moi … que M. Fournier feroit mieux d'exercer son art, que de critiquer les sçavans; qu'enfin M. Schoeplin doit écrire des livres et que M. Fournier doit fondre des caractères pour les imprimer.' Fournier, *Remarques* was the response to Baer's attack.

133 Fournier, *Observations*, review in *Journal de Trévoux*, p. 1386: 'C'est pour ainsi dire, l'érudition mise en parallèle ou même en contraste avec l'Art.'

134 Fournier, *Dissertation*, review in *Journal de Trévoux*, p. 1063: 'Cependant la vérité a des droits supérieurs.' Also on Fournier's polemical style in Fournier, *Remarques*, review in *Journal de Trévoux*. Baer, *Lettre*, review in *Journal de Trévoux*, p. 2394 equally deplored his tone: 'Nous désirerions que ce vengeur de M. Schoepflin eût fait l'honneur à l'imprimerie de traiter sa cause avec cette modération que la littérature recommande si fort.' (We would have wished that M. Schoepflin's avenger had respected the art of printing by treating his case with the moderation, which literature so strongly recommends.)

135 In *L'Année littéraire* (1761), VII, pp. 134–7 and 137–42.

136 Moxon, *Mechanick Exercises*. On the Royal Society see Hunter, *Establishing the New Science*, pp. 73–121; specifically on printing see Carter, 'Introduction'. In Fournier, *Manuel*, p. x in the 'Avertissement préliminaire', Fournier outlined the history of the interest in mechanical work on books in France, tracing it back to a project of the Académie des sciences from 1693 to describe printing and the

casting of type. He declared himself the author of the article called 'Caractères d'imprimerie', in *Encyclopédie*, II, 2, pp. 650–65. The article, however, refers to him not as author but as the main, much esteemed, source of information.

137 D'Alembert, 'Discours préliminaire', p. xiii: 'Le mépris qu'on a pour les arts mécaniques semble avoir influé jusqu'à un certain point sur les inventeurs mêmes. Les noms de ces bienfaiteurs du genre humain sont presque tous inconnus, tandis que l'histoire de ses destructeurs, c'est-à-dire des conquérans, n'est ignorée de personne. Cependant c'est peut-être chez les artisans qu'il faut aller chercher les preuves les plus admirables de la sagacité de l'esprit, de sa patience et de ses ressources. J'avoue que la plûpart des arts n'ont été inventés que peu-à-peu, et qu'il a fallu une assez longue suite des siècles pour porter les montres, par exemple, au point de perfection où nous les voyons. Mais n'en est-il pas de même des sciences?'

138 Dutens, *Inquiry*, p. xiii of the preface, first published in French in 1766. Dutens concentrates on discoveries in the fields of theology and philosophy.

139 See Chapter 1, note 47.

140 BL, Add. MS 76299, fol. 214, bill from Edwards receipted 30 March 1790, on 10 March: 'Schoeffelin Vind. Typogr. 7s.6d.' and on 15 March: 'Fournier, Origines de l'imprimerie 12s'.

141 This was printed in Schelhorn's edition of Quirini, *Liber singularis de optimorum scriptorum editionibus*.

142 Whatever our sensitivies, referred to by Schelhorn as 'inter praecipua Germaniae litteratae lumina suo iure referendus', Quirini, *Liber singularis de optimorum scriptorum editionibus*, p. 6.

143 Meerman, *Origines typographicae*, published in the Hague, Paris, and London.

144 For instance Bagford, 'Essay on the invention of printing'. I am grateful to Giles Mandelbrote for his suggestions on the importance of this article.

145 Palmer, *General History of Printing*.

146 As has been drawn out by Myers, 'Ames, Joseph'.

147 Hill, *The Inspector*, p. 90.

148 Grose, *The Grumbler*, no. XII, pp. 47–51.

149 Grose, *The Olio*, pp. 133–4.

150 Maittaire sought a technical, descriptive vocabulary, which developed concurrently with the language of bibliophile collectors, so well explored by Sordet, *L'amour des livres*, especially pp. 258–61, 'Une compétence du discours'.

151 Maittaire, *Annales typographici*, I, p. 58: 'Utinam quidem scirem multiformes litterarum, quibus illi utebantur typographi figuras adeo graphice verbis depingere, ut certis indiciis earum inter se discrepantia statim apparere posset, et suo typographo sua quaelibet editio assignari! Res ea foret immane quantum operosa, singulas typographorum classes perlustrare; singularum in iisdem litterarum ductus minutulos, apices et fastigia, extremitatum curvaturas,

lineolarum inclinationes et distantias, tenues subtilesque articulorum juncturas, universam denique elementorum composituram, faciem et proportionem attentius considerare; et in varietate typorum incredibili stylum dicendi prodigaliter variare. Metuo sane, ut in materia tam varia et multiplici verba deficerent. Non tamen parum ad hunc laborem levandum et rem tam utilem expediendam conduceret, si varia ex variis typographorum veterum editionibus selecta cum alphabetorum tum integrarum sententiarum specimina tabulis aereis inciderentur.'

152   For instance Jungendres, *Disquisitio.*

153   Laire, *Specimen historicum typographiae romanae.*

154   Braun, *Notitia historico-litteraria.*

155   Gras, *Verzeichniss typographischer Denkmäler* on Gerson, *De spiritualibus nuptiis.* Nuremberg: [Sensenschmidt, 14]70. Although modern bibliographers ascribe to Sensenschmidt, Gras identified the type correctly. Rummel financed Sensenschmidt, according to a note in a volume now in Erlangen, formerly in the Charterhouse in Nuremberg, where it was seen by Braun.

156   Hupfauer is especially interesting in this context. He was an Augustinian canon in Beuerberg until he became professor of philosophy in Munich in 1770. There he wrote about the uselessness of monastic learning in "Das Mönchsstudium in Baiern", was denounced as an Illuminate, and sent back to Beuerberg, resuming public offfice as Bavaria became more reform-friendly under French domination. See Knedlik, 'Hupfauer'.

157   Zapf, *Aelteste Buchdruckergeschichte Schwabens*, p. xiii.

158   Gras, *Verzeichniss*, review in *Allgemeine Literatur-Zeitung*, col. 554: 'Dass man seit einiger Zeit auch in dem katholischen Deutschland, besonders in den Klöstern, angefangen hat, den rühmlichen Vorschritten der Protestanten auch in Rücksicht der ehehin nur gar zu sehr vernachlässigten Literatur nachzufolgen, indem verschiedene würdige Männer, die unter ihrer Auffsicht stehenden [*sic*], bisher fast völlig vergessenem Schätze, für sich und auch für andere durch die dem Publikum vor Augen gelegten Verzeichnisse derselben, gemeinnütziger zu machen gesucht haben, verdient gewiss allen Beyfall.' (It deserves our full approval, that, for some time, in Catholic Germany especially in monasteries, people have begun imitating the admirable progress of Protestants, also concerning hitherto badly neglected literature, as worthy men have sought to make treasures in their charge, previously nearly totally forgotten, useful both to them and to others, through published catalogues.)

159   Hupfauer, *Druckstücke*, review in *Allgemeine Literatur-Zeitung*, at col. 686: 'Das, was vielleicht ein Paar Decennien rückwärts, in den Klöstern noch eine Seltenheit gewesen seyn würde, Männer in denselben anzutreffen, welche an derselben Geschmack gefunden, und denen auch die literarischen Schriften der protestantischen Gelehrten nicht zum Anstoss gereichten, das scheint jezt in vielen derselben zum guten Ton zu gehören.' (Perhaps just a few decades back it was rare to find men in monasteries who did not take offence at the

taste and at the literary works of learned Protestants, but now now they seem acceptable to many of them.)

160 Strauss, *Opera rariora*, review in *Historisch-litterarisch-bibliographisches Magazin*, pp. 169–70: 'Wieder eine neue Frucht des geschäfftigen Fleisses eines unermüdeten Klosterbibliothekars, der seinen zum Theil noch immer schläfrigen und saumseligen Herren Collegen nun schon das dritte Mahl … ein nachahmungswürdiges Exempel gibt. Zugleich aber auch ein neuer Beweiss, dass nicht alle Klosterbibliothecken, (welches freilich von einigen mit Recht behauptet wird,) aus blossen Asceten, Polemikern, Scholastikern, und andern dergleichen verrosteten Schofelzeug bestehen, sondern den forschenden Litterator mit wahren, zum Theil ausserordentlichen Seltenheiten befriedigen.' (Yet another fruit of the active diligence of a tireless monastic librarian; for the third time he has set an example for his often sleepy and dim-witted colleagues and also given new proof that not all monastic libraries … only consist of ascetics, polemicists, scholastics and this sort of rusty decrepitude, but can satisfy an investigating man of letters with true, sometimes extraordinary rarities).

161 See on this Wittmann, *Buchmarkt und Lektüre*, pp. 72–4 on 'Die Zerstörung des einheitlichen Buchmarktes' and pp. 74–6, 'Das "Nachdruckszeitalter"'.

162 Seemiller, *Bibliothecae academicae ingolstadiensis incunabula typographica*, review in *Allgemeine Literatur-Zeitung*, at col. 179: 'Dann erscheinen die Bücher, bey welchen sich keine Jahrzahl befindet. Hier macht Hr. S. wieder zwey Klassen. Einige eignet er nach der Aehnlichkeit der Lettern gewissen Druckern zu, und diese werden nach den Rubriken der Künstler zusammengestellt; die übrigen, bey welchen nichts dergleichen gemuthmasset werden konnte, machen den Beschluss. (Auch hier gibt es Bedenklichkeiten bey der ersten Classe. Die Uebereinstimmung der Typen kann bey verschiedenen Druckern statt finden, da Formschneider und Schriftgiesser nich oft für einen, sondern für mehrere arbeiteten).' (Next come books without year. Here Mr S again makes two groups. He assigns some to printers through the similarity of the types; these are organised by printer; at the end come those for which such assumptions cannot be made. Again, there are reservations about the first group. Several printers may have identical types, as engravers and type-casters did not work for one, but for many printers.)

163 Braun, *Notitia*, 1788, review in *Allgemeine Literatur-Zeitung*, cols 193–4: 'Da der Hr. Verfasser aus der Aehnlichkeit der Schriftzüge, Orte und Drucker ausfindig zu machen suchte, (weswegen er auch die 60 Alphabete verschiedener alter Typographen in Kupfer stechen liess) so erscheinen zuerst bis n. 142 diejenigen, welche nach seiner Meynung auf diese Art bestimmt werden können und zwar nach alphabetischer Ordnung der Städte und vorausgeschickter kurzer Geschichte der Druckerey an diesen Orten … (Rec. giebt gerne zu, dass man in einigen Fällen so glücklich ist, durch angestellte Prüfung der Lettern den Drucker zu errathen. Niemals aber ist diese Regel, allgemein angenommen,

sicher und zuverlässig. Druckereyen und Schriftarten können in kurzer Zeit auf andere Besitzer gekommen seyn. Formschneider und Schriftgiesser haben wahrscheinlich nicht immer nur für einen Drucker gearbeitet, diese Künstler haben auch vielleicht zuweilen einander nachgeahmt. Der Hr. Verfasser erinnere sich nur an das von ihm selbst S. 80 angeführte Beyspiel von der völligen Übereinstimmung der Valdarferischen und Reyserischen Typen).' (The author attempts to identify place and printer through the similarity of the typefaces. That is also why he had engravings made, reproducing 60 alphabets of old typographers. Those which he believes can be determined in this way feature, until no. 142, alphabetically by town, prefaced by a short history of printing of each place ... The reviewer concedes that in some cases one can be lucky enough to find out the printer by examining the letters. But this rule cannot be generally certain and reliable. Printing workshops and types can fast pass to another owner. Engravers and type founders probably did not work for one printer only; and craftsmen copied one another. The author should remind himself of his own observation on p. 80 of the similarity of the types of Valdarfer and Reyser.) Braun, *Notitia*, 1789, review in *Allgemeine Literatur-Zeitung*, at col. 594: 'S. 43 folgen die Schriften, deren Drucker der Verfasser aus Mangel der Kriterien nicht zu bestimmen im Stande ist. Einige davon aber haben auf dem Titel unter der Aufschrift einen Holzschnitt welcher einen Lehrer auf seinem Katheder nebst etlichen Zuhörern vorstellet. Sollten nicht manche davon bey Heinr. Quentell in Cölln geduckt seyn, weil sich dieser Drucker öfter einer solchen Abbildung bediente? Ueberhaupt kann man aus diesen Holzschnitten ... oft weit sicherer auf Ort und Drucker schliessen, als aus den Typen.' (On page 43 follow the works the printers of which the author lacks criteria to establish. Some have on the title page under the title a woodcut of a teacher at his desk with his students. Might many of these not have been printed by Quentell in Cologne, as he often used this illustration? In general, it is often far more reliable to determine a printer or a place from such woodcuts ... than from the types.) Hupfauer, *Druckstücke aus dem XV. Jahrhunderte*, review in *Allgemeine Literatur-Zeitung*, at col. 686: 'Eine der vorzüglichsten, aber auch verdienstlichen Bemühungen des Verfassers war dahin gerichtet, die ungenannten Drucker mancher Schriften zu entdecken, und dieses zwar durch Vergleichung der Typen. Rec. muss aufrichtig gestehen, das er, wenn Schriften einmal in die beiden letzten Decennien des 15. Jahrhunderts gehören, und wenn die Typen nicht etwas ganz eigenes und unterscheidendes haben ... es nie gewagt habe, bloss aus der Aehnlichkeit der Typen, über dieses oder jenes Produkt ein Urtheil zu fällen. Hr. H. hat dieses selbst eingesehen, und ist deswegen gar nicht in Abrede, dass er sich in seinen Muthmassungen und Behauptungen öfters könne geirret haben.' (One of the most valuable efforts of the author aimed at identifying the unnamed printer of many works, based on a comparison of typefaces. The reviewer must frankly confess that he has never dared to determine any one production only on the basis of the similarity of types, once works are from the last two decades of the fifteenth century, unless they are truly unusual. Mr H has himself realised this, and there is no suggestion that he has made numerous mistakes in his considerations and statements.)

164 Cicero, *Marius*, frag. 4.1.

165 Camus, *Voyage*, p. 33–4.

166 Seemiller, *Bibliothecae academicae ingolstadiensis incunabula typographica*, review in *Allgemeine Literatur-Zeitung*, at col. 179: 'Ohne gleich anfänglich darüber lange zu streiten, nach welchem Sprachgebrauche Schriften, die in den Incunabeln der Druckerkunst zum Vorschein kamen, selbst Incunabeln genennt werden können, – welches denn aber doch gewiss eben so unrichtig ist, als wenn man Kinder in der Wiege selbst Wiegen nennen wollte – ertheilt vielmehr Rec. der Arbeit des Herren Verfassers seinen volkommenen Beyfall.'

167 Seemiller, *Bibliothecae academicae ingolstadiensis incunabula typographica* (1789), pp. xiv–xv.

168 [Meusel?], 'Kleine Sammlung von Inkunabeln', p. 162: 'Über die Benennung: *Inkunabeln* wird sich hoffentlich niemand mehr ärgern. Ich weiß wohl, dass es Rezensenten giebt, die sie nicht leiden können.' (I hope nobody will take offence at the term 'incunabula'. I know that some reviewers cannot tolerate it.)

169 Murr, *Merkwürdigkeiten*, p. 130, on the Dominicans: 'Es sind 214 sogenannten Incunabeln da.' (There are 214 so-called incunabula.)

170 Schultes, *Briefe über Frankreich*, II, p. 374: 'Wie lange wird es noch hergehen bis unsere deutschen Bibliothekären, statt der elenden Incunabeln, die keinen anderen Werth als denjenigen haben, dass sie den Zeiten der Barbarey angehören … die Manuscripte beschreiben und würdigen, die sie besitzen.'

171 See the discussion on the 'commercialisation du champ du livre rare' in Viardot, 'Livres rares et pratiques bibliophiliques', pp. 451–5.

172 See for instance Jarausch, 'The institutionalisation of history', for Herder and Winckelmann as historians from outside the university environment.

173 Seeba, 'Zwischen Reichshistorik und Kunstgeschichte', for instance p. 323 referring to Lessing's *Literaturbrief* no. 52, from 1759: 'Our beaux esprits are rarely learned and our men of learning rarely beaux esprits. The former just do not want to read, to look anything up, to bring anything together. The latter do nothing but. The former have no material to work from; the latter lack the ability to give structure to their material.' Seeba suggests that Winckelmann belonged among the former from 1740 to 1754, among the latter from 1754 to 1768, subsequently combining the two.

174 Willett, 'Observations on the origin of printing' and 'Memoir on the origin of printing'. Here the latter at p. 307: 'Meerman may be excused in some of these mistakes, as probably he was not acquainted with the *practical* part of *letter-founding*, if he was even with that of printing. Sensible how much, in this enquiry, depended on a knowledge in both the branches, I have taken great

pains to make myself acquainted with them and I have found in Mr Martin, who hath so eminently distinguished himself in the types for the edition of Shakspeare, a ready and able master, who hath instructed me fully in the whole art of letter-founding.'

175 McKitterick, 'Bibliography, bibliophily and the organization of knowledge', p. 46.

176 Goethe, *Die italienische Reise*, entry for 25 December 1786. Here in the translation by W. H. Auden and Elizabeth Mayer.

177 Goethe, *Die italienische Reise*, entry for 28 January 1787.

178 While some have sought to diminish Winckelmann's importance, Édouard Pommier, *Winckelmann*, esp. pp. 150–74, has demonstrated, that in the eyes of contemporaries it was he who laid the foundations for a historical method based on the direct study of ancient monuments.

179 Quatremère de Quincy, *Considérations morales* and *Lettres sur le préjudice*, ed. Pommier, p. 103: '[Winckelmann] est le premier qui, en classant les époques … ait rapproché l'historie des monuments … Revenu enfin de l'analyse à la synthèse, il est parvenu à faire un corps de ce qui n'était qu'un amas de débris; s'il a servi la science, c'est peut-être encore plus par sa méthode que par ses écrits. Quelque estimable que soit son histoire de l'art, elle ressemble toujours plus à une chronologie qu'à une histoire.'

180 BL, Add. MS 76006, 5 October 1802: 'Il me paroit que bien de ces éditions sans datte ni signatures, et que nous appelons douteuses, et aux quelles nous n'avons pu jusqu'ici assigner ni l'époque ni l'imprimeur, commencent à être moins inconnues et moins incertaines.'

181 Lenoir, *Notice historique*, p. x: 'Ces monumens ainsi réunis ne doivent être regardés que comme un rassemblement de modèles vêtus selon les époques auxquelles ils appartiennent.' (The monuments brought together here should only be understood as a collection of models dressed according to their periods.)

4 Competing for authority

1 This has been described as a new cultural practice by Blechet, *Les ventes publiques de livres*, p. 17.

2 These have been listed and summarised in Batts, 'The eighteenth-century concept of the rare book'. See also Glomski, 'Book collecting and bookselling in the seventeenth century'.

3 Heumannus, *Conspectus reipublicae literariae*, pp. 97–9. For another use of the concept of causality see Wendler, *Dissertatio de variis raritatis librorum impressorum causis*.

4 Johannes Ihre, *Dissertatio historico-litteraria* (1741), all of section VI, p. 9: 'Scilicet is seculi nostri pruritus est ut scriptores quo atriore carbone a piis notantur eo vehementius a sciolis desiderentur, immo scripta atheistica et alia eiusdem furfuris, tanquam praecipua bibliothecarum ornamenta conquirantur, asserventur'. Ihre,

Dissertatio historico-litteraria (1743), section VIII, pp. 11–12: 'Sunt plurimi qui inter legendum delectari et ridere malunt quam instrui. Vnde etiam fere videmus, quod libri qui ludicra tractant, uel quouis alio modo frontem lectorum explicare norunt, studiose quaerantur.' In a French context, Viardot, 'Naissance de la bibliophilie' has explored how the apparently neutral interest in rarity could be a cover for subversive books.

5 Berger, *Diatribe de libris rarioribus*.

6 Debure, *Bibliographie instructive*, I, p. iii: 'Le premier de ces objets nous offre la connoissance propre d'un livre quant au fonds, qui puisse nous mettre en état de porter un jugement exact et certain sur sa bonté ou sur son inutilité.' At p. iv: 'Le second qui n'est purement que typographique, fait à proprement parler, la science d'un libraire; elle consiste dans la connoissance exacte et certaine des livres par rapport à leur valeur actuelle dans le commerce, à la différence des éditions, à leur mérite particulier et au choix que l'on en doit faire.' (The first of these aims gives the proper knowledge of the content of books, which can enable us to give an exact and definitive judgement on whether it is good or useful ... The second is purely typographical and, strictly speaking, constitutes the science of a bookseller. It consists in the exact and certain knowledge of books according to their current value in the market, the difference between editions, their special merits, and how to choose between them).

7 As suggested by Viardot, 'Livres rares et pratiques bibliophiliques', who talks of the establishment of the category of rare books as 'durable' through its institutionalisation in the marketplace. Similarly Hunt, 'Private libraries in the age of bibliomania', pp. 438–9.

8 Tocqueville, *L'ancien régime*, book III, chapter I: 'Comment des hommes de lettres qui ne possédaient ni rangs, ni honneurs, ni richesses, ni responsabilité, ni pouvoir, devinrent-ils, en fait, les principaux hommes politiques du temps, et même les seuls, puisque, tandis que d'autres exerçaient le gouvernement, eux seuls tenaient l'autorité?'

9 Debure, *Bibliographie instructive*, I, p. vi: 'Les critiques jaloux qui se sont élevés contr'eux, et qui auroient peut-être eux-mêmes été les plus ardens à se satisfaire dans ce genre, si les faveurs de la fortune les eussent mis en état de pouvoir les acquérir.'

10 Thompson, 'The moral economy of the English crowd', especially at p. 79. The 'moral economy' is, expressed by Douce, the book collector, in his legislative programme for an honest government: '1. The limitation of wealth in individuals ... 2. Annual or perhaps biennial parliaments ... 3. The fixing of prices of the necessaries of life ... 4. The abolition of all quack medics ... 5. The abolition in the most unqualified manner of the slave trade'; Bodleian, MS Douce e.36, fols 12 verso–13 recto.

11 Boyer d'Argens, *Mémoires secrets*, I, pp. 3–7.

12 Notably Viardot, 'Naissance de la bibliophilie'; also Chatelain, *La bibliothèque de l'honnête homme*; more recently Kenny, 'Books in space and time'.

13 As expressed by Hont, 'The early Enlightenment debate on commerce and luxury'.

14 Jaucourt, 'Imprimerie', p. 609: 'L' avantage que les auteurs ont sur ces grands maîtres, vient de ce qu'on peut multiplier leurs écrits, en tirer, en renouveler sans-cesse le nombre d'exemplaires qu'on désire, sans que les copies le cèdent en valeur aux originaux. Que ne paieroit-on pas d'un Virgile, d'un Horace, d'un Homère, d'un Cicéron, d'un Platon, d'un Aristote, d'un Pline, si leurs ouvrages étoient confinés dans un seul lieu, ou entre les mains d'une personne, comme peut l'être une statue, un édifice, un tableau?'

15 [Mercier], review of Debure, *Bibliographie instructive*. The review is the only contribution not included in Debure's re-publication of the controversy. Next followed [Mercier], 'Lettre … sur la *Bibliographie instructive*', followed by Debure, *Lettre … servant de réponse à une critique de la* Bibliographie instructive. Next came [Mercier], 'Seconde lettre … sur la *Bibliographie instructive*'. This letter ends with a note inviting Debure to respond, which is not included in Debure's reproduction. This was followed by Mercier, 'Lettre sur une réponse à deux critiques de la *Bibliographie*'. Finally, Debure, *Appel aux savans*.

16 [Mercier], 'Lettre … sur la *Bibliographie instructive*', pp. 1678: 'M. De B. parlant (pag. 425) de la traduction Françoise d'un ouvrage de Calvin, dit qu'elle est plus recherchée que l'original *à cause de la commodité de la langue*. Je crois sans peine que le François est *plus commode* pour ce Bibliographe que le Latin; mais je n'hésite point à dire que les deux morceaux que je viens de transcrire sont très-peu *commodes* pour les lecteurs les plus indulgens.' (Speaking of the French translation of a work by Calvin, Debure says that it is more sought-after than the original because of the convenience of the language. I find it easy to believe that our bibliographer finds French more convenient than Latin, but I do not hesitate to add that even the most indulgent of readers will find that the two French passages which I have quoted are far from convenient.'

17 Birgitta, *Revelationes*. Nuremberg: Koberger, 21 Sept. 1500. [Mercier], 'Lettre sur la *Bibliographie instructive*', pp. 1658–9; Debure, *Lettre … servant de réponse à une critique de la* Bibliographie instructive, pp. 49–52; and finally Mercier, 'Lettre … sur une réponse à deux critiques de la *Bibliographie*', pp. 2421–2. The word 'Septembris' is meaningless in the genitive unless construed with the preceding 'xxi' ('21st day of September').

18 Mercier, 'Lettre … sur une réponse à deux critiques de la *Bibliographie*', at pp. 2417–18: 'G. Martin dans son Catalogue de M. de Boze a pris pour un nom d'homme le mot GHEDRUCKT, qui en flamand et en Allemand signifie *imprimé*. Pour avoir fait une bévue pareille, ce libraire n'en est pas moins estimable; il n'avoit ni morgue ni prétentions, il rédigeoit tout bonnement des catalogues pour les ventes et vendait des livres sans se croire autre chose que ce qu'il était réellement; mais comment M. de B. a-t-il pû copier une faute aussi considérable dans un catalogue de Martin.' (In his de Boze catalogue G. Martin misunderstood as a personal name the word 'Ghedruckt', which in Flemish

and German means 'printed'. This bookseller is no less worthy for having made such a howler; he was neither proud nor pretentious, but simply edited sale catalogues and sold books without imagining himself to be anything other than what he truly was; but how could M. de B copy such a notable error from a catalogue of Martin's?'

19 Debure, *Appel aux savans*, p. 3: 'Messieurs, Occupé des soins de mon commerce, et cherchant à acquérir des connoissances dans l'état que mes pères m'avoient laissé, j'avois porté mes études sur la partie la moins connue de la librairie.' (Sirs, being engaged with my business and seeking to obtain knowledge in the state which my fathers have left me, I had brought my study to bear on the least known part of the booktrade.)

20 Bourdieu and Saint-Martin, *La noblesse d'état*, explored similar changes in mid twentieth-century France, analysing the dynamic between two social groups with opposing cultural values; the culture of the academic elite, previously closely associated with the governing class, was challenged by an emerging powerful social group with a different educational background, and with money.

21 Debure, *Supplément à la bibliographie*.

22 See Chapter 2, note 67.

23 Schwarz, *Bibliotheca schwarziana*. I am grateful to Giles Mandelbrote who drew this catalogue to my attention. Compare also with the Strasbourg bookseller's catalogue from 1745 of books printed not long after the invention of printing; Lesage, Netchine, and Sarrazin, *Catalogues de libraires 1473–1810*, no. 2530.

24 Debure, *Lettre … servant de réponse à une critique de la* Bibliographie instructive, p. 7: 'Il est nécessaire d'avertir le public, que si j'ai omis quelques fois de ces *éditions imprimées* avant 1500, c'est que la plupart d'entr'elles ne doivent pas être regardées comme des livres fort importants.'

25 See for instance Eberling, 'Upwardly mobile: Genre painting and the conflict between landed and moneyed interest'; Crow, *Painters and Public Life*, and, from the point of view proposed here, Chartier, *Les origines culturelles de la Révolution française*, p. 59.

26 See Coq, 'Le parangon'.

27 Rive, *Chasse*, p. 14: 'Cet infortuné bibliopole, que la nature n'a enrichi d'aucune sagacité, parce que le Génie et Plutus sont rarement d'accord, et qu'ils ne parcourent presque jamais ensemble la même carrière.' Debure had himself criticised Rive in strong terms in his 'avertissement' to La Vallière, *Catalogue des livres*.

28 Rive, *Chasse*, p. 189: 'Cet aide-de camp [of Desaulnays], étoit un petit garçon attaché au comptoir bibliopolique de mon bon ami Guillaume, Guillaume.' (Desaulnays's sidekick used to be a boy behind the book counter of my good friend, Guillaume, Guillaume.) At p. 190: 'Ce petit garçon de magasin bibliopolique' (this little bookshop drudge); at pp. 342, and 344: 'vil fripier de la librairie' (base junk dealer of the booktrade); at p. 346: 'loyal garçon de magasin' (faithful shop boy); etc.

29 Rive, *Chasse*, p. 40: 'Il s'extasie sur le prix de ce Virgile qui a été vendu, comme il le dit, 751 [livres] [*c*. £30]. Mais si ses leçons étoient aussi barbares que celle de son Térence, il ne valoit certainement pas la vingtième partie du prix auquel il a été vendu.'

30 Rive, *Chasse*, p. 46, on a copy of Antoninus Florentinus, *Confessionale*. Rome: Lauer, 1472.

31 Rive, *Chasse*, pp. 39–40: 'Si la valeur des éditions du quinzième siècle ne se tire pas de la blancheur de leur papier, et de l'analogie de leurs types inconnus, avec ceux des presses connues et célèbres de ce même siècle, comme le dit d'abord ce moine, mais si elle ne vient au contraire, que de la génuinité des leçons des manuscrits, d'après lesquels elles ont été exécutées, de leur correction et de la commodité de leur exécution, pourquoi ce moine nous dit-il ensuite … que l'édition de son Térence n'offre que des noms appellatifs …? L'ancienneté des éditions ne fait pas leur valeur, il n'y a que des bibliomanes et des brocanteurs qui se chauffent de cette idée.'

32 Rive, *Chasse*, p. 48. It is still believed to be by Zell, now dated about 1468–70. La Vallière's copy is now BnF, Rés. E. 3014.

33 *Bouquin* was also his word for another much treasured item, Caracciolus, *Sermones*. Cologne: Zell, 1473.

34 Sordet, *L'amour des livres*, part III, chapter III, especially pp. 242–8. In this important book Sordet explores how the intellectual price grew out of an estimated market price, but increasingly gained independence. On Cisternay Du Fay see Blechet, *Les ventes publiques de livres*, p. 76.

35 Coq, 'Le parangon', p. 319.

36 Rive, *Chasse*, vol. II, preface, p. ii: 'Est-ce, par ce qu'un Grand, qui n'a aucune connoissance bibliognostique, ou qui n'en possède qu'une très-médiocre, et qui est conséquemment dupé par des charlatans, fait l'acquisition de quelques objets bibliographiques, qu'il faut les préconiser? Les Grands ne sont-ils pas à plaindre, quand, sans aucune étude professionale, ils veulent se mêler de tout savoir?' The theme recurs, for instance at I, p. 46: 'Je plains les grands; ils veulent tout savoir sans avoir jamais rien appris; mais aussi les idées qu'ils ont sur la plupart des objets littéraires sont réellement pitoyable, et on ne peut les entendre discourir, surtout sur la bibliologie, sans les regarder comme des pauvres victimes de la charlatanerie.' (I deplore the lords; they want to know everything, having learnt nothing; but even the notions which they have on most literary matters are in truth pitiful, and it is impossible to hear them hold forth especially on bibliology, without seeing them as poor victims of charlatanry.)

37 Rive, *Chasse*, p. 52, note: 'Mais ce n'est pas moins un bouquin qui ne doit avoir entrée que dans les grandes bibliothèques publiques, qui doivent fournir un asile à ces sortes de livres, dont une très grande partie des hommes peuvent se passer; mais qui doivent néanmoins être conservés dans les grands dépôts pour y servir aux annales de la typographie et aider à accroître les connoissances de la société littéraire.'

38 See Chapter 1, note 70.

39 Rive, *Chasse*, preface, p. 8: 'Ne seroit-il pas à propos, que la surintendance littéraire … fît interdire à tous les journalistes l'accueil trop libre et trop facile, qu'ils donnent … aux ouvrages de bibliographie …? Sans l'intervention d'une semblable police, la profession de journaliste ne sera qu'un vil métier mercantile.'

40 Viardot, 'Naissance de la bibliophilie', p. 286.

41 Foxe, *the Benefit and Invention of Printing*, pp. 6–7.

42 *A Tower Conference*, pp. 1–2.

43 Seneca, *Ep.* 1.2.3–4.

44 On the 'stoicised Protestant' rejection of luxury and its political importance see Goldie, 'The English system of liberty', especially pp. 64–9. Stoicising morality was not confined to Protestantism. Thus Argonne, *Mélanges d'histoire*, I, p. 54, hints at Sen. *Dial.* 9.9.7: 'Innumerabiles libros et bibliothecas, quarum dominus vix tota vita sua indices perlegit. Jam enim inter balnearia et thermas bibliotheca quoque, ut necessarium domus ornamentum expolitur.' (Books without number and libraries of which the owner hardly reads the list in his entire life. A library is now considered a necessary amenity of a house, just like bathing facilities). The cultivated reader was expected to recognise the quote from Seneca.

45 La Bruyére, *Les caractères*, chapter XIII, 'De la mode', section 2.

46 Pope, *An Epistle to the Earl of Burlington*, p. 11.

47 Harwood, *A View*, preface, pp. x–xii.

48 Connell, *Portrait of a Whig Peer*, p. 40.

49 Reviczky, *Traité de la tactique*; Reviczky, *Specimen poeseos persicae*.

50 *Periergus*, a Greek equivalent of the Latin *curiosus*, careful and inquisitive but, adding to Reviczky's self-confident self-mockery, it has connotations of being a fuss-pot. *Deltophilus* is a freshly minted compound, 'lover of writing tablets': Reviczky was no common bibliophile.

51 Reviczky, *Bibliotheca graeca et latina*, 'Lettre à M. L'A. D.', p. 9: 'Les hommes sont trop heureux d'avoir quelque folie qui les amuse agréablement, et qui en charmant leur ennui, et en remplissant le vuide qui se fait toujours sentir au milieu de leurs plus grandes occupations, les détourne souvent de passions bien plus dangereuses, de l'ambition et de la cupidité. Qu'importe après tout de quelle manière on obtienne cet avantage, si c'est en poursuivant des papillons, ou en rassemblant des coquilles, en arrangeant ses jettons, ou en complétant ses auteurs? Je vous proposerois, Monsieur, de venir voir mes livres dans l'état ou ils sont actuellement, mais j'ai tout à craindre, qu'après les avoir vus vous n'en portiez un jugement semblable à celui de La Bruyère.'

52 Sordet, *L'amour des livres*, p. 260.

53 According to Cracherode, 'Obituary', p. 354.

54 Penny, 'Richard Payne Knight'.

55 See Chapter 2, note 65.

56 Dibdin, *Bibliographical Decameron*, III, p. 328. Spencer's earliest book-bill is from Elmsley for January to December, 1784. BL, Add. MS 76299, fol. 158.

57 BL, Add. MS 76016, Letters from Reviczky, the first dated 25 June 1789.

58 BL, Add. MS, 76321 covering 30 November 1797–7 July 1798.

59 See Vernus, *Une vie dans l'univers du livre*, p. 74.

60 Birkelund, 'Det Thottske bibliotek', p. 92, quoting from *Nyeste Kjøbenhavnske Efterretninger*, without indicating the date: 'For the first time in this place, we plan to save our catalogues from their previous fate, when distributed for free. Then the greater part fell into the hands of greedy paupers, who sold them to chandlers for a little coffee or snuff … That is why each catalogue is priced so that chandlers would not buy them for scrap, while any book lover will be happy to pay the small sum to avoid the destruction of the catalogues, not least because the profit of the sale will go to relief of the poor.'

61 Edwards, *Memoirs of Libraries*, I, p. 471. George III's distance from this world is compounded by the absence from the Royal Archives of material about the formation of his collection.

62 Welch, *Shopping in the Renaissance*, especially on Olivero Forzetta's acquisitions in Venice in 1335.

63 Bodleian, MS Douce c. 7, Paris 16 fructidor An VIII [3 September 1800]: 'Je regrette bien de ne l'avoir pas vu, j'aurois été très flatté de faire connaissance avec lui et de conférer sur tout ce que vous me demandez. Son nom est si fameux dans l'Europe littéraire, qu'il m'eut été très agréable de converser avec un tel amateur.' De La Rue had been in exile in England from 1792 to 1797.

64 Lord Glenbervie; see Douglas, *Diaries*, I, 27 July 1798, pp. 264–5. Bentley, 'The bookseller as diplomat' on Lord Grenville assisting Edwards's business trip to France in 1800; also another trip to France in 1801, before the peace of Amiens. The text of Edward's report to Lord Grenville of his political conversations, in Historical Manuscripts Commission, *Report on the Manuscripts of J. B. Fortescue*, VI, pp. 289–93.

65 See also Munby, *Connoisseurs*, pp. 4–7.

66 Perhaps Lyde Brown; see Grindle, 'Browne, Lyde'.

67 Presumably Joseph Ames.

68 Probably William Esdaile, although scarcely a clerk; see Vian, 'Esdaile', where Esdale's son is quoted saying that he 'knew little or nothing of what was passing out of banking hours'.

69 This may be Thomas Holcroft.

70 Bodleian, MS Douce e.29, fol. 17 verso, dated 1812.

71 BL, Add. MS 76083, copy of a letter from Spencer to George Augustus Herbert, eleventh Earl of Pembroke, 9 December 1799, asking to borrow Ovidius, *Opera*. Bologna: Azoguidus, 1471, in order to copy some pages which were missing in his newly acquired copy. And an answer from Pembroke 13 December 1799: 'With respect to that edition of Ovid to which you allude in my library at Wilton, tho' I am a very strict guardian of it in common with some other

valuables which perhaps from ignorance I do not price for their innate merit as highly as I ought to do I will trust it with you trusting also that you will not trust it in the hand of any of your fraternity of book collectors or their associates all of whom I have good reason to think are not quite so trustworthy as yourself.'

72 Bodleian, MS Douce e.29 fol. 24 verso. On Douce and Triphook see Feather, 'Robert Triphook and Francis Douce'.

73 The correspondence between Spencer and Burney 7 February 1815 and 24 February 1815 concerns an exchange completely detached from money; here Burney and Spencer were on an equal footing, despite class differences which were insurmountable in other contexts. I am grateful to Scot McKendrick for his observations on the correspondence between Burney and Spencer.

74 This is recounted in Munby, *Connoisseurs*, p. 49.

75 See Douce's note in Bodleian, Douce 270, that the offer was made long after he had acquired the book, in 1788, and MS Douce d.22, item 12, a letter concerning the matter from Spencer, 26 May 1810: 'The leaves that have been taken out in the middle of this volume were given by me to Lord Spencer to make his copy more perfect. I wish his librarian had been a little more careful in extracting them.'

76 BL, Add. MS 76067, letter from James Morrice, Flower, 20 March 1791: 'I am honoured with yr Lordship's letter respecting the copy of Livy which you were pleased to admire at Flower. I esteem myself happy in an opportunity of complying with your request. The Livy shall certainly grace the Library at Althorp. You were so good as to call it an obligation. I will not presume to appreciate it. Your Lordship will do me the honor to discharge it, if such, in any manner most agreeable and satisfactory to yourself. Mrs Morrice and I propose ourselves the pleasure of paying our respects at Althorp before you quit the Country.'

77 See BL, Add. MS 76066, letter from Cracherode, 27 January 1790. The Cracherode copy is now BL, C.19.e.4,5.

78 BL, Add. MS 76067, letter, 21 March 1791.

79 His hierarchical scorn of booksellers is brought out by Manzini, 'Biblioteche e libri', especially at p. 58.

80 See BL, Add. MS 76006, 20 August 1803.

81 See Carrier, *Gifts and Commodities*.

82 Rao, 'Cenni biografici su d'Elci', p. 18.

83 See also the letter from James Payne to Van Praet, Vienna, 28 September 1800 [for 1802], MS Fr. Nouv. acq. 3230, fol. 200: 'The Chevalier d'Elci is just arriv'd to my great joy, but his books are packed up in boxes at the Customhouse. He hopes soon to have them arrang'd at his apartments.'

84 Statius, *Thebais* [Rome: Printer of Statius, about 1470], dated by d'Elci to 'Romae 1470 vel 1471'. See BL, Add. MS 76006, 9 December 1802 and 1 February 1803.

85 In fact d'Elci had a copy of this edition, now in the Biblioteca Laurenziana in Florence, but that does not alter the financial nature of the transaction.

86 MS. Fr. Nouv. Acq. 3230, fols 58–60, Mainz, 28 fructidor an XI [15 September 1803], where Signor Podozzi first appears: 'Mr Podozzi avec une superbe collection de monuments typographiques qui sont tous très bien conservés, très précieusement reliés vient séjourner à Mayence. Il offre cette collection pour 125 Louis. Il pensait aller à Londres mais empêché par les circonstances, il croit la pouvoir placer à Manheim ou à Gotha.' Fischer's dealings with the Bibliothèque nationale have hitherto not been published, but for his dealings with Darmstadt, including the invention of Podozzi, see Knaus, 'Fischer von Waldheim'.

87 BnF, MS Fr. Nouv. acq. 3230, fol. 202, letter from Payne to Van Praet, Milan, 4 December 1802, concerning a copy of Valturius printed on vellum. JRL, 16122. First mentioned in a letter from Horn, 6 February 1811, subsequently 22 October 1813: 'Dans mes dernieres lettres j'avais indiqué a Milord Spencer une découverte bibliographique que je venais de faire. J'avais vu de mes yeux le livre suivant: Pius II Bulla ad principes christianos contra turcos 1463. fol. imprimé avec les caractères des litterae indulgentiarum Nicolas V 1454. On connait cette Bulle de Pie II en Latin mais celle-ci est en langue allemande, et c'est le seul exemplaire qu'on en connaisse. C'est un superbe exemplaire mais Dieu sait quel en est le prix.' On 2 March 1814 d'Elci set out clear instructions for the transfer of £100 through a banker who must have a draft on London, so that he could receive payment at the same time as Spencer received the Bull.

88 Through Horn, Spencer asked for additional information about an undated edition of Terence, JRL, 18028. D'Elci replied with full bibliographical details. The Terence is the only surviving copy of the edition so this is no exchange of duplicates. He also offered Spencer other books, now quite explicitly for sale. Correspondence with d'Elci ceased between 1804 and 1811, presumably because of the difficulty of wartime communication: the first letter from 1811, written in Vienna, reached Spencer via St Petersburg.

89 BL, Add. MS 75965, 5 August 1813.

90 See BL, Add. MS 76299, fol. 237, invoice dated 5 July 1790 from Antonio Longa who paid d'Elci 50 louis d'or for a box of books, a straight commercial deal which after the banker's commission amounted to £49 5s 6d. Including transport the total was £52 6s 7d.

91 Much the same could be said about other Italians collecting and dealing in this period, not least Canonici. For instance a note in BL, G.9030 states that it was acquired by Canonici during the upheavals follow the French incursions, and then sold to Edwards. Also Eusebio Della Lena risked the dangers of occupied Italy in 1797 to be able to sell to Spencer books made available by the unrest; see BL, Add. MS 76007.

92 Petrucciani, *Gli incunaboli della biblioteca Durazzo*, especially pp. 35–6. Also Petrucciani and Puncuh, *Giacomo Filippo Durazzo*.

93 Ratcliffe had fifty-four Caxtons, compared to Lord Harley's forty-nine, George III's thirty-eight and James West's thirty-seven. See Lucas, 'Book-collecting

in the eighteenth century', p. 269, on the collecting of Caxtons. See Ratcliffe, *Bibliotheca ratcliffiana.*

94 Nichols, *Literary Anecdotes*, VIII, pp. 456–7.

95 MS Douce e.36, fol. 12 recto–verso.

96 MS. Douce e.91, fol. 10 verso, July [1815].

97 MS Douce d.21, item 8, a letter from Blandford, 15 January 1802, in which he discussed in detail the text of a ballad and the relationship between the English, German, and Latin versions.

98 His relationship with Spencer was more complex in reality but not, apparently, very cordial. Cf. also note 75 above.

99 See Hillyard's excellent article, 'Ker, John'.

100 BL, Add. MS 18850 and IB.19756. This is far from being an isolated instance. *Douce Legacy*, item 212, records for instance the commentary of Primasius on the Apocalypse, a manuscript of the seventh or eighth century, now MS Douce 140 which was sold in 1742 for £27 17s 6d, to Joseph Ames. It was sold to Douce in 1801 for £2 9s. Also item 216, Berengaudus, a commentary on the Apocalypse. MS Douce 330, an English twelfth-century manuscript, was bought by Douce at the Sebright sale in April 1807, lot 2116, for 10s 6d.

101 The sale was reported in the *Morning Chronicle* (18 June 1812); *London Gazette* (20 June); *Derby Mercury* (25 June); *Ipswich Journal* (27 June); and *Caledonian Mercury* (29 June). I have identified these reports using the British Library's digital collection of nineteenth-century newspapers.

102 *The Times*, 18 June 1812, p. 2.

103 *The Times*, 16 October 1790, p. 2: 'Mr Fox disposed of two of his horses during the last Newmarket Meeting, viz. Seagul and Chanticleer. The sum for which they were sold was, four thousand four hundred guineas.' That is an average of £2,330 each. *Life of the Right Honorable, Charles James Fox*, p. 191.

104 Fletcher and Hanwell, *Catalogue*, 1798, no. 902: 'Aulus Gellius, Gronovii very neat and gilt 1£ 1s. L. Bat. 1706.' *Todd's Catalogue for 1798*, no. 5526: 'Aulus Gellius, Gronovii 18 shillings 1706.'

105 Bent, *London Catalogue*, 1799, pp. 34 and 56.

106 Purcell, '"A lunatick of unsound mind": Edward, Lord Leigh'; in 1764 this book cost Lord Leigh £53 10s.

107 Hunt, 'Private libraries', pp. 438–9.

108 *The Times*, 10 July 1793: 'Earl Spencer has, for some years past, been making very valuable additions to his library, which is now one of the largest and best in the kingdom. His Lordship's time is almost wholly absorbed in the researches of literature.'

109 BL, Add. MS 76016, 25 June 1789: 'Comme la seul idée, qu'un jour viendra, ou ma collection, assemblée avec tant de soins et de frais, deviendra le partage de quelque héritier idiot, et qu' elle sera éparpillée dans une vente, m'afflige dès à présent, mon plan favori a toujours été d'engager quelque prince ou souverain de s'en assurer de mon vivant pour une Bibliothèque publique et permanente,

en me donnant annuellement à peu près 300£ st.' (I am afflicted already now by the very thought that, one day, my collection, put together with such care and expense, will be the share of some idiot heir, and that it will be scattered in a sale, so my favourite plan was always to enlist a prince or a sovereign to secure it while I still live for a public and permanent library, giving me annually some £300.)

110 BL, Add. MS 76016, 10 September 1789, shortly after the sale of the library: 'Je vous supplie de ménager votre santé dans cette dangereuse saison de la chasse, et de tempérer cet exercice violent par la paisible lecture de Gratius de venatione et des κυνηγετικά d'Oppien, premières éditions in membranis.' (I implore you to take care of your safety in this dangerous hunting season, and to moderate this fierce activity by the peaceful reading of Gratius on hunting and Oppian on hunting with hounds, first editions on vellum.'

111 Quatremère de Quincy, *Considérations morales. Suivi de Lettres sur le préjudice*, ed. Pommier, fifth letter to General Miranda, p. 227: 'Après Italie, il n'est aucun pays plus riche en antiques, que l'Angleterre ... Qu'en résulte-t-il? Des richesses sont éparses dans tous les châteaux; il nous faut aller dans tous les comtés, faire plusieurs centaines de lieues pour voir ces recueils partiels: aussi, je ne connois rien de moins utile à l'Europe et aux arts même en Angleterre, que ce que l'Angleterre possède en ce genre.'

112 As suggested by August von Kotzebue, quoted by Haskell and Penny, *Taste and the Antique*, p. 35.

113 Cf. Chapter 2 notes 149 and 160.

114 Munby, *Connoisseurs*, p. 8.

115 See Feather, 'Triphook and Douce', pp. 468–79.

116 The prospectus for *Bibliographiana*, a publication bringing together the articles from the *Manchester Herald*, is found among Douce's paper, Bodleian, MS Douce d.23, item 167.

5 Commemorating and obliterating the past

1 Just two examples of this bureaucratic use of 'memory': Reading, 'Digital interactivity in public memory institutions'; and Dempsey, 'Scientific, industrial, and cultural heritage', who writes: 'Archives, libraries and museums are memory institutions: they organise the European cultural and intellectual record.'

2 Processes of forgetting the past have been analysed by Marc Augé in *Les formes de l'oubli*.

3 Most recently on Cracherode in Quarrie, 'Clayton Mordaunt Cracherode', p. 198.

4 Amory, *John Buncle, Esq.*, I, pp. 22–4, and II, p. 196.

5 BL, Add. MS 76067, 7 March 1791.

6 Grégoire, *Rapport sur la bibliographie*, p. 6: 'Les nobiliaires, les traités généalogiques, les ouvrages dans lesquels le despotisme consignoit ses extravagances et ses fureurs, avoient presque toujours les honneurs du maroquin, tandis que les livres

immortels d'Hubert Languet, d'Althusius, de Milton, de Williams Allen, n'echappoient au compas de la censure, de l'inquisition, des cours qu'en se réfugiant … sous la modeste enveloppe d'un parchemin. Les ouvrages qui revéloient les crimes des tyrans et les droits des peuples étoient les sans-culottes des bibliothèques.'

7 See Coq, 'Le parangon', p. 319.

8 BL, Add. MS 75964. The letter from the librarian of Roth is enclosed with Horn's letter to Spencer: 'Noch muß ich bemerken, daß unser Psalterium ein ziemlich dicker und schwerer Foliant ist theils wegen dem mit Messing beschlagenen Banddecke, theils wegen dem Anhang: weil das Psalterium noch vor 50 Jahren zum Gebrauch der jungen Herren im Chorstunden [benutzt wurde], wurden Psalmen, Hymni etc auf pergament geschrieben fast so stark als das Psalterium und dazu in Schweinleder gebunden. Doch kann dieser Anhang leicht abgesondert werden, wenn Sie das Psalterium ungebunden verlangen. Übrigens ist das Psalterium wohlbehalten bis auf ein Blatt vowon etwas abgerissen worden, welches aber nur als ein Merkmal seines hohen Alters anzuschauen ist.'

9 White, *Catalogue … January 19, 1790*, lot 7753, Isocrates in Greek and Latin, London, 1749, 'very neat, in the original binding'.

10 Cuthell, *A Catalogue of Books for the Year 1800*, nos 1324 and 1329.

11 Osborne, *An Extensive and Curious Catalogue*, for instance lot 62, Dio Cassius, Hanover, 1606.

12 James Edwards, *Bibliotheca parisiana*, for instance lot 189, where 'very neat, and original binding' is centred and on a separate, extra-leaded line.

13 Wagstaff, *Winter Catalogue of Rare Old Books*, no. 381: 'Opera domini Joannes Vigo, a curious antique edit. in the original binding, the covers curiously stampt. 5s.'

14 Dymott, *A Catalogue of Several Thousand Books*, no. 55: 'Biblia cum Glossa Ordinaria … with manuscript notes in the margin, the capital letters illuminated, exceeding fair, and in the original binding. Black letter, 5£ 5 s. *Imp. Koberger, 1487.*' Dymott, *Catalogue for MDCCLXXII*, contained several references to old bindings, which could be understood to be promoted because of their age, e.g. nos 3786, 3878, and 3896 (a manuscript).

15 Sordet, *L'amour des livres*, p. 251, and p. 277, on Adamoli's retention of parts of a historic binding.

16 Laire, *Index librorum*, pp. 5–11.

17 JRL, 3295; Aguesseau, *Catalogue des livres*, lot 2942: 'On sent bien qu'alors ce livre convenoit parfaitement à un jeune prince qui aimoit les lettres, et que ce présent étoit digne de lui être offert.'

18 Hobson, *Humanists and Bookbinders*, p. 103.

19 Reviczky, *Bibliotheca graeca et latina*, pp. 46–7, repeats the description from the d'Aguesseau catalogue, but omits the passage on the binding. On the binding with the pea-green lining see Dibdin, *Bibliographical Decameron*, II, p. 469.

20 BnF, Rés. A. 2298 and BnF, Rés. D. 67967, acquired by 1883; information on acquisition kindly provided by Nicolas Petit.

21 Letters to Spencer of 6 November and 8 December 1798: in November 1798 he sent Edwards four boxes with about 150 books weighing 935 pounds. It seems likely that this consignment formed the core of a sale held at Sotheby's six months later: *Catalogue of a Valuable Collection of Books Printed in the Fifteenth Century.*

22 Bodleian, Douce 192.

23 Lots 3, 8, 9, 11, 12, 18, 20, 23, 24, 25, 26, 32, 35, 39, 40, 42, 44, 50, 60, 61, 63, 64, 66, 67, 68, 78, 80, 86, 89, 95, 103, 105, 109, 114, and 127.

24 For instance lot 18: 'Gregorii (St.) Papae Pastorale, *circa* MCCCCLXVIII. *Typis Ulrici Zel de Hanau*, 1467. Thomas de Beatitudine Aeternitate et Divinis moribus. Gerson de Simonia. Lotharius (Card.) de Miseria Conditionis Humanae. Litigatio Satanae contra Genus humanum. *Haec quinque ultima opera sunt typis Therhoernen Coloniensis impressa, circa* MCCCCLXXI'. The lot was sold for 15s to Nicol who acted for George III; consecutive old foliation numbers indicate that six items now separately bound in Buckingham House bindings previously formed this tract volume: (1) BL, C.9.a.16; (2) BL, C.9.a.25/1; (3) BL, C.11.a.8/1; (4) BL, C.9.a.23; (5) BL, C.11.a.8/2; (6) BL, C.9.a.25/2.

25 BL, Add. MS 75965, 8 March 1802. See also Chapter 2, note 134.

26 Spencer's binders' bills for the period from the 1780s to 1813, with a few later ones, are held among BL, Add. MS 76299 to 73001, along with administrative notes and some letters relating to his collecting of books.

27 BL, Add. MS 76014, Erfurt, 9 August 1799: 'Je reviens à l'Histoire de Daniel dont votre excellence m'offre 1000# [livres]. Vous jugerez par vous même Mgr qu'il semble qu'il ne faut pas rompre la reliure de ce volume pour le séparer des autres ouvrages qui sont reliés ensemble, dont l'un est Biblia pauperum du même Pfister, l'autre l'histoire de l'anticrist. De ce qui me décide ou à garder le volume tel qu'il est ou à le céder tout ensemble. Si donc votre Excellence veut retenir le volume entier tel qu'il est, elle voudra bien m'en donner 1800#'. JRL, 9375; JRL, 9402; and JRL, 15019 (leaf 22) and 23127 (leaf 21). These items can now be associated because they have all been crudely repaired reusing paper from the same incunable edition.

28 Lister, 'The formation of the Althorp library', p. 86, referring to Dibdin, *Bibliotheca spenceriana*, II, p. 130. However, here Dibdin referred to a copy of the 1469 Pliny in the private collection of James Edwards.

29 Dibdin, *Bibliotheca spenceriana*, III, pp. 3–4.

30 Dibdin, *A Bibliographical, Antiquarian, and Picturesque Tour in France and Germany*, III, p. 593, on a copy of Dio Chrysostomus, *De regno*. [Venice: Valdarfer, not after 9 November 1471]: 'What renders this copy exceedingly precious is, that it is printed UPON VELLUM; and is, I think, the only known copy so executed. It is in beautiful condition, and I more than hinted that this precious tome ought to be covered (for it is now in old binding) by the morocco and gilt tooling of Charles Lewis.'

31 BnF, A.m., Carton 270, letter from Fischer to Van Praet, Mainz, '13 vendémiaire an XIII' [5 October 1804]: 'Ils sont tous d'une condition superbe, Horace est toute beauté et relié en marbre doré comme en général tous à l'exception des articles allemands qui ont encore la reliure en bois.'

32 BnF, A.1646. On the price see *1789 Le patrimoine libéré*, no. 57, pp. 93–4, signed by Coq.

33 Camus, *Notice d'un livre imprimé à Bamberg*, and Van Hulthem, *Discours prononcé ... en présentant la notice d'un livre imprimé à Bamberg.*

34 Wolfenbüttel HAB. 16.1 Eth.2°. In BnF, A.m., Carton 270, 'Notes de quelques livres extrêmement rares qui se trouvaient dans la Bibliothèque de Wolfenbuttel et qui manquant à celle de l'Empereur. Reçus le 10 janvier 1807.' It is noted in the margin, 'Il était dans son ancienne reliure en bois' (It was bound in its old wooden boards). This is not the list reproduced by Savoy, *Patrimoine annexé*, I, p. 132–3, and does not quite fit the chronology outlined there, but it was evidently drawn up in the Bibliothèque nationale. Uniquely a note with specifications for the rebinding of this book is enclosed with this list, underlining the importance attached to changing its status: 'Fables de Bamberg. Relié en M. R ... // en lettres d'or // Bibliothèque // L'aigle // Impériale // 1807.'

35 See Savoy, *Remarques sur le vol et la restitution des œuvres d'art*, pp. 86–91.

36 See Savoy, *Remarques sur le vol et la restitution des œuvres d'art*, p. 87.

37 BnF, A.m., Carton 55, pp. 91–3: 'Exposé du besoin de la Bibliothèque nationale pour l'An 8e'; p. 92: 'Reliures: Les reliures sont très arriérées. Un grand nombre de manuscrits et de livres imprimés encor couverts de leur ancienne reliure en bois sont exposés aux vers et à un dépérissement que chaque jour fait accroître. De ce nombre sont la plus part de ceux qui proviennent de nos conquêtes en Allemagne et en Italie et qui quoi qu'infiniment précieux nous sont parvenus dans état déplorable.' (Bindings. There is a substantial backlog. A high number of manuscripts and printed books, still in their ancient wooden boards, are vulnerable to worms and to a daily growing deterioration. The majority are those which come from our conquests in Germany and Italy, and while infinitely precious, they have arrived with us in a deplorable state.)

38 Harris, *A History of the British Museum Library*, p. 19.

39 BL, Add. MS 76300, fols 606–9 is Hering's bill for 1799, totalling £361 2s 3d; fol. 613–15 is Walther's bill for June 1799 to May 1800, totalling £150 18s 6d.

40 Quatremère de Quincy, *The Destination of Works of Art*, p. 10. The first French edition was *Considérations morales*, from 1815, here also p. 10.

41 It has been suggested in conversation that rebinding served to disguise provenance making restitution more difficult. This presupposes that restitution was long anticipated, which does not seem to have been the case, and that spoliated institutions had records which would have enabled them to rely on historic bindings for identifying their books. The list of books confiscated in Vienna in 1809 is unique in noting the bindings: BnF, A.m., boite 270: 'Etat des livres précieux de la Bibliothèque impériale de Vienne qui manquent à la Bibliothèque nationale de Paris ... à Vienne le 23 janvier 1809.' Several are

marked as being in red morocco, with the arms of Eugene of Savoy, or in the red morocco of the duc de La Vallière. Sampling has shown that the Bibliothèque nationale/imperiale did not rebind these books, although they could easily be identified as Viennese property. Rebinding Boner's *Edelstein* would not have disguised its Wolfenbüttel provenance: it was well recorded that the only surviving copy was held there.

42 Guyton and others, *Rapport sur la restauration du tableau de Raphaël*. On the controversy, see McClellan, 'Raphael's "Foligno Madonna"', especially p. 81.

43 Romme, 'Rapport au nom du comité d'instruction publique', p. 662.

44 Bodleian, Auct. 6Q 3.24,25.

45 The fifteenth century as part of the Renaissance is a later concept. For the eighteenth century, the revival of letters and of taste was a sixteenth-century phenomenon. The importance attached to illuminations ascribed to Giulio Clovio exemplifies this. See esp. Munby, *Connoisseurs*, pp. 25–6.

46 On the political background for the focus of historians on the 'vandalist' destruction compared with other more widespread destructions see especially Baczko, *Comment sortir de la Terreur*. Varry, 'Vicissitudes et aléas des livres', p. 283, has emphasised the importance of dispersals during the restoration and the empire.

47 I am grateful to the Earl of Crawford who generously allowed me to examine a substantial number of his Sweynheym and Pannartz editions of the classics, many formerly of the Sunderland collection. A few show signs of washing, but that may have been done at a later period.

48 Reviczky, *Bibliotheca graeca et latina*, p. 7: 'Comme malgré mon nom en *us*, je ne suis pas savant, et que probablement je ne le serais jamais … je ne me suis pas attaché à la recherche de certains exemplaires collationnés, avec des notes marginales manuscrites, très vantés par différens gens de lettres, et annoncés ainsi pompeusement dans quelques catalogues: *Exemplar collatum cum 3. Mss. Vaticanis, 2. Palatinis, 4 Mediceis etc.* ou bien ainsi: *Liber notatus manu Salmasii, Vossii, Scaligerii etc.* Ces exemplaires quoiqu'estimables, et d'un grand usage pour les éditeurs des auteurs anciens, n'en sont pas moins de vrais bouquins, où souvent le peu d'espaces épargnés par les vers, sont couverts d'encres de différentes couleurs, d'une manière très-désagréable à la vue, et qui donne au livre tout l'air d'un vieux grimoire.'

49 Urbanus Bellunensis, *Institutiones graecae grammaticae*. Venice: Aldus Manutius, January 1497/98.

50 BL, Add. MS 76016, letter from Reviczky, 10 September 1789: 'Les premiers dix feuillets sont piqués au bas de la page et ont besoin d'être raccommodés et les notes pourroient être effacées.' (The first ten leaves have worming at the foot of the page and need fixing and the notes could be effaced.) On 29 September he reported the return of the book and said that it looked good except for a few places where the ink has not come out completely, 'à l'exception de quelque peu d'endroits ou l'encre n'est pas entièrement sortie.' BL, Add. MS 76299,

fol. 204, bill for £57 2s from Kalthoeber, for September to November 1789, including: 'Urbani Grammatica graeca sm[all] 4to Blue turkey. G[il]t leaves. Extra. 12s. NB for mending and washing 4s 6d.'

51 Petrucciani, *Gli incunaboli della biblioteca Durazzo*, p. 155; on 15 January 1780 Durazzo wrote to the Fratelli Faure, binders in Parma: 'Si accingano dunque a lavarli, e ripulirli bene, affinché sembrino nuovi e della maggior bellezza.' (So prepare to wash them and to clean them well, so that they may seem new and beautiful.) Petrucciani mentions Durazzo's instructions for the use of *acqua forte* and of alum water for washing. Durazzo corresponded with Debure in 1783 about solutions appropriate for washing. See also p. 36: 'La smania per le belle editioni del 400 è divenuta così universale, che ogni angolo d'Italia mi sembra un Parigi.' (The mania for handsome fifteenth-century editions has become so universal that every corner of Italy seems to me to be a Paris.)

52 Augustinus, *De civitate dei*. [Subiaco: Sweynheym and Pannartz], 12 June 1467. Bodleian, Auct. 7Q 2.19. The barely visible inscription was noted in Jensen and Kauffmann, *A Continental Shelf*, no. 18. In all probability the copy which the monastery presented to Pius VI on 16 November 1776, it was subsequently owned by the duc de La Vallière and it seems likely that it was for him that the inscription was washed out; see La Vallière, *Catalogue des livres*, lot 448.

53 Bodleian, Auct. 2R 3.86.

54 The Bodleian Library appears not to have paid Walther or Kalthoeber to wash out manuscript notes, as they survive in books bound by them, e.g. Bodleian, Auct. O 3.2, Auct. N 2.2, Auct. L 2.1., Auct. K 4.11, and Auct. 7Q 2.1. Auct. L 2.25, rebound by Walther or Kalthoeber around 1790, preserves the notes for which it was acquired in 1697.

55 Didot, *Essai de fables nouvelles*, pp. 123–9, note, on French *papier-vélin* imitating paper used by Caslon for his type specimens which Didot had seen in 1779.

56 Renouard, *Annales*, II, pp. 19–22, here p. 21; his condemnation of French paper-makers is modified by a nationalistic praise of Angoulême paper: 'La France peut faire aussi bien et mieux que les étrangers … Angoulême fait maintenant des papiers non moins solides et plus beaux que ceux que depuis un temps immémorial elle fournit à l'Europe entière … Ses papiers vélins ont presque le bel apprêt et la solidité des papiers anglais de Whatmann et leur blanc naturel et sans azur est plus pur et plus ami de l'œil.' (France can do as well as foreigners, and better … Angoulême now makes paper which is no less solid and more beautiful than that which it since time immemorial provided to all of Europe. Its wove paper has nearly the beautiful sizing and solidity of the English Whatman paper and is a natural white without blue which is kinder to the eye.)

57 Renouard, *Annales*, II, pp. 19–22, here p. 19: 'Depuis que la fantaisie des papiers vélins est devenue presqu'universelle … les éditions de luxe sont, pour la plupart, des livres que le moindre usage détériore sensiblement. Ce défaut n'est cependant point inhérent à cette sorte de papier, mais à la manière dont il est le plus souvent fabriqué.' (Since the craze for wove paper has become nearly

universal … luxury editions have preponderantly become books which are noticeably damaged by the slightest use. This fault is not inherent in this type of paper, but depends on the way in which it is made.) On the French drive to compete with British manufacturing see Minard, *La fortune du colbertisme*, here especially pp. 212–24.

58 Spencer owned Berthollet, *Eléments de l'art de la teinture* from 1787; on the bleaching of paper esp. pp. 65–74. Now JRL, 7393, bound in elegant tree calf with a gold-tooled spine. By contrast, Berthollet, *Elements of the art of dying*. JRL, 25080.8, the English translation, was bound very plainly with eight other practical treatises on agriculture or finance.

59 For a discussion of its invention, application, and use see Kerr, *Memorial Relative to the Invention of a New Method of Bleaching*, from 1792.

60 *Whitehall Evening Post*, 14 October to 16 October 1794, issue 7475, continued in the issue for 15 November to 18 November: 'This liquor indeed has no effect upon spots of oil or other grease but it has long been well-known that a weak solution of caustic alkali furnishes a certain means of removing them.'

61 See MacCarthy Reagh, *Catalogue des livres rares et précieux* (1815), lot 507: 'Le papier en est d'une blancheur … qu'on le prendroit pour un livre qu'on vient d'imprimer.' This is now BL, G.9020.

62 On the society see William and Stoddart, *Bath: Some Encounters with Science*. Spencer began acquiring their publications when they started; see BL, Add. MS 76299, fol. 158, a bill from Elmsley 21 December 1784, including 'Bath Agriculture Society vol. 1, 5s'.

63 Archer, *Miscellaneous Observations on the Effects of Oxygen*, pp. 109–212: 'A brief account of the discovery, composition, properties, and uses in medicine, surgery, and the arts, of the oxygenated muriatic acid, or bleaching liquid', here p. 114.

64 JRL, 3341.

65 Twenty-three years later Dibdin, *Bibliotheca spenceriana*, II, p. 77, described it as being fragile.

66 JRL, 3231.

67 BL, Add. MS 76016, from Reviczky, London 11 February 1791: 'Il faut que ces sortes de livres lavés, comme celui-ci paroit l'être, et Dieu sait comment, se soutiennent assez longtemps lorsqu'ils sont fermés et serrés, mais dès que l'air les pénètre ils se roidissent, et les feuillets deviennent cassants. J'ai défendu au relieur de les mettre dans la presse, et même d'y toucher autrement que pour appliquer le maroquin au dos.' About this volume see Dibdin, *Bibliotheca spenceriana*, II, p. 499, who says 'Unluckily this copy is rather in tender condition'.

68 BL, Add. MS 76299, fol. 228, bill from Edward Jeffrey, Pall Mall, dated 20 May 1790.

69 In 1805 the Bodleian Library paid £36 15s for a copy of the 1466 edition. Bodleian, Auct. L 3.7.

70 Not in Dibdin's catalogue, the John Rylands Library, or the Rylands sale.

71 On experiments with bleaching in paper manufacturing in the 1790s, see also André, 'Au berceau de la mécanisation papetière', p. 278.

72 BL, Add. MS 76006, letter from d'Elci, 8 December 1819, who had heard that Spencer, having seen his books, had advised against bleaching 'parce qu'ils finissent par tomber en pièces'. D'Elci countered: 'Heureusement je me suis aperçu de cet inconvénient à temps, de la façon que à cet heure il n'y a pas un seul livre dans ma collection qui soit lavé avec de l'eau forte. J'ai changé tous les exemplaires qui l'avoient été et depuis ce temps la je me sers d'autres préparations qui n'ont ni peuvent avoir, aucune mauvaise suite.' (Fortunately I became aware of this drawback in time, so that there is no book now in my collection which has been washed in *eau forte*. I have long ago exchanged all the copies which had been, and since then I use another preparation which neither has nor can have a bad effect.)

73 For instance, BL, C.19.d.9, C.1.b.4; and C.19.d.11.

74 Bodleian, Auct. O inf. 1.24. It had lost its original covers by 1835, when it was bought.

75 Feijfer, 'Restoration and display', esp. pp. 89–93.

76 BL, C.7.e.7.

77 See Molli, 'La tarda miniatura', catalogue nos 198 and 199, with illustrations on pp. 449 and 451.

78 BL, C.6.d.1–3. Smith, *Catalogus librorum rarissimorum* [1724], p. 22: 'cum eleganti miniatura in frontispicio' (with an elegant miniature on the frontispiece); and Smith, *Catalogus librorum rarissimorum* [1737], p. 38: 'Pulcherrima editio, cum miniaturis affabre elaboratis in principio uniuscuiusque tomi appositis.' (A handsome edition with skilfully made miniatures at the beginning of each volume.)

79 I am grateful to Lotte Hellinga for this suggestion. The style is indeed very similar to Visentini's architectural fantasies, for instance one from 1764–72 in Gallerie dell'Accademia, Venice.

80 BL, IB. 17742; acquired by Cracherode in 1783.

81 JRL, 10547 and Florence, Biblioteca Laurenziana, d'Elci 749. This was discovered by Armstrong, *Renaissance Miniature Painters*, who reproduces both as plates 89–90. I am grateful to Lilian Armstrong for drawing d'Elci's decorations to my attention.

82 Florence, Biblioteca Laurenziana, d'Elci 753.

83 See Felicetti, *Cristoforo Unterperger*. See also Coltman, *Fabricating the Antique*, pp. 80–2 on the spread of the decorative style of the Loggia of Raphael, after the publication in 1776 of *Loggie di Raffaele nel Vaticano*.

84 Bussi, 'Le miniature nella collezione d'Elci', scheda 105, pp. 104–5, referring to Winckelmann, *Storia delle arti del dissegno presso gli antichi*, either Milan, 1779 or Rome, 1793. Dillon Bussi suggests that the decoration was made in Milan or probably Vienna. However, it seems to me that it was probably executed by Pietro Ciatti in Florence. Dillon Bussi has identified a blue band with the titles

of the books in gold letters as characteristic of the artist, no matter in which style he worked. This band is found in Biblioteca Medicea Laurenziana, MS. Fiesol. 182, which was missing the first leaves when it came to the Laurenziana in 1783. On the endleaves Bandini has recorded that the first three leaves were created by Ciatti, under his direction, and they carry Ciatti's signature where he describes himself as 'scriptor et codicum restaurator'. The decorated leaf is reproduced in *Biblioteca medicea laurenziana*, p. 286. Bandini and d'Elci were close friends.

85 Florence, Biblioteca Laurenziana, d'Elci 1034. Dillon Bussi suggested an eighteenth-century French sentimentalist model.

86 E.g. BL, G.11346.

87 Dillon Bussi suggests that the copies of d'Elci which received this grand treatment were rather poor copies. Perhaps it is more appropriate to see them as objects acquiring a new appearance to go with their new social status. They had been made poor copies, perhaps through excessive bleaching, only because they did not conform to the aesthetic demands of their owners.

88 Sordet, *L'amour des livres*, p. 283 on capital letters and paragraph marks supplied in BnF, Rés. R 587.

89 BL, Add. MS 76067, letter dated 7 March 1791.

90 Bodleian, Douce 270, and MS Douce d.22, containing a letter from Spencer, 26 May 1810. The entry in Dibdin's catalogue of Spencer's books makes no mention of this exchange. See also Chapter 4, note 75.

91 Investigated by Hellinga, *BMC*, XI, p. 148.

92 BL, 167.c.25 (George III's copy) and BL, G.9745 (Grenville's copy); *Catalogue of a Valuable Collection of Books Printed in the Fifteenth Century*, lots 60 and 61, both from St Anna, Bamberg.

93 Sig. z 4.5 (fols 220–1) and sig. Z5.6 (fols 453–4) have been moved from one copy to the other. Sig. M4.5 (fols 341–2), the leaves missing in Grenville's copy, are now in the king's copy, identifiable from the black ink note at the top left corner of M4. Grenville's comment on the former binding is found on a paper slip pasted in.

94 Since rebound by the British Museum bindery.

95 McKitterick, *Print, Manuscript, and the Search for Order*.

96 Bodleian, Auct. 2Q inf. 1.22(1).

97 Petrarch's *Canzoniere e Trionfi*, [Milan]: Zarotus, 1473. BL, G.11376. Panizzi wrote to Grenville: 'I am very much annoyed on finding that the first leaf of your Petrarch is not printed but a fac-simile uncommonly well executed.' In a note in his book Grenville was not entirely convinced; nor did *BMC*, VI, p. 710 agree. Panizzi did not say why he thought it a fake, but the leaf should have had a watermark which it does not. Maybe the leaf is supplied from another copy.

98 Hobson, *Humanists and Bookbinders*, pp. 100–3 points out that the vellum copies of the *Anthologia* were intended for potential patrons of Janus Lascaris, so the now lost decoration would have been intended for a person of some

significance. The decoration of JRL, 3295 indicates that that volume was intended for Cardinal Giovanni di Lorenzo de' Medici, the future Pope Leo X. The manuscript facsimile in Cracherode's copy, BL, IB.28002, is noted in Dibdin, *Bibliographical Decameron*, II, p. 469, note. Also Dibdin, *Bibliotheca spenceriana*, III, p. 3 note.

99 See MacCarthy Reagh, *Catalogue des livres rares et précieux* (1815), lot 2360, where it is stated: 'Les sept derniers feuillets qui contiennent une épitre latine de Lascaris sont manuscrits, mais exécutés avec le plus grand talent. Cet exemplaire a été acheté 45 liv. st à la vente de Pinelli.' (The last seven leaves which contain a letter in Latin by Lascaris are manuscript, but done with the greatest of talent. This copy was bought for £45 at the Pinelli sale.) See Edwards, *Bibliotheca pinelliana*, lot 8956: 'Praefatio miro artificio manu scripta est ad impressionis formam; quam equidem in exemplaribus membraneis impressam vix unquam reperire jam constat.' (The preface is written by hand imitating printing with great skill. It is hardly ever found in copies on vellum.) On the insertion of the pages, which came from a copy which had belonged to John Dent, see Payne and Foss, *Bibliotheca grenvilliana*, p. 29.

100 BL, Add. MS 76006, 20 April 1803: 'Je vous supplie, Mylord, d'une grâce; je vous prie de faire exactement copier moyennant un papier transparent le premier feuillet de Florus (Parisiis: par Gering, 1470) 4to. Première édition.' (I beg you a favour, my Lord; I pray you to have an exact copy made on transparent paper of the first leaf of Florus.)

101 Petrucciani, *Gli incunaboli della biblioteca Durazzo*, p. 160.

102 Dibdin, *A Bibliographical, Antiquarian, and Picturesque Tour in France and Germany*, II, pp. 402–3.

103 JRL, 18930. For the twelve pages supplied see de Ricci, *A Census of Caxtons*, no. 76, 2. Dibdin, *Supplement to the Bibliotheca spenceriana*, p. 213, identified eleven facsimile leaves and ascribed them to the 'incomparable skill of Mr. Whittaker'. Barry Gaines, 'A forgotten artist: John Harris', ascribes them to Harris, referring to a later description by Dibdin. Also Takamiya, 'John Harris'. See Middleton, 'Facsimile printing for antiquarian books', on the availability of matching old paper even in the twentieth century.

104 Here quoted from Grassinger, *Antike Marmorskulpturen auf Schloß Broadlands*, p. 46: 'Da die Art und Weise, wie Antiken aufgestellt werden, grösstenteils Auszierung von Palästen, Villen und Sälen ist: so ist freylich eine verstümmelte Statue, Büste oder erhobene Arbeit kein für das Auge gefälliger Gegenstand.'

105 The quotations from the Marquess of Tavistock and Thomas Jenkins are from Angelicoussis, *The Woburn Abbey Collection of Classical Antiquities*, p. 14. See also Ashby, 'Thomas Jenkins in Rome', and Ford, 'Thomas Jenkins: banker, dealer'.

106 Marvin, *The Language of the Muses*, p. 95; see in general pp. 87–93 on eighteenth-century aristocratic display of ancient sculpture and pp. 93–5 on its modification.

107 On the recreation of antique sculpture see Pinelli, 'Artisti, falsari o filologhi?' and Müller-Kaspar, *Das sogenannte Falsche am Echten*. On Cavaceppi see Gasparri and Ghiandoni, *Lo studio Cavaceppi*; still important is Howard, *Bartolomeo Cavaceppi*.

108 Bartmann, 'Piecing as *paragone*'.

109 Cavaceppi, *Raccolta d'antiche statue*, III, introduction, sig. E1 recto.

110 See Howard, 'Some eighteenth-century restorations'.

111 On the ideal notion of a statue compared with notions of correctness see Grassinger, *Antike Marmorskulpturen auf Schloß Broadlands*, especially p. 22. Grassinger takes as her point of departure the discussions of Townley's Discoboulos.

112 Blundell, *Engravings and Etchings*, here quoted from Michaelis, *Ancient Marbles in Great Britain*, p. 343. Also *The Age of Neo-classicism*, no. 375, and Southworth, 'The Ince Blundell collection'.

113 Musée du Louvre, Inventaire MR207 (no. usuel Ma 435).

114 Spence, *Polymetis*, first published in folio, since in radically revised versions in smaller formats.

115 Two separate editions appeared, one text-only, the other a deluxe illustrated version. Willett, *A Description of the Library at Merly*. He explained the historical or mythical scenes as a representation of the progress of human enlightenment.

116 *An Essay on the Original, Use, and Excellency, of the Noble Art and Mystery of Printing*.

117 Pegge, *Anonymiana*, p. 136.

118 Gibbon, *Miscellaneous Works*, III, p. 709.

119 Schelhorn, *Amoenitates historiae ecclesiasticae et literariae*, p. 779: 'Dignus est hic liber, qui servetur in bibliothecis, etsi futilissimus sit, musis plane iratis consarcinatus. Unde enim, quaeso, liquidius evinci potest, quae foeda et plus quam Thersitica fuerit temporum illorum facies, quae auspicatam illam bonarum literarum restaurationem et cum ea conjunctam ecclesiae emendationem praecesserunt, quam ex hujusce farinae scriptis, in quibus inanes apinae tricaeque [recalling Martial 14.1.7] horrido sermonis genere involutae, utramque farciunt paginam?'

120 Renouard, *Annales*, second edition (1825), I, p. 34, on Laurentius Maiolus, *Epiphyllides in dialecticis*. Venice: Aldus Manutius, 1497: 'Ces pièces, extrêmement rares, manquent à la plupart des collections Aldines. Elles sont au reste d'un intérêt à-peu-près nul, et au nombre de ces livres qu'on ne lit plus, et qu'on a raison de ne pas lire.'

121 For instance, Lambinet, *Recherches historiques, littéraires et critiques sur l'origine de l'imprimerie*, p. 177: 'Les caractères gothiques employés dans les éditions du 15ᵉ siècle n'ont rien de commun avec ceux que les Goths apportèrent en Italie et en Espagne, lors de leurs incursions … Le gothique moderne est la consommation de la décadence de l'écriture dans les 13ᵉ, 14ᵉ et 15ᵉ siècles. Né,

dans le moyen âge, avec la scholastique, époque de la décadence des arts et
des bonnes études, il est le fruit de la bizarrerie du plus mauvais goût. C'est
l'écriture latine dégénérée et chargée de traits absurdes et superflus.' (The
gothic characters used in fifteenth-century editions have nothing in common
with those which the Goths brought to Italy and Spain during their invasions.
The modern gothic is the consummation of the decadence of writing in the
thirteenth, fourteenth, and fifteenth centuries. Born in the Middle Ages with
scholasticism, the age of the decadence of art and learning, it is the fruit of the
vagaries of poor taste.)

122 Panzer, *Annales typographici*, Praefatio, sigs)()(1 verso–)()(2 verso: 'Quom vero
his novae artis peritis, genio seculi, quo vivebant, indulgendum esset, nemini
sane mirum videbitur, si primordia illa artis, huic ipsi genio ita adaptata inveniat,
ut politiorum ingeniorum, praeprimis veterum, foetus rari tantum, vasto quasi
gurgite nantes, appareant, locumque inter tot agmina sermonum, legendarum,
missalium, lecturarum, juris utriusque monarchiarum, scholasticarumque
Thomistarum Scotistarumque exercitationum vix habeant. Interim felici
admodum fato contigisse videtur, ut eadem haec ars divina quae prima aetate in
eo fere versaretur, ut hos foetus doctae ignorantiae e tenebris in lucem proferret,
exoptatam simul occasionem praebuerit, illos, luci iam expositos, spernendi,
perpetuisque imposterum tenebris committendi … Mutata hoc modo facie
eruditionis, profligatisque feliciter tenebris; et monumenta illa, typographicae
artis primordia illa inprimis, quae flebilem barbarae illius, immerito sic dictae
eruditionis, statum declarabant, aut penitus neglecta, aut ad summum in
bibliothecis monasteriorum, lusui blattarum tinearumque exposita, iacuerunt.
Dignum sane fatum, si argumentum maximae partis horum librorum spectes,
at deplorandum, si de arte, cuius initia ex illis, tanquam ex fonte haurienda
sunt … Non mirum igitur est accidisse tandem, licet post secula, ut viri quidam
eruditi, aequi rerum aestumatores, e somno quasi expergefacti, de restauranda
gloria artis, cui litterae earumque progressus omnia debent, serio cogitarent
… Ope horum virorum, laboreque illorum indefesso, novam ab eo tempore
induisse faciem studium historiae literariae videbatur. De origine nunc
typographicis … rebus disputabatur, quae in bibliothecis hactenus latebant
huius generis κειμηλια, non sine plausu in conspectum quasi omnium denuo
protrahebantur, aequumque illis pretium statuebatur.'

123 Maittaire, *Annales typographici*, I, pp. 2–3, the phrase used by Maittaire is 'Hi
quidem rari in vasto ignorantiae gurgite nantes apparebant'. Both Maittaire
and Panzer refer obliquely to Virgil, *Aeneid*, I, 118–19: 'Apparent rari nantes in
gurgite vasto / Arma virum tabulaeque et Troïa gaza per undas.'

124 Quoted by Sacquin, 'Bibliothèque royale et utopie', p. 20, who suggests
that one cannot accuse Ameilhon of involvement in the 'vandalism', but
see Edwards, *Memoirs of Libraries*, II, p. 273, who recorded that Ameilhon
led the destruction of archival material relating to nobility, heraldry, and
knightly orders.

125 Barruel, *Mémoires pour servir à l'histoire du Jacobinisme*, III, p. 91: 'C'est-là une de ces leçons que Weishaupt donne le plus formellement à ses adeptes, tantôt en leur disant de ne pas se faire un cas de conscience de donner aux Frères [i.e. the perfectibilists or Illuminates] ce qu'ils ont de la bibliothèque de la cour: tantôt en envoyant la liste de ce qu'ils peuvent prendre dans celle des religieux carmes, en ajoutant: *tout cela seroit bien plus utile chez nous. Que font ces drôles-là de tous ces livres?'* (This is one of the most categorical lessons which Weishaupt gives his followers, now telling them not to make it a matter of conscience to give to the Illuminates that which they have from the court library, now sending them a list of that which they can take from the Carmelites, adding 'All those things will be much more useful for us, for what use do those buffoons make of their books?')'

126 Bloch, 'La bibliothèque de Colbert', p. 161.

127 Brosses, *Journal*, II, p. 163: 'Le bon cardinal a souvent fait son main en Allemagne, où il furetait les couvents de moines, et se faisait donner, de bonne ou mauvaise grâce, quantité de livres curieux et d'éditions rares. Il assaisonnait le tout de beaux compliments; la pantalonnade italienne ne lui manque pas; on était assez embarrassé de savoir comment refuser Son Excellence Monseigneur le nonce, dont les remerciements précédaient toujours l'offre de la chose qu'il finissait par échanger contre une grave bénédiction.' Serrai, *Domenico Passionei*, pp. 270–1, does not refer to Brosses but mentions some donations made to Passionei while papal legate in Switzerland.

128 Sassi, *Historia literario-typographica mediolanensis*, p. dlviii: 'Dissimulare nequeo, plures in hoc catalogo libros recenseri inutiles ineptosque, sed praeter quam quod commune hoc fuit ceteris etiam urbibus infortunium, metropolis nostrae in typographicis rebus decus satis superque fulciunt tot libri nitidissimis caracteribus excusi … ut novum velut vultum induere viderentur.' (I cannot hide that many books in this catalogue are useless and foolish but, apart from this being a misfortune shared with other cities, books printed in such elegant characters that they seem to take on a new appearance sustain the dignity of our city in matters of printing.)

129 Rive, *Chasse*, II, p. xliii: 'Ne sçait on pas qu'il n'y a point de dépôts plus infidèles et plus risqueux que ceux que l'on a l'imbécilité de faire dans les agrégations séculières ou monachales ou religieuses?' Also quoted by Coq, 'Le parangon', note 45 at p. 331.

130 See McClellan, 'Raphael's "Foligno Madonna"', pp. 84–5.

131 See Cooper, 'Forgetting Rome', p. 113.

6 Conclusion

1 Este, *A Journey in the Year 1793*, pp. 284–5. He refers to Guilelmus Caorsin, *The Siege of Rhodes* [London, early 1483]. Spencer's copy, JRL, 3494, is listed as a Caxton by Dibdin, *Bibliotheca spenceriana*, IV, p. 349. There are four English

incunable editions of Jacobus de Voragine, *The Golden Legend*, the first being Westminster: Caxton, [after 20 Nov. 1483]. Raimundus de Vineis, *The Lyf of Saint Katherin of Senis*. [Westminster]: Caxton's device (Wynkyn de Worde), [about 1493]. The copy bought by the Duke of Roxburghe in 1794 is now BL, G.10542; the copy acquired by George III in 1776 is BL, C.10.b.14. Spencer's copy is JRL, 17317. Raoul Lefèvre, *Recuyell of the Historyes of Troye* [Bruges: Caxton, 1473?]. George III's copy is BL, C.11.c.1. Spencer's copy is JRL, 10863. *Blanchardyn and Eglantine*. Westminster: Caxton, [about 1489]. The only complete copy was acquired by Spencer for £215 at the Roxburghe sale: JRL, 15027. Walter Hylton, *The Ladder of Perfection*. [Westminster]: Wynkyn de Worde, 1494. Spencer's copy is JRL, 15046. There are two incunable editions of *Book of Hawking, Hunting, and Heraldry*, the first being from St Albans: Schoolmaster Printer, 1486. Spencer's copy is JRL, 10001. Raoul Lefèvre, *History of Jason*. [Westminster: Caxton, 1477]. The copy of the Duke of Roxburghe was bought for £94 10s by the Duke of Devonshire; see Dibdin, *Bibliographical Decameron*, III, p. 66. George III's copy is BL, C.10.b.3; Spencer's copy is JRL, 15391.

2 See Chapter 5, note 118.

3 Dupuis, *Origine de tous les cultes*.

4 Douce bequeathed his objects to Samuel Rush Meyrick who underlined the connection between the various parts of Douce's collection; see Meyrick, 'The Doucean museum', part 1, p. 246: 'I have little doubt but that, had he supposed his end so near, and had leisure and ability to make another will, he would have left me his illuminated MSS. as tending in an eminent degree to illustrate the collections of antiquities he has bequeathed.'

5 Such as Rock, *Hierurgia* from 1833.

6 MS Douce e.36, fols 7 verso–8 recto, an entry probably from 1799. Douce referred to the oppressive political environment but may also have had in mind men like John Carter, a 'pro-medievalist fanatic' who used 'the French revolution to cement a reaction rejecting foreign styles reverting to a true British style', in the words of Crook, *John Carter*, p. 6.

7 MS Douce e.37, fol. 9 recto.

8 Thus MS Douce e.30, p. 56: 'In 1825 at Paris on All Saints day no newspapers were suffered to be published. The reign of bigotry in France is restored and in England that of puritanism and hypocrisy.'

9 MS Douce e.30, fol. 48 verso, the note apparently from 1824, the year in which John Banks Hollingworth was elected Norrisian Professor of Divinity in Cambridge.

10 Douce, *The Dance of Death*, p. 2.

11 Douce, *The Dance of Death*, p. 8.

12 Bodleian, MS Douce d.22, fols 168 and 174, letters from Jonas Edwards, 2 July 1814 and 26 August 1814.

13 On this see Haskell, *History and Its Images*.

14 See generally Munby, *Connoisseurs*, specifically p. 146 on the early aesthetic appreciation of medieval decoration, shortly after Douce's death, mentioning

Edward Croft-Murray's *Decorative Painting in England* and Pugin's Red Drawing Room at Scarisbrick House, 1837, with gothic motifs derived from medieval miniatures. See also Humphreys, *The Illuminated Books of the Middle Ages*, from 1849.

15 Douce filled five notebooks with extracts and quotations systematically organised by a typology of fairies or devils. See Bodleian, MS Douce e.99–103, 'Fairies devils etc'.

16 Bodleian, Douce 274–5. See *Douce Legacy*, no. 102.

17 Douce, *Illustrations of Shakspeare*, II, pp. 431, in 'A dissertation on the English morris dance'.

18 Maugérard, *Notice de livres rares*, p. 3: 'Avertissement. La notice que nous présentons au public contient des livres moins importans par ce qu'ils renferment, que par leur antiquité; puisqu'il y en a qui précèdent l'invention de l'imprimerie, et d'autres qui datent de la naissance de cet art. Trois siècles, et sur-tout les trois dernières années, ont apporté tant de changemens dans la façon de penser des français, et dans l'objet de leurs études, que la plupart des livres imprimés par nos premiers imprimeurs nous sont devenus absolument étrangers.'

19 Maugérard *Notice de livres rares*, lot 25, Albertus Magnus, *De mysterio missae*. Ulm: Zainer, 29 May 1473, bound with Albertus Magnus, *De laudibus Mariae*. [Strasbourg: Mentelin, not after 1473]. Lot 68 is another copy of the *De laudibus*. Lot 74 is also described as *De laudibus Mariae* but is stated to be a different text from lot 25, suggested truly to be by Richardus de Sancto Laurentio, an ascription now generally accepted. Lot 74 is probably Albertus Magnus, *Mariale* [Cologne: Zell, not after 1473], which announces itself as 'Liber de laudibus gloriosissime dei genetricis Marie semper virginis'.

20 Maugérard, *Notice de livres rares*, p. 5: 'Nous savons que, si un jour on entreprend l'histoire des français, au lieu de l'histoire des rois de France, on ne le fera jamais bien sans connoître de quoi les français s'occupoient, et on ne le saura que dans des livres composés dans les siècles dont on écrira l'histoire; on y trouvera le principe de leur asservissement dans l'avilissement de leur esprit, qu'on accabloit de futilités.'

21 Bodleian, MS Douce e.33: 'We have little right to call ours an enlightened age, or to use the arrogant expression so frequent in the works of modern authors namely "the dark middle ages", when we reflect that within our own [century] we have endured the various frauds and quackeries under the name of scientific discoveries, in the shape of animal magnetism, Perkin's metallic tractors, acromatic belts, rules for bleeding in our almanacs (otherwise full of superstitious nonsense and catholic saints) and quack medicines.'

22 Bodleian, MS Douce e.29, fol. 24 verso.

23 Bodleian, MS Douce e.36, fol. 2 verso.

24 Douce adds. 83(1). One page has since been reinserted from fragments which came with Douce's books, while most of the woodcuts still live separate lives,

subsequently transferred to the Ashmolean Museum. *Douce Legacy*, no. 116 suggested that a man like Douce could not have mutilated books.

25 Bodleian, Douce 280*.

26 Sherbo, *Shakespeare's Midwives*, especially chapter 6, pp. 132–53, describes in detail Douce's contribution to the understanding of Shakespeare.

27 Bodleian, MS Douce d.23, fol. 130, a letter from George Hibbert, 1 June 1819, with a draft reply from Douce.

28 Douce, *Illustrations of Shakspeare*, especially II, pp. 281–5. See also Douce, 'Observations on certain ornaments of female dress', where a pair of knives is illustrated and discussed in association with literary references to wedding knives.

29 See Chapter 3, note 181.

30 Maitland, *The Dark Ages*, p. 416, and pp. 65–7 on the prices paid for manuscripts.

31 Jador, *Dialogue entre une presse mécanique et une presse à bras*.

32 Firmin-Didot, *Réponses aux questions soumises par les membres de la Chambre du commerce*.

33 12 December 1836.

34 As recorded by Proust, *Le côté de Guermantes*, I, p. 129 in the edition published by Gallimard, Paris: 1988.

35 Ruskin, *St Mark's Rest*, p. 262. On the importance of religion for Ruskin see Wheeler, *Ruskin's God*.

36 Knight, *William Caxton*, p. 84. Celebrations of Gutenberg provided opportunities for bourgeois opposition to aristocratic rule. In most Catholic cities in Germany they were either strictly censored or banned. See Estermann, 'O werthe Druckerkunst', pp. 118–76.

37 Knight, *William Caxton*, pp. 186–95.

38 See Tweedale, 'Days at the factories'.

39 See for instance the Religious Tract Society's *Caxton and the Art of Printing*, pp. 66–7.

40 Brunet, *Manuel du libraire*, 5th edition, in the 'avertissement', p. xiij: 'Pour terminer cet aperçu, nous dirons que jamais les traités sur l'art héraldique et l'histoire des familles nobles n'ont été aussi recherchés que depuis que la noblesse de France, dépouillé de ses anciens privilèges, ne conserve de son passé que des souvenirs, des titres et des blasons.'

41 Bodleian, MS Douce e.36, fol. 40 verso.

42 Brunet, *Manuel du libraire*, 5th edition, p. xxxiv.

43 These figures have to be read with caution. It has not been possible to establish the acquisition date for all volumes, but the graph probably represents reasonably accurately changes in purchasing patterns. However, it understates the number of editions acquired as many more volumes containing several incunabula were acquired in the mid nineteenth century than in the eighteenth and early nineteenth centuries, so the increase in the number of editions acquired is probably greater than the graph indicates.

44 Colclough, "'Purifying the sources of amusement and information'", p. 43: 'In January 1857 the *Saturday Review* noted that W. H. Smith's bookshop could be divided into the "two great classes of dear and cheap", using the halfcrown as a the limit.'

45 Bodleian, Mason H 173.

46 Bodleian, Auct. 7Q 4.32.

47 Bodleian, Auct. Q 4.27.

48 For instance Bodleian, Auct. 1Q inf. 1.52 was bought by Heber in 1816 for 3s 6d, according to a manuscript note in the book. It was bought by the Bodleian in 1837 for 1s, when the price index adjusted equivalent of the 1816 price would have been 3s 2d.

49 For details of the copies see Bod-inc A-467.

50 Clark, *The Gothic Revival*, p. 112.

51 For details of the copies see Bod-inc A-468.

52 The figures are derived from Oldman, 'Panizzi's acquisition of incunabula'.

53 See Miller, *Prince of Librarians*, p. 83.

54 *Hansard*, House of Commons Debate, 25 March 1833, XVI, columns 1003–4, reporting on the Committee of Supply, voting £16,000 to the British Museum.

55 Nicolas, *Observations on the State of Historical Literature*, pp. 21–2.

56 Harris, *A History of the British Museum Library*, p. 104, note.

57 *Hansard*, House of Commons Debate, 23 July 1832, XIV, columns 643–8 at column 643.

58 Whitehead, *The Public Art Museum in Nineteenth-Century Britain*, p. 20.

59 See Weimerskirch, *Antonio Panizzi*, p. 35. When arguing for purchase funds from the trustees he repeats that the collection is there to give access to books which most people cannot afford themselves; see also Weimerskirch, 'Antonio Panizzi's acquisition policies', pp. 202–7; quoting extensively from the Officers' reports 24 (4 February, 1840), 6813 verso and following.

60 On Panizzi's hostility to medievalism see Miller, *Prince of Librarians*, p. 273. The view that Panizzi was interested in acquiring medieval texts is expressed, without documentation, by Pollard 'The building up of the British Museum collection of incunabula', pp. 205–6.

61 See Whitehead, *The Public Art Museum in Nineteenth-Century Britain*, note 121 to p. 21, at p. 35, quoting Lord Aberdeen who distinguished between good pictures, from the time of Raphael and after, and earlier pictures which might be historical documentation, 'Lord Aberdeen noted "I do not think we [i.e. the trustees] have done ill in our purchases; our collection being so small, perhaps our first object ought to be to get good pictures, and after that the collection might be extended to antiquarian and mediaeval pictures with advantage; but if we were to make that too much of an object at present, the formation of a large collection of good pictures would, I think, be very much impeded."'

62 See again Estermann, 'O werthe Druckerkunst', here especially p. 184. It is worth underlining that although this sounds extreme, it is easily paralleled in most if not all European countries in the period.

63 Schulz, 'Gesamtkatalog der Wiegendrucke und Literaturwissenschaft'.

64 Leo XIII, *Aeterni patris*, an encyclical of 1879. The rejection of modern society, democracy, science, and religious toleration had already been formulated in the *Syllabus errorum*, of Pius IX, 8 December 1864, and the dogmatic constitution, 'De fide catholica' of the first Vatican Council in 1870.

65 See Baurmeister, 'Marie Pellechet', pp. 95–6, on her active engagement against Dreyfus and his supporters. As against Catholic anti-Semitism in Italy, Catholic anti-Semitism in France is the subject of an extensive literature. How pervasive a part of historiography it was can be exemplified by Mortier (OP), *Histoire des maîtres généraux de l'ordre des frères prêcheurs*, V, p. 571, who justified the expulsion of the Jews from Spain in 1492 on purely racist grounds.

66 Although Bradshaw published little, his importance has long been recognised. Proctor acknowledged Bradshaw in the preface to his *Index*, p. 8; also *BMC* I, p. xii and Harris, *A History of the British Museum Library*, p. 254. Wehmer, 'Zur Beurteilung des Methodenstreites in der Inkunabelkunde'. Needham, *The Bradshaw Method* has discussed his methodological contributions.

67 Bradshaw, *Collected Papers*, p. 221: 'In fact each press must be looked upon as a *genus*, and each book as a *species*, and our business is to trace the more or less close connexion of the different members of the family according to the characters which they present to our observation. The study of *palaeotypography* has been hitherto mainly such a *dilettante* matter, that people have shrunk from going into such details, though when once studied as a branch of natural history, it is as fruitful in interesting results as most subjects.' Quoted by Hellinga, 'Analytical bibliography', p. 49.

Bibliography

Manuscripts

BnF *Bibliothèque nationale de France*

A.m.   Archives modernes; Révolution, XIXe siècle, début du XXe siècle
Boite 55, Administration, Procès-Verbaux du Conservatoire. An IV-1922 (registres) An IV–XII
Boite 267, Acquisitions d'imprimés. Livres acquis ou saisis à l'étranger. Révolution et Premier Empire (cartons), Listes d'ouvrages à faire venir (Allemagne et Europe du Nord, Hollande, Angleterre, Italie, Espagne, Portugal, …)
Boite 270 (not foliated) Acquisitions d'imprimés. Livres imprimés achetés à l'étranger (Angleterre, Grèce) et imprimés saisis à l'étranger (Allemagne)
Boite 271, lettres et papiers de Maugérard concernant en particulier les saisies à l'étranger. L. Delisle, Notes
MS Fr. Nouv. acq. 3230, Papers and correspondence of Joseph van Praet

Bodleian *The Bodleian Library*

MS Broxbourne 84.10	Catalogue of John Selden's collection
MS Douce 330	Berengaudus, commentary on the apocalypse, England, twelfth century
MS Douce c.7	Letters from Abbé Gervais de la Rue
MS Douce c.8	Letters and drafts of letters from Douce, 1786–1831
MS Douce d.20–d.28	Letters to Douce, 1781–1824
MS Douce e.29–e.30	'Biguarrures modernes'
MS Douce e.33	'Maxims'
MS Douce e.36	'Occasional remarks'
MS Douce e.37	'Miscellanies II'
MS Douce e.91	'Political chronicle'
MS Douce e.99–103	'Fairies devils etc.'
MS Selden supra 111	Catalogue of John Selden's collection

BL *The British Library*

Add. MS 18850   *Horae et Officia*, the Bedford Hours, about 1423

Add. MS 53710	The chronicle of William Thorne, monk at St Augustine's, Canterbury, compiled at the end of the fourteenth century
Add. MS 75964–5	Althorp Papers, letters from Maurus Alexander Horne, 1794–1819
Add. MS 76004	Althorp Papers, letters from Bliss and Burney
Add. MS 76006	Althorp Papers, letters from the conte d'Elci 1802–24
Add. MS 76007	Althorp Papers, letters from Eusebio Della Lena
Add. MS 76014	Althorp Papers, letters from Renouard and from Maugerard.
Add. MS 76016–19	Althorp Papers, letters from Reviczky
Add. MS 76066–8	Althorp Papers, general correspondence
Add. MS 76077–8	Althorp Papers, general correspondence
Add. MS 76082–3	Althorp Papers, general correspondence
Add. MS 76107-8	Althorp Papers, general correspondence
Add. MS 76299-300	Althorp Papers, bills for books, with some correspondence, assembled between 1790 and 1819
Add. MS 763120–1	Althorp Papers, Earl Spencer's diaries 21 April 1796–7 July 1798
Add. MS 78010	Althorp Papers, list of books in the Althorp Library compiled by C. Bruce in 1875
Burney MS 3	Bible, 'The Bible of Robert de Bello', England (Canterbury?), between *c.* 1240 and 1253
Burney MS176	Aulus Gellius, *Noctes Atticae*, Italy (Verona?), third quarter of the fifteenth century?
C.1.a.25, C.1.a.26, C.1.a.27, C.9.a.13, C.8.a.4, and C.11.a.9	Incunabula with letters from Horn to Frederick Augusta Bernard pasted in
Sloane MS 722	Richard Smith (1590–1675), 'Of the first Invention of the Art of Printing'
Stowe MS 378	Gratian, *Decretum*, with gloss; list of popes and emperors, England, first half of the thirteenth century

Incunabula

Note: This list includes only specific copies which are referred to in the text and notes. Other incunabula appear in the general index.

Cambridge University Library (CUL)

Oates 754	Johannes Versor, *Quaestiones super libros Aristotelis*. [Cologne: Quentell], 1493

Oates 1949   Johannes Magister, *Quaestiones super tota philosophia naturali.* Venice: Locatellus, 30 May 1487

Oates 2181   Publius Ovidius Naso, *Epistolae heroides.* Venice: Tacuinus, 24 Jan. 1497/98

Copenhagen, Royal Library

Inc. 1314   Cyprianus, *Opera.* Rome: Sweynheym and Pannartz, 1471

Inc. 1315   Gaius Caecilius Plinius Secundus (Pliny the Younger), *Epistolae.* [Venice: Christophorus Valdarfer], 1471

Inc. 2001   Homerus, *Opera.* Florence: [Printer of Vergilius (C 6061)], 18 Mar. 1487/88

Inc. 2456   Constantinus Lascaris, *Erotemata.* Milan: Paravisinus, 30 Jan. 1476

Inc. 2492   Livius, *Historiae romanae decades.* [Venice]: Vindelinus de Spira, 1470

Inc. 3308   Gaius Plinius Secundus (Pliny the Elder), *Historia naturalis.* Venice: Jenson, 1472

Florence, Biblioteca Laurenziana

d'Elci 753   Tibullus, *Elegiae*; Propertius, *Elegiae*; Catullus, *Carmina*; Statius, *Silvae.* [Venice: Vindelinus de Spira], 1472

d'Elci 749   *Scriptores rei rusticae.* Venice: Jenson, 1472

d'Elci 1034   Quintus Curtius Rufus, *Historiae Alexandri Magni.* [Rome]: Lauer, [not after January 1472]

Harvard, Houghton Library

Inc. 6406   *Anthologia graeca Planudea.* Florence: Laurentius de Alopa, 11 August 1494

London, The British Library (BL)

167.c.25   Cato, *Disticha de moribus.* Augsburg: [Sorg], 2 November 1475

C.1.b.4   Demetrius Chalcondylas, *Erotemata.* [Milan: Scinzenzeler, about 1493]

C.6.d.1–3   Livius, *Historiae romanae decades.* [Venice]: Vindelinus de Spira, 1470

C.7.e.7   Dante Alighieri, *La Commedia.* Florence: Nicolaus Laurentii, Alamanus, 30 August 1481

C.9.a.16   Gregorius I, Pont. Max, *Pastorale.* [Cologne: Zell, not after 1470]

C.9.a.23   Innocentius III, *Liber de contemptu mundi.* [Strasbourg: Eggestein, about 1473]

C.9.a.25/1   Thomas Aquinas, *De beatitudine aeternitatis*. [Cologne: Printer of Dares, not after 1 December 1472]

C.9.a.25/2   Thomas Aquinas, *De divinis moribus*. [Cologne: Printer of Dares, not after 1472]

C.10.b.3   Raoul Lefèvre, *History of Jason*. [Westminster: Caxton, 1477]

C11.a.8/1   Johannes Gerson, *De simonia*. [Cologne: Printer of Dares, not after 1472]

C11.a.8/2   Johannes Gerson, *De remediis contra pusillanimitatem*. [Cologne: Printer of Dares, about 1472]

C.11.c.1   Raoul Lefèvre, *Recuyell of the historyes of Troye*. [Bruges: Caxton, 1473?]

C.19.d.9   Catullus, *Carmina* ... [Milan: Philippus de Lavagnia], 1475

C.19.d.11   Cicero, *De oratore*. Rome: Han, 5 December 1468

C19.e.4,5   Homerus, *Opera*. Florence: [Printer of Vergilius (C 6061)], 18 March 1487/88

G.8482   *Anthologia graeca Planudea*. Florence: Laurentius de Alopa, 11 Aug. 1494

G.9030   Livius, *Historiae romanae decades*. Rome: Sweynheym and Pannartz, [1469]

G.9745   Cato, *Disticha de moribus*. Augsburg: [Sorg], 2 November 1475

G.10542   Raimundus de Vineis, *The Lyf of Saint Katherin of Senis. The Reuelacions of Saynt Elysabeth of Hungarye*. [Westminster]: (Wynkyn de Worde), [about 1493]

G.11346   Dante Alighieri, *La Commedia*. Foligno: Johann Neumeister and Evangelista Angelini, Apr. 1472

G.11376   Francesco Petrarca, *Canzoniere e Trionfi*, [Milan]: Zarotus, 1473

IB.17118   Aulus Gellius, *Noctes Atticae*. Rome: In domo Petri de Maximis [Sweynheym and Pannartz], 11 Apr. 1469

IB.17366   Suetonius, *Vitae XII caesarum*. Rome: [Johannes Philippus de Lignamine], August 1470

IB.17742   Ammianus Marcellinus, *Historiae, libri XIV–XXVI*. Rome: Sachsel and Golsch, 7 June 1474

IB.19607   Cicero, *Rhetorica ad C. Herennium*. [Venice: Jenson, 1470]; bound with Cicero, *De inventione*. Venice: Jenson, 1470

IB.19658   *Scriptores rei rusticae*. Venice: Jenson, 1472

IB.19756   Giovanni Boccaccio, *Decamerone*. [Venice]: Valdarfer, 1471

IB.28002   *Anthologia graeca Planudea*. Florence: Laurentius de Alopa, 11 August 1494

Manchester, John Rylands Library (JRL)

15   Johann Brunner, *Grammatica rhythmica*. Mainz: [Schoeffer, about 1470–3] [but with a date of 1468]

3069	*Biblia latina*, [Mainz: (Gutenberg), about 1454–5]
3231	Honoratus Servius Maurus, *Commentarii in Vergilii opera.* [Rome]: Han, [about 1470–1]
3295	*Anthologia graeca Planudea.* Edited by Janus Lascaris. Florence: Laurentius de Alopa, 11 Aug. 1494
3341	Horatius, *Epistolae et carmina.* Ferrara: Carnerius, 1474
3494	Guilelmus Caorsin, *The Siege of Rhodes.* [London: Printer of Caorsin, 'The siege of Rhodes', early in 1483]
9375	Historie von Joseph, Daniel, Judith und Esther. Bamberg: Pfister, 1462, after 1 May
9402	*Biblia pauperum.* [German]. [Bamberg: Pfister, about 1462]
9784	*Psalterium.* [Mainz]: Fust and Schoeffer, 14 August 1457
10001	*Book of Hawking, Hunting, and Heraldry.* St Albans: Schoolmaster Printer, 1486
10547	Sallust, *Opera.* Venice, Johannes de Colonia and Johannes Manthen, 1474
10863	Raoul Lefèvre, *Recuyell of the Historyes of Troye.* [Bruges: Caxton, 1473?]
14387	Jacobus de Cessolis, *The Play of Chess.* [Bruges: Caxton], 31 March 1474
15019 (leaf 22)	*Ackermann von Böhmen.* [Bamberg: Pfister, about 1463]
15027	*Blanchardyn and Eglantine.* Westminster: Caxton, [about 1489]
15046	Walter Hylton, *The Ladder of Perfection.* [Westminster]: Wynkyn de Worde, 1494
15391	Raoul Lefèvre, *History of Jason.* [Westminster: Caxton, 1477]
15392	*Reinaert, The Historye of Reynart the Foxe.* [Westminster: Caxton, after 6 June 1481]
16122	Pius II, *Bul zu Dutsch widder die snoden ungleubigen Turcken.* Mainz: Fust and Schoeffer, after 22 Oct. 1463]
17249	'Christopher' (woodcut, dated 1424)
17250.1	Paulinus Chappe, commissary, *Indulgentia*, 1454 [30 lines]. [Mainz: Printer of the 42-line Bible, 1454–5]
17250.2	Paulinus Chappe, commissary, *Indulgentia*, 1454–1455. [Mainz: Printer of the 31-line indulgence and of the 36-line Bible, 1454–5]
17265	Johann Brunner, *Grammatica rhythmica.* Mainz: [Fust and Schoeffer], 1466
17317	Raimundus de Vineis, The Lyf of Saint Katherin of Senis. The Reuelacions of Saynt Elysabeth of Hungarye. [Westminster]: (Wynkyn de Worde), [about 1493]
17659	Giovanni Boccaccio, *Decamerone.* [Venice]: Valdarfer, 1471
18028	Terentius, *Comoediae.* [Rome: Riessinger, about 1469]

18930	Thomas Malory, *Le morte d'Arthur*. Westminster: Caxton, 31 July 1485
23127 (leaf 21)	*Ackermann von Böhmen*. [Bamberg: Pfister, about 1463]

Oxford, The Bodleian Library (Bodleian)

4° A20(1) Th. Seld.	*Appellatio Universitatis parisiensis de impositione decimae fructuum beneficiorum*. [Antwerp: Leeu, between 20 Sept. and 10 Nov. 1491]. Bod-inc A-362
4° T1 Th. Seld.	Petrus Bertrandi, Libellus de iurisdictione ecclesiastica contra Petrum de Cugneriis. Paris: Johann Philippi, 2 Apr. 1495. Bod-inc B-234, and Vita et Processus sancti Thomae Cantuariensis martyris super libertate ecclesiastica. Paris: Johann Philippi, 27 Mar. 1495. Bod-inc V-147(4)
4° A 31(1) Art. Seld.	Albumasar, *Flores astrologiae*. Augsburg: Ratdolt, 18 Nov. 1488. Bod-inc A-154
AA 127(2) Th. Seld.	Aegidius Romanus, *De regimine principum*. Venice: Bevilaqua, 9 July 1498. Bod-inc A-032
BB 17(3) Art. Seld.	Albumasar, *Flores astrologiae*. Venice: Sessa, [*c.* 1500]. Bod-inc A-156
Arch. B b.10,11	*Biblia latina*, [Mainz: (Gutenberg), about 1454–5]. Bod-inc B-237(1)
Arch. G d.36	John Mirk, *Liber festivalis*. [Oxford: Theodoricus Rood], 19 Mar. 1486/7. Bod-inc M-233(1)
Arch. G e.7(1)	Rufinus, *Expositio in symbolum apostolorum*. Oxford: 17 Dec. '1468' [1478]. Bod-inc R-148(2)
Auct. 1Q 5.15	Bartholomaeus de Chaimis, *Confessionale*. Mainz: Schoeffer, 25 May 1478. Bod-inc B-078
Auct. 1Q inf. 1.52	Albertus Magnus, *Compendium theologicae veritatis*. Ulm: Zainer, [not after 1481]. Bod-inc A-106
Auct. 2Q inf. 1.22(1)	Giovanni Boccaccio, *Genealogiae deorum*. Venice: Vindelinus de Spira, 1472. Bod-inc B-369
Auct. 4Q 1.3	Duranti, *Rationale divinorum officiorum*. [Mainz]: Fust and Schoeffer, 6 Oct. 1459. Bod-inc D-178
Auct. 4Q 1.7,8	Gratianus, *Decretum*. Strasbourg: Eggestein, 1471. Bod-inc G-178
Auct. 6Q 3.24,25	*Missale parisiense*. [Paris]: Jean Du Pré and Desiderius Huym, 22 September 1481. Bod-inc M-261
Auct. 7Q 2.1	Eusebius, *De evangelica praeparatione*. Venice: Jenson, 1470. Bod-inc E-047
Auct. 7Q 2.17	Cyprianus, *Opera*. Rome: Sweynheym and Pannartz, 1471. Bod-inc C-502
Auct. 7Q 2.19	Augustinus, *De civitate Dei*. [Subiaco: Sweynheym and Pannartz], 12 June 1467. Bod-inc A-517

Auct. 7Q 4.32   Augustinus, *De moribus ecclesiae.* [Cologne: Bartholomaeus de Unkel, *c.* 1482]. Bod-inc A-552

Auct. 7Q inf. 2.8   Leo I, *Sermones.* Rome: Johannes Philippus de Lignamine, 1470. Bod-inc L-063

Auct. 2R 3.86   Petrus Bembus, *De Aetna dialogus.* Venice: Aldus Manutius, 1495/6. Bod-inc B-143

Auct. K 4.11   Homerus, *Batrachomyomachia.* Venice: Laonicus [and Alexander], 22 Apr. 1486. Bod-inc H-137

Auct. L 1.8, 9   Livius, *Historiae romanae decades.* [Venice]: Vindelinus de Spira, 1470. Bod-inc L-116

Auct. L 2.1   Laurentius Valla, *Elegantiae linguae latinae.* Venice: Jenson, 1471. Bod-inc V-026

Auct. L 2.2   Aulus Gellius, *Noctes Atticae.* [Rome]: (Sweynheym and Pannartz), 11 April 1469. Bod-inc G-054

Auct. L 2.23   Silius Italicus, *Punica.* Rome: Sweynheym and Pannartz, [not before 5 Apr. 1471]. Bod-inc S-197(1)

Auct. L 2.24   Calpurnius, *Bucolica*; Nemesianus, *Bucolica*; Hesiodus, *Opera et dies.* Published as part of the above edition of Silius Italicus, *Punica.* Bod-inc S-197(2)

Auct. L 2.25   Vergilius, *Opera.* [Strasbourg: Mentelin, *c.* 1470]. Bod-inc V-074

Auct. L 3.7   Cicero, *De officiis*, [Mainz]: Fust and Schoeffer, 1466. Bod-inc C-308

Auct. L 3.9   Gaius Caecilius Plinius Secundus (Pliny the Younger), *Epistolae.* [Venice: Valdarfer], 1471. Bod-inc P-374

Auct. M 1.3   *Biblia latina.* Mainz: Fust and Schoeffer, 14 Aug. 1462. Bod-inc B-239(2)

Auct. N 2.2   Cicero, *Rhetorica ad C. Herennium.* Rome: Wendelinus de Wila, 1474. Bod-inc C-211

Auct. N 5.6   Hyginus, *Poetica astronomica.* Venice: Ratdolt, 14 October 1482. Bod-inc H-251(1)

Auct. O 3.2   Catullus, *Carmina* Parma: Stephanus Corallus, 31 August 1473. Bod-inc C-012

Auct. O inf. 1.24   Lucianus Samosatensis, *Vera historia.* Naples: Arnaldus de Bruxella, 6 Mar. 1475/76. Bod-inc L-176

Auct. Q 4.27   Marsilius Ficinus, *Commentaria in Platonem.* Florence: Laurentius de Alopa, 2 Dec. 1496. Bod-inc F-040

Auct. QQ sup. 1.15   *Cordiale quattuor novissimorum.* [Westminster]: Caxton, 24 Mar. 1479. Bod-inc C-457

Auct. QQ sup. 1.21   *Disticha Catonis.* [Westminster: Caxton, after 23 Dec. 1483]. Bod-inc C-137(2); Boethius, *De consolatione philosophiae.*

	[Westminster]: Caxton, [*c.* 1478]. Bod-inc B-403(2); Geoffroy de La Tour-Landry, *The Knight of the Tower.* Westminster: [Caxton], 31 Jan. 1484. Bod-inc L-001; Aesop, *Fables.* Westminster: Caxton, 26 Mar. 1484. Bod-inc A-054(1)
Douce 192	Johannes Salesberiensis, *Polycraticus.* [Brussels: Fratres Vitae Communis, 1479–81]. Bod-inc J-190(2)
Douce 270	Jacobus de Voragine, *Legenda aurea sanctorum.* Westminster: Caxton, [after 20 November 1483]. Bod-inc J-068(3)
Douce 274–5	Augustinus, *De civitate Dei.* Abbeville: Pierre Gérard and Jean Du Pré, 1486/7. Bod-inc A-533
Douce 280*	*Canon Missae.* [Mainz: Fust and Schoeffer, 1458]. Bod-inc M-284
Douce adds. 83(1)	*Die duythsche euangelien epistolen und lectien.* [Cologne: Ludwig von Renchen], 10 Apr. 1489. Bod-inc E-023
Mason H 173	Cherubino da Spoleto, *Regola della vita spirituale.* Venice: [Benalius, *c.* 1490]. Bod-inc C-176
S. Seld. d.4	*Chronicles of England.* Westminster: Caxton, 8 Oct. 1482. Bod-inc C-195(1)
S. Seld. d.5	*Myrrour of the Worlde.* [Westminster: Caxton, 1481]. Bod-inc I-002
S. Seld. d.6	Jacobus de Cessolis, *The Play of Chess.* [Westminster]: Caxton, [*c.* 1483]. Bod-inc C-169(1)
S. Seld. d.7	Ranulphus Higden, *Polychronicon.* [Westminster]: Caxton, [after 2 July 1482]. Bod-inc H-121
S. Seld. d.8(1)	John Mirk, *Liber festivalis.* Westminster: Caxton, 30 June 1483. Bod-inc M-232
S. Seld. d.8(2)	*Quattuor sermones.* Westminster: Caxton, [1482–3]. Bod-inc Q-007(1)
S. Seld. d.10	John Lydgate, *The Life of Our Lady.* [Westminster]: Caxton, [1484?]. Bod-inc L-204
S. Seld. d.11(1)	*Ars moriendi.* [Westminster: Caxton, *c.* 1490]. Bod-inc A-450
S. Seld. d.11(2)	*Directorium sacerdotum ad usum Sarum.* Westminster: Caxton, [*c.* 1489]. Bod-inc D-107
S. Seld. d.13	Christine de Pisan, *Faits d'armes et de chevalerie.* [Westminster]: Caxton, 14 July 1489. Bod-inc C-191(2)
S. Seld. d.14	Vergilius, *Aeneis.* [Westminster: Caxton, after 22 June 1490] Bod-inc V-109(1). Bound with Marsilius of Padua, *The Defence of Peace.* [London]: R. Wyer for W. Marshall, 1535

Paris, Bibliothèque nationale de France (BnF)

Rés. A.1646   *Historie von Joseph, Daniel, Judith und Esther*. Bamberg: Pfister, 1462, after 1 May

Rés. A.2298   Thomas Aquinas, *Commentaria in omnes epistolas Sancti Pauli*. Basel: Furter, 16 October 1495. CIBN T-134

Rés. D. 67967   Bartholomaeus de Chaimis, *Confessionale*. [Nuremberg: Fratres Eremitarum S. Augustini], 31 May 1480. *CIBN* C-239

Rés. E. 3014   Pius II, *Bulla retractationum. De curialium miseria*. [Cologne: Zell, about 1470]

Rés. R. 587   Rodericus Zamorensis, *Speculum humanae vitae*. Paris: Gering, Crantz and Friburger, not after 22 Apr. 1472

Rés. Velins 1149   Cicero, *Epistolae ad familiares*, [Venice], Jenson, 1475.

Wolfenbüttel, Herzog August Bibliothek

16.1 Eth.2°   Ulrich Boner, *Der Edelstein*. Bamberg: [Pfister], 14 February 1461

Printed primary sources

Académie royale, *Table de matières contenues dans l'Histoire et dans les Mémoires de littérature tirés des registres de l'Académie royale des inscriptions et belles-lettres* (Paris, 1751)

Aguesseau de Fresnes, Jean-Baptiste-Paulin d', *Catalogue des livres imprimés et manuscrits de la bibliothèque de feu monsieur d'Aguesseau* (Paris, 1785)

Alembert, Jean le Rond d', 'Discours préliminaire des éditeurs', in *Encyclopédie, ou Dictionnaire raisonné des sciences*, vol. I (Paris, 1751), pp. xxiii–xxiv

Ames, Joseph, *Typographical Antiquities, Being an Historical Account of Printing in England with Some Memoirs of Our Antient Printers and a Register of the Books Printed by Them from the Year MCCCCLXXI to the Year MDC* (London, 1749)

Amory, Thomas, *The Life of John Buncle, Esq., Containing Various Observations and Reflections Made in Several Parts of the World* (London, 1765)

Archer, Clement, *Miscellaneous Observations on the Effects of Oxygen on the Animal and Vegetable Systems* (Bath, 1798)

Argonne, Bonaventure d', *Mélanges d'histoire et de littérature ...* 4th edition (Paris, 1725)

Askew, Anthony [sale of], *Bibliotheca askeviana. Sive catalogus librorum rarissimorum Antonii Askew, M. D ... Quorum auctio fiet apud S. Baker & G. Leigh ... 13 Feb. 1775* (London, 1774)

   Bibliotheca askeviana manu scripta sive Catalogus librorum manuscriptorum Antonii Askew. His adduntur ... auctores classici in quorum marginibus scriptae sunt, suis ipsorum manibus, doctissimorum virorum notae atque observationes, nempe Bentleii magni, Chandleri, Chishulli, Joannis Taylori, Antonii Askaei, aliorum [London, G. Leigh et J. Sotheby, 7 March 1785]

Atkyns, Richard, *The Original and Growth of Printing, Collected Out of History and the Records of This Kingdome. Wherein Is Also Demonstrated, that Printing Appertaineth to the Prerogative Royal and Is a Flower of the Crown of England* (London, 1664)

Audiffredi, Joannes Baptista, *Catalogus historico-criticus romanarum editionum saeculi XV in quo praeter editiones a Maettario, Orlandio ac P. Laerio relatas … plurimae aliae quae eosdem effugerunt, recensentur ac describuntur: non paucae contra ab eodem P. L. aliisve memoratae exploduntur* (Rome, 1783)

Baer, Friedrich Carl, *Dissertatio logica de logices amplitudine* (Strasbourg, [1737])

Lettre sur l'origine de l'imprimerie, servant de réponse aux observations publiées par M. Fournier le jeune, sur l'ouvrage de M. Schopflin, intitulé Vindiciae typographicae (Strasbourg, 1761)

Review of *Lettre sur l'origine*, by Élie Catherine Fréron, in *L'année littéraire* (1761), 7, 134–7

Review of *Lettre sur l'origine*, in *Journal de Trévoux* (1761), 2392–407

Bagford, John, 'An account of several libraries in and about London, for the satisfaction of the curious, both natives and foreigners' first published in *Monthly Miscellany* (June 1708), here from *A Compleat Volume of the Memoirs for the Curious* (1710), pp. 167–82

'An essay on the invention of printing by Mr. John Bagford, with an account of his collection for the same, by Mr. Humfrey Wanley', *Philosophical Transactions*, 25, no. 310 (1707), 2397–410

Bale, John, *Illustrium Maioris Britanniae scriptorum, hoc est, Angliae, Cambriae, ac Scotiae summarium* ([Gippeswici in Anglia [i.e. Wesel], 1548)

Barruel, Augustin, *Mémoires pour servir à l'histoire du Jacobinisme*, 4 vols (London, 1797–8)

B—de, Monsieur, *Reflections on the Causes and Probable Consequences of the Late Revolution in France with a View of the Ecclesiastical and Civil Constitution of Scotland* (Edinburgh and London, 1790)

Beloe, William, *The Sexagenarian, or the Recollections of a Literary Life*, 2nd edition, 2 vols (London, 1818)

Bent, William, *The London Catalogue of Books, with their Sizes and Prices. Corrected to September MDCCXCIX* (London, 1799)

Berger, Joachim Ernst, *Diatribe de libris rarioribus horumque notis diagnosticis* (Berlin, 1726)

Berthollet, Claude Louis, *Eléments de l'art de la teinture* (Paris, 1787)

Elements of the Art of Dying Containing the Theory of Dying in General (Edinburgh, 1792)

Beughem, Cornelius à, *Incunabula typographiae sive Catalogus librorum scriptorumque proximis ab inventione typographiae annis, usque ad annum Christi M. D. inclusive* (Amsterdam, 1688)

Blundell, Henry, *Engravings and Etchings of Sepulchral Monuments, Cinerary Urns, Gems, Bronzes, Prints, Greek Inscriptions, Fragments &c in the Collection of Henry Blundell, Esq. at Ince*, 2 vols ([Ince?], 1809)

Bodleian Library, *A Catalogue of Books Purchased for the Bodleian Library. with an Account of Monies Collected for that Purpose* (Oxford, 1780–1861)

Bollioud de Mermet, Louis, *De la bibliomanie* (The Hague, 1761)

Boyer d'Argens, Jean Baptiste de, *Mémoires secrets de la république des lettres ou Le théâtre de la vérité*, vol. I (Amsterdam, 1744)

Bradshaw, Henry, *Collected Papers*, ed. F. Jenkinson (Cambridge, 1889)

Braun, Placidus, *Notitia historico-litteraria de libris ab artis typographicae inventione usque ad annum MCCCCLXXVIIII [ab anno MCCCCLXXX usque ad annum MD] impressis in bibliotheca ... monasterii ad SS. Vdalricum et Afram Augustae extantibus. Accedunt VIII [III] tabulae aereae sexaginta primorum typographorum alphabeta continentes*, 2 vols (Augsburg, 1788–9)

  Review of the 1788 part of *Notitia* ... in *Allgemeine Literatur-Zeitung* 25, 1 (1790, January), cols 193–6

  Review of the 1789 part of *Notitia* ... in *Allgemeine Literatur-Zeitung*, 165, 2 (1790, June), cols 593–6

Brosses, Charles de, *Journal du voyage en Italie, lettres familières* (Paris, 1799), here from the edition by Romain Colomb, 2 vols (Grenoble: Roissard, 1971)

Brunet, Jacques-Charles, *Manuel du libraire et de l'amateur de livres*, 5th edition (Paris, 1860)

Caledonian Mercury (Edinburgh, 1720–)

Camus, Armand-Gaston, *Notice d'un livre imprimé à Bamberg en M CCCCLXII, par Albert Pfister, et contenu dans un volume arrivé à la Bibliothèque Nationale au mois de pluviôse an 7 ... lue [à l'Institut national] le 23 germinal [12 April] an 7* (Paris, An VII [1799])

  Rapport fait à l'Institut national, le 5 ventôse an VI [24 February 1798] ... au nom d'une commission spéciale, sur l'édition de Virgile [Paris, 1798]

  Voyage fait dans les départemens nouvellement réunis et dans les départemens du Bas-Rhin, du Nord, du Pas-de-Calais et de la Somme, à la fin de l'an X (Paris, An XI [1802–3])

Catalogi librorum manuscriptorum Angliae et Hiberniae in unum collecti (Oxford, 1697)

Cavaceppi, Bartolomeo, *Raccolta d'antiche statue, busti, teste, cognite ed altre sculture antiche scelte restaurate*, 3 vols (Rome, 1768–72)

Cave, William, *Scriptorum ecclesiasticorum historia literaria, a Christo nato usque ad saeculum XIV facili methodo digesta ...* (London, 1688)

Caxton and the Art of Printing (London: The Religious Tract Society, [1853])

Chambers, William and Robert, *Exemplary and Instructive Biography for the Study of Youth*, Chamber's Educational Course (Edinburgh, 1836)

Chardin, Charles, *Section de Brutus. Discours prononcé à la section de Brutus, par le citoyen Chardin, commandant en chef de la force armée de la section de Brutus, dans le temple de la Raison et de la Vérité, décadi 10 ventôse [28 February 1794]* (Paris: Imprimerie de la section de Brutus, An II [1794])

Charlemagne, Jean-Philippe-Victor, *Section de Brutus, ci-devant de Molière et La Fontaine. Discours prononcé à la section de Brutus ... le 15 septembre 1793 ... jour où cette section célébra une pompe funèbre en l'honneur de Le Pelletier et de Marat* (Paris: Imprimerie de la section de Brutus, [1793])

Chateaubriand, François de, *Mémoires d'outre-tombe* (Paris, 1848–50; here Paris: Garnier, 1989)

Chevillier, André, *L'origine de l'imprimerie de Paris, dissertation historique et critique divisée en quatre parties ...* (Paris, 1694)

Cogan, Thomas, *John Buncle, Junior, Gentleman*, 2 vols (London, 1776–8)

The Rhine, or A Journey from Utretcht to Francfort; Chiefly by the Borders of the Rhine, and the Passage down the River from Mentz to Bonn, 2 vols (London, 1793)

Condorcet, Jean-Antoine-Nicolas de Caritat, marquis de, *Cinq mémoires sur l'instruction publique*, introduction by Charles Coutel and Catherine Kintzler (Paris: Flammarion, 1994)

Esquisse d'un tableau historique des progrès de l'esprit humain (Paris, An III [1794])

Esquisse d'un tableau historique des progrès de l'esprit humain, introduction by Alain Pons (Paris: Flammarion, 1988)

Essai sur l'application de l'analyse à la probabilité des décisions rendues à la pluralité des voix (Paris, 1785)

Oeuvres complètes, 21 vols (Braunschweig and Paris, 1804)

Outlines of an Historical View of the Progress of the Human Mind (London, 1795)

Vie de M. Turgot (Londres [i.e. Paris?], 1786) (ESTC number T130579)

Cracherode, Clayton Mordaunt, [Obituary], *The Gentleman's Magazine and Historical Chronicle*, 69 (1799), 354–6

Crevenna, Pietro Antonio; review of his *Catalogue raisonné*, 6 vols ([Amsterdam] 1775–6), in *Critical Review, or Annals of Literature*, 47 (1779), 467

Cuthell, John, *A Catalogue of Books for the Year 1800, in Various Languages and Classes of Literature, on Sale for Ready Money, by J. Cuthell ...* (London, 1800)

Debure, le Jeune, Guillaume-François, *Bibliographie instructive: ou Traité de la connoissance des livres rares et singuliers*, 7 vols (Paris, 1763–8)

Appel aux savans et aux gens de lettres, au sujet de la Bibliographie instructive ([Paris] 1763), signed G. F. De Bure, le Jeune, de Paris, ce 1 Décembre 1763

Lettre à M*** servant de réponse à une critique de la Bibliographie instructive, insérée dans le premier volume du mois de juillet 1763, du Journal de Trévoux, *page 1617* ([Paris], 1763), signed G. F. De Bure, le Jeune, de Paris, ce 25 Octobre 1763

Supplément à la Bibliographie instructive, ou Catalogue des livres du cabinet de feu M. Louis Jean Gaignat, 2 vols (Paris, 1769)

The Derby Mercury (1788–1933)

Des Essarts, Nicolas-Toussaint le Moyne, *Les siècles littéraires de la France* (Paris, 1800)

Dibdin, Thomas Frognall, *A Bibliographical, Antiquarian, and Picturesque Tour in France and Germany*, 3 vols (London, 1821)

The Bibliographical Decameron, or Ten Days of Pleasant Discourse upon Illuminated Manuscripts and Subjects connected with Early Engraving, Typography and Bibliography, 3 vols (London, 1817)

The Bibliomania or, Book-madness Containing Some Account of the History, Symptoms and Cure of This Fatal Disease. In an Epistle Addressed to Richard Heber (London: Longman, Hurst, Rees, Orme, and Brown, 1811)

Bibliophobia. Remarks on the Present Languid and Depressed State of Literature and the Booktrade (London, 1832)

Bibliotheca spenceriana, or A Descriptive Catalogue of the Books Printed in the Fifteenth Century and of Many Valuable First Editions in the Library of George John Earl Spencer, 4 vols (London, 1814–15)

Supplement to the Bibliotheca spenceriana (London, 1822)

Didot, Pierre, *Essai de fables nouvelles dédiées au Roi suivies de poésies diverses et d'une épître sur les progrès de l'imprimerie* (Paris, 1786, in 12°)

Douce, Francis, *The Dance of Death; Painted by H. Holbein and Engraved by W. Hollar* (London, 1794)

Illustrations of Shakspeare and of Ancient Manners with Dissertations on the Clowns and Fools of Shakspeare; on the Collection of Popular Tales Entitled Gesta Romanorum; and on the English Morris Dance, 2 vols (London, 1807)

'Observations on certain ornaments of female dress', *Archaeologia*, 12 (1796), 215–16

Douglas, Sylvester, Lord Glenbervie, *The Diaries of Sylvester Douglas (Lord Glenbervie)*, ed. Francis Bickley, 2 vols (London: Constable, 1928)

Dupuis, Charles François, *Origine de tous les cultes, ou religion universelle* (Paris, An III [1794–5])

Dutens, Louis, *An Inquiry into the Origin of the Discoveries Attributed to the Moderns: Wherein It Is Demonstrated that Our Most Celebrated Philosophers Have, for the Most Part, Taken What They Advance from the Works of the Ancients* (London, 1767)

Dymott, Richard, *A Catalogue of Several Thousand Books in Various Languages, in Manuscripts, (Very Early Printed) Black Letter, Many Printed by Aldus, Books in Alchemy Etc ...* [London, 1770]

Catalogue for MDCCLXXII of Several Libraries and Parcels of Books, in Various Languages ... Which Are Now Selling [London, 1772]

Eaton, Daniel Isaac, *The Pernicious Effects of the Art of Printing upon Society, Exposed. A Short Essay. Addressed to the Friends of Social Order* [signed Antitype] (London, [1794]). 'Price two pence'

Politics for the People, or A Salmagundy for Swine (London: printed for D. I. Eaton at the Cock and Hog-Trough, 1794)

Edwards, Edward, *Memoirs of Libraries: Including a Handbook of Library Economy*, 2 vols (London, 1859)

Edwards, James, *Bibliotheca pinelliana. A Catalogue of the Magnificent and Celebrated Library of Maffei Pinelli, Late of Venice: Comprehending an Unparalleled Collection of the Greek, Roman, and Italian Authors, from the Origin of Printing: with Many of the Earliest Editions Printed Upon Vellum, and Finely Illuminated* (London: [James Edwards], 1789)

Edwards's Catalogue of a Select Collection of Ancient and Modern Books, in Every Branch of Science, Valuable Drawings and Prints ... They Are Now on Sale, 1790 (London, 1790)

Bibliotheca elegantissima, parisina. Catalogue de livres choisis, provenants du cabinet d'un amateur très distingué par son bon goût ... La vente se fera à Londres, au plus offrant, le lundi 28 mars 1791 ... (Paris, 1790)

Bibliotheca parisiana. A Catalogue of a Collection of Books Formed by a Gentleman in France ... It Includes Many First Editions of the Classicks; Books Magnificently Printed on Vellum, with Illuminated Paintings; Manuscripts on Vellum, Embellished with Rich Miniatures ... 26th [Recte: 28th] *of March, 1791, and the Five Days Following ...* (London, 1791)

A Catalogue of Books in All Languages and in Every Branch of Literature Collected from Various Parts of Europe... (London, 1796)

Elgin Marbles; Letter from the Chevalier Antonio Canova on the Sculptures in the British Museum ... with the Report from the Select Committee of the House of Commons (London, 1816)

Encyclopédie méthodique (Paris, 1782–93)

Encyclopédie, ou Dictionnaire raisonné des sciences, des arts et des métiers (Paris, 1751–80)

An Essay on the Original, Use, and Excellency, of the Noble Art and Mystery of Printing (London, 1752)

Este, Charles, *A Journey in the Year 1793 through Flanders, Brabant, and Germany to Switzerland* (London, 1795)

Étienne, Charles-Guillaume, *La vie de Chrétien-Guillaume Lamoignon Malesherbes* (Paris, An X [1802])

Firmin-Didot, Ambroise, *Réponses aux questions soumises par MM. les membres de la Chambre du commerce de Paris ... sur la situation de la librairie, de l'imprimerie, de la fonderie de caractères, et de la papeterie* (Paris: Didot, [1831])

Fischer, Gotthelf, *Beschreibung einiger typographischen Seltenheiten nebst Beyträgen zur Erfindungsgeschichte der Buchdruckerkunst*, 6 parts (Mainz, 1800–4)

Essai sur les monumens typographiques de Jean Gutenberg Mayençais (Mainz, An X [1801–2])

Das Nationalmuseum der Naturgeschichte zu Paris: von seinem ersten Ursprunge bis zu seinem jetzigen Glanze geschildert (Frankfurt am Main, 1802–3)

Fletcher and Hanwell, *A Catalogue of Useful and Valuable Books ... Including the Libraries of the Late Rev. Dr. Randolph ... Rev. Dr. Harrison ... and E. Taylor* (Oxford, [1798])

Formey, Johann Heinrich Samuel, *Principes élémentaires des belles-lettres ... Nouvelle édition, augmentée par l'auteur, avec des réflexions sur les spectacles* (Amsterdam, 1763)

Elementary Principles of the Belles-Lettres ... with Reflections on Public Exhibitions (London, 1766)

Fournier, Pierre Simon, *De l'origine et des productions de l'imprimerie primitive en taille de bois avec une réfutation des préjugés plus ou moins accrédités sur cet art pour servir de suite à la Dissertation sur l'origine de l'art de graver en bois* (Paris, 1759)

Dissertation sur l'origine et les progrès de l'art de graver en bois, pour éclaircir quelques traits de l'histoire de l'imprimerie et prouver que Guttemberg n'en est pas l'inventeur (Paris, 1758)

Review of *Dissertation sur l'origine ...* in *Journal de Trévoux* (1758), 1061–74

Manuel typographique utile aux gens de lettres et à ceux qui exercent les différentes parties de l'art de l'imprimerie (Paris, 1764)

Observations sur un ouvrage intitulé Vindiciae typographicae pour servir de suite au traité De l'origine et des productions de l'imprimerie primitive en taille de bois (Paris, 1760)

Review of *Observations* in *Journal de Trévoux* (1760), 1386–1413

Remarques sur un ouvrage intitulé 'Lettre sur l'origine de l'imprimerie' etc, [by Baer] *pour servir de suite au 'Traité de l'origine et des productions de l'imprimerie primitive en taille de bois'* (Paris, 1761)

Review of *Remarques sur un ouvrage intitulé 'Lettre'* in *Journal de Trévoux* (1762), 329–44

Review of *Remarques sur un ouvrage intitulé 'Lettre ...'* by Élie Catherine Fréron, in *L'année littéraire* (1761), 7, 137–42

[Fox, Charles James] *The Life of the Right Honorable, Charles James Fox ...* (London, 1807)

Foxe, John, *The Benefit and Invention of Printing by John Fox ... Extracted out of his Acts and Monuments* (London, 1704)

Gando, François, *Lettre de François Gando le jeune, graveur et fondeur de caractères d'imprimerie* (Paris, 1758)

General Evening Post (London, 1733–1822)

The Gentleman's Magazine and Historical Chronicle (London, 1736–1833)

Gercken, Philipp Wilhelm, *Reisen durch Schwaben, Baiern, die angränzende Schweiz, Franken, und die Rheinische Provinzen, und an der Mosel etc. in den Jahren 1779–1782, nebst Nachrichten von Bibliotheken, Handschriften ... etc.,* 4 vols (Worms and Stendal, 1783–8)

Gibbon, Edward, *Miscellaneous Works* (London, 1796)

Goethe, Johann Wolfgang von, *Die italienische Reise.* Here from *Italian Journey, 1786–1788.* Tr. W. H. Auden and Elizabeth Mayer (London: Collins, 1962)

Gras, Franz, *Verzeichniss typographischer Denkmäler aus dem fünfzehnten Jahrhundert welche sich in der Bibliothek des regulirten Korherrenstiftes des heil. Augustin zu Neustift in Tyrol befinden* (Brixen, 1789)

Review of *Verzeichniss typographischer Denkmäler* in *Allgemeine Literatur-Zeitung*, 70, 1 (1791), cols 554–6

Grégoire, Henri, *Convention nationale. Instruction publique. Rapport sur la bibliographie, par Grégorie, séance du 22 germinal l'an IIe [11 April 1794] … suivi du Décret de la Convention nationale* (Paris, [1794])

Grose, Francis, *The Grumbler: Containing Sixteen Essays* (London, 1791)

The Olio: Being a Collection of Essays, Dialogues, Letters … Epitaphs, &c. (London, 1792)

Gude, Marquard, *Bibliotheca exquisitissimis libris in theologia, jure, medicina, historia literaria omnique alio studiorum genere instructissima: imprimis autem multorum a viris doctissimis Scaligero, Blondello, Salmasio, aliisque emendatorum ac eorum manibus notatorum … quae publica auctione distrahentur Hamburgi ad. d. 4 August. An. MDCCVI* (Kiel, 1706)

Guyton, Louis Bernard, Vincent, François-André, Taunay, Nicolas Antoine, and Berthollet, Claude-Louis, *Rapport sur la restauration du tableau de Raphaël, connu sous le nom de la vierge de Foligno, adopté par les classes des sciences mathématiques et physiques et de littérature et beaux art, dans les séances des 1er et 3 nivôse an X [22 and 24 December 1801]* (Paris, 1801)

Hansard, The Official Report of Parliamentary Debates (London, 1829–91)

Harwood, Edward, *A View of the Various Editions of the Greek and Roman Classics* (London, 1775)

Hearne, Thomas, *Reliquiae Hearnianae: The Remains of Thomas Hearne, MA, of Edmund Hall*, ed. Philip Bliss, 2 vols (Oxford, 1857)

Remarks and Collections of Thomas Hearne, ed. C. E. Doble and others, 10 vols (Oxford, 1885–1915)

Heinecken, Carl Heinrich von, *Idée générale d'une collection complette d'estampes. Avec une dissertation sur l'origine de la gravure et sur les premiers livres d'images* (Leipzig and Vienna, 1771)

Henderson, Alexander, *The History of Ancient and Modern Wines* (London, 1824)

Heumannus, Christophorus Augustus, *Conspectus reipublicae literariae* (Hanover, 1718)

Hill, John, *The Inspector*, vol. I (London, 1753)

Historical Manuscripts Commission, *Report on the Manuscripts of J. B. Fortescue, Esq. Preserved at Dropmore*, 10 vols (London, 1908)

Hogarth, William, *The Analysis of Beauty, Written with a View of Fixing the Fluctuating Ideas of Taste* (London, 1753)

Holbach, Paul Henri Dietrich, baron d ', *Théologie portative ou dictionnaire abrégé de la religion chrétienne* ('Londres' [i.e. Amsterdam?], 1768)

Homer, *Batrachomyomachia graece ad veterum exemplarium fidem recusa* (London, 1721)

Humphreys, Henry Noel, *The Illuminated Books of the Middle Ages: An Account of the Development and Progress of the Art of Illuminations as a Distinct Branch of Pictorial Ornamentation from the IVth to the XVIIth Centuries* (London 1849)

Hupfauer, Paul, *Druckstücke aus dem XV. Jahrhunderte, welche sich in der Bibliothek des regulirten Chorstiftes Beuerberg befinden … mit 23 Holzschnitten* (Augsburg, 1794)

   Review of *Druckstücke aus dem XV. Jahrhunderte*, in *Allgemeine Literatur-Zeitung*, 195 (1794, June), cols. 685–9

Hüttner, Johann Christian, *Englische Miscellen* (Tübingen, 1800–6)

Ihre, Johannes, *Dissertatio historico-litteraria de caussis raritatis librorum cuius partem priorem [posteriorem] … sub praesidio … Johannis Ihre … submittit Johannes Lexelius* (Uppsala, [1741]; Stockholm, 1743)

The Ipswich Journal (1739–1902)

Jador, Henry, *Dialogue entre une presse mécanique et une presse à bras. Recueilli et raconté par une vielle presse en bois* (Paris, 1830)

Jaeck, Heinrich Joachim, *Vollständige Beschreibung der öffentlichen Bibliothek zu Bamberg*, Dritter Theil (Bamberg and Nuremberg, 1835)

Jaucourt, Louis de, 'Imprimerie', in *Encyclopédie, ou Dictionnaire raisonné des sciences, des arts et des métiers*, vol. VIII (Neufchâtel: 1765)

Jondot, Étienne, *Observations critiques sur les leçons d'histoire du C. en Volney, ouvrage dans lequel est indiquée une nouvelle méthode d'apprendre l'histoire … Suivi d'un chapitre contre l'athéisme* (Paris, An VIII [1800])

Jones, William, *The Works. With the Life of the Author by Lord Teignmouth*, 13 vols (London, 1807)

Jungendres, Sebastian Jacob, *Disquisitio in notas characteristicas librorum a typographiae incunabulo ad an. MD. impressorum … in jubilaei typographici tertii mnemosynon conscripta* (Nuremberg, 1740)

Kerr, Robert, *Memorial Relative to the Invention of a New Method of Bleaching, Showing the Absurdity of Any Pretensions to an Exclusive Privilege for Using It* (Edinburgh, 1792)

Knight, Charles, *William Caxton, the First English Printer* (London, 1844)

Köhler, Johann David, *Hochverdiente und aus bewährten Urkunden wohlbeglaubte Ehren-Rettung Johann Guttenbergs, eingebohrnen Bürgers in Mayntz … wegen der ersten Erfindung der nie gnug gepriesenen Buchdrucker-Kunst in der Stadt Mayntz, zu unvergänglichen Ehren der Teutschen Nation, und insonderheit der löblichen uralten Stadt Mayntz* (Leipzig, 1741)

Kulenkamp, Lüder, *Bibliotheca Luderi Kulenkamp* (Göttingen, 1796)

La Bruyére, Jean de, *Les caractères* (1688) quoted from (Paris, 1990)

La Caille, Jean de, *Histoire de l'imprimerie et de la librairie, où l'on voit son origine et son progrès jusqu'en 1689* (Paris, 1689)

La Vallière, Louis César de La Baume le Blanc, duc de, *Catalogue des livres de la bibliothèque de feu M. le duc de La Vallière première partie … dont la vente se fera dans les premiers jours du mois de décembre 1783* (Paris: chez Guillaume De Bure fils aîné, 1783)

Labbé, Philippe, *Nova bibliotheca MSS librorum sive specimen antiquarum latinarum et graecarum lectionum* (Paris, 1653)

Laire, François-Xavier, *Catalogue des livres de la bibliothèque de M**** [Loménie de Brienne] *faisant suite à l'Index librorum ab inventa typographia ad annum 1500 … dont la vente se fera le lundi 12 mars 1792 et jours suivans* (Paris: G. De Bure l'Aîné, 1792)

   Index librorum ab inventa typographia ad annum 1500. Chronologice dispositus cum notis historiam typographico-litterariam illustrantibus, Part I (Sens, 1791)

   Specimen historicum typographiae romanae xv. saeculi (Rome, 1778)

The Lakelands Library. Catalogue of the Rare & Valuable Books, Manuscripts and Engravings of the Late W. H. Crawford (London: Sotheby, Wilkinson & Hodge, 1891)

Lamartine, Alphonse de, *Gutenberg, inventeur de l'imprimerie*, Bibliothèque des chemins de fer, sér. 2 (Paris, 1853)

Lambinet, Pierre, *Recherches historiques, littéraires et critiques sur l'origine de l'imprimerie; particulièrement sur ses premiers établissemens, au XVème siècle, dans la Belgique, maintenant réunie à la République française* (Brussels, vendémiaire, An VII [1798])

Langer, E. T., 'Noch etwas die älteste Buchdrukergeschichte von Bamberg betreffend', *Historisch-litterarisch-bibliographisches Magazin* (Zürich, [1788–]1794) (1794), 22–9 (signed W[olfenbüttel]. L[anger])

Lawrence, James, *A Picture of Verdun, or The English Detained in France from the Portfolio of a Detenu* [by James Lawrence] (London, 1810)

Le Camus de Limare [sale of], *Catalogue de livres rares dont la vente se fera le lundi 13 mars 1786*, par Guillame De Bure, fils aîné (Paris: G. De Bure, 1786)

Lenoir, Alexandre, *Notice historique des monumens des arts, réunis au Dépôt national, rue des Petits Augustins* (Paris, An IV [1795–6])

Leo XIII, Pont. Max., *Aeterni patris* [encyclical of 4 August 1879], in *Sanctissimi Domini Nostri Leonis Papae XIII allocutiones, epistolae, constitutiones, aliaque acta praecipua etc.*, 8 vols (Bruges and Lille, 1887–1910), pp. 88–108

Lévis, Gaston de, *Angleterre au commencement du dix-neuvième siècle* (Paris, 1814)

Lewis, John, *The Life of Mayster Wyllyam Caxton, of the Weald of Kent; the First Printer in England* (London, 1737)

London Gazette (1666–)

Mabillon, Jean, *De re diplomatica libri VI, in quibus quidquid ad veterum instrumentorum antiquitatem, materiam, scripturam et stilum; quidquid ad … notas chronologicas; quidquid inde ad antiquariam, historicam forensemque disciplinam pertinet, explicatur et illustratur* (Paris, 1681)

MacCarthy Reagh, Justin, Conte [sale of], *Catalogue des livres rares et précieux de la bibliothèque de feu M. le comte de Mac-Carthy Reagh* (Paris: chez De Bure frères, 1815)

Maitland, Samuel Roffey, *The Dark Ages; a Series of Essays, Intended to Illustrate the State of Religion and Literature in the Ninth, Tenth, Eleventh, and Twelfth Centuries* (London, 1844)

Maittaire, Michael, *Annales typographici ab artis inventae origine ad annum MD [ad annum MDLVII continuati]*, vols I–III (The Hague and Amsterdam, 1719–26)

 Annales typographici ab artis inventae origine ad annum MDCLXIV, vol. IV [with 2nd edition of vol. I; often refered to as vol. I] (Amsterdam, 1733)

 Annalium typographicorum, volumen V (London, 1741)

 Epistolaris de antiquis Quintiliani editionibus dissertatio [London, 1719]

Malesherbes, Chrétien-Guillaume de Lamoignon de, *Mémoires sur la librairie et la liberté de la presse* (Paris, 1809)

 Mémoires sur la librairie; Mémoire sur la liberté de la presse, with a preface by Roger Chartier (Paris: Imprimerie nationale, 1994)

 Les 'Remontrances' de Malesherbes 1771–1775, ed. Elisabeth Badinter (Paris: Union générale d'éditions, 1978)

Marchand, Prosper, *Histoire de l'origine et des premiers progrès de l'imprimerie* (The Hague, 1740)

Maugérard, Jean-Baptiste [sale of], *Notice de livres rares, la plupart imprimés dans le quinzième siècle, dont la vente se fera rue des deux Ecus, à l'hôtel Saint-Antoine, le 16 janvier 1792, et jours suivans après midi* (Paris, 1792)

Meerman, Gerard, *Origines typographicae* (The Hague, Paris and London, 1765)

Mentel, Jacques, *Brevis excursus de loco, tempore, et authore inventionis typographiae* (Paris, 1644)

 De vera typographiae origine paraenesis (Paris, 1650)

[Mercier, Barthélemy], review of Debure, *Bibliographie instructive*, in *Journal de Trévoux* (1763), fascicle viii, 1358–72

 'Lettre … sur la *Bibliographie instructive* de M. De Bure', *Journal de Trévoux* (1763), fascicle ix, 1617–782

 'Seconde lettre … sur la *Bibliographie instructive* de M. De Bure', *Journal de Trévoux* (1763), fascicle xi, 1994–2074

Mercier, Barthélemy, 'Lettre de M. Mercier, chanoine régulier et bibliothécaire de Ste Geneviève … sur une Réponse à deux critiques de la *Bibliographie* de M. De Bure', *Journal de Trévoux* (1763), fascicle xiii, 2407–22

Meusel[?], Johann Georg, 'Kleine Sammlung von Inkunabeln. Erster Abschnitt. Bücher in Folio', *Historisch-litterarisch-bibliographisches Magazin* (1791), 3. Stück, 162–74

Meyrick, Samuel Rush, 'The Doucean museum', *Gentleman's Magazine*, 106 (1836), part I, 245–53, 378–84, 585–90 and part II, 158–60; 378–84, 492–4, 598–601

Middleton, Conyers, *A Dissertation Concerning the Origin of Printing in England. Shewing, that It Was First Introduced and Practised by Our Countryman William Caxton, at Westminster: And Not, as Is Commonly Believed, by a Foreign Printer at Oxford* (Cambridge, 1735)

 A Letter from Rome, Shewing an Exact Conformity Between Popery and Paganism (London, 1729)

A Letter to Dr. Waterland; Containing Some Remarks on His Vindication of Scripture: In Answer to a Book Intituled, Christianity as Old as the Creation (London, 1731)

The Origin of Printing. In Two Essays: I. the Substance of Dr. Middleton's Dissertation on the Origin of Printing in England. II, Mr. Meerman's Account of the Invention of the Art at Harleim, and Its Progress to Mentz. With Occasional Remarks; and an Appendix (London: W. Bowyer and J. Nichols, 1776)

Milton, John, *Areopagitica, a Speech … for the Liberty of Unlicenc'd Printing, to the Parlament of England* (London, 1644)

Mirabeau, Honoré-Gabriel Riqueti, comte de, *Sur la liberté de la presse, imité de l'anglois de Milton* (London [i.e. Paris?], 1788)

Morhof, Daniel Georg, *Polyhistor, sive de notitia auctorum et rerum commentarii quibus praeterea varia ad omnes disciplinas consilia et subsidia proponuntur*, 2 vols (Lübeck, 1688–92) here from the posthumous edition (Lübeck, 1708)

Morning Chronicle (1789–1865)

Morris, Gouverneur, *The Diary and Letters of Gouverneur Morris*, ed. Anne Carey Morris, 2 vols (London, 1889)

Mosel, Ignaz Franz von, *Geschichte der Kaiserl. Königl. Hofbibliothek zu Wien* (Vienna, 1835)

Moxon, Joseph, *Mechanick Exercises, or The Doctrine of Handy-Works* (London: number I, 1 January 1677 [1678]–number XIV [1680])

Mulot, François-Valentin, *Discours prononcé à Mayence, le 1er ventôse de l'an VI [19 February 1798] … pour l'installation de l'administration centrale du département du Mont-Tonnerre* (Mainz, [1798])

Hymne à l'Être suprême. Discours sur le serment de haine à la royauté et à l'anarchie et imprécation contre les parjures, pour la fête du 2 pluviôse an VII [21 January 1799] (Mainz, [1799])

Murr, Christoph Gottlieb von, *Merkwürdigkeiten der fürstbischöflichen Residenzstadt Bamberg* (Nuremberg, 1799)

Napoleon, *Correspondance de Napoléon Ier*, 32 vols (Paris, 1858–69)

Naudé, Gabriel, *Advis pour dresser une bibliothèque*, 2nd edition (Paris, 1644)

Nichols, John, *Literary Anecdotes of the Eighteenth Century*, 9 vols (London, 1812–15)

Nicolas, Nicholas Harris, *Observations on the State of Historical Literature and on the Society of Antiquaries, and Other Institutions for Its Advancement in England* (London, 1830)

'Observation on oxygenated muriatic acid including a method of restoring the colour of old books and smoked prints by M. Chaptal of the royal society of Montpellier, from the memoirs of the academy of sciences in Paris', *Whitehall Evening Post*, Tuesday 14 October to Thursday October 16, 1794, continued Saturday 15 November to Tuesday 18 November

Orlandi, Pellegrino Antonio, *Origine e progressi della stampa o sia dell' arte impressoria e notizie dell' opere stampate dall' anno M.CCCC.LVII sino all' anno MD* (Bologna, 1722)

Osborne, Thomas, *A Catalogue of the Libraries of the Following Eminent and Learned Persons, Deceased, Viz. the Rev. Dr. Thomas Gale ... Which Will Begin to Be Sold ... at T. Osborne's and J. Shipton's ... for Two Years, Viz. to the First of January 1758* [London, 1756–8]

An Extensive and Curious Catalogue of Valuable Books and Manuscripts in All Languages ... (London, 1739)

Outreman, Philippe d', *Le pédagogue chrétien* (first edition identified by me is St Omer: Charles Boscart, 1626, recorded in the library of the Institut catholique de Lille. Many later editions)

Paine, Thomas, *The Age of Reason. Part the Second. Being an Investigation of True and of Fabulous Theology* (London, 1795)

Paitoni, Jacopo Maria, *Venezia la prima città fuori della Germania dove si esercitò l'arte della stampa* (Venice, 1756)

Palmer, Samuel, *The General History of Printing from Its First Invention in the City of Mentz to Its Progress and Propagation Thro' the Most Celebrated Cities in Europe. Particularly, Its Introduction, Rise and Progress Here in England* (London, 1732)

Panzer, Georg Wolfgang, *Annalen der ältern deutschen Litteratur oder Anzeige und Beschreibung derjenigen Bücher welche von Erfindung der Buchdruckerkunst bis MDXX [MDXXI bis MDXXVI] in deutscher Sprache gedruckt worden sind*, 2 vols (Nuremberg, 1788; Leipzig, 1802)

Annales typographici ab artis inventae origine ad annum MD., post Maittairii, Denisii, aliorumque doctissimorum virorum curas in ordinem redacti, emendati, et aucti [ad annum MDXXXVI. continuati], 11 vols (Nuremberg, 1793–1803)

Review of *Annales typographici*, vol. I, in *Allgemeine Literatur-Zeitung*, 258 (1793), cols 539–42

Paterson, Samuel, *Bibliotheca westiana: A Catalogue of the Curious and Truly Valuable Library of the Late James West ...* [London, 1773]

Payne, John Thomas and Foss, Henry, *Bibliotheca grenvilliana* (London, 1842)

Pearce, Zachary, *A Reply to the Letter to Dr. Waterland, Setting Forth the Many Falshoods Both in the Quotations and the Historical Facts, by Which the Letter-Writer Endeavours to Weaken the Authority of Moses* (London, 1731)

Pegge, Samuel, *Anonymiana, or Ten Centuries of Observations on Various Authors and Subjects* (London, 1809)

Pope, Alexander, *An Epistle to the Right Honourable Richard Earl of Burlington* (London, 1731)

Prévost, Antoine François, *Histoire du Chevalier des Grieux, et de Manon Lescaut* ('A Londres' [i.e. Paris ?], 1782)

Proust, Marcel, *Le côté de Guermantes*, I, (Paris: Gallimard, 1988)

Quatremère de Quincy, Antoine Chrysostôme, *Considérations morales sur la destination des ouvrages de l'art, ou de l'influence de leur emploi sur le génie et le gout* (Paris, 1815)

Considérations morales sur la destination des ouvrages de l'art. Suivi de Lettres sur le préjudice qu'occasionneraient aux arts et à la science le déplacement des monuments de l'art de l'Italie, le démembrement de ses Écoles et la spoliation des ses collections, galléries, musées etc. [1796], ed. Édouard Pommier (Paris, 1989)

The Destination of Works of Art and the Use to Which They Are Applied. Considered with Regard to Their Influence on the Genius and Taste of Artists and the Sentiment of Amateurs (London, 1821)

Quirini, Angelo Maria, *Liber singularis de optimorum scriptorum editionibus quae Romae primum prodierunt post divinum typographiae inventum, a Germanis opificibus in eam urbem advectum ... Recensuit ... Johannes Georgii Schelhornius* (Lindau, 1761)

Rabaut, Jacques-Antoine, *Rapport et projet de décret faits au nom des comités d'instruction publique et des finances, réunis, sur l'établissement d'un Muséum national d'antiques ... dans la séance du 20 prairial* [8 June 1795] (Paris, An III)

Ratcliffe, John [sale of], *Bibliotheca ratcliffiana: A Catalogue of the Elegant and Truly Valuable Library of the Late John Ratcliffe ... Comprehending the Largest and Most Choice Collection of the Rare Old English Black Letter ... Printed by Caxton, Lettou, Machlinia, the Anonymous St. Alban's Schoolmaster, Wynkyn De Word, Pynson ... and the Rest of the Old English Typographers* (London, 1776)

Réguis, François-Léon, *La voix du pasteur, discours familiers d'un curé à ses paroissiens, pour tous les dimanches de l'année* (Paris, 1773)

Renouard, Antoine-Augustin, *Annales de l'imprimerie des Alde, ou Histoire des trois Manuce et de leurs éditions*, 2 vols (Paris, An XII [1803]). 2nd edition, 2 vols (Paris, 1825)

Catalogue de la bibliothèque d'un amateur, avec notes bibliographiques, critiques et littéraires, 4 vols (Paris, 1819)

Au comité d'instruction publique ([Paris:] Par Ant.-Aug. Renouard [signed 2 du 2e mois de l'an II [23 October 1793]])

Manuel pour la concordance des calendriers républicain et grégorien ... nouvelle édition dans laquelle les tables de concordance sont portées jusqu'à l'an XLII–1834 (Paris: Chez Antoine-Augustin Renouard, 1822)

Observations de quelques patriotes sur la nécessité de conserver les monuments de la littérature et des arts (Paris, An II [1793])

Reviczky, Karl, *Bibliotheca graeca et latina, complectens auctores fere omnes Graeciae et Latii veteris quorum opera, vel fragmenta aetatem tulerunt, exceptis tantum asceticis et theologicis Patrum nuncupatorum scriptis. Cum delectu editionum tam primariarum, principum et rarissimarum, quam etiam optimarum, splendidissimarum atque nitidissimarum, quas usui meo paravi Periergus Deltophilus* (Berlin, 1784); *Supplément de quelques articles acquis depuis l'impression de ce catalogue* (Berlin, 1786). [second supplement] (Berlin 1788)

Specimen poeseos persicae, sive Muhammedis Schems-Eddini notioris agnomine Haphyzi Ghazelae, sive Odae sexdecim ex initio Divani depromptae, nunc primum latinitate donatae, cum metaphrasi ligata et soluta, paraphrasi item ac notis [translated by Reviczky] (Vienna, 1771)

Traité de la tactique ou méthode artificielle pour l'ordonnance des troupes, ouvrage publié et imprime à Constantinople par Ibrahim Effendi … l'an 1730 de l'ère chrétienne [translated by Reviczky] (Vienna, 1769)

Richardson, William, *A Christian Directory, or a Certain, Sure, and Safe Guide to Heaven; the One Thing Needful* ([London], 1711)

Rive, Jean Joseph, *La chasse aux bibliographes et antiquaires mal-advisés* (London [but truly Aix-en Provence], 1789)

Robelot, chanoine de Dijon, *De l'influence de la Réformation de Luther sur la croyance religieuse, la politique et le progrès des lumières* (Lyon, 1822)

Rock, Daniel, *Hierurgia, or The Holy Sacrifice of the Mass* (London, 1833)

Romme, Gilbert, 'Rapport au nom du comité d'instruction publique', in *Procès-verbaux du Comité d'instruction publique de la Convention nationale II (3 juillet 1793–30 brumaire an II (20 novembre 1793))* ed. M. J. Guillaume, Collection de documents inédits sur l'histoire de France (Paris, 1894), pp. 661–5

Ruskin, John, *St Mark's Rest; the History of Venice Written for the Help of the Few Travellers Who Still Care for Her Monuments*, vol. XXIV, *The Works of John Ruskin,* ed. E. T. Cook and A. Wedderburn (Orpington, 1884)

St James's Chronicle or The British Evening Post (1761–1866)

Sassi, Giuseppe Antonio, *Historia literario-typographica mediolanensis … et Catalogus codicum Mediolani impressorum ab anno MCDLXV. ad annum MD* (Milan, 1745)

Savoy, Bénédicte (ed.), *Remarques sur le vol et la restitution des œuvres d'art et des livres précieux, 1806–1815, avec divers témoignages sur les saisies d'art opérées en Allemagne par Vivant Denon* (Paris: La Vouivre, 1999)

Scaligerana, Thuana, Perroniana, Pithoeana et Colomesiana, ou Remarques historiques, critiques, morales, et littéraires de Jos. Scaliger, J. Aug. De Thou, le cardinal Du Perron, Fr. Pithou et P. Colomiès …, vol. I (Amsterdam, 1740)

Schaab, Carl Anton, *Die Geschichte der Erfindung der Buchdruckerkunst durch Johann Gensfleisch genannt Gutenberg, zu Mainz*, 3 vols (Mainz, 1830–1)

Schelhorn, Johannes Georgius, *Amoenitates historiae ecclesiasticae et literariae* (Frankfurt and Leipzig, 1737)

Schoepflin, Johann Daniel, 'Dissertation sur l'origine de l'imprimerie par M. Schepflin', *Mémoires de littérature tirés des registres de l'Académie royale des inscriptions et belles-lettres, depuis l'année M. DCCXLI, jusques et compris l'année M. DCCXLIII*, vol. XVII (Paris, 1751), 762–86

Vindiciae typographicae [with] *Documenta typographicarum originum ex argentinensibus tabulariis et bibliothecis nunc primum edita* (Strasbourg, 1760)

Schrevel, Dirk, *Harlemum, sive urbis harlemensis incunabula, incrementa, fortuna varia* (Leiden, 1647)

Schultes, A., *Briefe über Frankreich* (Leipzig, 1815)

Schwarz, Christian Gottlieb, *Bibliothecae schwarzianae pars I (–II). Seu catalogus librorum continens codices manuscriptos vetustos et libros saeculo XV ab incunabulis typographiae impressos quos olim possedit et notis adjectis recensuit Christianus Gottliebe Schwarzius* (Altdorf, [1769])

Primaria quaedam documenta de origine typographiae quorum illustratorum partem primam sub praesidio Christiani Gottlibii Schvvarzii ... disquisitioni academicae subiicit Benedictus Guilielmus Munch (Altdorf, [1740])

Primaria quaedam documenta de origine typographiae quorum illustratorum partem alteram sub praesidio Christiani Gottlibii Schvvarzii ... proponit Io. Guilielmus Schaubert (Altdorf, [1740])

Primaria quaedam documenta de origine typographiae quorum illustratorum partem tertiam sub praesidio Christiani Gottlibii Schvvarzii ... proponit Gustavus Philippus Negelein (Altdorf, [1740])

Seemiller, Sebastian, *Bibliothecae academicae ingolstadiensis incunabula typographica seu libri ante annum 1500 impressi circiter mille et quadringenti ... Fasciculus I qui libros complectitur nota anni insignitos ultra centum et viginti, eosque omnes ante annum 1477 impressos. Accedunt totidem fere libri nota anni impressa carentes, sed probabilissime ante annum 1477 vel certe ante annum 1480 impressi* (Ingolstadt, 1787)

Bibliothecae academicae ingolstadiensis incunabula typographica seu libri ante annum 1500 impressi circiter mille et quadringenti ... Fasciculus II qui libros complectitur nota anni impressa insignitos ultra ducento et viginti, eosque omnes septennii spatio ab anno 1477–1482 impressos. Accedunt quadraginta et amplius nota anni impressa carentes, sed probabilissime quoad majorem partem pariter ante annum 1484 impressi (Ingolstadt, 1789)

Review of *Bibliothecae academicae ingolstadiensis incunabula ...* in *Allgemeine Literatur-Zeitung*, 17b, 1 (1788), cols 179–82

Selden, John, *A briefe discourse concerning the power of the peeres and commons of Parliament in point of judicature* [ascribed to Selden] (London, 1640)

De anno civili et calendario veteris ecclesiae ... dissertatio (London, 1644)

The Historie of Tithes (London, 1618)

Θεάνθρωπος, or God Made Man: A Tract Proving the Nativity of Our Saviour to Be on the 25 of December (London, 1661)

Sénac de Meilhan, Gabriel, *Considérations sur les richesses et le luxe* (Amsterdam and Paris, 1787)

L'émigré (Braunschweig, 1797)

Senckenberg, Heinrich Christian, *Selecta iuris et historiarum tum anecdota tum iam edita, sed rariora*, 6 vols (Frankfurt am Main, 1734–42), I, part 3: 'Manipulus documentorum res francofurtenses et viciniam illustrantium'

Shepherd, William, *Paris in Eighteen Hundred and Two; in Eighteen Hundred and Fourteen*, 3rd edition (London, 1814)

Smith, Joseph, *Bibliotheca smithiana seu Catalogus librorum D. Josephi Smithii ...* (Venice, 1755)

   Catalogus librorum rarissimorum ab artis typographicae inventoribus aliisque eiusdem artis principibus ante annum millesimum quingentesimum excusorum [Padua, 1724]

   Catalogus librorum rarissimorum ab artis typographicae inventoribus aliisque eiusdem artis principibus ante annum millesimum quingentesimum excusorum [Venice, 1737]

Smith, Richard, *Bibliotheca smithiana, sive Catalogus librorum in quavis facultate insigniorum, quos in usum suum & bibliothecae ornamentum multo aere sibi comparavit Richardus Smith ... Horum auctio habebitur ... Maii die 15. 1682 per Richardum Chiswel* (London, 1682)

Sotheby, *A Catalogue of a Valuable Collection of Books Printed in the Fifteenth Century, Consigned from Abroad Containing Specimens of Most of the Early Printers; in the Finest Preservation and in the Original Monastic Bindings* (London: Leigh and Sotheby, 15 June,1799)

Spence, Joseph, *Polymetis, or An Enquiry Concerning the Agreement Between the Works of the Roman Poets, and the Remains of the Antient Artists* (London, 1747)

Steiner, Matthias Jakob Adam, 'Eine ganz neue Entdeckung, die den Freunden der ältern teutschen Litteratur, hoffentlich nicht unangenehm, und für die älteste Buchdruckergeschichte Bambergs, nicht unbedeutend seyn wird', *Historisch-litterarisch-bibliographisches Magazin* (1792), 5. Stück, 1–38

Stillingfleet, Edward, *Several Conferences Between a Romish Priest, a Fanatick Chaplain, and a Divine of the Church of England, Concerning the Idolatry of the Church of Rome* (London, 1679)

Strauss, Andreas, *Opera rariora quae latitant in bibliotheca canon. reg. collegiatae ecclesiae ad S. Joannem Baptistam in Rebdorf* (Eichstätt, 1790)

   Review of *Opera rariora* in *Historisch-litterarisch-bibliographisches Magazin* (1790), 1 Theil 3 B. and 4 B. 1 Abtheilung, pp. 169–74

Struve, Burkhard Gotthelf, *Introductio ad notitiam rei litterariae et usum bibliothecarum* (Jena, 1706)

Talleyrand, Charles Maurice de, 'Rapport sur l'instruction publique', in *Une éducation pour la démocratie*, ed. Bronisław Baczko (Paris: Garnier frères, 1982)

Thoresby, Ralph, *Ducatus leodiensi, or The Topography of the Ancient and Populous Town and Parish of Leedes* (London, 1715)

Thott, Otto, greve, *Catalogi bibliothecae thottianae tomi primi pars I* [–tomus quintus], 7 vols (Copenhagen, 1788–95)

The Times (1788–)

Tocqueville, Alexis de, *L'ancien régime et la Révolution* (Paris, 1856)

Todd, J., *J. Todd's Catalogue for 1798. A Catalogue of a Valuable and Curious Collection of Books in All Languages* ([York?], [1798])

A Tower Conference, Being a Dialogue between Robert Earl of Oxford and Earl Mortimer, and Sir W–P–l–e, a knight of Devon. On the Subject of the Earl's Approaching Tryal (London, 1716)

Trithemius, Johannes, *Tomus I [–II] annalium hirsaugiensium* (St Gallen, 1690)

Turgot, Anne Robert Jacques, 'Tableau philosophique des progrès successifs de l'esprit humain. Discours prononcé en latin dans les écoles de Sorbonne', in *Oeuvres de Turgot*, ed. Gustave Schelle, 5 vols (Paris, 1913–23)

Van Hulthem, Charles Joseph Emmanuel, *Corps législatif. Conseil des Cinq-Cents. Discours prononcé ... en présentant au Conseil la notice d'un livre imprimé à Bamberg en 1462 ... Séance du 24 fructidor an 7* [10 September 1799] (Paris, An VII)

Van Praet, Joseph-François-Bernard, *Essai du catalogue des livres imprimés sur vélin, de la Bibliothèque impériale* (Paris, 1805)

Vergilius, *Opera* (London, 1715)

   Opera varietate lectionis et perpetua adnotatione illustrata a Chr. Gottl. Heyne (Leipzig, 1767)

   Opera varietate lectionis et perpetua adnotatione illustrata a Chr. Gottl. Heyne ... 3rd edition, 8 vols (London: impensis T. Payne et ... J. Edwards, 1793)

   Bucolica, Georgica et Aeneis (Paris: in aedibus palatinis, M. DCC. XCVIII, reip. VI, excudebam Petrus Didot, natu major)

Villers, Charles François Dominique de, *Essai sur l'esprit et l'influence de la Réformation de Luther, ouvrage qui a remporté le prix sur cette question proposée dans la séance publique du 15 germinal an X [5 April 1802], par l'Institut national de France: 'Quelle a été l'influence de la Réformation de Luther sur la situation politique des différens états de l'Europe, et sur le progrès des lumières?'* (Paris, An XII [1804])

   An Essay on the Spirit and Influence of the Reformation of Luther: The Work Which Obtained the Prize on the Question Proposed in 1802, by the National Institute of France, translated by James Mill (London and Edinburgh, 1805)

Volney, Constantin François Chasseboeuf Boisgirais, Conte de, *L'École normale de l'an III: Leçons d'histoire de géographie d'économie politique*, ed. Alan Alcouffe, Giorgio Israel, Barthélemy Jorbet, and others (Paris: Dunod, 1994)

   Leçons d'histoire prononcées à l'École normale en l'an III de la république française, in *Séances des Écoles normales recueillies par des sténographes et revues par les professeurs. 1re partie, leçons* (Paris, An VIII [1800])

   Lectures on History, Delivered in the Normal School of Paris (London, 1800)

   Voyage en Syrie et en Égypte, pendant les années 1783, 84 et 85. 3rd edition (Paris, An VII [1798–9])

Wagstaff, George, *Wagstaff's Winter Catalogue of Rare Old Books for 1774 ... Monday the 7th of November 1774* [London, 1774]

Wanley, Humfrey, *The Diary of Humfrey Wanley 1715–1726*, ed. C. E. Wright and Ruth Wright, 2 vols (London: Bibliographical Society, 1966)

Wendler, J. C., *Dissertationem de variis raritatis librorum impressorum causis … publico eruditorum examini submittent praeses Magister Johannes Christophorus Wendler et respondens Christophorus Ungewitter* (Jena, [1711])

White, Benjamin and Son, *A Catalogue of the Library of the Rev. John Bowle … January 19, 1790* (London, 1790)

Willett, Ralph, *A Description of the Library at Merly in the County of Dorset. Description de la bibliothèque de Merly* (London, 1785)

   'Memoir on the origin of printing', *Archaeologia*, 11 (1794), 267–316

   'Observations on the origin of printing', *Archaeologia*, 8 (1787), 239–50

Wolcot, John, *The Poetical Works of Peter Pindar, Esq.* (Dublin, 1789)

Wuerdtwein, Stephan Alexander, *Bibliotheca moguntina libris saeculo primo typographico Moguntiae impressis instructa; hinc inde addita inventae typographiae historia* (Augsburg, 1787)

Yorke, Henry Redhead, *Letters from Paris 1802*, 2 vols (London, 1804)

Zapf, Georg Wilhelm, *Aelteste Buchdruckergeschichte Schwabens* (Ulm, 1791)

   Augsburgs Buchdruckergeschichte nebst den Jahrbuechern derselben. Erster Theil vom Jahre 1468 bis auf das Jahr 1599 (Augsburg, 1788)

   Ueber eine alte und höchst seltene Ausgabe von des Joannis de Turrecremata Explanatio in Psalterium und einige andere typographische Seltenheiten (Nuremberg, 1805)

Secondary sources

1789 Le patrimoine libéré: 200 trésors entrés à la Bibliothèque nationale de 1789 à 1799: 6 juin–10 septembre, 1989 (Paris: Bibliothèque nationale, 1989)

The Age of Neo-Classicism. The Fourteenth Exhibition of the Council of Europe. Royal Academy and Victoria & Albert Museum, London, 9 September–19 November 1972 (London: The Arts Council of Great Britain, 1972)

André, Louis, 'Au berceau de la mécanisation papetière: La papèterie d'Essonnes, des Didots à Robert', in *Les trois révolutions du livre: Catalogue de l'exposition du musée des Arts et Métiers*, ed. Alain Mercier (Paris: Imprimerie nationale, 2002), pp. 277–82

Angelicoussis, Elizabeth, *The Woburn Abbey Collection of Classical Antiquities* (Mainz: Philipp von Zabern, 1992)

Armstrong, Lilian, *Renaissance Miniature Painters and Classical Imagery: The Master of the Putti and His Venetian Workshop* (London: Harvey Miller, 1981)

Ashby, Thomas, 'Thomas Jenkins in Rome', *Papers of the British School in Rome*, 6 (1913), 487–511

Augé, Marc, *Les formes de l'oubli* (Paris: Payot & Rivages, 1998)

Baczko, Bronisław, *Comment sortir de la Terreur: Thermidor et la Révolution* (Paris: Gallimard, 1989)

'Vandalisme', in *Dictionnaire critique de la Révolution française*, ed. François Furet and Mona Ouzof (Paris: Flammarion, 1988), pp. 903–12

Bailey, Charles R., 'The French clergy and the removal of Jesuits from secondary schools, 1761–1762', *Church History*, 48 (1979), 305–19

Baker, Keith, 'Controlling French history: the ideological arsenal of Jacob-Nicolas Moreau', in *Inventing the French Revolution: Essays on French Political Culture in the Eighteenth Century* (Cambridge University Press, 1990), pp. 59–85

Bardiès-Fronty, Isabelle and Wagner, Pierre Édouard, 'Le retour à Metz d'un coffret reliquaire de l'abbaye Saint-Arnoul, une importante acquisition pour les musées de Metz', *La Revue du Louvre et des Musées de France*, 4 (2005, October), 36–42 and 110–12

Bartmann, Elizabeth, 'Piecing as *paragone*: Carlo Albacini's Diana at Ince', in *History of Restoration of Ancient Stone Sculptures*, ed. Janet Burnett Grossmann, Jerry Podany, and Marion True (Los Angeles: Getty Trust Publications, 2003), pp. 115–26

Batts, M. S., 'The 18th-century concept of the rare book', *Book Collector*, 24, 3 (1975), 381–400

Baurmeister, Ursula, 'Marie Pellechet ou l'"odyssée bibliothécaresque"', *Bulletin du Bibliophile* (2004), 91–147

Baxmann, Dorothee, *Wissen, Kunst und Gesellschaft in der Theorie Condorcets* (Stuttgart: J. G. Cotta, 1999)

Belhoste, Bruno, 'Condorcet, les arts utiles et leur enseignement', in *Condorcet, homme des Lumières et de la Révolution*, ed. Anne-Marie Chouillet and Pierre Crépel (Fontenay-aux-Roses: ENS, 1997), pp. 121–36

Bentley, G. E., 'The bookseller as diplomat: James Edwards, Lord Grenville, and Earl Spencer in 1800', *Book Collector*, 33 (1984), 471–85

Bentzen, Ruth, 'Lord Harley og Grev Thott: En studie i nogle af det Kongelige Biblioteks bind og bøger fra Harleys og Thotts bogsamlinger', *Fund og forskning*, 44 (2005), 277–369

Berkvens-Stevelinck, Christiane, 'Un cabinet de livres européen en Hollande: La bibliothèque de Prosper Marchand', in *Le magasin de l'univers: The Dutch Republic as the Centre of the European Book Trade*, ed. Christiane Berkvens-Stevelinck, Hans Bots, Paul Geradus Hoftijzer, and Otto Stephanus Lankhorst (Leiden: Brill, 1992), pp. 11–22

Bianchi, Serge, 'Le "vandalisme révolutionnaire" et la politique artistique de la Convention au temps des "terreurs": essai de bilan raisonné', in *Les politiques de la Terreur 1793–1794: Actes du colloque international de Rouen (11–13 janvier 2007)*, ed. Michel Biard (Rennes: Presses universitaires de Rennes and Société des études robespierristes, 2008), pp. 403–19

Biblioteca medicea laurenziana (Florence: Cassa di risparmio di Firenze, 1986)

Birkelund, Palle, 'Det Thottske biblioteks sidste dage', in *Fra de gamle bøgers verden: Festskrift fra en kreds af husets venner, udsendt i anledning af firmaet Herman H. J. Lynge & Søns 100-aarige bestaaen som videnskabeligt antikvariat 1853–1953*, ed. Arne Stuhr-Rasmussen (Copenhagen: Lynge, 1953), pp. 83–102

Birn, Raymond, 'Malesherbes and the call for a free press', in *Revolution in Print: The Press in France 1775–1800*, ed. Robert Darnton and Daniel Roche (Berkeley: University of California Press, 1989), pp. 50–66

Birrell, T. A., 'Books and buyers at seventeenth-century English auction sales', in *Under the Hammer: Book Auctions since the Seventeenth Century*, ed. Robin Myers, Michael Harris, and Giles Mandelbrote (London: British Library, 2001), pp. 51–64

Blanning, T. C. W., *The French Revolution in Germany: Occupation and Resistance in the Rhineland 1792–1802* (Oxford University Press, 1983)

Reform and Revolution in Mainz 1743–1803 (Cambridge University Press, 1974)

Blechet, Françoise, 'Le vandalisme à la Bibliothèque du Roi/Nationale sous la Révolution', in *Révolution française et 'vandalisme révolutionnaire'*, ed. Simone Bernard-Griffiths, Marie-Claude Chemin, and Jean Ehrard (Paris: Universitas, 1992), pp. 256–76

Les ventes publiques de livres en France 1630–1750: Répertoire des catalogues conservés à la Bibliothèque nationale (Oxford: Voltaire Foundation, 1991)

Bloch, Denise, 'La bibliothèque de Colbert', in *Histoire des bibliothèques françaises. II, Les bibliothèques sous l'Ancien Régime, 1530–1789*, ed. Claude Jolly (Paris: Promodis, 1988), pp. 156–79

BMC, *Catalogue of Books Printed in the XVth Century now in the British Museum* [British Library], 13 vols (London: The British Museum/The British Library, 1908–2007)

Bod-inc, *A Catalogue of Books Printed in the Fifteenth Century now in the Bodleian Library*, 7 vols (Oxford University Press, 2005)

Bourdieu, Pierre and Saint-Martin, Monique de, *La noblesse d'état. Grandes écoles et esprit de corps* (Paris: Minuit, 1989)

Bühler, Curt F., 'Manuscript corrections in the Aldine edition of Bembo's *De Aetna*', *Papers of the Bibliographical Society of America*, 45 (1951), 136–42

Bussi, Angela Dillon, 'Le miniature nella collezione d'Elci', in *Incunaboli ed edizioni rare: La collezione di Angelo Maria d'Elci*, ed. Angela Dillon Bussi, Anna Maria Figliolia Manzini, and Maria Dianella Melani (Florence: Nardini, 1989), pp. 171–215

Büttner, Johannes W. E., *Fischer von Waldheim* (Berlin: Akademie-Verlag, 1956)

Buzy, Jean-Baptiste, *Dom Maugérard: Histoire d'un bibliographe lorrain de l'ordre de Saint-Benoît* (Chalons-sur-Marne: T. Martin, 1882)

Carrier, J. G., *Gifts and Commodities: Exchange and Western Capitalism since 1700* (London: Routledge, 1995)

Carter, Harry, 'Introduction', in Joseph Moxon, *Mechanick Exercises on the Whole Art of Printing (1683–4)*, 2nd edition, ed. H. Davis and H. Carter (London: Oxford University Press, 1962)

Cave, Roderick, 'Richard Smyth and early English printing', *Bulletin/Bibliographical Society of Australia and New Zealand*, 5, 2 (1981), 41–59

Chambon, Ségolène, 'Le rôle de l'Abbé Leblond dans les Commissions de savants', in *Antiquité, lumières et Révolution: l'Abbé Leblond (1738–1809) 'second fondateur de la Bibliothèque Mazarine*'; ed. Isabelle de Conihout and Patrick Latour (Paris: Bibliothèque Mazarine, 2009), pp. 65–72

Chapiro, Adolphe, *Jean-Antoine Lépine, horloger (1720–1814): Histoire du développement de l'horlogerie en France de 1760 à l'Empire* (Paris: Éditions de l'amateur, 1988)

Charon, Annie, 'Un amateur russe à la vente Loménie de Brienne (1790–1792): Dubrovski', in *Le Siècle des Lumières. I. Espace culturel de l'Europe à l'époque de Catherine II* (Moscow: Nauka, 2006), pp. 213–30

Chartier, Roger, *Les origines culturelles de la Révolution française. Postface inédite de l'auteur* (Paris: Seuil, 2000)

Chartier, Roger, Julia, Dominique, and Compère, Marie-Madeleine, *L'éducation en France du XVIe au XVIIIe siècle* (Paris: Société d'édition d'enseignement supérieur, 1976)

Chatelain, Jean-Marc, *La bibliothèque de l'honnête homme: Livres, lecture et collections en France à l'âge classique* (Paris: Bibliothèque nationale de France, 2003)

Clark, Kenneth, *The Gothic Revival*, revised edition (London: Constable & Co., 1950)

Colclough, Stephen, '"Purifying the sources of amusement and information"?: The railway book stalls of W. H. Smith and Son 1855–1860', *Publishing History*, 56 (2004), 27–51

Coltman, Viccy, *Fabricating the Antique: Neoclassicism in Britain 1760–1800* (University of Chicago Press, 2006)

Connell, Brian, *Portrait of a Whig Peer Compiled from the Papers of the Second Viscount Palmerston 1739–1802* (London: André Deutsch, 1957)

Cooper, Tarnya, 'Forgetting Rome and the voice of Piranesi's "Speaking ruins"', in *The Art of Forgetting*, ed. Adrian Forty and Susanne Küchler (Oxford: Berg, 1999), pp. 107–25

Coq, Dominique, 'Le parangon du bibliophile français: le duc de La Vallière et sa collection', in *Histoire des bibliothèques françaises*, II, *Les bibliothèques sous l'Ancien Régime, 1530–1789*, ed. Claude Jolly (Paris: Promodis, 1988), pp. 317–31

Crisman-Campbell, Kimberley, 'L'Angleterre et la mode en Europe au XVIIIᵉ siècle', in *Modes en miroir: la France et la Hollande au temps des Lumières, Musée Galliera, 28 avril–21 août 2005*, ed. Pascale Gorguet Ballesteros (Paris: Paris musées, 2005), pp. 50–3

Crook, John Mordaunt, *John Carter and the Mind of the Gothic Revival* (London: Maney and Son, 1995)

Crow, Thomas E., *Painters and Public Life in Eighteenth-Century Paris* (London and New Haven, CT: Yale University Press, 1985)

Darnton, Robert, *The Great Cat Massacre and Other Episodes in French Cultural History* (Harmondsworth: Penguin, 1985)

Davis, Adina, 'Portrait of a bibliophile XVIII: Clayton Mordaunt Cracherode', *Book Collector*, 23 (1974), 339–54 and 489–505

Dempsey, Lorcan, 'Scientific, industrial, and cultural heritage: a shared approach', at www.ariadne.ac.uk/issue22/dempsey/

Desplat, Christian, 'Bibliothèques privées mises sous séquestre dans le Département des Basses-Pyrénées pendant la Révolution française', *Revue française d'histoire du livre*, 56 (1987), 439–62

Domingos, Manuela D., 'A caminho da Real Biblioteca Pública da Corte: dois documentos (1775–1795)', *Revista da Biblioteca Nacional, Lisboa*, 2, 5(1) (1990), 139–60

The Douce Legacy: An Exhibition to Commemorate the 150th Anniversary of the Bequest of Francis Douce (1757–1834) (Oxford: Bodleian Library, 1984)

Dupuigrenet, François, 'Les trésors d'Italie (1796–1798)', in *1789 Le patrimoine libéré: 200 trésors entrés à la Bibliothèque nationale de 1789 à 1799* (Paris: Bibliothèque nationale, 1989), pp. 264–5

Dussinger, John A., 'Middleton, Conyers (1683–1750)', in *ODNB*

Eberling, Jörg, 'Upwardly mobile: Genre painting and the conflict between landed and moneyed interest', in *French Genre Painting in the Eighteenth Century*, ed. Philip Conisbee, Studies in the History of Art, no. 72 (New Haven, CT, and London: Yale University Press, 2007)

Estermann, Monika, *'O werthe Druckerkunst/Du Mutter aller Kunst': Gutenbergfeier im Laufe der Jahrhunderte* (Mainz: Gutenberg-Museum, 1999)

Feather, John, 'Robert Triphook and Francis Douce: A bookseller and one of his customers', *Bodleian Library Record*, 15, 5–6 (1996), 468–79

Feijfer, Jane, 'Restoration and display of classical sculpture in English country houses', in *History of Restoration of Ancient Stone Sculptures*, ed. Janet Burnett Grossmann, Jerry Podany, and Marion True (Los Angeles: The Getty Museum, 2003), pp. 87–104

Felicetti, Chiara (ed.), *Cristoforo Unterperger: Un pittore fiemmese nell'Europa del Settecento* (Rome: Edizioni De Luca, 1998)

Ford, Brinsley, 'Thomas Jenkins: banker, dealer and unofficial English agent', *Apollo*, 99 (1974), 416–25

Furet, François, *La Révolution française* (Paris: Gallimard, 2007)

Gaines, Barry, 'A forgotten artist: John Harris and the Rylands copy of Caxton's edition of Malory', *John Rylands Library Bulletin*, 52 (1969), 115–28

Gasparri, Carlo and Ghiandoni, Olivia, *Lo studio Cavaceppi e le collezioni Torloni* (Rome: Musei di Villa Torlonia, 1994)

Gentil-Brasseur, Hélène, 'Le livre saisi en Picardie sous la Révolution française', *Bulletin du bibliophile*, 1 (2007), 38–69

Glomski, Jacqueline, 'Book collecting and bookselling in the seventeenth century: Notions of rarity and identification of value', *Publishing History*, 39 (1996), 5–21

'*Incunabula Typographiae*: Seventeenth-century views on early printing', *The Library*, 7th series, 2 (2001), 336–48

Goldie, Mark, 'The English system of liberty', in *The Cambridge History of Eighteenth-Century Political Thought*, ed. Mark Goldie and Robert Wokler (Cambridge University Press, 2006), pp. 40–143

Grassinger, Dagmar, *Antike Marmorskulpturen auf Schloß Broadlands (Hampshire)*, Monumenta artis romanae, XXI (Mainz: Philipp von Zabern, 1994)

Grell, Chantal, 'J.-D. Schoepflin et l'historiographie française des Lumières', in *Strasbourg, Schoepflin et l'Europe au XVIIIe siècle*, ed. Bernard Vogler and Jürgen Voss (Bonn: Bouvier, 1996), pp. 253–68

Griffiths, Antony, 'The prints and drawings in the library of Consul Joseph Smith', *Print Quarterly*, 8 (1991), 126–39

Grindle, Nicholas, 'Browne, Lyde (*d.* 1787)', in *ODNB*

Hamann, Günther, 'Prinz Eugen als Bibliophile, naturhistorischer Sammler und Freund der Wissenschaften', in *Prinz Eugen und das barocke Österreich*, ed. Karl Gutkas (Salzburg: Residenz, 1985), pp. 349–58

Harris, P. R., *A History of the British Museum Library 1753–1973* (London: British Library, 1998)

Häseler, Jens, 'Formey et Crousaz, ou comment fallait-il combattre le scepticisme', *International Archives of the History of Ideas*, 184 (2003), 449–62

Haskell, Francis, *History and Its Images: Art and the Interpretation of the Past* (New Haven, CT, and London: Yale University Press, 1993)

Haskell, Francis and Penny, Nicholas, *Taste and the Antique: The Lure of Classical Sculpture 1500–1900* (New Haven, CT, and London: Yale University Press, 1981)

Hellinga, Lotte, 'Analytical bibliography and the study of the early printed book with a case-study of the Mainz Catholicon', *Gutenberg-Jahrbuch* (1989), 47–96

   Catalogue of Books Printed in the XVth Century now in the British Library. BMC Part XI, England (Houten, The Netherlands: Hes & De Graaf, 2007)

   Caxton in Focus (London: British Library, 1982)

   'The Bibliotheca smithiana', in *Libraries within the Library: The origins of the British Library's Printed Collections*, ed. Giles Mandelbrote and Barry Taylor, (London: British Library, 2009), pp. 261–79

Hesse, Carla, 'Economic upheavals in publishing', in *Revolution in Print: The Press in France 1775–1800*, ed. Robert Darnton and Daniel Roche (Berkeley: University of California Press, 1989), pp. 69–97

   Publishing and Cultural Politics in Revolutionary Paris, 1789–1810 (Berkeley: University of California Press, 1991)

Hessels, J. H., *The Gutenberg Fiction: A Critical Examination of the Documents Relating to Gutenberg Showing that He Was Not the Inventor of Printing* (London: A. Moring, 1912)

Hillyard, Brian, 'Ker, John, third duke of Roxburghe (1740–1804)', in *ODNB*

Hobson, Anthony, 'Appropriations from foreign libraries during the French Revolution and Empire', *Bulletin du bibliophile* (1989), fascicle 2, 255–72

Humanists and Bookbinders: The Origins and Diffusion of the Humanistic Bookbinding 1459–1559, with a Census of Historiated Plaquette and Medallion Bindings of the Renaissance (Cambridge University Press, 1989)

Hont, Istvan, 'The early Enlightenment debate on commerce and luxury', in *The Cambridge History of Eighteenth-Century Political Thought*, ed. Mark Goldie and Robert Wokler (Cambridge University Press, 2006), pp. 379–418

Howard, Seymour, *Bartolomeo Cavaceppi, Eighteenth-Century Restorer* (New York: Garland Publishing, 1982)

'Some eighteenth-century restorations of Myron's "Discobolos"', *Journal of the Warburg and Courtauld Institutes*, 25 (1962), 330–4

Hunt, Arnold, 'Private libraries in the age of bibliomania', in *The Cambridge History of Libraries in Britain and Ireland. II, 1640–1850*, ed. Giles Mandelbrote and K. A. Manley (Cambridge University Press, 2006), pp. 438–58

Hunter, Michael, *Establishing the New Science: The Experience of the Early Royal Society* (Woodbridge: Boydell and Brewer, 1989)

Ilsøe, Harald, *Biblioteker til salg. Om danske bogauktioner og kataloger 1661–1811* (Copenhagen: Museum Tusculanum, 2007)

På papir, pergament og palmeblade. Skatte i det Kongelige Bibliotek (Copenhagen: Det Kongelige Bibliotek, 1993)

Irwin, Robert, *For Lust of Knowing: The Orientalists and Their Enemies* (Harmondsworth: Allen Lane, 2006)

ISTC, The Incunabula Short Title Catalogue: www.bl.uk/catalogues/istc/

Jacobs, Emil, 'Zur Kentniss Maugérards', *Zentralblatt für Bibliothekswesen*, 21 (1910), 158–62

Jarausch, Konrad H., 'The institutionalisation of history in eighteenth-century Germany', in *Aufklärung und Geschichte: Studien zur deutschen Geschichtswissenschaft im 18. Jahrhundert*, ed. Hans Erich Bödeker, Georg G. Iggers, Jonathan B. Knudsen, and Peter H. Reill. Veröffentlichungen des Max-Planck-Instituts für Geschichte, 81 (Göttingen: Vandenhoeck und Ruprecht, 1986), pp. 25–48

Jensen, Kristian, 'The Bodleian Library', in *Handbuch deutscher historischer Buchbestände in Europa*, ed. Bernhard Fabian, vol. X: *A Guide to Collections of Books Printed in German-Speaking Countries Before 1910 (or in German Elsewhere) Held by Libraries in Great Britain and Ireland*, ed. Graham Jefcoate, William A. Kelly, and Karen Kloth (Hildesheim: Olms, 2000), pp. 268–303

'Heinrich Walther, Christian Samuel Kalthoeber, and other London binders: books in the Bodleian Library bound by Germans settled in London in the eighteenth century', *Bibliothek und Wissenschaft*, 29 (1996), 292–311

Jensen, Kristian and Kauffmann, Martin, *A Continental Shelf: Books Across Europe from Ptolemy to Don Quixote: An Exhibition to Mark the Reopening of the Bodleian Exhibition Room* (Oxford: Bodleian Library, 1994)

Johns, Adrian, *The Nature of the Book: Print and Knowledge in the Making* (Chicago and London: University of Chicago Press, 1998)

Jolly, Claude (ed.), *Histoire des bibliothèques françaises. II, Les bibliothèques sous l'Ancien Régime, 1530–1789* (Paris: Promodis, 1988)

Kenny, Neil, 'Books in space and time: Bibliomania and early modern histories of learning and "literature" in France', *Modern Language Quarterly*, 61, 2 (2000), 253–86

Knaus, Hermann, 'Bodmann und Maugérard', *Archiv für Geschichte des Buchwesens* (1958), 175–8

'Fischer von Waldheim als Handschriften- und Inkunabelhändler', in *Festschrift Josef Benzing*, ed. Elisabeth Geck and Guido Pressler (Wiesbaden: G. Pressler, 1964), pp. 255–80

Knedlik, Manfred, 'Hupfauer, Paul', in *Biographisch-Bibliographisches Kirchenlexikon*, vol. XXIV (Hamm: Traugott Bautz, 2005), cols 882–6

Laboulais-Lesage, Isabelle, *Lectures et pratiques de l'espace: L'itinéraire de Coquebert de Montbret, savant et grand commis d'État (1755–1831)* (Paris: Honoré Champion, 1999)

Larsen, Knud, *Frederik Rostgaard og bøgerne* (Copenhagen: Gad, 1970)

Lehmstedt, Mark, '"Ein Strohm der alles überschwemmet", Dokumente zum Verhältnis von Philipp Erasmus Reich und Johann Thomas von Trattner', *Bibliothek und Wissenschaft*, 25 (1991), 176–267

Leniaud, Jean-Michel, 'Sur quelques délires parisiens et sur la fièvre des "massacres monumentaires": Les regrets de Grégoire', in *Les collections; fables et programmes*, ed. Jacques Guillerme (Seyssel: Champ Vallon, 1993), pp. 249–57

Le Roy Ladurie, Emmanuel, 'De la crise ultime à la vraie croissance', in *Histoire de la France rurale. II, L'Âge classique des paysans*, ed. Georges Duby (Paris: du Seuil, 1992), pp. 359–99

Lesage, Claire, Netchine, Ève, and Sarrazin, Véronique (eds), *Catalogues de libraires 1473–1810* (Paris: Bibliothèque nationale de France, 2006)

Levine, Joseph M., *The Battle of the Books: History and Literature in the Augustan Age* (Ithaca, NY: Cornell University Press, 1991)

Lister, Anthony, 'The Althorp library of the Second Earl Spencer, now in the John Rylands University Library of Manchester: its formation and growth', *Bulletin of the John Rylands University Library of Manchester*, 71 (1989), 67–86

'The formation of the Althorp Library', *Bulletin du bibliophile* (1989), 69–91

Lucas, Charles, 'Book-collecting in the eighteenth century: The library of James West', *The Library*, 5th series, 3 (1944–9), 265–78

McClellan, Andrew, 'Raphael's "Foligno Madonna" at the Louvre in 1800: restoration and reaction at the dawn of the museum age', *Art Journal* (summer 1995), 80–5

McKitterick, David, 'Bibliography, bibliophily and the organization of knowledge', in *The Foundations of Scholarship: Libraries and Collecting 1650–1750: Papers Presented at a Clark Library Seminar 9 March 1985*, ed. David Vaisey and David McKitterick (Pasadena, CA: Clark Memorial Library, 1992), pp. 29–61

Print, Manuscript, and the Search for Order, 1450–1830 (Cambridge University Press, 2003)

Madsen, Victor, *Katalog over det Kongelige Biblioteks inkunabler*, 3 vols (Copenhagen: Levin & Munksgaard, 1935–63)

Mandelbrote, Giles and Taylor, Barry (eds), *Libraries Within the Library: The Origins of the British Library's Printed Collections* (London: British Library, 2009)

Manzini, Anna Maria Figliolia, 'Biblioteche e libri per studio e per diletto', in *Incunaboli ed edizioni rare: La collezione di Angelo Maria d'Elci*, ed. Angela Dillon Bussi, Anna Maria Figliolia Manzini, and Maria Dianella Melani (Florence: Nardini, 1989), pp. 53–113

Marvin, Miranda, *The Language of the Muses: The Dialogue Between Roman and Greek Sculpture* (Los Angeles: Getty Publications, 2008)

Mazal, Otto (ed.), *Bibliotheca eugeniana. Die Sammlungen des Prinzen Eugen von Savoyen: Ausstellung der Österreichischen Nationalbibliothek und der Graphischen Sammlung Albertina, Prunksaal, 15. Mai–31. Oktober 1986* (Vienna: Nationalbibliothek, 1986)

Michaelis, Adolf, *Ancient Marbles in Great Britain*, translated from the German by C. A. M. Fennell (Cambridge University Press, 1882)

Middleton, Bernard, 'Facsimile printing for antiquarian books', in *Bookbindings 2000 Proceedings. A Collection of Papers from the June 2000 Conference Celebrating the Installation and Opening of the Bernard C. Middleton Collection of Books on the History and Practice of Bookbindings* (Rochester, NY: Cary Graphic Arts Collection, 2002), pp. 21–32

Miller, Edward, *Prince of Librarians: The Life and Times of Antonio Panizzi and the British Museum* (London: André Deutsch, 1967)

Minard, Philippe, *La fortune du colbertisme: État et industrie dans la France des Lumières* (Paris: Fayard, 1998)

Minois, George, *Censure et culture sous l'ancien régime* (Paris: Fayard, 1995)

Mohr, Louis, *Die Jubelfeste der Buchdruckerkunst und ihre Literatur* (Vienna: F. Jasper, 1992)

Molli, Giovanna Baldissin, 'La tarda miniatura', in *La miniatura a Padova dal medioevo al settecento*, ed. Giovanna Baldissin Molli, Giordana Canova Mariani, and Federica Toniolo (Modena: Panini, 1999), pp. 533–43

Mortier, Daniel Antonin, OP, *Histoire des maîtres généraux de l'ordre des frères prêcheurs*, 8 vols (Paris: Alph. Picard, 1903–20)

Müller-Kaspar, Ulrike, *Das sogenannte Falsche am Echten: Antikenergänzungen im späteren 18. Jahrhundert in Rom* (Bonn: Rheinische Friedrich-Wilhelm-Universität,1988)

Munby, A. N. L., *Connoisseurs and Medieval Miniatures 1750–1850* (Oxford: Clarendon Press, 1972)

'Jacob Bryant and the Sunderland library', *The Library*, 5th series, 2 (1947), 192–8

Müntz, Eugène, 'Les annexions de collections d'art et de bibliothèques et leur rôle dans les relations internationales, principalement pendant la Révolution française', *Revue d'histoire diplomatique*, 8 (1894), 481–97, 9 (1895), 375–93, and 10 (1896), 481–508

Myers, Robin, 'Ames, Joseph (*bap.* 1687, *d.* 1759)', in *ODNB*

Needham, Paul, *The Bradshaw Method: Henry Bradshaw's Contribution to Bibliography* (Chapel Hill, NC: Hanes Foundation, 1988)

Nexon, Yannick, 'La bibliothèque du chancelier Séguier', in *Histoire des bibliothèques françaises. II, Les bibliothèques sous l'Ancien Régime, 1530–1789*, ed. Claude Jolly (Paris: Promodis, 1988), pp. 147–55

Nixon, Margaret, Goldfinch, John and Hellinga, Lotte, 'The formation of the collection of English incunabula in the British Library (formerly the British Museum) 1753–2006', in *Catalogue of Books Printed in the XVth Century now in the British Library. BMC Part XI, England*, ed. Lotte Hellinga (Houten, The Netherlands: Hes & De Graaf, 2007), pp. 71–84

Oates, J. C. T., 'Booksellers' guarantees', *The Library*, 5th series, 6 (1951), 212–13

'The "Costerian" *Liber precum*', *The Library*, 5th series, 3 (1948–9), 65–6

ODNB, Oxford Dictionary of National Biography (Oxford, 2004); www.oxforddnb.com

O'Donoghue, Jim, Goulding, Louise and Allen, Grahame, 'Consumer price inflation since 1750', *Office for National Statistics: Economic Trends*, 604 (March 2004), pp. 38–46

Officer, Lawrence H., 'What were the UK earnings rate and consumer price index then? A data study', www.measuringworth.com/calculators/ukcompare/ukcompessay.htm

Oldman, C. B., 'Panizzi's acquisition of incunabula', in *Essays in Honour of Victor Scholderer*, ed. Dennis Rhodes (Mainz: Karl Pressler, 1970), pp. 284–91

ÖNB-Ink, Österreichische Nationalbibliothek Inkunabelkatalog. Band 1, A–B, ed. Otto Mazal and Konstanze Mittendorfer (Wiesbaden: Reichert, 2004)

Parshall, Peter and Schoch, Rainer, 'Early woodcuts and the reception of the primitive', in *Origins of European Printmaking: Fifteenth-Century Woodcuts and Their Public*, ed. Peter Parshall and Rainer Schoch (Washington, DC: National Gallery of Art, 2005), pp. 1–17

Pasta, Renato, 'Tra Firenze, Napoli e l'Europa: Giuseppe Molini senior', in *Editoria e cultura a Napoli nel XVIII secolo: atti del convegno / organizzato dall'Istituto universitario orientale, dalla Società italiana di studi sul secolo XVIII e dall'Istituto italiano per gli studi filosofici, Napoli 5–7 dicembre 1996*, ed. Anna Maria Rao, Quaderni del Dipartimento di filosofia e politica; 17 (Napoli: Liguori, 1998), pp. 251–83

Penny, Nicholas, 'Richard Payne Knight: A brief life', in *The Arrogant Connoisseur: Richard Payne Knight 1751–1824*, ed. Michael Clarke and Nicholas Penny (Manchester University Press, 1982), pp. 1–18

Petrucciani, Alberto, *Gli incunaboli della biblioteca Durazzo*, Atti della società ligure di storia patria, nuova serie, vol. XXVIII (102), fasc. 2 (Genoa: Società ligure di storia patria, 1988)

Petrucciani, Alberto and Puncuh, Dino, *Giacomo Filippo Durazzo (1729–1812): il bibliofilo e il suo 'cabinet de livres'* (Genoa: Società ligure di storia patria, 1996)

Philip, Ian, 'The background to the Bodleian purchases of incunabula at the Pinelli and Crevenna sales, 1789–90', *Transactions of the Cambridge Bibliographical Society*, 7 (1979), 369–75

The Bodleian Library in the Seventeenth and Eighteenth Centuries (Oxford: Clarendon Press, 1983)

Piggott, Stuart, 'Antiquarian studies', in *The History of the University of Oxford. V. The Eighteenth Century*, ed. L. S. Sutherland and L. G. Mitchell (Oxford: Clarendon Press, 1986), pp. 757–77

Pinelli, Orietta Rossi, 'Artisti, falsari o filologhi? Da Cavaceppi a Canova, il restauro della scultura tra arte e scienza', *Ricerche di storia dell'arte*, 14 (1981), 41–56

Podany, J., 'Restoring what wasn't there: Reconsideration of the eighteenth-century restoration to the Lansdowne Herakles in the collection of the J. Paul Getty Museum', in *Restoration: Is It Acceptable?* British Museum Occasional Papers, 99, ed. A. Oddy (London: British Museum, 1994), pp. 9–18

Pollard, Alfred W., 'The building up of the British Museum collection of incunabula', *The Library*, 4th series, 5.3 (1924), 192–214

Pommier, Edouard, 'Discours iconoclaste, discours culturel, discours national, 1790–1794', in *Révolution française et 'vandalisme révolutionnaire'*, ed. Simone Bernard-Griffiths, Marie-Claude Chemin, and Jean Ehrard (Paris: Universitas, 1992), pp. 299–313

Winckelmann, inventeur de l'histoire de l'art (Paris: Gallimard, 2003)

Poulot, Dominique, *Musée, nation, patrimoine 1789–1815* (Paris: Gallimard, 1997)

Surveiller et s'instruire: La Révolution française et l'intelligence de l'héritage historique (Oxford: Voltaire Foundation, 1996)

Proctor, Robert, *Index to the Early Printed Books in the British Museum: from the Invention of Printing to the Year MD, with Notes of Those in the Bodleian Library* (London: K. Paul, Trench, Trübner, and Co., 1898)

Purcell, Mark, '"A lunatick of unsound mind": Edward, Lord Leigh (1742–86) and the refounding of Oriel College library', *Bodleian Library Record*, 17, 3–4 (2001), 246–60

Quarrie, Paul, 'Clayton Mordaunt Cracherode', in *Libraries within the Library: The Origins of the British Library's Printed Collections*, ed. Giles Mandelbrote and Barry Taylor (London: British Library, 2009), pp. 187–201

Raeder, Joachim, *Die antiken Skulpturen in Petworth House (West Sussex)*, with contributions from Norbert Ehrhardt and Christian Ede, Monumenta artis romanae, 28 (Mainz: Philipp von Zabern, 2000)

Ramsay, Nigel, 'Libraries for antiquaries and heralds', in *The Cambridge History of Libraries in Britain and Ireland. II, 1640–1850*, ed. Giles Mandelbrote and K. A. Manley (Cambridge University Press, 2006)

Rao, Ida Giovanna, 'Cenni biografici su Angelo Maria d'Elci', in *Incunaboli ed edizioni rare: La collezione di Angelo Maria d'Elci*, ed. Angela Dillon Bussi and others (Florence: Nardini, 1989), pp. 13–19

Rau, Arthur, 'Bibliotheca parisina', *Book Collector*, 18 (1969), 307–17

Reading, A., 'Digital interactivity in public memory institutions: the uses of new technologies in Holocaust museums', *Media Culture and Society*, 25 (2003), 67–86

Ricci, Seymour de, *Catalogue raisonné des premières impressions de Mayence (1455–67)*, Veröffentlichungen der Gutenberg-Gesellschaft, 8–9 (Mainz: Gutenberg-Gesellschaft, 1911)

   A Census of Caxtons (London: Bibliographical Society, 1909)

   English Collectors of Books and Manuscripts (1530–1930) and Their Marks of Ownership (Cambridge University Press, 1930)

Robbins, A. F., rev. Matthew Kilburn, 'Morice, Humphry (1723–1785)', in *ODNB*

Roche, Daniel, 'La censure', in *Histoire de l'édition française. II, Le livre triomphant 1660–1830* (Paris: Promodis, 1984), pp. 76–83

   'La police du livre', in *Histoire de l'édition française. II, Le livre triomphant 1660–1830* (Paris: Promodis, 1984), pp. 84–91

Rogers, David, *The Bodleian Library and Its Treasures 1320–1700* (Henley-on Thames: Aidan Ellis, 1991)

Römer, Gerhard, '"Lediglich ein Bücherwust ohne vollständige Ordnung", Die Bibliotheksordnung des Praemonstratenserstiftes Allerheiligen im Schwarzwald von 1788', in *Literatur und Kultur im deutschen Südwesten zwischen Renaissance und Aufklärung*, ed. Wilhelm Kühlmann (Amsterdam: Rodopi, 1991), pp. 395–416

Rowe, Michael, *From Reich to State: The Rhineland in the Revolutionary Age, 1780–1830* (Cambridge University Press, 2003)

Sacquin, M., 'Bibliothèque royale et utopie', in *1789 Le patrimoine libéré: 200 trésors entrés à la Bibliothèque nationale de 1789 à 1799* (Paris: Bibliothèque nationale, 1989), pp. 18–20

Savoy, Bénédicte, 'Codicoloque, incunabuliste et rabatteur: La mission de Jean-Baptiste Maugérard dans les quatre départements du Rhin (1802–1805)', *Bulletin du bibliophile* (1999), fascicle 2, 313–44

   Patrimoine annexé: Les biens culturels saisis par la France en Allemagne autour de 1800, 2 vols (Paris: Maison des sciences de l'homme, 2003)

Schaab, Rupert, 'Universitäts- und Forschungsbibliothek Erfurt/Gotha', in *Regionalbibliotheken in Deutschland mit einem Ausblick auf Österreich und die Schweiz*, ed. Bernd Hagenau (Frankfurt am Main: Klostermann, 2000), pp. 290–5

Schandeler, Jean-Pierre, *Les interprétations de Condorcet: Symboles et concepts (1794–1894)* (Oxford: Voltaire Foundation, 2000)

Schmidt-Künsemüller, Friedrich-Adolf, 'Gotthelf Fischer von Waldheim und die Gutenberg-Forschung', *Börsenblatt für den Deutschen Buchhandel*, 17 (1961), 2372–80

Scholderer, Victor, 'The beginnings of printing at Basel', in Scholderer, *Fifty Essays in Fifteenth- and Sixteenth-Century Bibliography*, ed. Dennis Rhodes (Amsterdam: Hertzberger, 1966), pp. 192–5

Schottenloher, Karl, 'Beiträge zur Geschiche der Inkunabelkunde in Franken', *Zentralblatt für Bibliothekswesen*, 29 (1912), 64–75

Schulz, Ernst, 'Gesamtkatalog der Wiegendrucke und Literaturwissenschaft: ein kritische Beurteilung des ersten Bandes', *Archiv für Bibliographie, Buch- und Bibliothekswesen*, 1 (1926), 113–27

Seckel, Raymond-Josué, 'La Bibliothèque nationale et les dépôts littéraires', in *1789 Le patrimoine libéré: 200 trésors entrés à la Bibliothèque nationale de 1789 à 1799* (Paris: Bibliothèque nationale, 1989), pp. 23–4

Seeba, Hinrich C., 'Zwischen Reichshistorik und Kunstgeschichte. Zur Geschichte eines Paradigmawechsels in der Geschichtsschreibung', in *Aufklärung und Geschichte* (Göttingen: Vandenhoeck und Ruprecht, 1986), pp. 299–342

Serrai, Alfredo, *Domenico Passionei e la sua biblioteca* (Milan: Sylvestre Bonnard, 2004)

Sherbo, Arthur, *Shakespeare's Midwives: Some Neglected Shakespeareans* (Newark: University of Delaware Press, 1992)

Shtrum, Batyah, 'LACMA's classical sculpture collection reconsidered – again', in *The Object in Context: Crossing Conservation Boundaries. Contributions to the Munich Congress 28 August–1 September 2006*, ed. David Saunders, Joyce H. Townsend, and Sally Woodcock (London: International Institute for Conservation of Historic and Artistic Works, 2006), pp. 197–203

Snoek, Jan A. M., '"De vele énorme en schreeuwende faiten teegen de broederschap begaan" door [John] George Smith (*ca.* 1728–*ca.* 1785)', in *De andere achttiende eeuw: opstellen voor André Hanou*, ed. Cis van Heertum, Ton Jongenelen, and Frank van Lamoen (Nijmegen: Vantilt, 2006), pp. 201–29

Somov, V., 'Les aristocrates russes acheteurs de livres en France pendant la Révolution', in *Le Livre voyageur: Constitution et dissémination des collections livresques dans l'Europe moderne (1450–1830)* (Paris: Klincksieck, 2000), pp. 227–49

Sordet, Yann, *L'amour des livres au siècle des Lumières: Pierre Adamoli et ses collections* (Paris: École des Chartes, 2001)

Sorel, Albert, *L'Europe et la Révolution française*, 12th edition, 9 vols (Paris: Plon, 1908)

Southworth, E., 'The Ince Blundell collection: collecting behaviour in the eighteenth century', *Journal of the History of Collecting*, 3, 2 (1991), 219–34

Sparrow, John, 'The earlier owners of books in John Selden's library', *Bodleian Quarterly Record*, 6 (1931), 263–71

Spencer, Charles, *The Spencer Family* (London: Viking, 1999)

Swift, A. K., 'The formation of the library of Charles Spencer: A study in the antiquarian booktrade', unpublished D.Phil. thesis, University of Oxford, 1981, The Bodleian Library, MS.D.Phil c.6554

Takamiya, Toshiyuki, 'John Harris and the facsimile pages', www.bl.uk/treasure/caxton

Thompson, E. P., 'The moral economy of the English crowd in the eighteenth century', *Past and Present*, 50 (1971), 76–136

Traube, Ludwig, and Ehwald, Rudolf, *Jean-Baptiste Maugérard, Ein Beitrag zur Bibliotheksgeschichte*, Abhandlungen der historischen Klasse der Königlichen Bayerischen Akademie der Wissenschaften, 23 (Munich: Königliche Bayerische Akademie, 1904); Ehwald, *Besonderer Teil* is at pp. 341–87.

Tweedale, Geoffrey, "'Days at the factories": A tour of Victorian industry with the *Penny Magazine*', *Technology and Culture*, 29, 2 (1988), 888–903

Varry, Dominique, 'Joseph Van Praet', in *Histoire des bibliothèques françaises. III, Les bibliothèques de la Révolution et du XIXe siècle*, ed Dominique Varry (Paris: Promodis, 1991), pp. 302–3

'Quand l'incunable paraît: les catalogues de ventes lyonnais d'Ancien Régime', *Revue française d'histoire du livre*, 118–21 (2003), 397–402

'Vicissitudes et aléas des livres placés "sous la main de la Nation"', in *Révolution française et 'vandalisme révolutionnaire'*, ed. Simone Bernard-Griffiths, Marie-Claude Chemin, and Jean Ehrard (Paris: Universitas, 1992), pp. 277–84

Vernus, Michel, *Une vie dans l'univers du livre: François-Xavier Laire (1738–1801)* (Besançon: Les Bibliophiles comtois, 2001)

Verwey, H. de la Fontaine, 'Frederik Corcellis, knecht van Laurens Jansz Coster of de gevolgen van een drukfout', *De Gulden passer*, 28 (1950), 87–103

Vian, Alsager, rev. Holger Hoock, 'Esdaile, William (1758–1837)', in *ODNB*

Viardot, Jean, 'Livres rares et pratiques bibliophiliques', in *Histoire de l'édition française. II, Le livre triomphant 1660–1830*, ed. Henri-Jean Martin and Roger Chartier (Paris: Promodis, 1984), pp. 447–67

'Naissance de la bibliophilie: les cabinets de livres rares', in *Histoire des bibliothèques françaises. II, Les bibliothèques sous l'Ancien Régime, 1530–1789*, ed. Claude Jolly (Paris: Promodis, 1988), pp. 269–89

Voss, Jürgen, *Universität, Geschichtswissenschaft und Diplomatie im Zeitalter der Aufklärung: Johann Daniel Schoepflin, 1694–1771* (Munich: Fink, 1979)

Wasson, E. A., *Whig Renaissance: Lord Althorp and the Whig Party, 1782–1845* (London: Garland, 1987)

Wehmer, Carl, 'Zur Beurteilung des Methodenstreites in der Inkunabelkunde', *Gutenberg-Jahrbuch* (1932), 250–325

Weimerskirch, Philip John, 'Antonio Panizzi's acquisition policies for the Library of the British Museum', unpublished PhD dissertation, Columbia University, 1977

Antonio Panizzi and the British Museum Library (Clifton, NJ: Bookman's Weekly, 1982)

Welch, Evelyn, *Shopping in the Renaissance: Consumer Culture in Italy 1400–1600* (London and New Haven, CT: Yale University Press, 2006)

Wheeler, Michael, *Ruskin's God* (Cambridge University Press, 1999)

Whitehead, Christopher, *The Public Art Museum in Nineteenth-Century Britain: The Development of the National Gallery* (Aldershot: Ashgate, 2004)

William, David, 'New constructions of equality', in *Condorcet and Modernity* (Cambridge University Press, 2004), pp. 139–71

William, W. J. and Stoddart, D. M., *Bath: Some Encounters with Science* (Bath: Kingsmead Press,1974)

Wittmann, Reinhard, *Buchmarkt und Lektüre im 18. und 19. Jahrhundert: Beiträge zum literarischen Leben 1750–1880* (Tübingen: Niemeyer, 1982)

Wonderful Things from 400 Years of Collecting: The Bodleian Library 1602–2002. An Exhibition to Mark the Quartercentenary of the Bodleian. July to December 2002 (Oxford: Bodleian Library, 2002)

Zorzi, Marino, 'Les saisies napoléoniennes en Italie', in *Le livre voyageur: Constitution et dissémination des collections livresques dans l'Europe moderne (1450–1830)* (Paris: Klincksieck, 2000), pp. 251–70

Index

Page numbers with 'fig' are the illustrations; with 'n' are notes; with 'g' are graphs.

Lightning Source UK Ltd.
Milton Keynes UK
UKOW06f1838201014

240312UK00006B/189/P

9 781107 687837